STEPHEN CLARKSON is a member of the Department of Political Economy at the University of Toronto.

Until now the innumerable and widely distributed Soviet writings on the third world have been scrutinized for the clues they contain on the Kremlin's aid, trade, and foreign policies, on Soviet strategies for local communist parties, and even on shifts in the Sino-Soviet relationship. But they have rarely been analysed in their own terms and for what they are – the application of marxist-leninist theory by Soviet scholars to the problems of Asia, Africa, and Latin America. Based on research in Paris, New York, the Soviet Union, and India, this book provides a long needed insight into how Soviet thinkers understand such crucial problems in development as planning in mixed economies, foreign aid from socialist and capitalist donors, agrarian reform, and the class struggle.

A concerned observer of Soviet development theory for some fifteen years, Stephen Clarkson is neither hostile nor uncritical. He argues that western students and third world policy-makers alike have a good deal to learn from marxist-leninist political economy because it presents an integrated approach to understanding the dilemmas of underdevelopment. Although Soviet scholarship benefits from some important theoretical advantages, it also suffers, in Clarkson's view, from severe intellectual handicaps. The book examines the Soviet analysis of third world development as a whole, drawing particularly on the most extensive and sophisticated school of interpretation, the Russian writings on India.

This book makes an important contribution to Soviet and third world studies by offering the reader a guide to the publications on development, a complex and evolving aspect of the Soviet view of the world.

'This is undoubtedly a highly perceptive piece, lucidly presented and well organized. It addresses itself to a very important problem and it is likely to be of value to social scientists in various fields as well as to the interested intelligent layman.' Alexander Ehrlich, Columbia University.

STEPHEN CLARKSON

The Soviet Theory
of Development:
India and the third world in
marxist-leninist scholarship

UNIVERSITY OF TORONTO PRESS
TORONTO   BUFFALO

© University of Toronto Press 1978
Toronto Buffalo London
Printed in Canada

Library of Congress Cataloging in Publication Data

Clarkson, Stephen.
The Soviet theory of development.

Includes index.
1. Marxian economics. 2. India – Economic policy.
3. Underdeveloped areas – Economic policy. I. Title.
HB97.5.C63   338.9'001   78-1771
ISBN 0-8020-5391-2

This book has been written by a member of the Centre for Russian and East European Studies, University of Toronto. A list of other books sponsored by the Centre appears at the back of the book.

I dedicate this book
to my old friend BHABANI SEN GUPTA
for his cheerful inspiration, profound
integrity, and irrepressible originality
and to my young daughter BLAISE CLARKSON,
trusting that these same qualities
will blossom in her person

Contents

Preface

This book is going to press some sixteen years after it was begun. Between the summer of 1962, before Khrushchev met his third-world nemesis at the Cuban missile crisis, and the spring of 1978, when Indira Gandhi had been a year out of power, the analysis contained between these covers has matured as it has come into contact with different readers and different realities.

Its first two years' gestation was in the womb of the Fondation Nationale des Sciences Politiques in Paris where it developed as a dissertation under the doctoral supervision of Alfred Grosser, with Hélène Carrère d'Encausse acting as midwife and such scholars as the late Daniel Thorner, Stuart Schram, and Basile Kerblay lending their generous intellectual advice.

While this French manuscript was being prepared for publication in France, I was able, thanks to the Canadian-Soviet cultural exchange, to go to Moscow and discuss the entire work with leading members of the Indian Department of the Institute of Asian Peoples and thus benefit from their often heated criticism of my own analysis – a particularly rewarding experience in any event and a rare opportunity in Soviet studies.

The chance to broaden my study of Soviet indology until it embraced the Russian view of development throughout the third world was given me by the Research Institute on Communist Affairs at Columbia University, where such fellow Senior Fellows as Bhabani Sen Gupta helped temper my judgments with his third worldly wisdom. To Bhabani Sen Gupta I also owe the inspiration, as to the Canada Council I owe the financing, of my research trip to South Asia, which allowed me to see how Soviet development writings were actually appreciated by their southern readership.

At each stage of this long journey, I have reworked and revised the analysis and the judgments of my manuscript. While I can identify some of the most important influences on my work, there are many I cannot acknowledge. Those dozens of scholars with whom I conversed in the Soviet Union on two visits must remain anonymous for reasons familiar to all who pursue Soviet studies. Several western colleagues gave detailed readers' reports; their anonymity did not prevent my profiting greatly from their pre-print critiques. Finally, to University of Toronto Press I must confess my debt.

Delays in bringing a manuscript to press may impose costs, but they can also produce benefits in terms of the maturity of an analysis that has, in this case, been revised for a last time in 1977. Judgments made as a result of the first research have been reviewed in the light of developments in subsequent years. In some cases Soviet scholars have changed their stands; in others they have reaffirmed their positions; in still others they have opened up new areas in which they had previously been quite deficient. While I can make no claim to provide a final view, since Soviet thinking will continue to evolve, my decade and a half of monitoring their publications gives me some confidence in the assessments I now bring to the anglophone reader.

* * *

Discrepancies in spelling may be noticed between Soviet translations of Russian texts and my own translations. Different spellings of Soviet writers' names also occur, a result of different forms of transliteration. In the text a simplified form is used, for example Ulyanovsky; in the notes, where the reference is in Russian, scholarly transliteration is used, for example Ul'yanovskii, but where Soviet English-language editions are cited, their transliterations, generally simplified, are retained and may vary.

An earlier version of this work was sponsored by the Research Institute on Communist Affairs at Columbia University. This book has been published with the help of grants from the Social Science Federation of Canada, using funds provided by the Canada Council, from the University of Toronto, and from the Publications Fund of University of Toronto Press.

PART ONE

INTRODUCTION

1

Questions and methods

In the last analysis, the outcome of the struggle will be determined by the fact that Russia, India, China, etc., account for the overwhelming majority of the population of the globe. And during the past few years it is this majority that has been drawn into the struggle for emancipation with extraordinary rapidity, so that in this respect there cannot be the slightest doubt what the final outcome of the world struggle will be. In this sense, the complete victory of socialism is fully and absolutely assured.

V.I. Lenin, 'Better fewer but better,' March 1923.[1]

Interest in the impact of communism on the third world has long crossed all ideological lines. Among communists themselves the role of the socialist camp has been seen as the guarantor of their ultimate triumph at the vanguard of the national liberation movement. The new nations, desperately struggling with their unsolved dilemmas, have looked hopefully towards the socialist camp for concrete help – crucial sources of foreign aid (Guinea), vital trade outlets (Cuba), ways to improve their bargaining position with Washington (Pakistan) or Paris (Algeria), and diplomatic support for their own national objectives (India). Observers of underdevelopment – economists, anthropologists, sociologists, technical experts – have periodically looked to the socialist bloc, wondering what solutions the marxist-leninists might have for the desperate problems with which they were trying to cope. If Atlantic world capitalism did not provide an appropriate formula for resolving rather than deepening the dilemmas of development in Africa, Asia, and Latin America, did the marxist-leninists have a key to unlock the problems of poverty that kept widening the gap between nations of the North and those of the South?

Western scholars through the 1950s and early 1960s had great difficulty not projecting their culture's own perspective of a dangerous cold war into their analysis of the new nations. The issue as they saw it was a life-and-death struggle for supremacy. They anxiously measured the penetration of socialist bloc diplomats in the ex-colonial world;[2] they tabulated figures of socialist aid programmes;[3] they measured Chinese against non-communist economic growth in Asia;[4] they scrutinized every published word of third world leaders looking for signs of western attachment or eastward vacillation.[5]

THE MODEL MUDDLE

With the normalization of the East-West confrontation towards the end of the 1950s, the reluctance of the newly independent countries to fall like dominoes around the border of the communist bloc, the schisms within the socialist bloc itself, and the transformation of the very tense cold war into a decidedly less brinksmanlike cold peace, scholarly interest shifted from the communist offensive to the communist model. Would it, like some international Pied Piper, entice the elites of the Afro-Asian nations into the socialist bloc?[6] Just what constituted this model, however, was never absolutely clear. Was it the historical experience of development in the Soviet bloc?[7] If so there would be a multiplicity of models, one based on each revolutionary regime – Lenin's or Tito's, Mao Tse-tung's[8] or Ho Chi Minh's. Worse, in the case of the more long-lived leaders such as Stalin there would be a distinct model for each stage of communist construction over which he had presided: that of NEP, or his primitive socialist accumulation and forced industrialization,[9] the patriotic war's nationalist mobilization, or the stage-skipping industrial development of feudal Central Asia under Soviet direction,[10] and so on.

In this expanding showroom of models, the political controls, the economic priorities, the agricultural programme and the class tactics of each model presumably responded to the national situation in each communist regime for the given period. But which part of which model was relevant to the problems of a particular developing country grappling with its situation of the 1970s?[11] Who would decide what was relevant in a particular communist model and what was not? If the ruling group in each country made this decision, then the communist model would vary with the needs and ambitions of each nation's leadership: Nehru was impressed above all by the Soviets' claimed solution to their nationality question and rapid industrialization through the magic of long-term economic planning;[12] for Nkrumah it was, if anything, the disciplined single party system;[13] for Sékou Touré it was the state control of foreign trade;[14] for others it could be the armed mobilization of the peasantry, the nationalization of foreign companies, the cultural revolution, or some mix of these and other features identified with the socialist countries' experiences.

If elite subjectivism leads to unmanageable multiplicity, so does recourse to the claims of the communist leaderships. The communist model might be defined as the packaged historical experience of individual members of the socialist camp containing a real, if general, appeal to the emerging leaderships of the decolonized world. But when it came down to specifying its precise characteristics, the rival claims to revolutionary orthodoxy coming from the USSR, China, and lesser communist powers shattered the claimed coherence of a socialist model.[15] Was it not too diverse in its components and too subjective in its perception to provide the developing countries' ruling elites with a coherent guide for political survival and economic growth?

THE SOVIET SCHOOL

If we abandon the hope of discovering a general communist development model in the minds of the practitioners of development there is still another but more concrete sense in which a communist model specifically relevant to each developing country might be found. This is the analysis of a nation's problems by communist bloc scholars. By taking communist publications on development in the third world we find marxist-leninist theory applied to the specific conditions in each country. From these analyses and policy recommendations a model can be assembled.

But to speak of marxist-leninist development theory requires a choice to be made between its different national versions since scholars and research institutions are working and publishing on the third world in several socialist countries. The Soviet analysis of the third world constitutes a natural body of writings for making this search for a specific communist model. Of all the marxist-leninist states, the Soviet Union has devoted by far the most resources and the longest time to studying the colonies and developing countries. Khrushchev's revision of Soviet foreign policy from 1954-6 led to a thorough reformulation of the stalinist axioms about the colonial and ex-colonial world.[16] With the rejection of other evil effects of the 'cult of personality' in orientology there came a call for new research.[17] The Institute of Eastern Studies was refurbished and directed to create a basic Soviet expertise on the economics, politics, and geography of the third world.[18] As more colonies gained independence, new institutes were created, one specializing in Africa (1959)[19] and another in Latin America (1961);[20] as more students graduated, research teams expanded and scholarly production soared.

More western writings made their way to Soviet libraries both in the original and in Russian translation.[21] The establishment of diplomatic relations, commercial links, and cultural exchanges with the ex-colonies allowed Soviet scholars for the first time to do field work in the countries of their specialization. Soviet writings on Asia, Africa, and Latin America over the past two decades are thus abundant enough to stand consideration.[22] The spectacular increase in the quantity of Soviet writings was matched by a striking improvement in their quality.[23]

Nevertheless, a wide credibility gap has long made serious consideration of the marxist-leninists' point of view intellectually unrespectable in western academic circles. Soviet experts on any political or economic questions have been dismissed as lost to social science: are they not writing under impossible constraints of censorship, political control, and intellectually crippling ideological dogmas which prevent them from reaching anything but ideologically preconceived conclusions?[24] As for Soviet writings on the third world, they have been used by western scholars primarily to shed light on current shifts in Soviet foreign policy[25] or on relations between the CPSU and either its rival or client communist parties.[26] Soviet writers have been thought to be too cut off from the reality of the African village or the Latin American city: can they then have anything significant to say to a non-communist public concerning serious solutions for a particular new nation's immediate economic problems?

The preoccupations of cold war kremlinology have tended until recently to depreciate all Soviet scholarship on the developing countries as being of less inherent interest in itself than as evidence concerning other questions. Certainly we should not ignore what the Soviet writings on the developing countries can tell us about other problems. As long as there is a direct link between marxist-leninist ideology and power,[27] the development output of Soviet scholars and journalists can be searched for the light it sheds on Soviet third world policy.[28] So long as we can assume a close control over Soviet publications by the Kremlin's ideological mentors, Soviet writings on the outside world can be interpreted as reflections of Moscow's current strategy. As long as local communist parties look to Moscow or Peking or other socialist capitals for guidance and support in dealing with their own problems, marxist-leninist publications can be probed for insights on directives to local communist parties. Since the Soviet scholarly community is an integral part both of the academic and the political process, the output and the characteristics of the research institutes studying foreign countries can be scrutinized for clues to the working of the Soviet academic and political system.[29] All these facets of Soviet marxist-leninist writing ensure that the printed word in socialist countries will continue to be exploited by sovietologists in lieu of more satisfactory research tools for many types of secondary political analysis. However, this study proposes to join the small body of literature that takes Soviet writings at their face value and examines them in their own terms as intellectual contributions to the understanding of specific problems.[30]

READING THE LINES THEMSELVES

There are good reasons for simply reading Soviet writings on the developing countries rather than scrutinizing what lies between the lines because what is actually written has a real interest of its own. First there is the Soviets' own claim that their analysis provides the exclusive solution to the problems of the third world. No less an authority than Academician R.A. Ulyanovsky could write: 'Naturally, it is the communists and not the us capitalists and politicians who are able to offer the people of the developing countries constructive ideas about the shortest roads and successful methods for eliminating their age-old backwardness. No one except the communist knows and is able to offer such roads and methods which, moreover, have stood the test of history.'[31] The Soviet claim is no longer that marxism-leninism holds a single formula but that it is a dynamic corpus of knowledge adapting to problems as they evolve. 'Marxism has been finding the right solutions for all the problems of current development, including the complicated processes and phenomena of the third world, because it has never stood still but ceaselessly developed, adding new propositions and conclusions to its body of theory.'[32] A dramatic claim to offer the only truth may not of itself attract attention unless the claim is taken seriously by others. Some western scholars do indeed regard it with respect: 'At the crucial point of transition from a pre-industrial society to a modern, at least partly industrialized state, Marxism becomes in a sense the natural ideology of that society and the most alluring solution to its problems.'[33]

In any case, the wide distribution of Soviet publications throughout the third world means that this claim is being made before a far wider readership than in the past. Moscow's multilingual weekly *New Times* and monthly *International Affairs* have long brought the Soviet view to a broad public throughout the non-communist world. The scholarly quarterly *Social Sciences* carries regular academic articles on the third world, and the yearbook *Africa* brings a solid offering of Soviet africanists' specialized monographs to an anglophone readership. Besides these periodical publications there is a growing library of local language translations of Soviet writings aimed at the literate public and students of individual countries. Local elites can read for themselves both the marxist-leninist analysis of their development problems and the Soviet policy recommendations for their solutions. Marxist-leninist vocabulary is now an established part of the ideological and intellectual environment into which the modernizing elites are exposed in their socialization process, whether in the University of Dar-es-Salaam, at the Sorbonne, or at Patrice Lumumba University in Moscow.[34] The very fact that the analysis in these books and articles comes not from the capitalist west but from the socialist east can make the marxist-leninist analysis attractive a priori for the intelligentsia in the ex-colonial world. The anti-imperialist, strongly nationalist, and explicitly state-centred orientations of the marxist-leninist correspond closely with the attitudes of both the leaders from the liberation movement days and those even in the second generation of leadership for whom solutions coming from western sources have proven disillusioning in the face of their enormous, intractable problems. Now that the first enthusiasm of independence has passed in most new nations and now that the leaderships are having to confront worsening situations (deteriorating trade terms, declining flows of foreign aid, increasing competition on world markets, and unyielding internal bottlenecks) their search for new solutions, new policies, and new ideologies to arouse popular enthusiasm and relegitimize their flagging charisma could move them to take the Soviet ideological claims more seriously.

There is a third and more important reason to justify taking the lines of the Soviet development analysis at face value. At a time when western development analysis is under attack for conceptual degeneracy, it may be opportune to look further afield for intellectual cross-fertilization.[35] The general attributes of marxist-leninist scholarship seem at first glance to meet the criticisms of the radical academic. Those who decry the static quality of the traditional institutional concerns of political science will find the marxist-leninist giving low priority to considerations of formal political structures. Anyone uneasy with the effervescent individualism of the theoretical systems of western development scholars may be attracted by the historical stability of the marxist-leninist concepts. Those who find the theoretical frameworks of the structural-functionalists hard to apply in the real world of empirical analysis may find the Soviet concern for state power, class, and industry more relevant to the new nations' pressing problems. And any who feel that the fragmentation of the social sciences into autonomous disciplines has let the major national issues fall between the separate academic stools of politics, economics, and sociology could find that the integrated social-economical-political approach of the marxist-leninist school better corresponds to their methodological preferences. While highly sophisticated in their theory and elaborate in their methodology, western social sciences have been criticized as unable to see the forest for the trees – or rather notice the forest fire for their concern for tree disease. Those making this reproach should at least consider the Soviet claims to offer a 'political economy' that is historically dynamic, conceptually stable, socially relevant, and disciplinarily integrated.

One's first discovery is that Soviet analysis is quite different from anything produced in the west. Indeed, since the marxist-leninist is ideologically alien to all non-communist systems, one should expect his application of the marxist critique to provide a strikingly distinct impression of the problems of development. The communist scholar is an outsider to the ex-colony. He neither bears a sense of guilt for colonialism nor feels a need to defend the metropolitan record. His ideological commitments favour revolutionary change and independence from neo-imperialism rather than stability and maintenance of ex-colonial ties with the west. The questions asked by the marxist-leninist differ from those posed by the western analyst; we should expect the answers offered also to be different. Since these questions are centred on the problem of class struggle and socioeconomic transformation, we should anticipate the analysis to be dynamic rather than static. In short, marxism-leninism is a different intellectual language, whether written in Russian, English, or French. As an analytical system, it has its own assumptions, concepts, norms, and methodology; it raises specific types of problems, uses distinct sources of information, and produces its own kind of analysis and policy recommendations.

Notwithstanding the fluctuations of Soviet ideological positions following political shifts in the Kremlin, another distinguishing characteristic of Soviet social science over the decades is the stability of its conceptual system. The marxist-leninist vocabulary, its general approach, its normative assumptions, and its methodology have remained very markedly constant for over half a century. While it is true that some notions such as the 'Asiatic mode of production' have been discredited only to be rehabilitated later, and while some formulations like 'national democracy' have been created to conceptualize new phenomena in the independent ex-colonies, a Soviet Rip Van Winkle who went to sleep in 1928 would have little difficulty comprehending the texts of Soviet works when awakening in 1978.

THE CENTRALITY OF INDIA

The objective of this monograph is to provide the non-marxist reader an exposition and interpretation of the Soviets' development theory. It must be confessed at the outset that this is a forbidding project. Since new books and articles are appearing in Moscow every week, it is a gargantuan task to keep up with the flow of Russian publications, let alone analyse all the material that has been produced on all the questions of interest to Soviet scholars on all the countries about which they have written. This problem would be insuperable were it not for an imbalance in the Soviet opus.

Any extensive bibliographical study reveals that India enjoys a predominant place in Soviet orientology. The factors that caused this special Soviet scholarly attention to India are also reasons to give India a central place in the exposition of the Soviet development theory. As the opening quotation to this chapter indicates, the history of marxist-leninist concern for India's strategic international position goes back to the first days of the October Revolution. As late as 1924 India was still the colony which Stalin considered held the greatest hope for rapid revolutionary overthrow.[36] Since 1922, when M.N. Roy, one of the most influential non-Russian intellectuals in the early years of the Communist International, wrote a book giving the first extensive post-revolutionary Bolshevik analysis of India's problems, there has been a continuous flow of marxist-leninist publications on India. This provides us with a historical depth to the Soviet view of development which is unique to the Soviets' third world analysis. The India department of the Institute of the Peoples of Asia also happens to have the longest tradition and the highest standards of scholarship in Soviet orientology, tracing its roots back to tsarist days. By comparison, the writings on Africa and Latin America were superficial and dogmatic until the late 1950s.[37] Furthermore, since English is the intellectual language of India, Soviet scholars for whom English is the first foreign language find less difficulty doing research there than in non-English-speaking countries.

India is a subcontinent of great social and economic complexity. With some of the world's most backward agrarian sectors, it lends itself to the study of precapitalist forms of production. While in many ways underdeveloped, the country already possesses advanced industrial sectors operating in a variant of a mixed economy which gives the marxist-leninist ample scope to apply the major lines of his classical critique of capitalism. In fact, as we shall see, India became central to the Soviet analysis in another sense. The rehabilitation of Mahatma Gandhi as a progressive leader of the national liberation movement was considered a crucial change in the Soviet assessment of the whole national bourgeoisie throughout the third world.[38] The concept of state capitalism, central to Soviet development theory, was articulated most fully for independent India.[39] Even though in the Soviet evaluation India has shifted from being at the vanguard of the non-aligned countries to constituting their prime example of a capitalist albeit still progressive power, it has maintained its leading position as the Soviets' most analysed third world country. This has made the Soviet assessment of the Indian scene a bellwether of Soviet development analysis even in Africa.[40]

The general significance of Soviet writings on India is greatly increased by the universalism of the marxist-leninist approach. 'While making certain allowances for important differences in the various countries, Soviet Asian and African experts have always tended to regard the colonial world and the dependent countries as a whole' wrote Walter Laqueur.[41] Until the 1960s Soviet scholarship tended 'to treat Latin America as one big undifferentiated area.'[42] If, in the Soviet academy, a country is considered the same until proven different, then what is written about India will apply *mutatis mutandis* to the rest of the third world.

India enjoys a pre-eminence among Soviet scholars not only because of its inherent interest and importance but also because it is most accessible to research. The Indian subcontinent is crucial for the Soviet analysis of underdevelopment for the good reason that the statistical information for research purposes is better there than for any other developing area. In an important study on small-scale industry, for instance, Kuzmin did his work 'chiefly on the basis of statistical materials of India, Burma and Pakistan because these materials are the most complete and comprehensive. Unfortunately, statistics on other countries do not permit us to arrive at any kind of coherent idea as to the basic indicators of the activity of small-scale industry and are therefore used only as supplementary illustrative material for the basic conclusions.'[43] The better scholars make traditional cautionary observations that in other countries the situation may be quite different and that more research must be done, but until that additional work is done India often remains the major case study of a problem.

Since India has practised what the Soviet government has defined as a progressive foreign policy and a relatively progressive internal policy, the Soviet analysis of India has not been clouded by the type of distortion that can mar their analysis of a regime considered hostile and reactionary. The fact that India was one of the first independent countries of the third world with whom the Soviet Union established diplomatic relations deepens the historical perspective from which one can observe post-war Soviet analysis. Since diplomatic relations between these two countries have remained friendly and, by comparison with the violent swings of Soviet relations with other ex-colonies,[44] relatively stable since Stalin's death,[45] this continuity in foreign policy has provided the framework for a generally stable, though not static, ideological stance towards India. That the major lines of the Soviet analysis of India – its anti-imperialist foreign policy, the progressive historical role of its national bourgeoisie, the positive contribution of state capitalism – have remained constant themes in the Soviet writings in the period since 1955, this body of literature can be studied as a relatively homogeneous whole, even though there have been significant variations in particular aspects of the Soviet view.

PROBLEMS OF METHODOLOGY AND RESEARCH

For the social scientist concerned above all with the verification of all propositions it is important to note that this study shares the methodological limitations of all sovietology. The quality of evidence and conditions of research are such that many statements can only be made as speculations. Foreign scholars, for example, can utilize Soviet writings that are available in the Soviet libraries, but access to Soviet dissertations is generally restricted to the twelve-page printed summaries filed in the Lenin Library. The private papers that circulate within research institutes, especially research reports written expressly for the CPSU secretariat, are strictly inaccessible. It is even difficult to be sure that one has kept track of all the openly published works: books promised in pre-publication notices do not always see the light of day. The Soviet book distribution system is so disorganized that it is often difficult for the foreign library or scholar ordering a book at long distance to obtain copies. One scholar I interviewed in Moscow apologized that he could not show me a copy of his most recent book: he had been out of the country when it was published so had not been able to obtain a copy even for his own use.

The interview is of unpredictable and varying value. Even when one gains access to the Soviet scholarly establishment, one's ability to discuss academic topics fruitfully is severely restricted by the power of each institute's academic secretary who decides which scholars will be interviewed – regardless of whom the researcher wishes to see.[46] If the foreign researcher is to respect the anonymity demanded by his Soviet interviewees, he must either abstain from using the insights gained from direct conversations with the authors whose work he is studying or use the material without attributing a source. This is not to say that fruitful discussion could not take place with groups of Soviet scholars. In fact one of the reasons the Soviet analysis of India has proven most susceptible of careful analysis is the self-confidence of the Soviet indologists whose institute is among the oldest, whose quality is among the best, and whose scholars are among the most forthright in the whole area of Soviet orientology.

Research facilities are not the only methodological constraint. No less important is the author's own intellectual perspective. It is especially clear in a study of this kind that the character of the analysis will be largely determined by the bias of the analyst. While not a marxist-leninist, but what the Soviets might label a 'progressive,' my most obvious ideological bias is a distaste both for the tensions of the cold war and for that scholarship in the East and in the West which has contributed to the perpetuation of a great power confrontation whose major consequence is to keep the third world vulnerable and destitute.

To undertake a study of part of marxist-leninist thought is to open up the same possibilities and to run the same risks as making an inquiry into another faith or a study of another language. Scholars raised in the Judaeo-Christian tradition and studying Moslem thought bring to that inquiry a range of questions arising from their own tradition. They have the opportunity to open up new perspectives, just as they run the danger of so missing the essential truths that their distortions do more damage than can be compensated for by their insights. Similarly, the study of a language by someone with a different linguistic background can produce an awareness of syntactical structure that escapes the native-born. Yet not having been steeped since birth in the literature and the oral tradition, outsiders may miss subtleties that would be second nature to scholars studying their mother tongue.

The analogies of comparative religious and linguistic studies are chosen advisedly. For a non-marxist to venture into the world of Soviet thought is to be suddenly lifted into an intellectual world where words have different meanings, where rules of logic are not the same, where simple assumptions that are the foundations for his normal intellectual intercourse do not hold true. While the general patterns of language are similar, the actual linguistics are quite different. The meaning of a concept such as 'democratic' or 'exploitation' or 'contradiction' is likely to be quite different from his own connotation of the word. And yet it is not simply a question of making accurate translations from one language of political analysis to another. What strikes the liberal intellectual in talking with a Soviet scholar or in reading a Soviet book is the metaphysical distance that separates their two mental worlds. Axioms unquestioned in one vision of the world may be totally unacceptable in the other.

If I cannot claim to possess the inner comprehension of a believer in marxism-leninism, I hope to transcend the passions of the cold war in an attempt to convey to the non-communist reader the essence of the Soviet marxist-leninist vision of development problems in the third world. Good intentions do not of course guarantee the successful achievement of an exercise in impartiality. It is at times difficult to retain an open mind when reading Soviet writings that are often tendentious, badly constructed, contradictory, or just poorly written. Nor should impartiality preclude critical comment. If marxist-leninists are misapplying the limited resources that they do allocate towards the study of development problems, then this should be stated, not with the aim of scoring cheap debating points, but with the hope that justified criticisms will in fact be taken as intended – to improve the product of the Soviet development research effort. If Soviet scholars know they are read abroad they may increasingly accept international standards of scholarship, rather than the more parochial norms applied to writing designed for internal consumption within the Soviet Union.

Another consequence of being an outsider to the Soviet school must be acknowledged. Even in describing one must obviously make choices about what is worth reporting and what is not, about what is more important and what is less. In many cases one is obliged to extrapolate from a statement necessarily quoted out of its full context in order to make a coherent presentation of the point being analysed. In some cases the extrapolated version may be more coherent than the original – a particularly great danger with the Soviet type of writing in which unresolved contradictions are often left for the reader to cope with himself. Since it is impossible to distinguish exposition from commentary completely, I have tried to let the analysis 'speak for itself' as much as possible without drowning the reader in quotations. It is my hope that the discussion of the Soviet writings on state capitalism, foreign aid, and agrarian reform will provide a means of access and insight into the whole Soviet conception of under-development.

An assumption which underlies this study is reflected in the title. To talk of the 'Soviet' analysis may imply there is a single Soviet view. Yet a book titled 'The American Theory of Development' would appear strange to anyone familiar with the many disparate schools of thought in the United States. The high degree of control exercised over all publications in the Soviet Union allows us to use as a working hypothesis that all publications which appear in the USSR have an official nature, especially in such a delicate realm as international relations. Furthermore, the ideological homogeneity inculcated through the Soviet educational process and enforced by the whole system of collective scholarly enterprise, gives Soviet writing a uniformity distinct from the multiplicity of schools of thought to be found in the western academies. This does not imply, for instance, that all Soviet indologists have identical views concerning all Indian problems or that analysts of Tanzanian agriculture will parrot their colleagues' views on latifundia in Brazil. There are divergencies among the different Soviet authors on many particular points both of principle and detail. But there is a unity in the organization of the Soviet academia, despite the existence of separate institutions in the federated republics, that allows one to talk of a Soviet school in the simple sense of there being an identifiable core of leading scholars and their students.

Other factors make it more difficult to interpret the significance of Soviet writings. Quite apart from the difficulties noted above in plumbing the personal depths of the Soviet analyst, there is an intellectual art to identifying such obviously important factors as the condition at any particular time of the Soviet strategic evaluation of the different members of the third world. The impact of internal political changes within the Soviet Communist Party on the fortunes of the Academy of Sciences in general and the particular institutes is, as a rule, hidden behind a solid and impenetrable screen of silence.[47] So too are the repercussions on particular theories and areas of thought of such international factors as the Sino-Soviet conflict. The relationship between Soviet foreign policy as decided in the Ministry of Foreign Affairs or the secretariat of the Communist Party and the main lines of the Soviet analysis as decided in the institutes' party committee and secretariat is even better hidden from scholarly view. The relevance of a developing country's political situation to the Soviets' appreciation of its world role and its local revolutionary prospects can only be perceived indirectly and with the aid of considerable doses of intuition.[48] These are all critical factors which must influence in varying degrees the written output of the Soviet scholars. But to what extent and in what order these factors play a role an outside observer cannot establish precisely. Certainly it would be desirable to be able to evaluate the exact role of each of these variables in determining the character of the Soviet analysis. Even in a reasonably open political system it is extremely difficult to identify causal links between policy and ideology with any certainty. Yet if this study were postponed until the necessary research facilities were provided in the Soviet Union we would have a very long wait indeed.

This book therefore does not offer a political sociology of Soviet development studies. It is not duplicating the existing studies of Soviet doctrine at the level of strategy for the communist movement. It does not deal with the non-ruling communist parties of the third world. Instead its attention is focused on the developmental and theoretical significance of the officially published Soviet texts. It is to the analysis of these texts that we now turn.

2

The first four decades

The Soviet comprehension of development did not spring fully grown from the ashes of the Russian revolution to remain constant from the inflammatory exhortations of Leon Trotsky through to the administrative sermons of Leonid Brezhnev. Nor did marxism-leninism evolve exclusively in response to the praxis of the Bolshevik leaders pulling themselves up to great power status by their Russian bootstraps. It is important for the investigator searching for the Soviet analysis of underdevelopment to keep in mind that their theory derives from a number of elements. Some of these factors, such as Marx's writings, date back a century and more; others, like the current concerns of Soviet foreign policymakers, are responding to the pressures of the present; all are subject to a constant process of re-evaluation and redefinition in the analysts' minds, as they wrestle with their ongoing intellectual tasks.

First of the pre-revolutionary components is Marx and Engels's own opus, which established a foundation and a direction to subsequent revolutionary thinking. Although they did not conceive of the colonial peoples playing a revolutionary role and though they felt colonialism to be a historically necessary and objectively progressive process – both themes that were to be reversed by their ideological descendants – they did establish a number of paradigms that were to mould the contours of subsequent marxian analysis. The historicist evaluation of national movements, with its dialectical appreciation of the bourgeoisie's role, was developed in the context of European nationalist movements but was to be applied later to national movements in the 'East.' Making the judgment of a particular national movement's progressiveness depend on the historic role it might be playing at the moment in furthering or impeding the supreme goal of undermining reaction (tsarist Russia) and furthering the proletarian revolution, for instance, was a relativism that was easily adapted by communist ideologues who were later to judge the progressiveness of any national bourgeois government in the third world by the extent to which it supported or opposed the interests of the socialist fatherland.[1]

Of equal importance were the fragmentary applications of their theory of economic development to what they considered backward areas. In raising the question of Russian, Indian, and Chinese undevelopment, Marx and Engels debated why feudalism had not taken over, experimented with a new concept of an Asiatic production mode, and theorized on the progressive developmental impact of the British colonial penetration.[2] In confrontation and correspondence with Russian revolutionaries interested in advancing direct from their 'asiatic despotism' to socialism without passing through a capitalist stage, Marx and Engels accepted the possibility of using the communal property of the peasant commune as the point of departure for communist development, subject to world proletarian support.[3]

The next major contribution to the marxist-leninist background was the revolutionaries' debates at the turn of the century that formed the intellectual climate in which Lenin and his fellow Russian marxists cut their own ideological teeth. This factor is best understood as negative since Lenin's ideas largely emerged in battle against what he considered the erroneous formulations of his rival revolutionary theorists in Europe and in Russia. It was through interaction with the Austro-Marxists and in reacting against Rosa Luxemburg's and Kautsky's Eurocentric internationalism that he worked out his ideas on the nationalist question for Russia. In Russia the debate on overcoming backwardness had centred on the issues of industrialization versus the defence of peasant society.[4] When Plekhanov for the first time seriously applied Marx's economic theory to the Russian situation, he precipitated the debate with the dominant populists over the extent of capitalist development in Russia that Lenin was to make his own,[5] berating the utopian narodniks for refusing to recognize a process that he laboured to prove was objectively gaining ground.[6] While Lenin reacted against the populists for being insufficiently determinist, he opposed the Mensheviks for their excessive determinism which kept them from revolutionary activity on the grounds that Russia's capitalist development was insufficiently advanced to create appropriate revolutionary conditions for the proletariat.

Lenin's own decisive contribution made the crucial adaptation of a western revolutionary theory to a relatively backward and semi-oriental society. His voluntarism, which refused to wait for history to catch up with revolutionary urgency, his organizational sleight-of-hand, which created a party to act in the name of an admittedly weak proletariat, and his sensitivity to the revolutionary potential inherent in nationalist and peasant discontents made Lenin not just the successful revolutionary strategist but the crucial mediator of marxist thought for the pre-capitalist third world.[7]

Among the post-revolutionary components of marxist-leninist theory, there are five that must be borne in mind if one is to comprehend the Soviet consciousness. First in importance is the impact of strategic considerations. If world revolutionary strategy dictated a priority to fomenting revolution in the East, then large efforts would be expended to analyse the balance of class forces, the current stage of development, and the peculiarities of nationality problems of the various peoples. But if it looked as if the revolutionary fires were burning hottest in Europe, then analysis of the East would be dropped in favour of concentration on the West. This strategic vacillation between East and West had two major consequences for the ultimate Soviet development theory. First of all, it caused crippling gaps in the intellectual development of Soviet orientalists. Since investment in research on the third world depended on a strategic judgment that the colonies had a high revolutionary potential, Stalin's downgrading of the East necessarily led to a dark age in Soviet orientology lasting for the final twenty-five years of Stalin's rule. A second consequence emerged from the unresolved debate over granting priority to revolution in the East or in the West. With the Chinese communists fighting for the former position, the whole corpus of Soviet writings on the third world since destalinization has been moulded by the less leftist, more determinist view that the future of the world revolution rests primarily in the West.

Following this strategic judgment comes the tactical assessment. What prospects a communist party had in a particular country could and did have a discernible impact on Soviet thinking concerning that country. The weakness of communist parties in Latin America and their apparently bleak prospects for revolutionary breakthroughs accounted for the general Soviet disinterest in that area and the consequent weakness of Soviet Latin American studies until the Cuban revolution boosted their hopes in the western hemisphere.[8] Tactical considerations could work against local communist parties as well as in their favour. Optimistic assessments of the revolutionary potential of the radical one-party states in the third world led to a marked improvement in Soviet relations with them, despite these regimes' outright discrimination against local communists.[9] Tactical shifts from left wing to right wing, from violent to non-violent, or from coalitions 'from above' to coalitions 'from below' would be expressed in analysis and transmitted in print, often dramatically changing the Soviet perspective on a country. When a local communist party was largely directed by advice from Moscow, the tactical component of Soviet writings had a considerable importance for the writers, as for the readers.[10]

Often, and more recently of greater importance, considerations of Soviet foreign policy have been determinant. Once Soviet relations with the United Arab Republic improved, the dictates of national interest far outweighed concerns about Egyptian communists in determining the scale of Soviet military and economic aid and so the content of the Soviet analysis of Nasser's socialism.[11]

Side by side with Soviet concerns about relations with non-communist countries are relations with other communist powers. Given the acuity of the Sino-Soviet conflict for power and prestige in the third world, intracommunist considerations must also be rated as an important input into Soviet analysis both at the strategic level as noted above and in more immediate ways. The impact of the Sino-Soviet rivalry on Soviet policy towards, and analysis of, Pakistan is a case in point.[12]

Once of crucial weight, now seemingly insignificant, is the impact of internal Soviet politics. Stalin's struggle for power was inextricably linked with the politics of the Comintern during the 1920s and had startling effects on the violent shifts in international communist strategy, tactics, and analysis.[13] By comparison, the ouster of Khrushchev and his replacement by Brezhnev had much less impact on the content of Soviet analysis of the third world. While this implies neither that major upheavals in the Kremlin could not again affect Soviet development writings nor that the politics of the Academy of Sciences is a negligible factor in creating the climate of socialist collectivism within which Russian academics must operate, Soviet internal politics can be left at the bottom of our list of factors providing the ideological inputs into Soviet development theorizing and research.

Two implications of this analysis are worth noting immediately. As the Soviet Union has become consolidated in its superpower status with a decreasing interest in external revolutions that could endanger its position, research by intellectuals has been increasingly possible for its own sake. Whereas any scholarly interest in Bolshevik writings was entirely derivative from their essential revolutionary function in the early years after the October Revolution and were completely subservient to Stalin's international obsessions for the second leadership phase of the USSR, a large proportion of Soviet writing now seems largely free of direct policy considerations. Written from a concern for the subject matter, considerable amounts of Soviet writing can now be read as contributions to the understanding of development problems.

With this growing commitment to the international status quo has come a reversion in the Soviet perspective from the leninist or voluntarist emphasis that characterized the first decade of the Comintern to a more marxist or determinist stance that finds it easier to accept - and to analyse - situations where revolution may have only poor prospects.

Some countries, such as most African states now subject to Soviet scrutiny, have practically no background of marxist-leninist analysis. Others, like China and India, fascinated Marx and his successors since the 1850s. It would be tedious to sketch the history of the Soviet 'line' on every major colony and third world state, not just because of the number of separate stories to tell and because of the low quality of the Soviet early writings on the majority, but because 'Soviet Asian and African experts have always tended to regard the colonial world and the dependent countries as a whole.' If it is 'impossible to retrace the discussions and disputes about the Middle East except in the wider framework of the great Soviet debate on the coming Asian revolution,'[14] it also follows that there is more to be learned about the background of Soviet orientology by following with care the vicissitudes of the Soviet writings on one particular country. From the first months after the Russian Revolution to the years following Stalin's death in 1953, the Soviet line on the colonial question went through five major phases. The broad lines of the evolving marxist-leninist approach to development emerge with greatest clarity from Soviet publications on India, the country where they first expected a successful colonial revolution and which became the symbol, after the dark decades of stalinist neglect, for the Soviet Union's rapprochement with the third world.

THE BOLSHEVIK CALL TO ARMS

While Soviet diplomats are fond of tracing Soviet relations with India to the Russian merchant Athanasi Nikitin and his exploratory trek to India in the late fifteenth century, tsarist interest in India was imperial rather than commercial, spasmodic rather than compulsive.[15] The bolshevik revolution transformed this interest from occasional schemes of military campaigns to a much more active concern for revolution. While the tsars dreamed of pushing the English out of their empire by military force, the Bolsheviks hoped to kill two birds with one stone: continue in the East the chain reaction of the world revolution and cut off their principal enemy, British imperialism, from its strategic supply base in the colonies.

The Bolsheviks did not lose much time in directing their revolutionary message towards India, considered to be the most advanced of the colonial areas and so the ripest soil for insurrectionary seed. Already on 7 December 1917 the Soviets launched an appeal to the Muslims of Russia and the East in which they maintained that 'even distant India ... has raised the standard of the revolution.'[16] The first Soviet texts devoted to the East express the definite hope to find in India the avant-garde of the socialist revolution on the Asian continent: 'India can and must become for the East what Russia today has already become for the West ... the hearth of the revolution proclaiming liberation from imperialist exploitation for the oppressed nations and their toiling masses, an anti-imperialist force on both the national and the class fronts.'[17] Though these first hopes were disappointed, India remained a central focus for such Bolshevik propaganda as Zinoviev's passionate appeal for a crusade against British imperialism at the Congress of the Peoples of the East at Baku in September 1920.[18]

THE FIRST MARXIST-LENINIST ANALYSIS

The second period of the Soviet analysis bears the intellectual imprint of M.N. Roy, the Indian Communist, who had already made his mark in the Comintern by successfully having his theses on the colonial problem adopted at the second Congress of July 1920 even though they were diametrically opposed to Lenin's views. His book, *India in Transition*, hailed in the foreword to its Russian translation of 1923 to be the 'first Marxist research on India,'[19] remained still in 1925 'almost the only one in Russian literature on contemporary India.'[20]

According to Roy, India had already entered the stage of capitalist development, 'the last vestiges' of feudalism having disappeared as a result of the failure of the Indian mutiny of 1857. Despite Great Britain's resistance to the establishment of native Indian enterprise, a huge expansion of modern industry had in fact taken place in the two decades preceding the outbreak of the first world war. When the military situation prevented the export to India of English products and increased the mother country's need for the economic support of its major colony, Great Britain made a drastic revision of its colonial economic policy. It now actively encouraged the expansion of local industries, even going so far as to permit tariff protection of India's textiles. The revolutionary significance of the prodigious industrial expansion that resulted was clear to Roy. The capitalist class that by 1922 already controlled 75 per cent of Indian industry, railroads, mines, and plantations excepted, would be at the head of the movement to overthrow foreign domination. But the bourgeoisie would not be able to maintain its leadership of the national movement because only a 'radical agrarian revolution' would be able to solve the principal Indian crisis, that of agriculture.[21]

The Soviet writings devoted to India until the stalinization of the Bolshevik regime reflect the influence of Roy's book. These works emphasize the extremely rapid development of Indian industry, whose domestically owned capital rose by 2000 per cent during the first world war.[22] The significance of India's industrialization was seen to transcend the colony's frontiers; it 'creates the economic basis for the national revolutionary movements in the East.'[23] That India was already a 'modern capitalist country' was not seriously doubted: 'During the last decade, India had rapidly been transformed from a furnisher of raw materials for the industrial countries into an industrial country itself ... During the war, the export of raw materials, cotton and jute, diminished but the export of finished cloth doubled. India's railroad network is growing now, thanks to the participation of local capital and a rapid growth of industries extracting metals, manufacturing industries and machine tools.'[24] Given Stalin's priority expectation for revolutionary outbreak in India, Soviet writers were still emphasizing by 1925 the importance of Indian industry and its vast proletariat, estimated at eight million workers,[25] although the rapid expansion of Indian industry did not mean an end of British exploitation. On the contrary, capitalist development stimulated English exploitation of India, but under a new form. As Indian products cost less than English, the English transferred their economic activity to the colonial country itself. 'Now they import their capital, open their factories there and, with their own hands, seize local industry.'[26]

The class situation was analysed in terms familiar to any leninist: the national bourgeoisie vacillates between its national resistance to foreign domination and its need for international class support against internal revolutionary pressures. If the national bourgeoisie, under its 'petty bourgeois' leader Mahatma Gandhi, makes a compromise with Great Britain, then the 'success of the revolutionary red trade unions in India is assured.' As for the peasantry, some 220 million strong, it 'forms the principal base for India's national liberation struggle.' Leadership, however, must be in the hands of the conscious revolutionary group. If the struggle against the English is not led by the bourgeoisie 'but by the progressive proletariat and the revolutionary intelligentsia, then the [tactical] union with the peasantry will be decisive for victory.'[27]

STALINIZATION

After the decimation of the Chinese communists by the Kuomintang in 1927, the consequent belated swing to the left of the Comintern, and the purge of Trotsky and other potential rivals to Stalin's authority within the Soviet Union, Soviet orientology entered its dark decades. Although during the quarter-century that Stalin was in power there were many changes of strategy (from maximum confrontation to alliance with British imperialism) and of tactics (from co-operation to subversion by the communists of the Indian National Congress, the political arm of the national bourgeoisie),[28] what is important to notice here is the poverty of the few writings devoted by the Soviets to India up to the end of the second world war. The whole period of the Soviet analysis was dominated by the remarks Stalin had made on 18 May 1925 during his much celebrated speech to the students of the Communist University of the Workers of the East. In this address he classified India as the most capitalistically developed of the dependent countries, having a 'more or less numerous national proletariat.' He denounced the 'conciliatory part' of the Indian bourgeoisie, Gandhi included, for already having made a compromise with English imperialism. As a result, it was necessary to 'prepare the proletariat for the leadership of the liberation movement.' The hegemony of the proletariat, of course, 'can only be prepared and realized by the Communist Party.'[29]

As part of their function, the writings of this period join the witch-hunt of those who deviated from the jagged line of marxism-leninism-stalinism. Thus a book devoted to the famous Meerut trial of Indian communists (1929-33) denounced the 'counter-revolutionary Menshevik policy of the former Indian communist Roy.' According to these authors, 'Roy had obstructed by all possible means the creation of an Indian Communist Party.'[30]

Roy had joined the ranks of the heretics of Stalinism upon the condemnation at the sixth Comintern Congress in 1928 of his 'decolonization theory' and his expulsion from the Comintern the next year.[31] He had maintained that imperialism had changed its strategy, now favouring economic development in the colonies, a process that would inevitably lead to decolonization. Since this view was now officially anathema, a second preoccupation of the writings of this period was to insist that imperialism was trying to prevent economic development in the colonies, a theme that permeates Soviet writings to this day.

The preface to a book published in 1935 clearly defined the Stalinist theory on this topic: 'Aiming to strengthen its domination in the colonies, imperialism does not develop their productive forces; it impedes their development. However, the role of imperialism in the colonies is contradictory. Because of its interest in strengthening its colonial domination, England ... is forced to permit a certain amount of development, not only of its own industry but even of native industry.'[32] A small book written by Pronin in 1940 shows to what extent this denunciation of Roy's thesis was solidly established. The structure of Indian industry makes it absolutely self-evident that 'the alleged "theory" of decolonization' promoting the free development of India's productive forces, was 'fundamentally erroneous and counter-revolutionary.' Although this analysis insisted on imperialism's resistance to colonial development, it nevertheless maintained that India was sufficiently developed for her proletariat to be able to dominate the revolutionary struggle. Thus Pronin denounced the 'complete inconsistency of counter-revolutionary Trotskyist-Zinovievist agrarianism (*agrariatorstvo*)' which denies the existence of industrial capitalism in the colonies. This other heresy 'denies the presence in India of the proletariat and its leading role in the national liberation struggle against British imperialism.'[33]

The years of military collaboration with Great Britain in the war against Nazi Germany were to cause a relaxation in the hostility of the Soviet analysis towards imperial rule. In her 1943 book Sofia Melman put less stress on the revolutionary character of the proletariat than on the large role played by India as 'an important military and economic base against the Fascists.' Although she pointed to the feeble development of heavy industry as a whole, she now praised the significant expansion of the chemical and metallurgical sectors under English encouragement.[34]

The period of bonne entente was short-lived. As cold war tensions escalated between the communist and Atlantic blocs, they extended to the third world. After a period of uncertainty from 1945 to 1947, the Soviet line hardened into hostility toward any country, new or old, that was not an explicit ally. Under the two-camp thesis and the Cominform, India with its bourgeois government, like every other developing country or colonial leadership, was denounced as a lackey of British-American imperialism.

An instructive way to follow the impact of the ups and downs of Stalinist strategy on post-war Soviet development analysis is to trace the vicissitudes of the theses defended by Eugene Varga, the prominent Hungarian economist who in 1928 had launched the campaign against M.N. Roy's theory of decolonization[35] but who was to suffer for adopting Roy-like views two decades later. The publication in 1946 of his pioneering study, *Changes in the Economy of Capitalism Resulting from the Second World War*, was taken as a major revision of the Soviet view of the state of world capitalism. Documented in the chapter devoted to the economic situation in the colonies was Varga's proposition that, by the reduction of imports, particularly of textiles, and the need to feed the European army, the war had fostered in the colonies and in India especially the 'tendency toward the development of its own industry.' Varga did not challenge the marxist-leninist stand that British policy was hostile to India's industrial development, but he noted that the Americans had opposed this policy by sending machinery and machine tools to India in application of its Lend-Lease programme.[36]

The recognition of the progress achieved by Indian industry during the war did not in itself constitute a striking innovation for the Soviet analysis. The originality of Varga's chapter lay in his emphasizing a fact which was 'completely new, without precedent in the history of imperialism': the reduction of the colonial countries' financial dependence on their metropolitan power. India, for example, had accumulated by the end of the war a £ 737 million credit with Great Britain, representing a reversal of the debt relationship by £ 1,045 million in India's favour. Although this credit was frozen, Great Britain had undertaken to liquidate it by delivering capital goods over a ten-year period which itself would give 'the development of India's productive forces a strong push forward.' The resulting industrial expansion 'would in turn strengthen both India's economic position and that of the Indian bourgeoisie in its competition with Britain.' Thus, Varga concluded, 'the economic dependence of the majority of the colonies on their mother countries will never be as great as it had been before the war.'[37]

Varga's reappraisal soon fell victim to the Soviet response to the Cold War. For the colonies the left turn in Stalin's foreign policy announced by Zhuhov in 1947 spelled a strategy for local communist parties of radically anti-bourgeois opposition in which Varga's attribution of pre-eminence to the local bourgeoisie was no longer tolerated. During a debate organized in Moscow at the Institute of World Economics and Politics, of which he was director in May 1947, Varga was accused of having given the impression in his book that the colonies could achieve independence by purely economic means. V.V. Reichhart, for example, insisted that, on the contrary, the only possible road leading to independence was revolution. Another hostile colleague, A.N. Shneerson, stated that, Varga's evidence notwithstanding, the colonial situation had not changed in principle; only the forms of imperialist exploitation had been altered – not its substance.[38]

The attack on Varga's theses was followed the next month by a meeting of the Soviet Academy of Sciences devoted to India.[39] The condemnation of the Indian National Congress as a reactionary bourgeois party was the official indication of the re-revised hard line vision of the colonial world in general and of hostility to Nehru's bourgeois regime, which on 15 August 1947 became a Dominion within the Commonwealth.

During this last phase of the stalinist period, Soviet writings on India grew in quantity if not in quality. The major themes of this analysis are summarized in the 1953 edition of Varga's book, reissued to correct the errors of his 1946 volume. The starting point for Varga's revised analysis of the colonial and ex-colonial world is India's position in the struggle between the capitalist and socialist camps. The colonial system was disintegrating from within under the stress of the 'general crisis of capitalism.'[40] India's relationship to this process was seen in exactly the same terms as Stalin had used in his speech of 1925 which Varga dutifully quotes on page 330: The creation of the Indian Dominion is merely symbolic of the compromise made between the English imperialist bourgeoisie and the Congress's ruling puppet bloc of big capitalists and landowners. By granting formal independence, English monopoly capitalism was trying to conserve its economic position in India with the aid of the native ruling classes, while the latter were trying, with imperialist aid, to defend the existing social structure against the growing revolutionary movement of the workers and peasants. Although the end of direct political domination over India marked an important stage in imperialism's decline and fall, Varga argued that the British imperialists had fallen back on 'positions prepared in advance' in order to conserve their control of the economy's 'key positions.' Thus India's Dominion status has done nothing to alter the colonial character of her economy.

As for India's wartime credit, which Varga had originally pointed to as a sign of the changing colonial relationship, India was only 'formally' England's creditor. In fact the debt actually tied India to Great Britain, which continued its colonial exploitation by draining from the Dominion some £ 50 million each year.

As a direct consequence of its compromise, Congress abandoned its promised nationalization of the British firms operating in India. Moreover, these companies were merging with Indian capital to form 'mixed companies.' Furthermore, capital equipment continued to be supplied by the English, who thereby retained both technical and financial control. 'Indianization' served only to camouflage the continuing dominance of English capital in the country.

As another dimension of the general crisis of capitalism, India had become a battlefield of the contradictions tearing apart the imperialist camp. The United States was trying to wrench India from England's control especially in the area of foreign trade. Despite this underlying Anglo-American conflict, India still played an important military role in the over-all imperialist scheme against the 'democratic camp.' The concessions given by the Nehru government to Standard Oil and Burma Shell for the construction of large oil refineries were used by Varga to demonstrate not just India's dependence but her place in the American and British imperialists' anti-Soviet strategic design.

At the same time as Congress's compromise had conserved India's colonial external relationships, it had failed to break out of the country's internal economic stagnation. After five years of bourgeois rule, India remained 'a backward agrarian country without machine-building capacity, without machine tool factories and unable to produce locomotives.' As for the planning process, Varga spoke of 'the five year plan' between ironical quotation marks because only $346 million of the total $4,138 million of planned investments are allocated to industrial development. Since British capital was strengthening its positions by new investments, India was becoming 'more and more' a semi-colony of England.

Because the small size of India's internal market remained the principal obstacle to industrialization, the broadening of its capacity by transforming agrarian relationships should have been regarded as an urgent necessity. But the bourgeoisie was sabotaging the agrarian reform. After five years in power, the government had done nothing to accomplish a real transformation of the agrarian scene because overpopulation assured a supply of cheap labour for industry. As the bourgeoisie was continuing the British policy of conserving the feudal conditions of the country's agriculture, it will only be possible to liquidate feudalism 'by a struggle of all the workers, the proletariat in the van, led by the Communist Party, as in China.'

There was no better indication of how the stalinist analysis was locked into a formula perception of the Indian scene than the extent to which the Chinese example dominated Varga's whole political vision. He flatly identified the Indian situation of the 1950s with that of China in 1927. 'After its compromise with English imperialism, Congress has lost its *raison d'être*, just as the Kuomintang did after Chiang Kai-chek's treachery of 1927.' Congress itself was disintegrating from an internal struggle of its different cliques, 'following the example of the Kuomintang.' Moreover, the peasantry was made to fit the model: it was no longer the strategic political base of the bourgeoisie but had become 'the principal reserve of the Indian proletariat in its struggle against the large landowners and the bourgeoisie.' Indeed the large peasant insurrection in Telengana, Hyderabad, in 1948 showed the great potential for a 'revolutionary agrarian transformation.'[41]

DESTALINIZATION

For all their volte-faces, the theses of Varga's 1953 edition were not to remain in style any longer than had those of his original volume. For with the death of Joseph Stalin and the accession to power of a new leadership, the Kremlin's foreign policy was reviewed.

The post-Stalin reversal of Soviet policy towards the third world had been long in preparation as the world situation changed in the early 1950s: Korea being stalemated, India was perceived to be more genuinely non-aligned in practice than had been anticipated; China already represented a great extension of communist power and the Americans were no longer monopolists of nuclear know-how. Symbolized by such dramatic gestures as the Bulganin and Khrushchev trip to India in December 1955, the Soviet change of policy towards the ex-colonies of the third world took the material form of diplomatic support and economic aid. These political changes demanded a total rethinking on the part of Soviet ideologues. The establishment of commercial and diplomatic relations required reliable information and assessments of these countries' economic and political situations. The Soviet research establishment had to be revived. During the 20th Congress of the Communist Party of the Soviet Union, the weakness of Soviet orientology and the errors of the previous analysis were denounced as products of the cult of personality by the same writers who had originally propagated them. The authenticity of the former colonies' political independence and their autonomous, even anti-imperialist, foreign policy; the leading role played by the local bourgeoisie, Gandhi in particular, in the national liberation movement; the possibilities of real economic development under capitalist regimes: these were the new doctrines on which good relations with the ex-colonies were to be based. The newly reactivated research institutes would have to pursue these themes in their academic plans.

As we shall be examining in detail three main aspects of the post-Stalinist development analysis, it is sufficient at this point to sketch the main features of

this new interpretation. The general exposition of this new ideological orientation is best found in the final edition of Varga's book, published in 1957 to correct Stalin's 'erroneous positions' which had been 'repeated without critical
examination' in the 1953 volume, reflecting, he noted, the 'influence of the
personality cult.'[42]

The starting point for Varga's reassessment of the Indian scene was the country's international position. Accepting that India had already won political independence in August 1947, Varga observed that she 'rapidly conquered her full
independence in foreign policy.' Her foreign policy of peace was quite distinct
from that of the imperialist powers. Great Britain had to take India's policy into
consideration just like that of any other independent country. That the Americans were sometimes unhappy with such Indian policies as support for the admission of Communist China to the United Nations was further proof of Indian
diplomatic independence, US loans notwithstanding. India was now seen as a
progressive 'member of the peace zone' at the side of the Soviet Union and
China.

Varga's new analysis of the Indian economy now emphasized the improvements effected since independence – changes that contrasted with the sorry heritage left by imperialism. 'The decade following Indian independence was a
period of considerable progress for the Indian economy, but it was naturally far
from sufficient to liquidate the deathly consequence of two centuries of English
colonial rule.'[43] In industry, production had increased by 80 per cent over nine
years. Another positive sign was the rate of growth of heavy industry, surpassing
that of industry in general, 'which indicates the beginning of the country's industrialization process.' In the agrarian sector Varga noted that the harvest was considerably greater than before the war, thanks to favourable rains and the agrarian
reforms which the Nehru government was gradually introducing. Now that India
was liberated from the 'yoke of the English colonizers who deliberately did not
permit the country's industrialization,' the state's economic intervention by
means of the five-year plans 'plays a major role in gradually changing the economy.' The proportion of manufactured articles had diminished in Indian imports but had increased in its exports, while the share of raw materials had
increased in imports while decreasing in exports. This meant that 'India's position
is changing from being an agricultural and raw-material producing country.'[44] On
this decidedly optimistic note the post-Stalin analysis of India's development
problems was inaugurated.

Over the four decades since 1917 the Soviet analysis of India passed through
several quite distinct stages. During the period when Roy's theses received official approval they eulogized the capitalist and industrialized qualities of India's
economy. After the condemnation of the decolonization theory and the imposi-

tion of Stalin's ideological dead hand, the Soviet writings insisted on the lack of economic development, even after colonies had won their political independence. Backwardness was regarded as primarily due to the resistance by the imperial powers to their colonies' industrialization. Finally the post-stalinist re-evaluation focused on the 'progressiveness' of the states under national bourgeois leadership and again underlined the economic progress achieved since their liberation. The political and ideological conditions were now ripe for a thorough analysis of the social, economic, and political development problems in every third world state in which the Soviet leaders were to take a serious interest.

PART TWO

STATE CAPITALISM

3

The political economy of state capitalism

It does not take the foreign reader of Russian publications long to discover that Soviet marxism-leninism has produced a literature of development analysis unique in the world. Most obviously, marxism-leninism is not an umbrella for a series of isolated social science disciplines each with its own methodology and jargon, its own practitioners and journals. It has no one-dimensional economics in which economic problems are discussed in isolation as technical questions of growth rates or capital/output ratios. Even the quite specialized economics monograph will relate the topic under analysis to its sociopolitical context thus situating the study in a commonly accepted theoretical framework. Similarly, political problems are not presented as an autonomous system that can be analysed in its own right without reference to the economy's mode of production or the sociology of its class dynamic. As a result there is no third world political science in Soviet writings in which interest groups or political parties are taken as objects of separate study. Nor is there a sociology which analyses classes without these social formations being seen in terms of the dominant power structure and the contradictions at work in the economy. Quite distinct from the bulk of Western scholarship, Soviet 'political economy' is an integrated discipline with a common methodology. Third world political economists in the Soviet Union may be divided into area research institutes within which scholars specialize by topic, such as industrialization or agrarian reforms, but very consciously apply a standardized approach linking history, ideology, sociology, politics, and economics into one interlocking analysis. One cannot proceed to read – and comprehend – the Soviet analysis without acknowledging in advance its holistic striving.

THREE-DIMENSIONAL ANALYSIS

The newcomer to Soviet political economy would do well to visualize it as trying to situate a particular country at a specific point along each of three axes: eco-

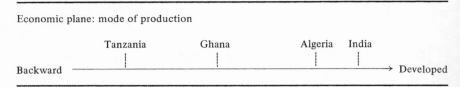

FIGURE 1 First Dimension of the Soviet Political Economy

nomic, political, and historical. On the economic axis, Soviet scholars attempt to define the mode of production that predominates in a given country at a given point in time. In third world countries this is no easy task, since, 'because of their general backwardness, imperialism's continuing influence, the relative weakness of national capitalism and immaturity of socio-class relations in the majority of the young states,' there is an intermixing and preservation of several modes of production – 'tribal, communal, feudal, early capitalist and developed capitalist relations.'[1] India presents a difficult challenge. Its modern heavy industrial sector coexists with an equally large pre-capitalist handicraft economy, while in agriculture large plantations operating on capitalist principles and small independent 'kulak' farmers account for less production than the vast numbers of sharecropping tenants. In the final analysis, India is placed along with Mexico, Brazil, and Egypt quite far along the spectrum from Backwardness to Industrialization, as is suggested by Figure 1.

In describing a third world country the Soviet writers also seek to situate it at some point along a political axis that shows the orientation of its development. Two prime factors determine this assessment: the nature of the ruling class (feudal, national bourgeois, petty bourgeois, etc.) and this ruling group's major development policy thrust (capitalist closely linked with foreign capital or anti-capitalist striving for independence from imperialism). Even if the leadership of independent India has consistently claimed that it was bent on building a socialist type of society, Soviet analysts note that the Indian National Congress primarily consists of and serves the interest of the national bourgeoisie that itself nourishes close ties with imperialist monopoly capital. Nevertheless the Indian leadership's policy orientation is considered more progressive than that of Pakistan whose class essence is very similar but whose political orientation is more reactionary.

Although a country cannot change its mode of production even over a decade of great effort, it can rapidly change its position on the political plane. Literally overnight a country can switch from a reactionary monopoly capitalist orientation to a progressive anti-capitalist stance, as Cuba did when Fidel Castro took

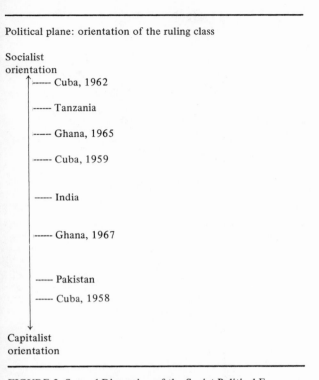

Political plane: orientation of the ruling class

Socialist
orientation

----- Cuba, 1962

----- Tanzania

----- Ghana, 1965

----- Cuba, 1959

----- India

----- Ghana, 1967

----- Pakistan

----- Cuba, 1958

Capitalist
orientation

FIGURE 2 Second Dimension of the Soviet Political Economy

power from Batista in 1959. Three years later, when Castro officially declared himself a marxist-leninist and *Pravda* formally recognized Cuba as socialist, Cuba left the third world category entirely to become a full-fledged member of the socialist camp.[2] In this shifting snakes-and-ladders analysis, a regime can fall as well as rise in its classification. Ghana was a prime example of a country on a non-capitalist path that fell back to a capitalist orientation when a military regime took power from Nkrumah, as Figure 2 represents graphically.

Plotting the economic against the political planes produces a two-dimensional presentation of the Soviet political economy. India's economy may have been gradually advancing along the difficult path of industrialization, but Shastri's political vacillations in the face of the big bourgeoisie's assertion of its monopoly interests clearly reduced that country's progressiveness in the Soviet writers' eyes. Economic growth in the early 1970s was not dramatic, but Indira Gandhi's

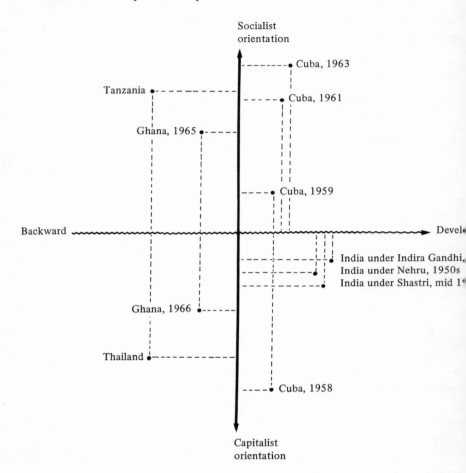

FIGURE 3 Two-Dimensional Presentation of the Soviet Political Economy

more resolute nationalization programme and other radical measures produced a revision in the previous downgrading of India's position. Schematically a two-dimensional representation as in Figure 3 can show how the Soviet concern with the policy orientation of a government's ruling class can produce great oscillations in their treatment of the same country. Tanzania's level of industrial development may be low, but its 'revolutionary-democratic' leadership puts it squarely in the non-capitalist group of young nations.

The capitalist/socialist axis is not a static spectrum. It embodies a tension between two polar opposites, capitalism and socialism, straining to attract each country into their orbits. Socialism-oriented states are presented as trying to rebuild their socioeconomic system along a transitional 'non-capitalist' path of development that should bring them to full socialism. On the other hand states taking a capitalist path have no such prospects for a rapid elimination of their backwardness: 'The fact that specific forms of pre-capitalist, early capitalist and so-called transitional and intermediate forms of relations continue to exist on a fairly large scale is due to the fact that these countries in general follow a conservative path of capitalist development.'[3]

It is of course true that many scholars in the west reject a unidimensional professionalism in their work. Certainly there are those who explicitly claim to practise 'political economy' by accepting the analytical interdependence of economic and political factors. Among such political economists some marxists also add a third, historical dimension as an integral part of their methodology. What role, they ask – progressive or reactionary – is a particular country playing on the stage of world history? Is it progressive in its contribution to undermining capitalism's global system of imperialism or is it reactionary in actually supporting the consolidation of neo-colonialism? Even if Soviet scholars used the same concepts as western marxists for identifying the economic mode of production and asked the same questions about the class nature of state political power, their Soviet-centric conception of world history would distinguish their work from that of their fellow researchers in different lands. Soviet marxist-leninists define the progressiveness of a country's world historical position not just in terms of its anti-imperialism but also as a function of the friendliness of its foreign policy towards the Soviet Union and its hostility to China. Thus during the last years of the Stalin period, when Soviet ideology considered all who were not in the Soviet bloc to be hostile, India was thought to be a lackey of imperialism and just as retrograde as Pakistan. When the Soviets reassessed the South Asian continent after Stalin's death they found that India's non-alignment had considerable anti-imperialist qualities, whereas Pakistan's participation in American military alliances clearly kept that country in the imperialist, anti-Soviet camp, as is indicated in Figure 4.

The tension along this global spectrum is more overt since the world capitalist system is seen as straining with all the power and devices at its command (colonial domination, neocolonial aid and investment, military alliances) to keep the third world in its camp. On the opposite pole the socialist camp, led since the Great October Revolution by the Soviet Union, offers a staunch moral support as the hearth of socialism as well as the military shelter, the diplomatic support, and the economic assistance necessary to help the former colonies to pull themselves out of the grips of imperialist dependence.

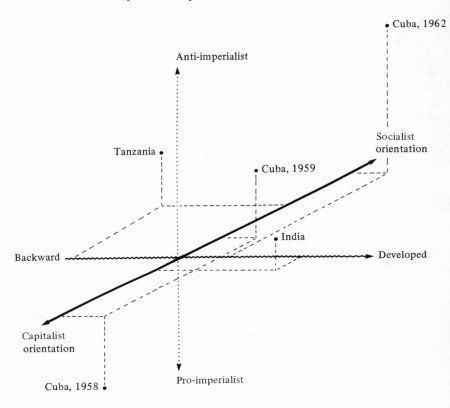

FIGURE 4 Three-Dimensional Presentation of the Soviet Political Economy

If the multi-dimensional integration of its different analytical axes into one comprehensive analysis is the first striking characteristic that distinguishes Soviet political economy from its international rivals, a powerful manicheism is the second. From backwardness to industrialization, from capitalist to socialist development, from imperialism to the world socialist camp: the countries of the third world are seen to be constantly caught in a herculean global struggle between the forces of evil and good. The focus of these global and ideological tensions is the economic and political role played by the state in the life of each third world country.

THE STATE IN THE THIRD WORLD'S ECONOMIC LIFE

The student in search of the Soviet model of development for the third world cannot look far before coming upon their overriding concern for the direct economic role of the state. To V.V. Rymalov, for instance, it was simply an 'unquestionable truth that the state sector in industry and other branches of the national economy of the former colonies and semi-colonies is the decisive instrument for attaining the economic aims of the liberation revolution. Its all-round development is designed to create the strongest possible economic basis for their further anti-imperialist struggle for independence and social and economic progress.'[4] While the state's industrial sector is the most important, it is not the only way that the state asserts itself in developing countries. State power is used to destroy outmoded production relations, to mobilize national resources, to free the economy from the control of foreign monopolies, and to broaden the internal market by generating industrialization and agrarian reforms.[5] How the state goes about these tasks, who controls it, and in what form, are questions the Soviet scholars ask about all the countries in Africa, Asia, and Latin America. Whether the state is used for independent economic development or to conserve outmoded and stagnant colonial structures depends on who holds power and who the government serves. For the social and economic significance of the state sector in particular and the state's economic role in general 'is defined at each stage of a country's development by the classes and strata holding power.'[6]

Progressive forces may be in power in relatively advanced countries such as Algeria or backward societies like Tanzania. Reactionary forces may equally control semi-feudal countries like Gabon or relatively well-off countries like Brazil. Feudal forces may use the state to modernize their economy, as in Afghanistan, or to hold it back, as in Thailand. In some cases, the use of the state may objectively have consequences not intended by those in power.

In Thailand, where the ruling group defends the interests of the big bourgeoisie and large landowners, 'the state is a weapon of the ruling classes who, acting in their own interests, assist ... the accelerated development of backward productive forces.'[7] But demands for accelerating economic development force the ruling summit to introduce measures both of trade and tariff regulation and of direct participation in industrial enterprises, despite the big bourgeoisie's opposition to state competition.[8] In the feudal society of Afghanistan, the state makes possible the mobilization of the nation's material and financial resources. The state participates to extend industrial construction, control foreign trade, extend the credit system, and drastically limit the big private landowners. Helped by long-term planning and Soviet co-operation, it is speeding up the historical process of economic development.[9]

STATE CAPITALISM AS A KEY CONCEPT

The central concept for the Soviet view of the state in the third world is state capitalism, a concept refurbished for application to the ex-colonies during the post-stalinist re-evaluation of development theory. Once the emerging nations were no longer written off as hopelessly enmeshed in the world capitalist economic system, they were seen to have a real opportunity to develop through a transitional phase towards socialism. It was this transitional phase that was labelled state capitalist, a category around which was constructed a framework for analysing the strengths and weaknesses of a new nation's development thrust. When Soviet scholars introduced the notion of state capitalism into their analysis of third world development, they were not talking solely about the public sector in a capitalist economy or the capitalist aspects of a statist system. Originally state capitalism had been a marxist term describing the European capitalist systems of the early twentieth century. After the October Revolution state capitalism had then taken a specific meaning in the Soviet revolutionary context when temporary concessions were 'tolerated by Soviet power, controlled and limited by the proletarian state' in the transition from capitalism to socialism.[10] Now they were adapting this theoretical construct to categorize the whole political and economic system at the post-colonial stage of an emergent country's development. Illustrating how marxist-leninist political economy rejects the analytical isolation of economic problems from their political or social context, state capitalism is presented as the product of a particular historical development, a specific international situation, and a definite constellation of political forces within the country. As A. Levkovsky put it: 'the objective role of state capitalism in national development is determined by who is at the helm of state rather than by the level of development of state capitalism in the given country. The more radical the class forces in power are, the faster does state capitalism develop, the more effective are its efforts to boost the economy, and the greater is the possibility for its democratisation and for utilising it for the switch-over to the non-capitalist path of development.'[11]The overriding polarization between a capitalist or a socialist orientation imbues their approach to state capitalism. 'There are countries where state capitalism serves as a bulwark for the emerging large-scale bureaucratic and monopoly capital, while in others it acts in the interests of petty-bourgeois circles and assists national governments in curbing the plunderous ambitions of the bourgeois "upper stratum," protecting the national economy against the detrimental influence of the imperialist monopolies and bringing the country out of her economic backwardness.'[12] The most complete illustration of the Soviet three-dimensional state capitalism paradigm is provided by India.

STATE CAPITALISM IN INDIA

Since India was used as the prime specimen on which to try out the post-Stalin development framework, the analysis of Indian 'state capitalism' provides an example of great relevance for the study of other developing countries. India's complexities presented no small challenge for any school of analysts. It was industrially quite developed and had a predominantly pre-capitalist agriculture; its foreign policy was anti-imperialist, yet imperialist monopolies were firmly implanted on its soil; its internal political orientation had been continuously progressive, though strong reactionary forces contended for power. Under Nehru's Fabian leadership India had been the first major third world power to commit itself to a decisive economic role for the state. It was also one of the most capitalist of the colonies, having by the time of independence a series of advanced industries under free enterprise, notably the world's second largest cotton industry, a large jute and tea industry and an extensive railroad network.[13]

The historical perspective in which the Soviets place state capitalism was, as we have seen, the global confrontation between the forces of decaying capitalism and rising socialism: 'In India state capitalism could only arise in the conditions created by the general crisis of capitalism when the forces of imperialism were greatly weakened and when the powerful socialist camp had been formed.'[14] Shaken to its foundations by the first general crisis when the socialist revolution occurred in Russia, and weakened still further by its second general crisis culminating in the second world war, world capitalism was being forced into a tactic of retreat by decolonization in this, the third stage of its general crisis.

While the formation of the socialist camp had been the general factor forcing decolonization and establishing an international environment favourable to the more independent development of the Afro-Asian world, the necessary cause precipitating the birth of state capitalism was the capture of political power from the colonial rulers by the national liberation movement. Up to the acquisition of independence, for example, the Indian system was a 'very special colonial state monopoly capitalism which had served the English monopolies' interests by exploiting the Indian peoples.' With the transfer of control, the new government received as a direct institutional inheritance from the colonial regime the state's instruments of economic control together with the publicly owned enterprises providing the 'material base' for the new state capitalist system that 'appeared in the Indian Republic on August 1947, that is at the moment that independence was achieved.'[15]

The determinant of the new system's character was the class composition of the new nation's leadership. Had the proletariat taken power led by its vanguard communist party, India would have become a socialist country directly; had a revolutionary-democratic group taken over, with proletarian support, it could have started along a non-capitalist path of development as a 'national democratic state.' As it was, the assumption of power by the Indian National Congress, the political party of the national bourgeoisie who had led the struggle for independence, ensured that the country would not be developed on a socialist path. On the other hand the interests of the national bourgeoisie precluded a Western style, free market capitalism.

State capitalism (as opposed to straight capitalism) was essential for the new national bourgeois government since only vigorous governmental measures could begin to cope with the urgent problems confronting the economy. Industrial groups demanded accelerated capital accumulation and the opening up of new branches of production. But the growing demand of national capitalists for economic expansion was in contradiction with the 'impossibility of achieving this on the basis of private capitalist enterprise.' This is why 'state capitalism was required to create the basis for Indian capitalism's new stage of development.'[16] State capitalism, in other words, was the means used by the national bourgeoisie to overcome the tension in an extremely backward economy needing to develop its productive forces by the industrialization of its economy and the transformation of its agriculture.

THE PROGRESSIVENESS OF STATE CAPITALISM

Western social science generally attempts to erase value judgments from all analysis, since its prime commitment is to 'objectivity' interpreted as the effacing of the author's personal opinions and the striving for universal truth. Given their commitment to what they claim is the only scientific social theory, Soviet marxist-leninists on the contrary feel obliged to make a basic value judgment at a very early stage of their analysis. Objectivity for them is historical, not personal. Historical forces in a particular situation are either objectively favourable to realizing the goal of world communism, in which case they are labelled progressive, or they resist this development, in which case they are reactionary.

Central to the marxist-leninist development analysis is the preliminary historical judgment of how progressive a particular state's role is on the stage of world history. For instance, in the original Soviet reassessment of India in the mid-

1950s what was decisive was the very high 'progressiveness' (*progressivnost'*) accorded state capitalism. It is because 'in India state capitalism is aimed at solving the important historical task of making the semi-colonial economy independent by the development of its productive forces that it therefore has a progressive character.' In political terms this meant that 'the objective achievement of this aim (of independence) creates an anti-imperialist and anti-feudal force' by uniting the nation against internal reaction and Western interference.[17] State capitalism was anti-imperialist because in generating any independent national development it would necessarily undermine the external hegemony of the imperialists, who aim to maintain their former colonial empires intact. Internally, any development of a capitalist economy would shatter the still powerful feudal forces that have their economic base in pre-capitalist feudal landlord-type exploitation of the peasantry.

In economic terms state capitalism was progressive since it was the necessary precondition for accelerated growth: 'without the creation of a powerful state capitalist sector it is impossible to expand capitalist reproduction in modern India in a short space of time.'[18] The weakness of private local capital combined with the resistance of foreign capital to India's industrialization required an acceleration of capital accumulation by the state if the many branches of heavy industry needed for capitalist reproduction were to be established.[19] 'The development of the productive forces based on modern techniques ... requiring large capital investment ... inevitably provokes an abrupt increase in the Indian economy's state sector, i.e. the development of state capitalism.'[20] State-inspired industrial development was thus the key to the forced development of the country's economy.

Given the opposition by imperialism to the creation of heavy industry in India, the systematic promotion of state capitalism constituted the most efficient means of political and economic defence against the penetration of foreign capital and the new forms of colonialism, since this defence required an attack on the privileges of foreign-controlled corporations and a limitation of their activity in favour of national enterprise. 'State capitalist development weakens foreign capital's position and, by this token, encourages the growth of national capital.'

In addition, state capitalism played a beneficial role by limiting the 'primitive forms' of capitalism and by channelling surplus capital towards industrial development. 'State capitalism is a significant means of limiting and shortening the primitive forms of capitalist accumulation, partially controlling its rapacious character and even utilizing these types of capital for the country's industrial development.'[21] While it helped shorten the painful early phase of free enterprise capitalism, state capitalism simultaneously counteracted local monopolies which had developed during the colonial regime.[22]

All these positive characteristics of state capitalism led the Soviet writers of the late 1950s to consider it to be a historically more advanced, even if economically less developed, form of capitalism than the 'state monopoly capitalism' found in the West. Far from being a fusion of the monopolies with the apparatus of the state as in imperialist industrialized countries, state capitalism in a country such as India was evolving in the quite different conditions of a huge agrarian country in an epoch when the colonial system was collapsing and the socialist bloc standing by to offer support. By its very industrialization and suppression of technological and economic backwardness, state capitalism was reinforcing India's political and economic independence and so contributing to the favourable transformation of the international situation by its appropriate foreign policy. This reciprocal link between the socioeconomic and the international factors was made explicit: 'the government, in implementing this [state capitalism], conducts a peaceloving foreign policy thus strengthening the forces of peace.'[23] State capitalism could blossom only in the world historical situation of a weakening imperialism and the consolidation of the 'mighty socialist camp'; conversely, because the establishment of state capitalism was increasing Indian autonomy from the world imperialist system, it was 'an important factor in the further sharpening of the general crisis of capitalism.'[24]

Just how progressive is a particular country's state capitalism becomes the subject for careful assessment among Soviet analysts. The deemed progressiveness of Indian state capitalism has fluctuated: for some time it followed a declining curve. Originally, according to R.A. Ulyanovsky, writing in 1957, it was 'the highest form of capitalism' because the state appropriates different forms of property, thereby accelerating the process of historical development and already introducing the 'supreme forms of bourgeois property.' By abridging the painful road of primitive capitalist accumulation, it 'accelerates by this means the creation of the material conditions favouring the transition to socialism.' Even though he found the signs presaging further socialist development to be hopeful, Ulyanovsky clearly distinguished promise from reality. State capitalism 'is a step towards socialism, but it is neither socialism itself nor the starting point for the country's non-capitalist development.'[25] However advanced its capitalism might be, some authors wrote, it was capitalism nonetheless.

The state still continued to serve the interests of the ruling bourgeoisie, for whom it played the role of a 'collective industrial capitalist.'[26] What was worse, the socialist possibilities inherent in the development of the state sector were offset by the state's relationship with the large landowner class in the country and with foreign monopoly capital in the private sector. While in theory the national bourgeoisie should want to accelerate economic development by expropriating foreign companies and liquidating the large feudal landowners, in practice it feared the social consequences of such a decisive attack against these groups, worrying particularly about activating the class struggle and the further socioeconomic transformations that such radical reforms might bring in their wake.

State capitalism necessarily reflected the contradictory nature of the bourgeois ruling groups whose interests were opposed to imperialism and the large landowners and at the same time connected socially and economically with these two reactionary forces. It was these internal contradictions which explained the 'limits and incoherence of state capitalism's development in India.'[27]

What must also be added to the negative side of the ledger in the Soviet assessment of state capitalism is the impact of the private capitalist sector, which, 'with its anarchy [competition among enterprises], its spontaneity [unplanned activity] and its unevenness [unequal degrees of development of different sectors of the economy], has a decisive influence even on the state's economic activity,' so that the economy still suffers from the uncontrollable action of capitalism's laws of value. The public sector is in conflict with the private, trying to control it. Still, the contradictions between the private and public sectors are not antagonistic or irreconcilable. On the contrary, the state follows a conscious policy of aiding private enterprise through such devices as raising protective tariffs and providing public credit. While the private capitalist component is noted, the active role of the government in state capitalism's development proves that capitalism itself as a pure economic system has been discredited as a vehicle of social and economic construction.[28]

These serious imperfections did not prevent the Soviet theoreticians from elevating state capitalism in the third world to the status of a new 'law of development' (*zakonomernost'*), a unique historical stage distinguished both from primitive capitalism and western monopoly state capitalism. They were careful to refute the claim that this was a 'third option,' separate from capitalism or socialism, as many third world scholars maintain. The mixed economy is not a separate development *path* implying a stable, long-term form that will not become socialist. It was, however, a transitional *stage*. Without obligating them to talk of a third path, state capitalism thus provided an over-all conceptualization for the transitional stage of an emerging nation by relating its internal social, political, and economic development problems to its historical and international context.

This paradigm of state capitalism gave Soviet scholars an analytical framework which could serve several functions. It provided an ideological sanction for Soviet scholarship to approach non-communist developing countries with a more open mind, since capitalism no longer prevented their being considered progressive. In fact the rash of articles and books on African and Asian state capitalism which appeared in Moscow through the late 1950s and early 1960s is ample evidence of how useful the concept was for reassessing the economic and political systems of the newly liberated ex-colonies. It was hardly coincidental that the restoration of state capitalism as an analytical model accompanied the dramatic warming of Soviet foreign policy to the non-aligned new nations. The ideological reappraisal helped legitimize Khrushchev's new commitment to distribute economic aid in the third world, a foreign policy change that, according to the old stalinist line, would have implied that the Soviet Union was supporting reactionary capitalist systems. It was here that the dialectic of the analysis could be put to use. Since the new state capitalism was not old colonial capitalism, India could be seen to be in a period of historical transition with the potential for making further dramatic progress towards the next historical stage. In pointing out the unreformed capitalist elements of the Indian system, Soviet indologists could both protect their flank from the accusation of revisionism and keep an ideological escape route: if India should waver from its non-alignment, it could be reclassified as a system of reactionary state monopoly capitalism.

Attributing a progressive historical role to state capitalism in its struggle to suppress the vestiges of the colonial heritage had another implication. It shifted the major blame for the economy's backwardness from the governing group to the colonial regime. The notion of historical stage attributes to state capitalism the nuance of the 'right' to direct a country's development for the ensuing period. To designate the Indian National Congress as a 'national bourgeois' regime and to endorse its system as progressive was to accept a non-revolutionary perspective for the foreseeable future. When presenting the national bourgeois leadership as appropriate to the historical stage for the country, the Soviet analysis accepted the two propositions that the 'bourgeois-democratic revolution' still had to run its course and that the national bourgeoisie was a sufficiently progressive ruling class to be able to execute the historical and economic transformation from feudal colonialism to pre-socialist capitalism.

What might appear on first glance to be a static paradigm turns out to have a dynamic capability. Built into the political assessment is a critical variable containing the possibility of either progressive or regressive change. Should the reactionary class forces – some combination of the big capitalist bourgeoisie, the large landowners in the country, and foreign monopoly capital – push out the progressive elements of the national bourgeoisie from effective rule, then the country would be reassessed as having degenerated into state monopoly capitalism. From the interdependence of the component factors of the model one would expect that the different constellation of class forces would engender different economic policies oriented to favouring private enterprise rather than the public sector. Greater dependence on imperialist aid and closer relations with foreign monopolies together with worsening relations and reduced economic links with the socialist camp would likely ensue, as was the case for Ghana after the coup against Nkrumah.

Should the communist party take power in New Delhi, India would be reclassified as having embarked on the socialist path of development, cutting down its dependence on the capitalist camp and benefiting fully from its fraternal links with the socialist countries. Castro's adoption of marxism-leninism, plus the radical socioeconomic reforms he implemented, brought Cuba into full membership in the socialist camp. Or, if it were a 'revolutionary-democratic' coalition of forces that took power, with the participation, but not the dominance, of the communist party, the appropriate model applied to India would be that of the national democratic state pursuing a non-capitalist path by adopting more radical economic and social policies aimed at reducing the capitalist sector of the economy if not actually abolishing it in the immediate future, as happened in Egypt, Guinea, Tanzania, or Algeria. Egypt, which was seen to be state capitalist under the early years of Nasser's rule, was promoted to the category of non-capitalist when the leadership carried through a vigorous programme of liquidating the positions of big capital through nationalization, carrying out a radical land reform programme, establishing close relations with the socialist camp, and introducing proletarian or revolutionary elements into the ruling circles. There is no precise weighting attached to the relative importance of a country's economic structure or balance of class forces as opposed to its foreign policy or, more exactly, its relationship with the Soviet Union. The judgment that Nehru's India was playing an anti-imperialist role on the world scene resulted from a consideration of all these factors.

Soviet marxism-leninism does not leave much room for doubt about what the analysis of state capitalism would be once the general tendency of a country's development has been labelled as reactionary, for reasons internal or external. 'With the progress of capitalism and the concentration of production which characterizes it, the state sector becomes the economic support of a reactionary regime in which power falls into the hands of the big, essentially monopolistic national corporations.'[29]

By looking at the various aspects of monopoly state capitalism as defined in the official marxist-leninist manual, one can see with what ease India could find herself demoted to this category. Monopoly state capitalism is first of all described as the transformation of the state 'into a committee administering the affairs of the monopolistic bourgeoisie.' In this committee 'the interpenetration of the state apparatus and the monopolies is so close that it is often difficult to distinguish them.'[30] It would not take much effort for Soviet specialists to revive the Stalinist analysis which showed that the huge consortia like the Tatas and the Birlas had infiltrated the whole governmental apparatus in order to control

it.[31] In state monopoly capitalism the power of the government is used to benefit the interests of the large corporations: by its 'public works' the state con-
structs roads to reduce the transport costs of the monopolies and installs electric
generators to reduce their costs of electric energy consumption.

Given the large concentration of the Indian five-year plans on the creation of
the infrastructure necessary for industrial development, no Soviet analyst would
have any difficulty in showing that India demonstrates this reactionary quality.
Not just the policy of improving the infrastructure, but the whole state capitalist
activity, including such positive actions as nationalization, is liable to an adverse
interpretation, for in the marxist-leninist theory of monopoly state capitalism
'the state takes different measures destined to regulate the economy and proceeds to nationalize certain sectors.' India has carried out enough nationalization
for her to qualify under this reactionary label too. Even the most normal of government policy is eligible for classification as monopoly state capitalist. 'Under
the guise of direct and indirect taxation, the state concentrates in the hands of
and redistributes in favour of the monopolies an increasingly large part of the
national income.'[32] Soviet analysis already complains about the Indian policy of
capitalist taxation. What is more, the Congress policy of state capitalist expansion of the economy could also provide proof of monopoly capitalism, for in
this system 'the monopolies try to make the state assume the role of creating
new branches of industry necessitating large investments.'

In addition, all the general aspects of India's current political life could be
given a reactionary characterization. The Soviet commentary on the repression
of Indian communists during the Sino-Indian conflict, for instance, could easily
be transformed into a condemnation of the 'military and police functions of the
state in the service of the monopolies to crush the workers.'[33] Soviet indologists
would thus have no difficulty in using their current typology and the existing
data to find state capitalism, in an India which had become less friendly towards
the Soviet Union, to be monopolistic and reactionary.

While a reversal of Indo-Soviet foreign policy friendship would be the most
drastic indicator requiring India's reclassification in the marxist-leninist development typology, a sufficiently important shift in the other major elements of the
model could also necessitate a Soviet reappraisal of India's 'progressiveness.' In
fact a long debate took place in the Soviet academy, with some claiming that the
big bourgeoisie had become so powerful while the encouragement of private
capitalism was so major an element in the country's economic policy that India
should already be denounced and reclassified as a state monopoly capitalist system. For example, the unpublished doctoral thesis of S.A. Bessonov showed in
1961 that India was half way towards a reactionary position. According to him
there was a double danger: the Indian monopolies were controlling the govern-

ment, with the result that the state sector was being transformed into a mono-poly state capitalist system. Originally the national bourgeoisie had been progres-sive in its world orientation, but during the 1950s it had changed from opposi-tion to frank co-operation with imperialism.[34] That this thesis was not published may say more about Soviet politics than Soviet scholarship. Disturbed only slightly by the Soviet rapprochement with Pakistan, relations between Moscow and Delhi remained warm and steady whether measured by their political soli-darity or by their economic transactions. Though Indo-Soviet relations have re-mained excellent since the mid-1950s, the initial enthusiasm of the state capital-ist analysis as formulated in the first flush of destalinization cooled noticeably over the years. In the interregnum period between Nehru's death and Indira Gandhi's accession to power Soviet hopes for planning and the public sector were repeatedly dashed and shattered.[35] As it became apparent that, far from restricting the monopolies' sphere of influence, state capitalism was actually helping them expand and consolidate, Soviet scholars became more critical about the institution. In the turbulent politics of the post-Nehru years, growing Soviet apprehensions were expressed in print. In an important series of articles appraising the over-all socioeconomic and political situation in India, O.V. Maev noted that the reduced effectiveness of state capitalism had been accompanied by a strengthening of the largest corporations having the highest concentration of capital. The high level of organization and technology of 'monopoly capital,' according to Yu.I. Loshakov, was due to its close links with the imperialist mono-polies.[36] What made these links with the Western corporate giants a serious mat-ter for the Soviet analysts was their implication for the general trend of India's economic development. In his report on the rise of big business in India, Maev emphasized the threat that the reactionary strategy of the monopolies presented in economic policy: they were striving to transform India's economy along the lines of the Western model.[37] Although he considered in 1964 that monopoly capitalism – the subordination of the state to the monopolies – had not yet tri-umphed in India, his later assessments showed a growing pessimism in this re-gard.[38] To make the political point very clear, N. Savelev warned in *International Affairs* in April 1967 that the growing activity of the Indian monopolist bour-geoisie was seriously threatening to deflect India from 'its established path of neutrality in foreign policy.'[39] The threat of India's state capitalism being trans-formed into its reactionary essence became greater as the progressive aspects of the state's regulatory activity were overshadowed by the independent activity of private enterprise. In one later article, the concessions made by the government to free enterprise were seen as the possible 'starting point for the country's slide into the state monopoly capitalist path.'[40] Subsequently Indira Gandhi's consoli-dation of power and radicalization of policy were seen to have reversed this incipient tendency. State capitalism in the 1970s emerged as progressive as it had been in the 1950s. As one analyst of the third world scene wrote in 1976, 'On the whole, state capitalism is undoubtedly a more mature form of bourgeois property promoting the development of the productive forces, eradication of pre-capitalist survivals, consolidation of the national economy and, to a certain extent, an improvement of the people's welfare ... The overall establishment of state capitalism which substantially modifies the entire socio-economic situation in each individual country is an objective necessity for the development of the young states.'[41]

4

The state sector

Soviet political economy makes a basic distinction between state capitalism, understood as the whole mode of production including the system of direct and indirect measures that the state can use to achieve its social and economic development goals, and the state sector, in which the government itself runs publicly owned enterprises in industrial production, trade, banking, the infrastructure, and even agriculture. For example, in Africa 'only the state sector can transform the backward economic and social structures of the African countries into a modern one within a short historical period.' It is the only sector that can withstand the pressure of foreign competition, that can proceed rationally on a planned basis and can meet the interests of the working people.[1] If Tanzania is praised as a progressive non-capitalist state, it is largely because 'the state has taken over the commanding heights of the economy: it controls the entire banking and insurance network, 75 per cent of the mining and manufacturing industries, 75 per cent of the country's foreign and domestic trade.'[2]

On the other hand the state sector can be misused. In Pakistan proper development was frustrated by the big bourgeoisie's failure to use the state sector to its full potential. The state's Industrial Credit and Investment Corporation was used to promote private industrial enterprise, rather than the state sector. This 'policy of developing the private sector and curtailing the sphere of the public sector inevitably accentuated Pakistan's dependence on the imperialist powers.'[3] Here state capitalism was not sufficiently oriented to the state sector, heavy industry, and fighting foreign investment to be progressive.

GOVERNMENT ECONOMIC POLICY

Since the nature of a country's state sector reflects in the Soviet mirror the complex contradictions of state capitalism, 'evolving and progressing in its development by well-defined stages,'[4] a general perception of the Soviet view of state sector development can emerge from their critique of the government's official economic policy. Their analysis generally starts with the government's formal statements of policy and then goes on to examine the actual performance of the government in the economy. These periodical policy statements are taken very seriously as an earnest of governmental intentions.

Early Soviet discussions of the Indian state sector examined the Nehru government's programmatic statements on industrialization starting with its 1948 resolution on industrial policy. Interest centred on two indicators, the proposed size of the public sector and the intended degree of governmental control over the state sector's antithesis, the private industrial sector.

The Soviet commentators noted with satisfaction the declaration of intention in the first resolution of 6 April 1948 that 'the Government must play an increasingly active role in the development of industry.'[5] Reported without any adverse comment was the postponement for ten years of Congress's pre-independence promise to nationalize the basic industrial sectors.[6] V.A. Kondratev cited the prudential reasoning in the resolution that blamed the resources and apparatus of the state for being too limited to permit it to operate in industry as fully as desired. As a result the state's activity was to be concentrated on new productive enterprises rather than acquiring and managing existing ones. As for private enterprise it was invited to play a central role provided it was duly directed and controlled by the state.[7]

The policy consequence of this declaration of principle was the delineation of three spheres of influence for the public and private sectors. In the first sphere the public sector was to maintain an exclusive monopoly in such public utilities as railway transport and was to develop a similar monopoly in such economic sectors affecting national security as the production of armaments and atomic energy. The second economic sphere of influence was one of shared jurisdiction. The government assumed the responsibility for the creation of all new enterprises in key branches where private enterprise was still predominant: coal, oil, iron and steel, and others. As for the third sphere it was left open to private enterprise, but the state was to participate progressively, intervening without hesitation in case the progress in any industrial sector should be deficient. While it assumed the responsibility for developing a whole group of industries in a separate state sector, the government declared at the same time that it was ready to assist private enterprise solve its basic problems such as insufficient transport facilities, securing vital imports, protection against foreign competition, and help in exploiting the country's resources. 'Thus a few months after the proclamation of India's independence, its first bourgeois national government already declared its involvement in the sphere of industrial production, intending by this means to stake out a path for the country's industrialization.'[8]

The 1951 law on the development and control of industry was also thoroughly approved in the first Soviet writings on state capitalism because it promised a stronger economic role for the state. It required government approval before any new private enterprise could be established, and it gave the government power to investigate and even take over firms whose production had declined, deteriorated, or become overpriced. In the view of the Soviet commentators of the late 1950s, this legislation 'proved the definitely regulatory role of the state in relation to private capitalist industry.'[9]

Later interpretations found these early judgments too enthusiastic. One writer complained in 1961 that the government's powers to intervene were not applied because of bourgeois resistance.[10] In 1962 Kondratev pointed out that there was a large gap between the legislated possibility of government control over industrial development and the actual 'anarchical process of capital accumulation.' The anticipated transfer to governmental control of private companies in a number of industries had not taken place, and the state's theoretical control over the establishment of new firms had not led to an effective channelling of investments in the desired areas of heavy industry. Of 3,500 requests for governmental permits for the creation or enlargement of plants, 2,300 were in light or food industry and the rest were for consumer goods production. 'In actual practice, the regulatory functions of the state are subordinated to the initiatives and selfish interests of private capitalist enterprise.'

Similarly in discussing the government's resolution on industrial policy of 30 April 1956, Kondratev pointed out that, though the resolution proclaimed significant widening of the state's sphere of activity in industry, this area of monopoly prerogatives only applied to a relatively narrow group of producer-goods industries which were either non-existent in India or barely developed. More important, he noted the discrepancy between the claimed extent of the state's responsibility for exclusive economic activity and the actual practice which made self-defeating concessions to private enterprise. Despite the state's exclusive responsibility for the expansion of the iron and steel industry, for example, the government has actively encouraged the doubling of Tata's steel capacity amounting to 'not just an enlargement but the construction of a powerful supplementary plant in the private sector.'[11]

This apprehension of the late 1950s turned to real alarm in the mid and late 1960s when the monopolies succeeded in winning major concessions from the government in economic policy. The state limitations on the sphere of heavy private enterprise were substantially weakened; 'ever more frequently the monopolists received permission to establish enterprises in the branches that had been reserved for the state sector.'[12] The Indian government has been under combined attack from local big capital and external reaction. Local big capital, growing despite governmental regulation in the early 1960s, started insisting on a role in defining economic policy. At the same time the World Bank recommended a loosening of policy on licensing and taxing foreign capital and put open pressure on the government to force concessions and 'improvements' in its economic policy before giving aid to the fourth five-year plan. As a result, government control over the production and distribution of cement was abolished in January 1966, foreign companies were given the right to establish mixed companies under their control in the fertilizer industry in April of that year, and the following month government licensing control over eleven other branches was terminated.[13] As a result of the diminution of state control and regulation of the private sector,' the significance of the planned bases of the economy has been significantly lowered.'[14] Lowered, but not extinguished. Soviet writers continued to watch the political struggle between the left and right wings of the Indian National Congress over the state's economic policy, with close attention for indications as to which direction the country's state sector was taking. With obvious relief they noted the strengthening of the Indian public sector through the early 1970s. Reporting the growing 'share of the public sector in India's reproducible tangible wealth' from 15 per cent in 1950-1 through 25.6 per cent in 1960-1 to 43 per cent in 1970-1, I. Egorov could conclude that the 'growth in domestic means of reproduction has been of tremendous significance to building up India's economic independence.'[15]

THE FORMATION OF THE STATE SECTOR

The Soviet preference for giving highest priority to state sector development emerges unambiguously from their critique of a country's economic policy. The way a new nation should go about building up its state sector is spelled out explicitly in their discussion of the different techniques available to the developing nations for creating the public sector. Of the four sources of state industrial property, two (inheritance from the colonial power and nationalization of foreign private enterprises) involve the takeover of existing plant; the other two (joint private-state sector operations and pure state enterprises) are techniques requiring new construction. The Soviet view on the best way to proceed in this critical development strategy is quite clear. Though the strategy followed by the Indian government is not in fact the one the Soviet scholars consider most progressive, their critique shows what they consider to be the best approach.

Inheritance from the colonial regime
The first component of any new nation's public sector is the property taken over from the colonial regime at the acquisition of independence. This normally in-

cludes the government's funds (or debts), telecommunications, public utilities such as electric power, and any irrigation system along with occasional industrial enterprises. 'The material base of Indian state capitalism – state property of several means of production – was inherited to a significant degree from the colonial period,' wrote A.I. Levkovsky who evaluated the government's productive capital at the time of independence at Rs 8.75 billion.[16] Government funds transferred to the new state were considerable, amounting to Rs 16.2 billion.[17] While this included the large railway and irrigation systems, the public sector only constituted 7 per cent of Indian industry, insufficient on its own for creating a state sector that would dominate the economy's development.[18] For the colonies, the 'free enterprise system' meant having their economies dominated by a small number of metropolitan companies. With independence, this left the new nations with more industrial plant outside the public sector than inside it. Outside meant not just in the private sector but also still under the control of the former colonial power. Since the Soviet view is less interested in the levers of government economic regulation than actual state industrial property to guarantee state capitalism's ability to develop, nationalization of the foreign monopolies' colonial branches is thus their favourite means to achieve instant state sector growth.

Nationalization for instant state sector

Marxist-leninists leave no doubt about their belief in nationalization as an essential factor for a new nation's independent economic and political progress. 'As many years of experience show, the fight for democracy in *all* the underdeveloped countries is *above all* the fight for the nationalization of foreign capital, for the limitation of the economic power of big capital and the monopolies.'[19] Politically the nationalization of foreign capital is seen to be the natural result of the liberation revolution and the change from colonial rule to national state power. Ideologically it is an indicator of the new state's desire for real independence from the imperialist system. In economic terms nationalization can create the basis for the public sector economy. At one blow it 'undermines foreign influence on the internal life of the country and creates the best conditions for ... the reconstruction of its economy.'[20]

Nationalization is not presented as a magic panacea that can solve the dependence and growth problems of every new nation. There are two types of nationalization – as there are two general types of development paths: radical or moderate. Radical nationalization of private foreign enterprises that took place in such countries as Algeria, Burma, Egypt, and Guinea go beyond the simple transfer of property because they lead to social transformations by attacks on the big and middle bourgeoisie. This is not to be confused with nationalization that serves the interest of the bourgeoisie itself by restricting expropriation to firms that are making losses or to the natural resource sectors such as the oil industry, nationalized in Mexico and Ceylon.[21] 'In the actual conditions of the Third World, nationalization may be bourgeois or anti-bourgeois. In the former case, it helps to strengthen the anti-imperialist character of independent capitalist development and has a limited progressive significance. In the latter case, it is a vigorous measure for accelerating the transition of the immediate construction of the basis of Socialism, because the state sector itself is anti-capitalist and transitional to Socialism.'[22]

Whatever theoretical advantages nationalization offered the state sector, the Indian government took the bourgeois path, and on 30 April 1956 postponed for the second time the original Congress promise to nationalize foreign firms in the key industries.[23] The Soviet explanation for this second refusal lay in the closely interlocking interests of British and Indian big capital through joint Indian-foreign companies and the big Indian industrialists' fear that the nationalization of foreign firms might sound the death knell of their own corporate holdings. What nationalization took place under Nehru was the typical bourgeois state's buying up of firms that were making a loss, as in the case of the Indian aviation industry.[24] Faced with the constitutional obligation of paying full compensation for expropriated private property, the New Delhi government was showing a marked preference for using its limited capital resources to create new industrial enterprises rather than to take over existing plant. Thus it was with unconcealed approval that Indira Gandhi's programme of nationalization was greeted. Noting the state takeover of 64 national and 42 foreign insurance companies, 62 per cent of the country's import trade, 678 coal mines, and 103 textile mills between 1971 and 1973, I. Egorov concluded that one could not overestimate the 'significance of the public sector's role in eliminating the country's uneven development.'[25]

As a result of its nationalization of the oil industry in 1975, 'Venezuela, which had been the country with the largest amount of foreign capital investment in Latin America, became the country with the highest level of state control over its economy.' Even if the regime is not radical, its action is clearly deemed progressive: 'All these measures are indubitably of a positive nature, although they ... are being carried out to suit the interests of the national bourgeoisie which is striving to eliminate the overly great influence of the foreign oil concerns and of the latifundists and to make use of the extra means accruing in the state budget to accelerate capitalist development.'[26]

The developmental potential of rapid state sector growth through expropriation is illustrated by Egypt's record. 'In the Arab Republic of Egypt the public sector, which plays the dominant part in the national economy, was created as a result of the determined and consistent state policy of nationalising the property of foreign and national capital ... The public sector in the ARE is the largest in developing countries ... The economic activity of the state has transformed Egypt from a backward British colony into an industrial-agrarian country, in which the value of the output of the manufacturing, extractive and power industries is almost twice as much as that of agricultural production.'[27]

Bitter experience of hasty nationalizations by the radical developing countries in the 1960s has led to a modification of the simple marxist-leninist slogan of immediate and general nationalization. Dislocations caused to the economy may outweigh the advantages gained by the new state property. 'In effect, it should be remembered that the folding-up of operations by nationalised enterprises, especially in countries with a single-commodity economy, may disrupt the country's life and seriously harm economic progress. This may be utilised by the imperialist and reactionary forces in their efforts to discredit the idea of nationalisation and to stage a reactionary coup d'état. The Communist Party of Iraq, for instance, does not put forward the task of immediately nationalising the oil concessions.'[28] R.N. Andreasyan also notes that, while the developing countries have 'scored major successes' in nationalizing foreign-owned credit and financial institutions, transport and communications facilities, and public utilities, there have been far fewer cases of nationalization in the important export industries like mining or plantation crops, which still depend on the foreign monopolies for transportation and marketing of the export. As a means of achieving economic independence, Andreasyan admonishes that 'nationalization can help to liquidate only the direct means of control exercised by imperialism over the economy.'

Other commentators have pointed out that nationalization often produces a false sense of independence, since, through lack of trained cadres, the nationalized companies have been obliged to keep on as advisers the same foreign personnel they had been trying to get rid of. Nevertheless the qualifications on the economic side of the ledger do not override the overwhelmingly positive political attributes that the Soviets see in nationalization. Although the Soviets concentrate their talk on the nationalization only of the foreign monopolies, at the early stages of the national democratic revolution, this is not because they are against the nationalization of the property of the national capitalists. On the contrary, the former should lead to the latter. As Andreasyan puts it, 'The nationalisation of the property of the imperialist monopolies is also of great social and political importance. The slogan of nationalisation frequently serves as a preliminary to a mass anti-imperialist movement or is put forward when such a movement is under way. The success of nationalisation depends on the success of this movement and in turn helps to raise it to a new stage. The struggle for nationalisation helps to mount an offensive against the reactionary classes and sections of the population – the social agents of imperialism – and to carry the national-liberation revolution to a new stage, that of the struggle for transition to the non-capitalist way.'[29]

Joint state-private construction

Nationalization may be effective in weakening the foreign monopolies' position and giving the state stronger economic levers, but it does not of itself change a country's backward economic structure or create new economic activity.[30] Once the new state has expropriated what it intends to nationalize, the only way its state sector can expand is by applying additional capital in constructing new industrial projects – either jointly with private entrepreneurs or entirely on its own.

In the Indian experience the third means of socializing industry by state co-operation with private capital in joint industrial development has proven less significant than nationalization. Although the power to attract foreign capital is often cited as one of the positive features of state capitalism, the actual proliferation rate of these mixed enterprises has been low. By 1958 only seven joint companies existed in which the government owned the majority of shares, and of these only two had been founded since independence. In the decade since then the few joint state-private ventures have not changed the situation significantly. 'It would thus appear that in India's complex conditions neither the transfer to the new state of the property belonging to the colonial administration, nor nationalization, nor participation in private enterprise can lay the material and productive foundations creating a state capitalist industrial sector. As a result new capital construction effected by the state through the industrial development programmes of the Indian five-year plans takes first place.'[31]

New state sector construction

The creation of new plant by fresh governmental expenditure clearly comes last on the Soviet list of methods for creating a public industrial sector, though it has come first in India's practice. Building new plant by public investment is in their view a long and difficult path which 'provokes considerable, sometimes critical tension' in the country's weakly developed economy.[32] This tension, as we see below, leads to such undesirable consequences as inflationary financing and increased dependence on foreign funds, as well as problems affecting the technology and personnel employed.

Soviet critics nevertheless note with satisfaction the important place assigned to industrial construction in the public sector by India's five-year plans. Credits allocated to industrial development, mining included, increased by 365 per cent: from Rs 1,890 million in the first to Rs 8,800 million in the second five-year plan. Still, comparing the second with the first plan, government investment in the productive industrial sectors as a whole increased by 720 per cent, which in iron and steel industry reached 1600 per cent and in the chemical industry 900 per cent.[33] Even if nationalization is the shortest and sweetest route to a dominant public sector, the Soviet analysts still would rather expand the state sector by the most difficult route of new investment than leave new industrial construction to the private sector.

The analysts writing in the light of India's ambitious second five-year plan (1956-61) could see in the plan's projections and initial results the validation of these propositions. New industries were in fact to be created in the state sector where private enterprise had not ventured. The ratio of public to private investment in such capital-intensive industries as mining and manufacturing had risen from 4:96 to 11:89 during the first five-year plan and was to reach 30:70 by the end of the second.[34] While keeping its monopoly in transportation and communications, the state was devoting a growing proportion of its investments to new industry and energy production, the general volume of public investments having largely surpassed the combined rate of local and foreign private capital investment in the country. Hopeful data were easily available. Citing 1958 statistics, V.A. Kondratev reported that state enterprises already accounted for 70 per cent of the country's machine tool production, 80 per cent of its locomotive equipment, and 100 per cent of its telephone equipment output. Once the three public iron and steel mills at Bhilai, Rourkela, and Durgapur were completed, the state sector would produce 51 per cent of the country's iron and steel.[35] By 1972, 'enterprises of the public sector produced 62 per cent of all the pig iron, 45 per cent of the steel, 60 per cent of the zinc, 48 per cent of the machine-tools, 77 per cent of the mineral fertilisers and 52 per cent of the oil.'[36]

THE DYNAMICS OF THE STATE SECTOR

Concern with the growth of the state sector has both a quantitative and a qualitative aspect. For in the final analysis it is the strength of the public sector relative to that of the private sector which will determine the fate of state capitalism. Either the public sector grows at the expense of the private as the whole system progresses towards the non-capitalist stage, or it will be brought under the private sector's control as the economy regresses to a condition of monopoly state capitalism.

Furthermore, publicly owned enterprises demonstrate many qualitative advantages. They provide the most direct means of government control of the economy since through them the state can develop the exact branches it needs as well as the most effective contribution to economic growth since there is no draining away of profits to private owners. In addition they offer the instrument for freeing the economy from the domination of foreign capital in the short term and from capitalism generally in the longer term. They constitute a growing material base for the system's ultimate transition to the next historical stage of non-capitalist development. Although the nature of the productive relations in public enterprises is the same in a bourgeois state as those of private sector firms, 'they represent in their capacity of state enterprises the most advanced degree of socialization of labour that is possible under the capitalist mode of production.'[37] Ultimately it is through the state sector that the new nations will achieve the industrialization they need to solve their basic economic and political problems. 'The new industries and enterprises created in the public sector are becoming (as demonstrated by the experience of the Arab Republic of Egypt, India and other countries) the outposts of industrialisation, its strategic points of support in the offensive on economic backwardness. They are in fact the material basis of state control over the accumulation and distribution of resources on a nationwide scale.'[38]

As L.I. Aleksandrovskaya put it, industrialization changes the nature of the third world's external economic links, ends the domination of the imperialist states, and so promotes national independence. The process of industrialization also serves to push ahead the national liberation movement, liquidate colonialism, develop national self-consciousness, and stimulate the political activity and organization of the broad masses. When the desire to liquidate backwardness is transformed into a political movement, one of the popular demands is industrialization, with the destruction of the colonial or semi-feudal system of administration and the democratization of social life. Industrialization requires successful capital accumulation but depends on the material conditions in each country. In the small countries of Africa which suffer from a very low level of economic development, regional co-operation is essential for heavy industrial development. More solid economies such as Nigeria's, Kenya's or Ghana's are pursuing industrialization in light industries, while only the most powerful, such as Brazil, Argentina, Mexico, or Egypt, are introducing heavy industry.

There are four methods for developing industry – state creation of industry and energy sectors, mixed state-private enterprise, light industry built up by local capital, and the use of foreign capital. The majority of the developing countries recognize the utility of all four methods since the use of different social forms allows the fullest mobilization of their own internal as well as external resources. Aleksandrovskaya agreed that co-operation was needed between these different social forms of industry, although this did not qualify her basic preference for industrialization via the state sector: industrialization is more successful when there is full national control on all energy and material resources.[39]

Though recognizing the greater difficulties that the weaker economies have in introducing heavy industry, Soviet scholars do not condone development by light industry alone. Nor does the acceptance of the fact and utility of foreign aid reconcile them to what they consider the latter's pernicious influence on the direction of industrialization. In Pakistan, for instance, 'no amount of foreign aid can lead to a healthy economy if it is not based on heavy industry. Western aid has actually hindered, not facilitated, the development of heavy industry. The light industries started in recent years have not given the country anything resembling economic independence.'[40] A compelling reason for the Soviet preoccupation with India is that country's level of heavy industrial development, which they consider the highest in the third world, as indicated by the growth of industrial products in her exports.[41] Despite unevenness in the planned growth of different branches of the economy and despite serious problems of unused capacity, Soviet analysts continue to make clear their general approval of the government's economic policy of industrialization by creating a first subdivision of the economy able to produce the means of production.[42]

An integral part of the industrialization process is the use of modern technology, a force that has a 'colossal action on the developing countries' social life,' revolutionizing society, accelerating its progress and allowing it to jump whole historical epochs of socioeconomic development. Modern technology is in conflict with the entire system of socioeconomic relations preserved by the colonial regime. But technology is costly and demanding. It is very capital-intensive, requiring a heavy concentration of capital at a time when private capitalism is still embryonic. Furthermore, it needs a broad energy base and an efficient transportation system as well as qualified cadres.[43]

This is why, in India, state sector enterprises are the harbingers of modernization: they can profit from the latest technological developments and so have a positive influence on the Indian economy's development. Distinguished from the diffuseness of private investment by its ability to concentrate on heavy industry using the most modern and costly technology required for accelerated development, government industrial investment is seen to be superior to private sector investment both in the volume of capital applied and in its more advanced technology. 'In its attempt to shorten the period of technical backwardness and the dominance of primitive capital relations linked to this backwardness, India must develop its own productive forces to reach the level attained by the latest technological progress and consequently having a high organic content of capital.'[44] There was no hint in this analysis, at least until the mid 1960s, that with India's scarcity of capital and overabundance of manpower, some more labour-intensive approach using small-scale organization and traditional technologies should be used to speed up economic development. On the contrary, industrialization for the Soviet analyst meant two things: high capital intensity and heavy industry.

As nothing succeeds like success, so the state sector does best in the Soviet view when it dominates the economy both selectively by holding its 'commanding heights' and over-all by outweighing the private sector. This means that new state capitalist investment has the greatest economic effectiveness where the state sector is already the 'main base of economic development.' Egypt is an example to all developing countries for having concentrated all production in the state's hands.[45]

That bigger means better for India's state sector is conveyed both by its Soviet critics and by its apologists. Those who were sceptical about state capitalism's success gave a severe criticism of the Indian public sector's insufficient growth record. Kondratev noted, for instance, that actual state investments in industry were far less than the investments projected in the first two five-year plans.

Those who approved of India's state capitalist development did so by emphasizing such aspects of the state sector as its growth at a rate faster than that of private enterprise.[46] E.A. Bragina took Charles Bettelheim to task for writing that the state sector was and remains the simple appendage of the private sector. She insisted the public sector was growing steadily, as indicated by the fourth five-year plan's targets. Once these were achieved the state sector would produce articles of broad consumption and so increase its influence on the economy.[47]

Since state capitalism was born to resolve the contradiction between the new nations' urgent needs to develop rapidly and the inability of private enterprise to perform this task, it was self-evident in the Soviet theoretical structure that the huge investments needed by these economies were beyond the capacity of private national capital. As neither imperialism nor the foreign monopolies wanted to industrialize India, only the state apparatus was both willing and able to raise the rate of capital accumulation necessary for undertaking such large investments.[48] Evidence that private enterprise, whether national or foreign, is alive and living distressingly well in the heavy industrial sectors is taken not as an invalidation of the Soviet hypothesis about private capital but as a failure in the performance of the Indian state sector.

Thus N. Savelyev could write of the 'social emasculation' of India's state sector by the admission of national and foreign monopolies to seven out of sixteen vital industries, by the fact that private capital controls 80 per cent of the exports of iron ore, by the situation in the coal industry where the state sector's National Coal Development Corporation has fallen in its output to 8 to 9 million tons, while private sector production increased to 40 to 50 million tons or by private foreign and national capital having captured 60 per cent of mineral fertilizer production.[49] In the final analysis state control through direct government involvement in industrial production is a zero-sum game: the private sector's gain must be the state sector's loss.

According to socialist theory, state sector enterprises make a superior contribution to economic growth because their profits are not lost to the country by flowing to the head offices of the foreign monopolies or lost to the economy by ending up in the profligate pockets of the big bourgeoisie. Run in the national interest, their profits go directly to the state budget for financing further development – an important advantage in the original state capitalist model for which forced capital accumulation was an urgent need. Soviet observers now agree that there is a considerable gap between socialist theory and third world practice. In fact low profit rates are a major bane of public sector industrial activity. Because of failures to master production problems, insufficiencies in adminstration, and politically induced low prices, 'a large number of state enterprises don't make profits.'[50] Discussing this problem in the African context, V.G. Solodovnikov cites inexperience and the lack of skilled personnel as the main reasons that state enterprises 'sometimes are hardly paying propositions.' Somewhat defensively he says that, since socialist experience proved that the state sector can be highly profitable, 'it is necessary to work out measures aimed at making the state enterprises profitable rather than denounce this form of social production.'[51]

India has also disappointed its Soviet analysts in not managing to increase the state's power to generate its own capital accumulation. Despite its growth from Rs 400 million to Rs 1,200 million between 1948-9 and 1956-7, Indian government income from public corporations' profits was still 'insignificant.'[52] G.K. Shirokov produced a startling comparison of the profit record of Indian public and private enterprises: the former made on the average 5.6 per cent, the latter 27.4 per cent, on their invested capital. He explained this by a number of causes. Most of the state sector development has been in heavy industry where the turnover of capital is slower. In the state enterprises the expenditure on variable capital (wages, holidays, health, and cultural benefits) is higher because there is a lower exploitation rate in the socialized sector. In addition there have been specific shortcomings such as overcentralization, insufficiently trained cadres, and unused capacity.[53] He does mention the 'indirect profits' made by public corporations, which are mainly the external economies produced by infrastructure development, but these he dismisses as a subsidy, given private enterprise in a mixed economy.

The record of the 1960s was no better. Public enterprises absorbed very large amounts of state capital but made very small profits. As a result the government directed its investments toward light and food industries where the return is more rapid but the development impact is less progressive.[54] In doing this it offended yet another of the Soviet principles of state capitalist development.

Just as the historical progressiveness of the state is defined by which classes hold power, so the economic thrust of the state sector is determined by the social origins of the personnel who run it. In African countries where the ruling group is often labelled the 'bureaucratic bourgeoisie,' Soviet observers decry the state sector officials' cultivation of personal enrichment, their increasing corruption and plunder of state property which frustrates the state capitalist purposes of public enterprise. It is not enough to have an economic base for state capitalism in a state sector. The 'essence of the dialectical interconnection between form and content of this or that phenomenon' is that there must be 'a corresponding socio-political structure for each economic base.' The development of the state sector and planning calls for 'certain social transformations which will make it possible and profitable to use these new forms of social production.'[55] What is needed is the democratization of the state sector through the broad participation of the working masses in running the economy. Only such devices as the Burmese workers' soviets will keep bourgeois elements from penetrating the administration.[56]

The Indian state sector plants are run by representatives of the big bourgeoisie. The monopoly families like Tata make every effort to have relatives or caste members or former employees put in management positions so that there will be no clash of interests between state sector enterprises and their own. The upper echelons of the state sector are also populated by representatives of foreign monopolies.[57]

It is bad enough that, in the attempt to build an independent, state-owned industrial sector, India is obliged to seek finance and technology from the very powers whose control she is trying to break. What is worse, the lack of trained national cadres both restricts the construction of new projects and opens further doors for foreign penetration of the Indian public sector. The transfer of technical supervision or financial management of new state firms to private or foreign hands defeats the prime purpose of public sector development under state capitalism. 'The penetration of foreign firms in the management of public enterprises reflects their desire to exploit the state's difficulties in obtaining experienced economic and technical cadres. By this foreign capital counts on monopolizing as its privileged function the organization of the technical process of production, thus enabling it to keep public enterprises under its control.'[58]

The development of the state sector depends on the country's economic potential, external as well as internal. Although Egypt and India dispose of much greater internal resources than their other third world partners, even these countries' state sectors have not been able to solve the problem of capital accumulation.[59] State enterprises have a low profitability. There are definite limits to foreign aid, since donor countries are reluctant to donate. The state sector progresses in the framework of general financial weakness.[60]

The picture of state capitalism painted thus far in the Soviet analysis is a system whose progressiveness and effectiveness is directly proportional to the relative size of the public industrial sector, its financial independence and strength, its technical and managerial autonomy from outside control, and the number of industrial fields it dominates directly or influences by threat of intervention. If the state sector is sufficiently developed, it will itself provide the momentum for further capital accumulation and more progressive development. When, as in India, the 'state sector is gradually gaining strength and acquiring domination in some branches,' it plays 'an important part in weakening the power of the monopolies, [in undermining] the positions of foreign capital and in reducing the disparity in the level of economic development in different parts of the country.'[61]

STATE CAPITALIST COMMERCIAL VENTURES

The state capitalist analytical schema is applied as much to micro analysis of the firm or to non-industrial, non-fiduciary activities such as transport or insurance as to macro analysis of the whole economy. The Soviet treatment of India's State Trading Corporation (STC), founded in May 1956, demonstrated on a smaller scale that you only control what you own. According to L. Vladimirsky the motive for setting up the STC was to achieve the aims of the second five-year plan more rationally by increasing the government's control over internal commerce and by stimulating exports. Apart from using commercial activity to finance some projects, expand exports, and so pay for the growing imports needed for the plans, the monopoly granted the STC for the import and export of certain kinds of merchandise allowed India to utilize the world capitalist market more judiciously and to resist foreign monopoly competition more effectively. It was especially helpful in battling the component of 'non-equivalent exchange' in trade with imperialist nations offering lower prices for Indian exports. but demanding higher prices for imported finished products.[62]

The class essence of the STC remains nonetheless. It serves the interests of the Indian ruling class by consolidating the economic position of the national bourgeoisie on the world market. Its aim is not to force private commercial firms out of business by nationalization but to supplement their activity by co-operation between the state corporation and private commercial capital. These narrow class aims notwithstanding, the STC 'objectively' does narrow private capital's area of operation to the extent that it has its own defined spheres of trading activity. More important, it concentrates in the government's hands commercial relations with the state trading firms of several other countries, particularly those in the socialist camp. Thus even if the STC only accounted for 5 per cent of Indian commerce, 30 per cent of its trade is carried out with socialist countries through a system of blocked accounts.[63]

BANKING

While direct state productive enterprise may be the bellwether of a new nation's development health, there are other organs of the economy where the state can – and must – have a decisive development impact. In the whole area of finance, for instance, state capitalism can use its tax apparatus to accelerate capital accumulation in the public sector by significantly broadening its financial base. Both indirect taxes, which fall more heavily on the shoulders of the workers or the poor, and direct taxes, which touch the better off, broaden the base of the state's resources. Thus strengthened financially, the state's budget can more effectively redistribute the national income and use the nation's resources for accelerated economic development.[64] Outside the state's fiscal apparatus, the commanding heights of the economy's finances are the banking and credit system.

In a relatively complex economy such as India's, the banking system provides a critical link in the chain of state capitalism. Here too, Soviet analysts make the same condemnation of the distorting impact of the colonial period, show the same concern for state ownership as the only sure way to control, have the same preoccupation for the alarming growth of the private sector, evince the same pessimism about government regulation, and end up with the same overriding sense that the political situation is the ultimately decisive factor.

One of the reasons for the disproportions in the development of industry and agriculture – a major factor holding back the Indian economy – has been the social structure of the banking industry that took shape in the colonial period. In this period British monopoly capital established a dominating position and already achieved a high degree of concentration in banking. This favoured the development of the big businesses which were under the control of the bank directors but resulted in starving small business and agriculture of much-needed credit.

The Congress's state capitalist banking policy advocated a parallel growth of the state sector, the monopolies, and small enterprise in the towns and villages. The most important aspect of this mixed economy approach was the appearance of a state banking sector, created from the same four sources used to build the state industrial sector. As an inheritance from the colonial regime came the country's central Reserve Bank of India which was nationalized in 1949 to strengthen the government's control over the private banks and to influence the direction and size of their credit. 'It set the level of bank interest, limited loans for non-productive uses, regulated the industrial distribution of loans, etc.'[65] The second expansion of the public financial sector came with the nationalization in 1955 of the nation's largest bank, the Imperial Bank of India. Thirdly, by co-operating with private capital in setting up the Industrial Finance Corporation under direct parliamentary control with half its capital of Rs 100 million furnished by the state, the government strengthened its own position, reducing thereby the role of private capital in the financial field. Less progressive was the creation of the Industrial Credit and Investment Corporation, which had a preponderance of foreign capital but no state participation in its administration or profits. It showed nevertheless the state's desire 'to attract private, even foreign capital for the country's industrial development.'[66]

Although the state banking sector had grown to the point that it held Rs 10.8 billion or 28 per cent of the economy's commercial banking deposits, the industry was mainly in the hands of private banks, which grew 4.2 times from 1956 to 1968, when they held deposits of Rs 38 billion. During this period there had been a significant concentration and centralization in banking, the number of banks having declined from 561 to 100 between 1951 and 1966.[67] By 1962 the five biggest banks, with 38 per cent of the industry's capital, had 57.3 per cent of the deposits, gave 58.6 per cent of the credits, and held 47.7 per cent of the state treasury bills.[68]

Banking has shown the same 'rapid growth of monopoly and concentration of capital in the hands of a small and steadily narrowing group of big capitalists' as other branches of the private sector. From 566 banks with deposits of Rs 9,000 million in 1951, the number of banks fell to 58 while their deposits rose to Rs 38,000 million by 1968. The process of concentration allowed the biggest banks to conclude monopolistic agreements. Beginning in October 1958, the biggest commercial banks periodically made agreements about interest rates. As a result the differential increased between the rate paid for deposits and the rate asked for loans – as did the banks' profits. Monopolization in banking was accompanied by a linking of finance and industrial capital. Expressed in interlocking directorships, the 188 directors of twenty banks in 1962-3 occupied simultaneously 1,640 seats on the boards of industrial and commercial firms.[69] This gave monopoly capitalists the opportunity to use the savings of the broad masses of the people to finance their own operations, while agriculture and small and medium industry still experienced extremely sharp financial difficulties.[70]

Although the government's fiscal system had successfully used the banking system for financing the five-year development plans, governmental regulation had failed to restrict this monopolistic linking of finance and industrial capital. The obvious marxist-leninist solution was complete liquidation of both the Indian and foreign banks. Bank nationalization would provide many advantages. As B. Brodovich explained, this would end the concentration of finance capital in the hands of the biggest industrial monopolies. It would use the public's savings for general national purposes, not those of the monopolies, guaranteeing supplementary resources for financing the five-year plans, and so use state control of a key sector to speed the economy's growth rate. At the same time as it would stop the outflow of currency and save the country's foreign exchange reserves, public control would also prevent speculators from getting credit to collect stocks and speculate on prices.[71] Nationalization was the necessary prerequisite for democratizing the credit system in the interests of the peasantry and small industry.

Nationalization might well be the indicated solution, but it could only come as a result of a growing political strength of the progressive forces. After a long struggle between the left and right forces within the Congress party and after the success of the democratic parties in the elections of February 1969, Congress approved Indira Gandhi's proposal for nationalization of the fourteen biggest private Indian banks, giving the state sector a commanding 85 per cent of all the commercial banks' deposits.

But form does not necessarily determine content. The real significance of the nationalization would depend on the character of the banks' future policy. Maev recalled that there were ten representatives of the big monopolies on the board of the state bank nationalized in 1955. So it was no accident that the state bank took a greater part in financing the monopolies whose representatives sat on its Board than even the biggest private banks. 'It goes without saying that, if the nationalized banks follow the former policy, the fact of nationalization will of itself change little. For this reason the country's progressives advise nationalization at the same time as they demand the democratization of the banks' administration, a change of their credit policy and the further development of anti-monopolistic measures.'[72] Other commentators on the nationalization were more willing to give the government the benefit of the doubt. For M. Stasov, bank nationalization will have an impact on the whole economic activity of the state. Not only will the measure 'definitely strengthen the state sector'; the nationalization will also 'act as a big stimulus to the adoption of other progressive measures mapped out at the last conference of the Indian National Congress in Bangalore.'[73] For G. Mirsky, a leading iconoclast of the Soviet school, this nationalization had a general significance by indicating the direction the Indian economy was taking under Gandhi. It showed that India was not after all 'firmly embarked on a practically classical capitalist road of development,' as some of his Soviet colleagues, he implied, were inclined to think. The polarization of forces within the Congress party was proof that there was a growing conviction that 'this country will not be able to win complete economic independence and wipe out poverty and backwardness by following the capitalist path.'[74]

Other things – especially the balance of class forces – being equal, Soviet approval of a country's economic policy is directly related to the growth of its public sector. If Academician Ulyanovsky could write enthusiastically about the main trends of India's socioeconomic development at the end of 1971 it was largely because 'the state sector in the economy is steadily growing in size and strength. At the end of the 1960s it accounted for 12.5 per cent of the gross national product. State involvement is being especially strengthened in such key industries as iron and steel, heavy engineering and power generating equipment, oil extraction, aircraft and others. The banks, imports of major goods, the production and distribution of electric power and air transport are largely under direct state control.'[75]

5

Planning

Planning is to state capitalism in the Soviet political economy what the brain is to the body. Long-range capital investment programmes direct the public economy's limited energies into constructive activity in the state sector. Long-range co-ordinated plans projecting the future growth of all the economy's sectors are what give order and impulses to co-ordinate the action of its various sectors and branches. Just as a deranged brain can incapacitate the best built body, so can a misdirected planning process nullify the potential of a nation's economy, however large and complete its public industrial sector may be.

Soviet analysts take obvious pride in any evidence of planning in developing countries since its general introduction in the countries of the third world 'took place to a significant degree under the influence of the planning experience in the USSR.'[1] Planning is the irrefutable example of how the socialist model has been borrowed by the have-not nations; the 'recognition of the necessity of planning and its presence as an indispensable aspect of governmental economic policy in the underdeveloped countries is one of the indicators of the influence of the world socialist system in general.'[2] Of course, the similar nomenclature of five-year plans does not imply an identity between socialist and third world planning. The former requires a socialist structure with a corresponding anti-capitalist economic policy, so that the plans can direct activity in the whole national economy. Since planning is meaningful only in the state sector,[3] the developing countries labour under a number of crippling difficulties.

The strength of pre-capitalist survivals, the consequent under-development of capitalist production relations, the large size of the primitive natural economy – as much as 50 per cent in Latin America, and 60 per cent of the economies in Africa – results in a limited demand for industrial production and the predominance of small-scale production beyond the control of any state planning measures. The narrowness of the internal market and the resultant limited means of capital accumulation are aggravated by unemployment and the one-sided specialization that is the hallmark of ex-colonial economies.[4]

Nevertheless, planning has enormous potential. It is the most efficient weapon for mobilizing human and economic forces to overcome economic backwardness and to concentrate these energies on the decisive development areas.[5] Five-year plans have an 'all-national' character since the plans answer the interests of all classes and receive general support. There is no doubt that the Soviets place critical importance on planning: 'Under certain conditions the plans can be the concentrated expression of an economic policy aimed at changing the colonial structure of the economy, achieving industrialization and raising the standard of living.'[6] 'Can be' does not mean 'necessarily are.' As all structures can be used for better or worse, so planning is bi-valent. It can have a positive, anti-imperialist developmental thrust, or it can be used conservatively to reinforce the surviving colonial and pre-capitalist obstacles to development. It is, in other words, the political factor which determines planning's economic effectiveness. What has 'primary importance' is the nature of the government and 'its resolution to carry through a break of the existing social relations and forms of property.' Where this political situation does not exist, as in the majority of the capitalist countries of Asia and Latin America, planning favours the strengthening of the productive forces in the framework of the existing production relations. Much depends on 'how much the local bourgeoisie has formed and what its place in the country's economic life is'; in African countries, where it has not developed and has no place in the economy, the creation of industry becomes the state's function and is achieved through the plans.[7]

In Asian countries where the bourgeoisie is in power, the fight is over the limitation of the state's investment in industry. In Thailand, for instance, where the state has been in the hands of reactionary groups dominated by imperialist advisers, state capitalism has played a secondary role, so that planning did not prepare for a breakup of the old economic structure. The planning commission attempted to develop capitalism without affecting the feudal survivals. It was indeed making a step backwards, not trying to end the colonial structure of the economy but on the contrary aiming to deepen the old specialization.[8] Fulfilment of the 1961 six-year plan would increase dependence on the world capitalist market, particularly on raw material export prices.

In Pakistan, where the 'ruling bourgeois-landlord summit' has not even started on the path of liquidating feudal relations in agriculture or decisively limiting the activity of foreign monopoly capital, there was no question of national planning being adequate.[9] The government Corporation for Industrial Development has played an important role in jute, paper, sugar, cement, and shipbuilding, but with the aim of stimulating and complementing the private sector. The plans were simply 'transformed into a supplementary instrument for private enterprise.'[10]

Under revolutionary-democratic leadership, plans are used with radical effect. The big bourgeoisie is liquidated by the nationalization of industry and banking. Private enterprise is subordinated to state regulation, so that the plans are realized on the basis of the public sector holding the key positions in a series of branches, and being further strengthened by the state investments. In Egypt, for example, the increased strength of the state sector has allowed planning methodology to be perfected and used more effectively.[11]

INDIAN PLANNING IN THE SOVIET PERSPECTIVE

It is in India that the Soviet analysts have had the example of the longest and most ambitious sustained planning experience in the third world. They have in fact been watching it since before destalinization, when they considered that planning in a non-socialist system could have no progressive potential. Their re-evaluation has varied with their assessment of the ruling summit's class essence and historical orientation. 'The most important and essential part of India's economic plans is the fight for economic independence realized along the path of the country's industrialization.'[12]

Since the planning process in India was founded on state capitalist property in a national bourgeois state, its objective purpose reflected its class base as the 'consolidation of the anti-imperialist positions of the national bourgeoisie.'[13] But just as the construction of a state sector is a contradictory combination of anti-capitalist tendencies and pro-capitalist policies, expressing the social crises within the developing nation, so planning is seen by Soviet eyes as evolving in a continuing dialectical tension. It is the product of the struggle between the exploited, to change their social conditions, and the exploiters, who are compelled to make changes.[14] Planning strengthens the positions of the ruling national bourgeoisie against imperialism by building up state control mechanisms while conserving the capitalist mode of production. To the extent that the bourgeoisie still plays a progressive role in the national liberation revolution, its planning reflects in addition the anti-imperialist dispositions of the broad masses. This means that tactically planning provides the basis for a national united front, while strategically it represents for the peasantry and the proletariat a potential vehicle for an eventual non-capitalist development.[15] While the contradictions between these two tendencies will 'sooner or later' rise to the surface in a crisis, until then the left-wing forces support the government in its planning strategy against the reactionary opposition from the right.

Two alternating tones run through the Soviet assessment of Indian planning, one sympathetic and understanding of the many difficulties facing the planners, the other critical of what is seen to be a reorganized but failing capitalism. The more favourable line dwells on the progressive character of Indian planning, seeing it as the expression in public policy terms of a historically necessary state capitalism. The more hostile approach has less illusions about the plans, which are labelled as 'nothing other than a specific form of the bourgeois national state's interference in the economy with a view to insuring its stable development on the basis of complex and elaborate programmes called five-year plans.'[16] This severe view is based on a more sceptical judgment about the uncontrollable action of the private sector. In the Indian mixed economy, planning consists of nothing more than 'governmental recommendations' to 'anarchic private enterprise' on the desirability of a certain volume of investments, their allocation by industrial branches, the quantity and mix of products, etc. Apart from these resolutions, which have only limited authority, the state has no more effective means of controlling private enterprise than the indirect instruments of fiscal policy, credit control, or the allocation of resources and equipment. The 'spontaneous laws' by which private enterprise continues to flourish are 'far stronger than bourgeois programming.' To the extent that the major process of development in Indian industry takes place under the auspices of private capital, this development is 'in principle outside the sphere of government control.'[17]

For the public sector on the other hand the planning system is the necessary corollary of the state's industrial power because it is only in the public sector of Indian industry that the government exercises the direct control required for implementing long-range development programmes. Whether indulgent or critical, the Soviet commentators have all agreed on the imperfect nature of the Indian planning system, which is far from being socialist either in theory or in practice. Yet they have also taken equally seriously both the contents and the implementation of those five-year plans that India has undertaken. Their reports on the successive plans reveal the Soviet appreciation of the mechanics of state capitalism at the level of concrete governmental policy planning.

In interpreting this analysis one must recall both that the Indian planning picture was continually changing and that the Soviet perspective itself altered with the passage of time. The first five-year plan (1951-6) was virtually an accomplished fact when the original destalinized views on Indian planning were expressed. The second five-year plan was digested by Soviet analysts at the first blush of their new-found enthusiasm for Asian state capitalism. When the Indian economy subsequently ran into difficulties, forcing a revision in 1958 of the second plan, the Soviet observers were already taking a second look at the obstinately capitalist nature of the Indian economy. The problems encountered in implementing the third plan (1961-6) were complicated by India's grave internal political problems, caused by its two succession crises and its two border wars. When the planning process was put into dry dock for an overhaul, a further reassessment of the whole significance of planning was made by the Soviet school.

THE FIRST FIVE-YEAR PLAN, 1951-6

While stalinist observers scoffed at the very idea of 'planning' in a capitalist neocolony, the post-Stalin reappraisal discovered in the first Indian experiment in planning a response to a serious contradiction between the needs of coherent development and the insufficiencies of the economic control system inherited from the colonial regime under very chaotic political conditions and considerable inflationary pressures. 'The plan reflected the objectively ripened necessity for instituting some kind of planning to make possible state capitalist construction of such new enterprises as hydro-electric installations, irrigation works, etc.'[18] While those parts of the plan concerning state sector construction did have an 'authentic imperative character' since they were tied to the 'direct utilization of the available budgetary means,' the parts of the plan affecting the private sector and agriculture only comprised 'distant forecasts' and 'indications merely concerning the advisability of achieving certain economic objectives.' But by its volume of Rs 23,568 million in planned public expenditures, by its long-range perspective, and by its scope, the plan far surpassed the budgetary projections of the normal corporate capitalist consortium.

The general tone of the Soviet reassessment of the first five-year plan is one of tolerant forbearance. The severe difficulties of the economic situation in India made truly rigorous planning impossible. 'The plan could not embrace all the phases of the production process in this vast, small-peasant country with its different economic sub-systems, their complex inter-relationships, the dominant role of the capitalist economic structure and the country's great dependence on the world capitalist market and foreign capital.'[19] The most severe critic pointed out that the first plan was severely hampered by a lack of capital for investment – 4 or 5 per cent of the gross national product.[20] The government's indirect means of acting on private enterprise through taxation, loans, and market operations were insufficient to direct the private sector, which did not achieve the objectives set for it in the plan either by volume or by industrial branch. (Although private sector performance in actual fact exceeded the plan's targets, achieving an investment of Rs 18 billion, an overfulfilment of Rs 2 billion, the theme of private capitalism's inability to develop needed industries was heavily emphasized.) The profits available in the food and light industries, plantations, and banks attracted foreign and national private capital, which would not flow to the heavy industry branches controlled by the government and thus were un-profitable.[21]

The Soviet analysts' approval of the first Indian five-year plan's giving top priority to agricultural and infrastructural development reveals the concept of a pre-industrialization stage for weak economies. The plan created the 'important economic, industrial and technological prerequisites' for the future industriali-zation of the country.[22] The gross national product increased by 18 per cent (11 per cent per capita), the production of consumer goods by 34 per cent, the growth of industrial production by 38 per cent, and the production of the means of production by 70 per cent. 'For this period and in these conditions, this represented a significant success.'[23] 'In these years the main difficulties of the transitional period were overcome and the losses suffered by the country's par-tition made good. The general level of economic activity rose as India turned to the future with considerable confidence.'[24]

THE SECOND FIVE-YEAR PLAN, 1956-61

The first plan had in fact been a hastily assembled collection of projects already on ministerial drawing boards or even in process of implementation. They were brought together virtually after the fact in a plan document giving the aura of purpose and co-ordination to what would otherwise not have been as coherently articulated an over-all investment strategy. The second plan was quite different. The Planning Commission had settled down under the direction of Professor P.C. Mahalonobis who had the time and the staff to approach long-term planning in a more rational way. Of obvious interest to Mahalonobis, as to Nehru himself, was the Soviet planning experience, to which most credit for the USSR's dramatic economic expansion was generally laid. This interest was not simply platonic; since the dramatic improvement of Indo-Soviet relations, the Polish and Soviet economists Oskar Lange and M.I. Rubinshtein had contributed to the Planning Commission's work. As the economy's performance during the first plan had been most encouraging (largely because of good weather increasing agricultural output and slack being taken up in the previously disrupted economy), the plan-ners were encouraged to shift the priorities from agriculture and infrastructure to make a massive and daring push at heavy industrialization, hoping to achieve that self-sufficiency in the production of the means of production that was the hallmark of the Soviet model.

If one adds to this background the fact that the second five-year plan was published in 1955 just as the Soviet re-evaluation of the developing countries and the proclamation of Soviet friendship for India was in full, exuberant swing, it should be clear why the initial Soviet exposition of the second plan was highly sympathetic. The Soviet public was introduced to the second five-year plan by two articles which are notable for the absence of any criticism. The first simply reproduced without comment the plan's investment and growth projections as published in India.[25] The second, a detailed report by M.I. Rubinshtein, who had just returned from participating with Indian planners, gave a highly informative account of the many dimensions of the plan, clearly approving its priorities and letting the mass of detail speak for its great significance in the achievement of state capitalist development in India.

It was the plan's commitment to rapid industrialization by the forced development of heavy industry that Rubinshtein selected as most significant. From a realized investment of only Rs 750 million, or 6 per cent of the first plan, the allotment to mining and heavy industrial investment in the second plan increased 900 per cent to Rs 6,910 million, or 15 per cent of the second plan's total investment. Rubinshtein regaled his readers with a profusion of information conveying the clear impression that the second plan would create foundries, electrical equipment plants, factories of locomotives and railway cars, huge chemical complexes ... so many signs of a rapidly industrializing nation.[26]

The large role allocated to private capital in the predicted industrial development, especially in the production of means of production, which was to absorb 70 per cent of the private sector's investment, did not provoke any adverse comment or explanation on Rubinshtein's part, despite the fact that he himself had elsewhere maintained that private capital was unable and unwilling to develop heavy industrial sectors in the developing countries.[27] Of the Rs 6.2 billion which the private sector was to invest, the Tata consortium alone was to invest Rs 1.15 billion, which would double its production of steel.

Infrastructural development was not to be neglected. Electrification, 'one of the most important conditions for industrialization,' was to progress by doubling the national capacity from the 1956 level of 3.4 million kilowatt hours to 6.9 million kwh in 1961. The transportation system was to be modernized, old rolling stock renovated, and the rail network expanded, so that the volume of transported merchandise would increase by 50 per cent.

Labour-intensive industry was also to benefit by major increases in investment allocations, the handicraft and artisanal industry getting Rs 2 billion for expansion compared to the Rs 312 million it had received in the first plan. A systematic aid programme for small manufacturing by financial aid, technical instruction, training of cadres, organizing research, supplying raw materials, and selling finished products would attempt to reduce unemployment and decentralize production.

Rubinshtein did not restrict himself to reporting the economic aspects of the plan. Despite the measures envisaged to increase employment by 8 million jobs, he noted that the expected increase of the working force by 10 million persons in five years, combined with the existing unemployment and underemployment in the cities and villages, would produce an acute employment crisis by the end of the second plan. He noted nevertheless the growing effort in social welfare expenditures (from Rs 1.31 billion to Rs 2.67 billion), the increase in projected housing construction, and the vast Rs 3.2 billion programme for public, professional, and scientific education.[28]

The over-all impression conveyed by Rubinshtein's introductory report was that the plan was doing everything economically possible. The next series of articles, which appeared in 1958 and 1959, maintained the same approving tone for the principles of the second plan. One author felt that, though the second plan was still far from constituting authentic socialist planning, 'the fact that India is borrowing from the planning experience of the socialist countries in its effort to escape from its backwardness and to suppress its economic dependence on foreign capital by the country's industrialization is a fact of enormous progressive significance.'[29] For another the second plan was a vital element in the process of economic liberation: 'the fulfilment of the second five-year plan will mark a new step on the road towards the achievement of economic independence.'[30] While these commentaries praised the intentions of the plan, they took a critical look at its implementation problems, particularly with respect to its financial base. The increase in the amount of state capitalist construction was going to cause an increase in expenditures which in turn would have serious repercussions on the balance of payments and the country's internal financial stability.[31]

The commentators who wrote after the economic crisis of 1958 and the subsequent reduction by 13 per cent of the plan's targets placed particular emphasis on the financial question. Of the Rs 48 billion allocated for state capitalist construction, the government had hoped to raise 41.8 per cent (Rs 20 billion) by two methods of which Soviet observers strongly disapproved: inflationary deficit financing and the 'slippery path of accepting foreign aid in ever increasing proportions.'[32] The point is simple: while ambitious plan targets are approved, they should be covered by the country's internal financial resources. Despite the doubling of taxes to Rs 12 billion and the increase of the internal debt (Rs 12 billion), one half of the plan's investments had to be sought from other sources. During the plan's first fiscal year the consequences of this financial policy were already noticeable in the 13.8 per cent increase in the country's money supply.[33] The government's debt to the Reserve Bank of India rose by Rs 1,630 million and the private sector's debt rose by Rs 1,380 million. The increase in the demand and the insufficiency of supply in 1956 raised wholesale prices by 15 per cent.

The Soviet analysts did not criticize the plan's deficit financing for lack of an alternative to propose. The government could and should have sought the necessary means for forced development in the revenue and property of the monied classes. In clear, fraternal support, the Indian Communist Party position is quoted at length:

The Communist Party observes that ... sufficient measures have not been taken to limit the monopolies' profits; a programme to nationalize the plantations, the banks, the foreign firms and consortia has not been proclaimed; a monopoly of foreign trade in the major raw materials exported has not been established. The Communist Party also draws attention to the necessity for severely taxing the income of the propertied classes to achieve economic recovery, most especially by establishing a ceiling for the profits of the big capitalists, to restrict the export of profits abroad and to use the funds available above these limits as forced loans; by mobilizing the financial resources of the large corporations (used usually to camouflage profits), raising the taxes on corporate profits, introducing heavy direct taxes on family income derived from personal fortunes and capital, postponing the compensation payments to large landowners, suppressing the payments for the personal expenses of princes, requisitioning the princes' excessive riches by forced loans, reducing the salaries and subventions which the overly paid civil servants receive.[34]

On the external front the modernization of industrial equipment had led to a great increase in the import of means of production. For the fiscal year 1955-6, imports of cast iron and steel rose from Rs 286 to 707 million and producer goods from Rs 1,277 to 1,653 million. The annual average of imports was to increase by 128 per cent over the imports of 1955-6 to Rs 8,680 million while for the same period the forecast of exports was only in the area of Rs 5,930 million. In fact already in the first ten months of 1957 a 9 per cent decrease in the export of traditional goods combined with a decline in their prices on the world market had further increased the trade deficit from Rs 584 million in 1954-5 to Rs 815 million the following year and Rs 1,722 million in the first ten months of 1957. As a result the country's gold and currency reserves fell from Rs 7.7 billion at the end of 1955 to Rs 6.4 billion a year later and a mere Rs 3.4 billion by the end of 1957.[35]

It would be wrong to infer that in the final analysis the Soviet indologists were hostile to the second five-year plan. Quoting the Communist Party of India in its support as well as its criticism, they note the CPI's endorsement of the high priority assigned to the expansion of heavy industry in the state sector and for the increased production of consumer goods through the 'development of artisanal industry and a more complete utilization of the [capitalist] enterprises' productive capacity.'[36]

The same over-all approval, seasoned by some reservations, characterized E.A. Bragina's review, drawn after the first decade of Indian planning: 'the former colony deprived of its own industrial base has, in the course of two five-year plans, laid the foundations for the development of the domestic production of its producer goods.'[37] She cited the statistics of the first planning decade: 42 per cent increase of gross national product or 16 per cent per capita rate of capital investment from Rs 5 billion in 1951-2 to Rs 8.5 billion in 1955-6 to Rs 16 billion in 1961-2; production of machinery from Rs 40 million at the beginning of the first plan to Rs 250 million by 1955 and Rs 2.500 million by mid-1962. The public industrial sector's share of manufacturing had grown from 1.5 per cent to 8.4 per cent and the number of state firms multiplied from 36 with a capital of Rs 263 million in March 1951 to 140 firms ten years later with a capital of Rs 5,452 million.[38]

THE THIRD FIVE-YEAR PLAN, 1961-6

Though Bragina voiced criticism of the first planning decade's experience, particularly the precarious nature of its financial base, the critical imbalance in foreign trade, and the worsening unemployment situation, her generally sympathetic attitude was maintained towards the third five-year plan despite the increasingly serious difficulties that the Planning Commission was encountering. In striking contrast to Bragina's benefit-of-the-doubt approach to the objectives of the third plan was R.S. Gorchakov's suspect-the-worst interpretation of the same subject published a year later. A comparison of their views is instructive.

State sector investments
Bragina noted that the allocation of state funds for heavy industry development was rising from Rs 1.7 billion in the first plan through Rs 7.9 billion in the second to Rs 15 billion in the third. This public sector investment created capacity in heavy industry branches that were either not in existence before or were entirely insufficient, thus laying the foundations for the national production of the means of production. Though imports must still supply the major part of the country's equipment needs, by the end of the third plan internal production should cover 75 per cent of the national demand for machinery and equipment. 'The increased allocation of funds reflects a desire to strengthen the government's influence on the economy and to consolidate the state sector.'[39]

Gorchakov agreed that statistics did indeed show a large increase of public investment in mining and manufacturing, so that Indian industry would make great progress thanks also to the Soviet Union's participation in the construction of twenty-six of these projects. While the targets were impressive, 'in actual fact the real situation is quite different' from the picture painted by the projections. Taking the rupee's devaluation into account, the real value of public investment if fully achieved would fall to Rs 58 billion from Rs 72.5 billion or a 16 per cent shortfall in the targets set in 1956 for the decade ahead. 'All this testifies to a definite slowdown in the growth of the Indian economy's state sector and to the government's considerable reduction of its original targets for the economy's long-term growth.'[40]

Financing
Bragina noted with satisfaction that new public sector enterprises were to furnish a supplementary revenue of Rs 4.5 billion to the state budget. Deficit financing was to fall in both relative and absolute terms from Rs 11.5 billion (23.9 per cent of the second plan's expenditures) to Rs 5.5 billion (7.6 per cent of the third plan's projected expenditure). On the other hand she pointed out such difficulties as the increased taxation, which would restrict the internal market by reducing the purchasing power of the masses. The lack of free resources among the population was indicated by the insignificant growth of small savings and the stability of internal loans. She noted the tension in the economy resulting from internal resources only covering 70 per cent of the forecast investments. Rs 22 billion or 30.5 per cent of the total would have to be found from foreign aid. While obtaining such a sum was not categorically out of the question, it would certainly be very difficult to find.[41]

Gorchakov considered that, though the share of deficit financing had fallen by 50 per cent (reflecting the bourgeoisie's fear of inflation), the increase of taxation would conceal the same inflationary methods that had been used before. What was more, the forecast increase of taxation from 8.5 per cent to 11 per cent of the gross national product would not be feasible, given its previous increase by 60 per cent from 1950 to 1960. These increases simply lead to the familiar results: price rises, increased inflation, and worsening conditions for the labouring masses. The public's reduced purchasing power for consumer goods would narrow the internal market and so aggravate the contradiction between production and demand. As for the income forecast from the public sector, Gorchakov had grave doubts about the profit target of Rs 4.5 billion; revenue from public sector enterprises had already fallen from Rs 16 million to Rs 13 million from 1958-9 to 1960-1. His most violent attack was made on the plan's second 'vulnerable point,' the dependence on foreign aid, which he estimated to be 44.4

per cent of the plan's needs – Rs 22 billion as stated in the plan plus the Rs 5 billion needed to amortize previous debts and Rs 6 billion to pay for American wheat imports. One could hardly talk of a 'plan' if half of it depends on foreign assistance: 'The trend towards [reliance on] foreign capital aid threatens the fulfilment of the anti-imperialist aims of the national liberation revolution and is completely incompatible with the plan's proclaimed intentions of strengthening the country's economic independence.'[42]

Private capital
Bragina observed that the increase of private investment from Rs 24 billion in the second plan to Rs 40 billion in the third represented a relative decline from 38 per cent to 36 per cent of total planned investments. However, private capital was no longer limiting itself to light industry but wanted to operate in the branches which had originally been reserved as governmental spheres of influence. Taking advantage of a series of political concessions, capitalists were constructing factories for chemical fertilizers and synthetic rubber and aluminum production and participating in metallurgical complexes.[43]

Gorchakov denounced the 'extremely dangerous tendency' of the private sector continually to surpass the targets fixed for it: by Rs 2 billion over the first plan's target of Rs 16 billion and by Rs 7 billion over the second plan's target of Rs 24 billion. As for foreign capital, its investments have risen from Rs 2.9 billion in 1948 to Rs 5.9 billion in 1958. As these dangerous trends were increasing, the declared aims of the national bourgeois policy were unrealizable. The concessions made to foreign and national capital, the efforts to avoid difficulties at the expense of the masses, and the refusal to make a radical break with the past all constituted 'a serious obstacle to the country's possibility of non-capitalist development.'[44]

General assessment of the third plan
Gorchakov's pessimism was seasoned with a ritually optimistic conclusion: 'It would be incorrect to believe that the prospect [of non-capitalist development] has disappeared in India. The facts prove that the contradictions between the national bourgeoisie and imperialism are still very severe. This still creates favourable conditions for a great surge of the anti-imperialist struggle for the foundation of a national democratic state in the country.'[45] Bragina felt that despite such negative factors as the unsolved unemployment crisis and the increased activity of private capitalism in heavy industry nevertheless 'the Indian government retains for the state sector the dominating position in the country's economic development ... The large industrial plant constructed during the second plan now allows the government to play an important role throughout the eco-

nomy ... The considerable industrial expansion in the public sector during the third plan will strengthen still further the government's position.'[46]

A more penetrating analysis appeared in 1966 when N.G. Lozovaya could assess the experience of the three plans as a whole. Although she judged the 1956-61 plan to have marked the country's entry into the second stage of its industrial revolution and obviously approved of the third plan's redoubling the state sector's investment for manufacturing industry, Lozovaya noted that even if the objectives were to be realized the nation's industry would still not be able fully to satisfy the country's demand for the most important aspects of industrial production. The projected increase of machine building and mining machinery production would fully satisfy the country's needs. But only 97 million tons of coal would be produced by the end of the third plan, as against a planned consumption of 110 million tons; nor would the economy's needs for electricity be met. Lozovaya's chief criticism was summed up in a single concept: disproportion. 'Disproportions of industrial development are seen in the fact that the demands of the economic law of priority growth for the production of the means of production will be insufficiently observed: imports will be used to supply the needed capital goods not produced at home.'[47] More complex than the failure to achieve self-sufficiency in producing capital goods is a series of different disproportions. 'Besides the process of overcoming the old disproportions inherited from the colonial past, new ones are appearing, such as the unused capacity of enterprises, the temporary inactivity of a significant part of the invested capital, the low technical-economic level of a series of new production operations, the disparity in the development of adjacent branches, the growth or creation of dependence on imports of some types of equipment, materials and patents, backwardness in the development of the fuel-energy base as compared to the needs for the economy's development.'[48]

It was in the mid-1960s that the Soviets were becoming increasingly alarmed by the growing dominance of the monopolies and the undeniable vitality of private enterprise capitalism. Thus, although Lozovaya's 1966 assessment gave full credit to the planning system for having overcome the economic consequences of colonial rule, broken the country's economic dependence, and created the conditions for enlarged reproduction by industrialization, and although the plans were seen as the most important means of accelerating the development of capitalism, they were also judged unable to resolve the country's contradictions of socioeconomic development. The third plan's rate of growth was insufficient to absorb the industrial unemployment, agriculture lagged half-stagnant behind industrial development, while on the accumulation front foreign investment increased in sixteen years from Rs 2.5 billion to Rs 7 billion. On one level Lozovaya could be read as making a policy critique. She pointed out the planning commission's failure to foresee all the necessary types of steel and to build up the widened energy base required by the planned heavy industrial plants. She presented as a serious causal factor the failure to break up the administrative machine inherited from the colonial period. She considered the continuation in power of the anglicized upper caste of civil servants to have induced the bureaucratism, inefficiency, corruption, and nepotism which reduced the viability of the planning practice.

At another level Lozovaya was making a more serious political judgment about the role and significance of planning in the Indian policy. In answering the question 'whose interests does planning serve?' she found state regulation and planning to be the key factors in the high rates of growth of Indian monopolies. In fact the various measures of state regulation were completely opposed to their official aims of creating a socialistic pattern of society. The state's regulating activity was 'objectively directed to accelerating and strengthening the processes of concentration and centralization of capital and the enrichment of the monopolistic summit of the Indian bourgeoisie.' Politically the general all-class support for the plans concealed their real class nature and allowed the ruling classes to use them as a 'means of weakening the class struggle and a supplementary subjection of the broad popular masses to the ruling circles.'[49]

Planning was no longer what it was seen to be ten years previously – the means for leading Indian state capitalism onto the non-capitalist path by an anti-imperialist, anti-monopolist programme of state sector industrialization: 'Planning is the all-embracing form of the state's economic policy in the framework of the fight to keep India in the capitalist system of the world economy and accelerate the rate of capitalist development.'[50]

ON TO THE FOURTH PLAN

If the pendulum of the Soviet assessment of Indian planning had swung so far back from progressive towards reactionary on the marxist-leninist scale towards the end of the third five-year plan, it seemed for a considerable length of time that the abandonment of the fourth five-year plan by Indira Gandhi's government in 1967 would be the final straw. With planning linked in dialectical dependence to state capitalism and with the increasingly vocal denunciations of the monopolies' growth coming from Moscow, it looked as though the planning process and state capitalism were to be stripped of their last shreds of progressiveness. For a long two years the Soviet academic and political press was silent on the subject of planning. It was only in October 1968 when the fourth five-year plan was about to be relaunched after a considerable period of revision that an article appeared. With all the facts available about the failures of the third plan and the weaknesses of the planning system, this could have been a scathing *coup de grâce*. Instead, the article, by V. Vasilev, could not have been more sympathetic and understanding. He was not entirely uncritical. He considered that the third five-year plan did not correct the interbranch disproportions that had developed in the second but had caused even more deformations. It had been a plan without an over-all conception, unlike the second plan whose guiding principles Vasilev strongly endorsed for future planning: a double thrust of heavy industrialization by capital-intensive projects in the state sector and widening employment by aid for labour-intensive, small-scale manufacturing.

While he pointed out how the slow 2.9 per cent growth of national income during the third plan was slower than the population growth rate of 3.2 per cent and how agriculture continued to dominate the economy in production and employment, his conclusions were optimistic. An end had been put to the critical trend at the end of the colonial period of a lowering of national per capita income. The state sector had become the vital instrument for the reconstruction of the industrial structure. Vasilev did not turn a blind eye to the problems of inflation, stagnant agricultural production, insufficient accumulation rates, and external trade crisis. But he did say 'it would be incorrect to explain these difficulties only by economic causes and, in particular, by mistakes made in planning.' External factors beyond the government's control played an essential role; in particular, worsening relations with China and continuing tension along the Indo-Pakistan borders loaded growing military expenditures onto the Indian economy's shoulders.

The three-year break in planning was a 'needed pause' in the working out of the fourth plan, which 'doubtless will answer all the more the essential needs of the country's economic development.' The first three plans were an important stage in the nation's development, 'a difficult stage, but a very essential one for the country's further advancement along the path of progress.'[51]

Explanations for this sudden change of tone, from critical to favourable, can only be speculative. Perhaps in the intervening two years too many disasters occurred to planning in such model non-capitalist states as Ghana, Indonesia, Egypt, and Algeria for India's comparative stability to remain underappreciated. If it was a case of comparing planning failures, India's stood out as a temporary hiatus in a system undergoing strong political and ideological struggles, not as an outright reversal. If a Soviet author had to choose between mediocre planning and abandoned planning, he would still take the former. Vasilev's article represented the restoration of this more appreciative view that had been in eclipse during the mid-sixties but had resurfaced with the consolidation of Gandhi's progressive rule. By 1971 the Soviet line was back in the groove of the Nehru era: 'The [fourth] plan provides for increasing the national income by 32 per cent and per capita income by more than 16 per cent. The state sector retains definite priority in the allocation of the planned capital investments.'[52] As another scholar confirmed, the Indian National Congress has underscored 'the government's intention to develop the state sector intensively as the main prerequisite for economic and social progress.'[53]

PLANNING PRIORITIES

In examining the nuts and bolts of five-year plans the Soviet analysts were very much on their own home ground, observing what was closest to their own historical experience. We can rightly expect to gain from their critique a sharper insight into their policy recommendations for Indian state capitalism. Yet lacking most in this literature was any fundamental theoretical analysis beyond the broad discussion of planning as a function of the country's class character or a historical description of the planning process.[54] At best the reader can extrapolate from the description of the particular plans and the more general statements on the subject the basic Soviet attitudes towards the major planning problems.

No specific critique of investment priorities was made. The first Indian five-year plan was approved as a fait accompli providing a necessary transition to the second. The second was endorsed in full knowledge of the plan's designs: heavy emphasis on forced industrialization. But so too were the priorities of the third and fourth plans: balanced development of industry, agriculture, infrastructure, handicraft, and labour-intensive industry. One looks in vain for a separate Soviet scale of priorities for public investments in India or for planning in other third world countries.

One can assemble a number of general propositions from the Soviet observation of planning in Africa and Asia over the past years. Introducing a collection of monographs on planning in individual third world countries, for instance, A.Z. Arabadzhyan makes two points. First, planning is a necessarily imperfect system since plans define targets for the whole economy but can only be 'imperative' in the state sector. The decisive factor defining the possibilities of planning is the relationship between the state and private sector because much of the plans' success depends on what happens in the private sphere, which can only be influenced indirectly by such instruments as fiscal, commercial, and credit policies. Secondly, planning is complex. All plans deal with the simultaneous development of agriculture, industry, communications, and social conditions. 'Such a complicated approach to the problem is determined by the low level of economic and social development of these countries which, by the interdependence of these branches, makes this complexity especially unavoidable.'[55] Nevertheless, a 'main direction' is still needed, though this can change from plan to plan.

Infrastructure

It is infrastructural development that takes first place as the 'main direction,' taking from one-third to over one-half of resources in most third world plans. Given the 'low level of development of their productive forces, attention to the infrastructure is dictated by these countries' national economic development needs.'[56] Because of the huge capital needs and the long waiting period before receiving a return on the investment, infrastructure development answers the interests of all classes. The big bourgeoisie wants to extend its influence to new regions, exploiting cheaper working forces and accelerating the export of goods and raw materials to the world market; the national bourgeoisie sees in infrastructure development the foundations for a capitalist development both in breadth and in depth. Since this is the precondition for changing the emphasis of later plans in favour of industrial expansion, the working class also supports state investment in infrastructure.[57] Arabadzhyan points out in addition that the possibility of genuine planning in infrastructure is greater since transportation, communications, irrigation, hydroelectric power, and mining are generally in the public sector and construction projects are financed by state funds.[58]

If the reader was searching for a distinctive Soviet view, he would be disappointed, for the Soviet consensus rejects both the position that belittles the importance of infrastructural development and the opposite line which urges a concentration on infrastructure. 'Realities have demonstrated the untenability of such extreme solutions. Many socio-economic factors have to be considered in determining the scale and sequence of building infrastructure projects ... The rational scale of developing the infrastructure can be determined only in the context of a general analysis of the entire pattern of the economy and the interaction of a country's different sectors and regions.'[59] If a position can be detected here it is a preference for the bland and cautious middle of the road. Equally vague is the Soviet position on investment in the social infrastructure. The high amounts devoted to non-economic social expenditures in the plans is noted, though the attitude to this is unclear. While all classes are said to support expenditures on the satisfaction of social needs, the ruling classes, in the Soviet view, see this as a means of weakening social contradictions and conveying their ideology to the masses.[60] Aware of the miserable living conditions in the third world, Soviet observers do not condemn programmes of social security. They also perceive the economic utility of social expenditures like education: the new systems of education reduce the dependence on foreign specialists by training experts locally at the new technical institutes.[61] Still, there is scepticism that any social welfare system can really work in a capitalist economy and concern about non-economic expenditures that will not lead to a direct increase in per capita national product.

Financing

The problem of financing the plans is approached with greater consensus and certainty. Planning is generally recognized as being accompanied by a tense financial situation. The third world economies start with a difficult inheritance from colonialism: to cope with inflation they have only weakly developed forms of modern capitalist credit, while the credit system is dominated by foreign banks. Furthermore, planning uses government debt as its most important source of financing.

The basic reason for most countries' failure to achieve the planned levels of state capitalist investment is the insufficient mobilization of the country's internal resources. Great inequalities in the distribution of the national income mean that those with high income spend it not on accumulation but on luxury consumption, while farmers have too little to save for the capital needs of reproduction. Yet the developing countries suffer also from unutilized reserves, as the flight of national capital abroad from Latin American countries demonstrates.[62] It is impossible to increase internal accumulation, to accelerate economic development sharply and thus liquidate the centuries-old backwardness of the developing countries - writes V.L. Tyagunenko, the dean of the development school - without (internally) radical socioeconomic transformations and (externally) a change in the nature of the relations between industrially developed capitalist states and the developing countries.[63] The non-capitalist states who have taken steps to liquidate feudal survivals and abolish foreign monopoly oppression have set a good example.

Egypt's agrarian reforms, which undermined the economic position of feudalism, permitted the development of productive forces in agriculture with the expansion of co-operatives and the enlargement of the area of cultivated land. A series of nationalizations - the Suez canal, whose revenue provided (at the time of writing) 40 per cent of the annual foreign currency needs of Egypt's five-year plan, the banks, and the enterprises of both the big and middle bourgeoisie - made the state the decisive force in the accumulation of capital.

Burma's radical measures of nationalization, which closed the road to foreign private capital investments as well as to the private sector's expansion 'create real bases for Burma's subsequent development on socialist principles and for the country's accelerated economic growth.' The only qualification to the recipe of radical socioeconomic transformations is a reference to local conditions: the objective possibility of enlarging social production is determined by concrete economic conditions and depends to a large extent on such factors as the amount of raw material and energy resources available, the size and training of the working force, the capacity - actual and potential - of the internal market.[64]

In some countries, especially in Africa, these concrete economic conditions are not very promising. According to Y.N. Cherkassov, the possibilities for financing development programmes with internal resources are very limited. 'The slow development of production relations, the low standard of living (the national revenue per capita is $100-110) the limited development of monetary and commodity relations (the proportion of consumer economy being 25 to 50 per cent of the GNP), the narrowness of the budget-base, the small size of the amortization fund (3 to 8 per cent of the GNP) all combine to determine the low proportion of financing by means of internal sources.'[65] Africa is thus obliged to look to foreign aid for initial support. External capital should not be regarded as the main source of accumulation, since servicing the growing debt becomes itself a stumbling block to economic growth.

Hence the solution to the problem of finance consists in making the utmost use of internal sources, regarding these as fundamental, while at the same time attracting foreign capital. This makes the planned state sector an important factor and its own capital investments 'one of the most essential forms in the unfolding of the production forces in Africa.' But the basis for its budget is very narrow because of the feeble development of commodity-monetary relations. Furthermore, a very high proportion of state expenditures is non-productive, going to the administration, the army, and the police.

Taxation is an important instrument of state accumulation. Customs duties form 65 per cent of Egypt's indirect taxation (1963-4) and 87 per cent (1961-2) in Ghana's case. As for state sector profits, they have little significance as a whole. Nor are internal loans very significant, because of the limited capital markets. These financial straits make deficit financing, once treated with great venom by Soviet observers, a tolerable device: 'at the present stage of development in the African economy, inflation is, to a certain extent, justified and is assuredly more advantageous than economic stagnation.'[66] The majority of the underdeveloped countries raise their funds through indirect taxes, since the pressure of the propertied classes on the government's economic policy is great enough to prevent high direct taxation.[67]

Despite the difference in complexity and industrial base between Africa and South Asia, the Soviet advice for India is remarkably consistent with the rest of their analysis. The problems are similar: the enormous amount of petty commodity production with a low productivity and non-productive consumption by the wealthy; surplus money is not invested in production but in precious stones, real estate, and parasitic capital (trade profiteering), thus depressing the reproduction process; economic policy must remove the barriers to both production and accumulation.[68]

India uses government debt as the most important means of financing the plans. Through loans floated on the market, small savings and deficit financing, 60 per cent of the first five-year plan's investments and 80 per cent of the second plan's investments were raised. While this shows the 'growing significance of state credit for capital accumulation,' the growing government debt is alarming (1962: Rs 71 billion; 1965: Rs 100 billion). The increase in deficit financing means a growth of inflation. In the third plan India had to use the whole deficit financing planned for the five-year period in its first three years because of its failure to mobilize enough capital through state loans. The subsequent growth of indirect taxes and deficit financing led to further inflation. The mobilization of internal resources is difficult, Lozovaya conceded, when there is a national growth rate of only 2.5 per cent, a deteriorating world price situation, and growing expenditures for military operations and food imports.[69]

The narrow base for internal accumulation and the failure of those in power to infringe on the interests of the bourgeoisie by direct taxing of the private sector leads to the search for external means of finance. The growing dependence on foreign sources of finance is a matter of record. From 9.6 per cent of India's first plan, foreign aid rose through 23.7 per cent of the second to financing 29.4 per cent of the third plan's investments. In Pakistan foreign aid accounted for 39.9 per cent of the first plan's financing and 47.6 per cent of the second. While this dependence on foreign loans is noted by all, not every Soviet analyst has the same attitude towards the problem. Arabadzhyan remarked that 'practically speaking, without aid from the outside, the achievement of economic development plans would be impossible.'[70] Others see the resulting dependence as incompatible with independent, anti-imperialist planning. In his study of the financing of the Indian five-year plans, I.I. Egorov underlined the inadequate revenue coming from the public sector. Observing that the plans' financing depends more and more on foreign sources of capital, especially through enticing private foreign capital, he expressed serious doubts about the planning system's capacity to direct the nation's economic development. Bragina considered that the foreign financing of development created a vicious circle: Western advisers who accompany their loans offer the bad financial advice which leads to a further growth of the third world's indebtedness. In thirty-four countries the international indebtedness rose from $6 billion in 1955 to $16.3 billion in 1962. From 1963 to 1966 their international indebtedness doubled. By 1966, seventy-four underdeveloped countries owed $40 billion, having to make repayments of $5 billion each year.[71] For all its criticism, the Soviet judgment of third world planning remains tolerant, even in the area of financing. Despite their limitations, the plans are a 'significant factor in mobilizing ways and means for liquidating backwardness.'[72]

Industrialization

In this passive reporting of the five-year plans' different investment programmes, an implicit priority pervades the Soviet view: the industrialization imperative. There may be certain obstacles in the way of the rapid creation of a complete and self-sufficient economy producing all the means of production on the basis of its own resources and technology, but it is simply a question of time and technique before, say, India catches up. All in all it is clear that the large project is preferred to the small. Capital-intensive investment is preferred to labour-intensive. The employment of large numbers of workers per plant is preferred to the small factory using a few workers. And of course all these priorities are themselves preferred when they are operated in the public rather than the private sector and financed by domestic capital accumulation or socialist credits rather than by private foreign investment or imperialist 'aid.' 'The essence of industrialization consists in the extensive introduction of the latest scientific and technological achievements in production, in the comprehensive technical re-equipment of the national economy.'[73]

Industrialization does not carry such a strong imperative in the Soviet development perspective just because it stands for progress and because the Soviets consider that they themselves did master the major development problems by a programme of forced industrialization. More fundamental in the marxist-leninist theory, industrialization connotes the establishment of a whole new mode of production in which all the socioeconomic relations are qualitatively transformed into a historically superior economic system. Large capital-intensive projects using the latest technology allow greater accumulation and faster improvement in the wages of the workers; they make the benefits of social ownership of the means of production increasingly obvious since the need for economy-wide planning of a complex system becomes ever more essential. It may have its social and human costs; it may create economic tensions. But every marxist-leninist knows that forced industrialization is the real way to break the chains of dependence and backwardness. Everything that facilitates movement towards this inevitable stage is historically progressive; everything that impedes the necessary industrialization is objectively reactionary since it holds back the historical laws of development.

If concessions have to be made to small-scale and light industry because the government does not have the financial resources to follow through with its heavy industry programme or because it must create more employment, then this is grudgingly accepted as a poor second best, and the consequent delays in the progress of industrialization have to be suffered. The objective – an industrialized, productive economy using modern, efficient (and expensive) technology – is clear. Any marking time in the form of aid for small-scale industry is seen as a deviation that may even strengthen the already overpowerful archaic forms of production which are themselves obstacles to industrialization.

In making his case for the support of small-scale industry, S.A. Kuzmin may have been challenging the conventional Soviet wisdom that the road to industrialization is paved with heavy industrial complexes, but he did not abandon the objective of industrialization, 'the creation of their own production of the means of production on the basis of modern science and technology.'[74]

Serious doubts have nevertheless been sown. The enormity of the problem is no longer evaded by inspiring exhortations but faced as the conundrum it is. 'Industrialisation in developing countries thus runs up against the need to mobilise huge resources. But the problem is further complicated by the fact that a modern works can function properly only if there are a number of allied sectors which provide raw materials, power and semi-manufactures, process the by-products, transport the goods, and so on. In other words, capital has to be invested not in one enterprise, but a whole complex, which further sends up the scale of resources that must be mobilized and invested in the national economy more or less simultaneously.'[75] For all the rhetoric, the Soviet analysts no longer claim to have an answer in the form of a standard formula. 'The choice of the development strategy, specifically industrialisation, is an intricate process which requires not only a detailed analysis of diverse trends in the national economy as a whole, but also consideration of tendencies of both economic and social development, their interaction and at times contradictions. It is clear that there is no "single," "universal" solution. A proper approach is arrived at only on the basis of a most thorough examination of the concrete conditions ... This, in turn, demands very flexible forms and methods of planning and a correct system of criteria and planning evaluations.'[76] Rather than concluding that Soviet analysts have no answer, we should note their acknowledgement that there are many answers. The summary of one study stated the new agnosticism:

Thus, owing to the diversity of objective and subjective factors, as we hope our study has shown, many alternative approaches to formulating the strategy of the initial stages of industrialisation in various less developed countries of Asia, Africa and Latin America are possible. For some countries it may be more expedient to concentrate on building the infrastructure and expanding the existing export sectors and the greater processing of their output to increase accumulations. For others, it is more advisable to step up the development of light industry and small-scale production so as to increase employment and accumulations. The third group of countries may begin development with several, most promising sectors (from the viewpoint of the availability of raw materials and know-how and the size of the market) for the accumulation of the necessary resources and training personnel for the subsequent reconstruction of the entire national economy. Some of these countries are already able to undertake the building up of heavy industry and engineering and reconstructing, on their basis, the entire economy. For many of them a combination of these alternatives in one or another proportion is optimal.[77]

The Soviet assessment of planning ends where its analysis began – with a political judgment. Without a doubt a 'progressive phenomenon' given the anti-imperialist direction of their social content, the plans have great potential in the struggle for a democratic solution of the objective economic problems confronting the developing countries. 'By having long-term planning as the basis of its economic programme, Indira Gandhi's Government has been trying to combat the haphazard nature of private capital in the economy. India's plan is a well-based effort to ensure the planned growth of production, to carry out social changes on a vast scale and develop science and technology, the transport system and foreign trade.'[78] Since the 'degree of progressive social potentialities realized in the plans depends on the concrete class relations,' the implementation of the plans presents progressive forces with the task of fighting for more democratic solutions.[79] However, a major impediment to plan implementation in India, as in any non-socialist country, is the presence of a private economic sector.

6

The private sector

If the state sector and planning represent all that is positive in state capitalism, the private sector constitutes its dialectical opposite. Whereas the state sector embodies the possibility of making a transition to a non-capitalist and eventually socialist path of development, the private sector provides the material base for the development of pure capitalism and even state monopoly capitalism. While on the one hand the state sector can profit from the planning experience of the socialist countries and bring a country's economy under a more rational law of development, on the other hand the private sector can borrow the latest organizational techniques of imperialist monopolies and bring the colonial economy under the sway of the anarchic laws of capitalist evolution.

Indeed Soviet writing about developing economies uses two separate vocabularies, one for the state sector employing a socialist terminology and another for capitalism with a conceptual apparatus taken straight out of *Das Kapital.* Free enterprise capitalism is regarded as a separate economic structure distinct from if coexisting with the state sector. Even though capitalist development cannot achieve economic independence or liquidate age-old backwardness,[1] and even though capitalism is no longer the dominant or progressive social force in the modern world (since socialism is now the decisive tendency of contemporary development thanks to the growing strength of the socialist camp) various sections of the bourgeoisie and landowners are in power in a considerable number of Asian, African, and Latin American countries. Whether their leaders want it or not, these countries are moving towards capitalism. For where the position of the imperialist monopolies is strong, where the activity of the local bourgeoisie is unhindered, where corruption permits officials to enrich themselves at the state's expense, where the petty bourgeoisie is also given a free rein, a passive government stand is objectively helping capitalism to develop spontaneously.[2] In Latin America the capitalist path was taken after independence was achieved in the 1800s and before there was a socialist option available. A brand of semi-colonial capitalist system developed that still has pre-capitalist as well as imperialist obstacles to overcome.

India, as we have seen, has been the most fascinating specimen for the Soviet assessment of third world capitalism. The most industrially advanced of the colonies, it had the biggest proletariat and the most firmly established bourgeoisie, the richest natural resources, the most efficient administrative system, and the most complete infrastructure. Since Stalin's death the Soviet evaluation of national capitalism in India has evolved noticeably. In the 1950s when the state capitalist model was first being articulated there was little concern for the private sector compared to the tiny but historically more progressive public sector. Since Soviet observers perceived state capitalism to be taking India via industrialization towards socialism, straight capitalism was no longer thought to be the dominant structure. It might be growing, but it was being harnessed by state capitalism to achieve India's aims of economic independence. By the early 1960s, however, it had become clear that the private sector was indeed flourishing, and Soviet writers became somewhat more alarmed about which economic structure was in control. Was state capitalism harnessing the private sector, or was it the reverse?

The Indian private sector has appeared in the Soviet analysis as the classic capitalism of Marx's analysis, following its own patterns of development according to its own law of value. Having grown at an increasing rate since the acquisition of independence, 'big capital' showed the traditional signs of concentration of production and centralization of capital. Using estimations of stock values, Soviet scholars observed in the 1950s a growth of private capital between 1948-9 and 1956-7 at 9.6 per cent per annum, compared with the previous colonial rates of accumulation of 2.6 per cent between 1918 and 1940 or 4.5 per cent between 1941 and 1945.[3] The strong position occupied by national capital in the cotton industry (91 per cent), jute (75 per cent), coal (86 per cent), sugar (76 per cent), paper (62 per cent), and food (68 per cent) indicated the private sector's strength in some key industries. This considerable growth of capital had been accompanied by a process of concentration, the number of corporations having fallen by 8.9 per cent between 1951 and 1961 while the size of their capital assets measured by value of share capital rose by 57.4 per cent.

Liberated from the colonial yoke and supported by the national bourgeois government, the country's 'capitalist industry is developing both in depth and breadth.'[4] Capitalism was consolidating in depth because large corporations employing five hundred workers or more were growing rapidly. The sixty-two biggest private companies (12 per cent of all the Indian corporations) had, by 1955, 44 per cent of the nation's share capital.[5] Between 1947 and 1953, 40 per cent of all new investment was made by these firms. By 1968, seventy-five of the biggest Indian companies (out of 25,000 private firms) owned 54 per cent of all the assets of the private sector.[6] 'The concentration of production, the centralization of capital and the strengthening of big capital's economic power on this basis in India's private sector are obvious facts.'[7] All these statistics marshalled by anxious Soviet observers in the early sixties pointed to a continuous concentration of capital that is 'leading inevitably to the monopolies' growing influence.'[8]

At the same time as this concentration of capital illustrated the law of capitalist development 'in depth,' India's economic development showed a growth of capitalism 'in breadth' by the proliferation of small and medium enterprises at the economy's base. This was confirmed by the decline in the average number of workers per enterprise between 1947 and 1953 from 264 to 207 in heavy industry and from 138 to 98 in light industry and showed the results of the bourgeois state's post-independence policy of support for small- and medium-sized enterprise.

Accompanying this flowering of private capitalism, profits and productivity had risen by 314 per cent in the fifteen years since 1939. Placed in a context of huge unemployment and underemployment, the worker had been subjected to increasing capitalist exploitation and productivity had grown by 53 per cent between 1947 and 1953, while the number of workers remained the same and real wages had hardly regained the level of 1939.[9] The share of wages in the gross national product had fallen from 53 per cent in 1939 to 39 per cent in 1958.[10] While private capitalism was surging ahead in industry at a rate three times higher than before the second world war, 'the mass of new surplus value obtained from each worker rose in six years by about 40 per cent.'[11]

Despite this capitalist expansion and proletarian exploitation, the general Soviet judgment on the evolution of the private sector in India has been favourable. That even private enterprise was considered progressive under a state capitalist regime can be seen by Ulyanovsky's quotation from an Indian Communist Party statement: 'The progressive nature of national capitalism's development in India in the present concrete conditions compared to the preceding periods of its development ... is indisputable. The Communist Party of India supports the widening of consumer goods production by a more complete utilization of the available [capitalist] productive forces and the development of the handicraft industry.'[12]

MONOPOLIES REASSESSED

The growing politicoeconomic strength of right wing forces in India during the frequent political crises following Nehru's death brought to a boil the debate that had long been simmering among the Soviet analysts of India. With the difficulties experienced by the planning system, with the concessions made to foreign investment, with the resulting growth of both foreign and local monopolies, it was no longer possible to maintain the original post-stalinist hope that state capitalism would lead India directly to the non-capitalist path. No formal reassessment was made in an ideological declaration by Soviet authorities. State capitalism was not deconsecrated. India was not declared to have passed to the reactionary state monopoly capitalist path. But the reader of Soviet writings gradually became aware of shifts in the analysis that made no bones about the capitalism of India's economy. Without going so far as to condemn it as reactionary, the Soviet writers made it clear that this capitalism no longer contained the promise of an early or easy socialist transformation. This reassessment was expressed retroactively in a greater emphasis on the capitalist content of India's heritage from the colonial period.

The important point now for the Soviet analysis was that independent India had started with an already established capitalist base, since 'the capitalist structure had long been the leading one' in colonial times. Although it had no facilities for producing the means of production, no machine-building, and no heavy chemical industry, India was the 'most capitalist' of the colonies. While 'developing capitalism' was distinguished from Western capitalism by its absorption of some feudal socioeconomic forms, N.G. Lozovaya insisted that it was 'necessary to underline that the deformed development of capitalism was still above all the development of capitalism.'[13] What differentiated the Indian bourgeoisie from other third world bourgeoisies was the existence of a monopoly stratum within it at the time independence was gained.[14]

The colonial monopolies had developed through a process of 'borrowing' the oppressing colonialists' own techniques. 'Borrowing,' seen historically, was a form of self-defence by the national bourgeoisie who had to use the methods of the colonialists to fight foreign capital. The British industrialists' use of trade associations led to Indian counteractions. In 1915, for instance, the Association of Indian Tea Planters had been founded to counter the Indian Tea Association, a group of British planters set up back in 1884. Similarly, the British use of managing agencies to augment their control of the subcontinental economy was adopted by their Indian rivals to give the local monopolistic bourgeoisie far more power than its relatively weak capital base would have allowed it without these corporate devices. Since independence the borrowings of Indian monopoly capital have taken more regular European forms, such as holding companies, investment trusts, and insurance societies. This structural transformation of local monopoly capital was facilitated by the fact that these forms have already been developed in the West.

While the socialist model of the Soviet Union plays an important role as inspiration for and accelerator of state capitalist developments towards socialism, the monopoly capitalist model can serve an equal and opposite role for spurring third world monopolies. These firms borrow the methods of Western monopolies, although this is only possible once a definite minimum level of capitalist development and industrialization has been achieved. In India this basic growth of monopoly capitalism was, in the Soviet view, produced by three main factors, the evolution of the managing agencies (the dominant form of foreign control of Indian business in the colonial period), the high concentration of production in the new branches of industry (which required large capital investments), and the growth of private banks (which provided the financial base). Without this borrowing from monopoly-capitalist imperialism, however, the emergence of national monopolies at such an early stage of capitalist development would 'obviously be impossible.' Monopoly capitalism in the third world is thus a kind of historical export of capitalism, for 'if the Western countries were less mature, the monopolies could not have appeared in a series of under-developed countries,'[15] such as Pakistan, Turkey, and the Philippines. If India's class forces were such that she developed quickly along capitalist lines, then the laws of capitalist development would have led quite naturally to the emergence of monopolies. Borrowing introduces their activity at a much earlier stage of capitalism and had a perceptible impact on independent India's development.

In a series of articles published between 1964 and 1967 O.V. Maev presented the monopoly sector as growing more from foreign stimulus than from governmental support. The government's industrial policy of 1956 had clearly opposed the growth of monopolies and was in fact implemented by a whole series of measures hostile to big capital. 'But by virtue of its bourgeois character, the ruling circles of India did not launch a resolute pursuit of an anti-monopoly course.' In fact, despite the bourgeoisie's hostility to big capital, the government's policy of encouraging private capital to develop in weak areas of the economy (for lack of adequate capital resources of its own) led to a close collaboration between the government and the monopolies, with a resultant parallel growth of state capitalism and monopoly capital. Any concession made to private capital at the expense of the state sector was in practice a concession to the monopolies.[16]

The external stimulus to monopoly development was more direct, though it varied with the geographical areas. In eastern India, the predominance of British colonial capital had made it difficult for national enterprise to get established. This diverted such big entrepreneurs as Marwari capitalists into investments in the traditional spheres of usury, landholding, trade, and financial speculation. After independence their growth in industrial production was not by building new enterprises but by purchasing foreign-owned plants in the existing branches of the economy. In buying shares in British managing agencies and changing them into Indian-foreign companies, Indian entrepreneurs established close and growing relationships with foreign capital resulting in large credits from imperialist governments.[17] In western India, where there had not been much colonial investment in industrial enterprise, the Indian monopolists could not expand by buying British firms.

More important than reaction against the old colonial capital was co-operation with foreign capital in creating new operations under joint control. In western India co-operation with foreign capital was mainly in trade, thirty of the forty-one biggest western Indian groups having agreements with foreign monopolies to set up mixed companies.[18] For their part the foreign monopolies had a strong interest in this collaboration with Indian monopolies as they adapted to the new conditions created by the independent government's limitations on the activity of foreign capital. To get around the numerous obstacles placed in their way, the foreign monopolies decided to operate under the mask of national capital as joint companies with Indian labels. Collaborating with local big capital gave them distinct advantages. It was more efficient to deal with a few big monopolies than with many small capitalists. Working in unison with local monopolies guaranteed the safety of their capital as well as higher profits in a protected market and a foreign outlet for their industrial equipment.

The Indian monopolies also found distinct advantages in these arrangements. They obtained the right to use the patents and the highest technology of the foreign corporations and could thereby reduce the capital outlay needed to create the production facilities and obtain western capital equipment without foreign exchange problems. These unions of big capital made possible investment in new branches requiring from tens to hundreds of millions of rupees. This allowed the big Indian bourgeoisie to establish itself in new branches and broaden its market at the expense of the non-monopolistic sectors of the economy. Yu.I. Loshakov described this process as a self-reinforcing causal chain: 'Thus the domination of foreign capital in India stimulated the borrowing of monopolistic practice by the big Indian bourgeoisie. The establishment of individual monopoly agreements leads to the elaboration of other agreements in related branches of industry. The foundation of monopolies quickens the concentration of production and capital and leads to the rise of new monopolies.'[19] N.A. Savelev provided figures on concentration: by the end of the 1950s the 596 firms employing more than one thousand workers constituted only 7.5 per cent of India's factories, but accounted for 62.6 per cent of India's capital investments, employed 68.4 per cent of the country's working force, and produced 53.7 per cent of her industrial output. By 1963 one hundred of the biggest industrial concerns with over

Rs 100 million capital had almost one-half of the capital of all the registered companies in the country.[20] Other figures indicated the absolute dimensions of this explosive growth. In Eastern India, twenty-two groups controlled 770 companies with capital of Rs 10.88 billion.[21] Tata, a vast empire of companies in all branches of the economy, had grown from a capitalization of Rs 700 million to Rs 4,000 million in 1963. Its influence 'defied assessment'; it exploited over 80,000 people. Seventy-five monopoly groups virtually ran the Indian economy, controlling 1,536 companies with assets of Rs 26 billion. As recorded by Savelev, the rapid growth of the number and power of the national monopolies, the concentration of vital links of the economy under their control, and the co-operation with foreign monopolies in joint investment projects (totalling 2,358 by 1966) indicated the existence of a monopolistic sector permeating the economic system.[22]

What is the significance, the reader might ask, of these figures? Do the Soviets perceive more than just quantitative expansion; do they see qualitative change as well? With its rapid rate of concentration of capital, with its control becoming truly monopolistic, Savelev indicated that Indian big business was throwing off its semi-feudal shell and making fundamental structural shifts. Despite the figures and the analysis it is impossible to conclude from these studies of the Indian monopoly sector just what was the significance of these fundamental shifts. The authors provide themselves ample ammunition to conclude that the monopolies had taken over, but they do not go so far. Relative to the middle or small capital, was the monopolistic bourgeoisie dominant or just growing faster? Relative to the state sector was monopoly capitalism now the controlling agent or just becoming stronger? The Soviet writers come to the brink of answering these questions but hesitate to make the leap. When they come to the edge of their socioeconomic analysis, they quickly shift ground to their political concerns. The political implications of the monopolies' progress appeared to be the major concern of the Soviet writers. The monopolies may or may not be the historically dominant economic trend, but the renascence of their political activity clearly was threatening to make them the dominant political force by taking over state power and diverting India from its independent path. The basic problem was that the 'economically strong financial and industrial magnates of India are now persistently reaching out towards the levers of governmental power in an effort to change the [country's] domestic and foreign policy.'[23] It was not news that the monopolies and other forces of right reaction had always fought the development of the state sector, long-term planning, and an independent foreign policy. What was new was the emergence of the monopolies into the open in their strong campaign to seize power and radically reorganize the Indian state. Not content with the Swatantra party as the rallying point for extreme reactionary forces, big monopoly capital participated in the 1967 general elections with its own list of candidates. Candidates were selected for the Congress party by big business who threatened to cut off their financial contributions if these nominees were rejected. In Bihar state, candidates linked to the Birla monopoly contended for ten of the fifty-three national seats and for 'dozens' of the state-level seats. Big business politics extended from electoral tactics to parliamentary intrigue, when the right wing of Congress exerted strong pressure in economic and military matters.

The real significance of the monopolies' development was seen in their relationship with the politics of right reaction. Because the right was headed by the top crust of the bourgeoisie who were experienced in politics and had big financial and economic resources, supported by the international financial oligarchy, the threat of a reactionary onslaught was very acute.[24] The importance of the threat could be seen from the monopolies' economic programme. Tactically they were pressing for a limitation of the state sector's activity, the abolition of governmental regulation of the private sector, and a free rein for their foreign monopoly partners. Their strategic programme was worse: sale of government firms to monopoly capitalists, transformation of the economy to a free market system on the Western model, full domination by monopoly capital over the government, and a firm tie to the world imperialist system.[25]

The Soviet writers' medium was an analysis of monopoly economic concentration, but their message was political. It was a notice to Indian 'patriots' who 'are recognizing increasingly the necessity of a continual fight against the reactionary sociopolitical forces, whose activization is one of the characteristic peculiarities of the contemporary stage of India's capitalist development.'[26] It was also a warning to the Indian government not to let things go so far that the Soviet Union might be forced to change its Indian policy. In an unusual departure from the apolitical tone of the Soviet texts, Savelev openly admonished the Indian authorities: 'It cannot be said that scientists [Soviet scholars] have been unaware of these economic, social and political processes in India. More is now being said and written about them in view of the increased political activity of the Indian monopoly bourgeoisie and, consequently, of imminent serious clashes in Indian society and potential departures from the established neutral course in foreign policy.'[27]

The struggle between the two paths of development that had gone on since the first day of India's state capitalism had reached a new climax, though right reaction had by no means won. In 1964 O.V. Maev gave what seemed the best summary of the tortuous Soviet debate: 'As opposed to the imperialist countries, there has not yet been a splicing of the government apparatus and the monopolies with the submission of the former to the latter and the formation of state monopoly capitalism.'[28] Monopoly capital might be strong, but state capitalism was still stronger. Maev may have had to hold his breath several times in the succeeding years as state capitalism suffered from the declining fortunes of Congress and the serious difficulties of planning. But what boosted his morale was Indira Gandhi's nationalization of the fourteen biggest private banks, a 'serious blow at the positions of local reaction.'[29] Since the banks were one of the main supports of the monopolies, their nationalization had become a political focus for the democratic forces and was thus a sign of their growing strength. Even at this moment of triumph, Maev was cautious. The monopoly sector might not have full power, yet it could still achieve its ends by bringing political pressure to bear behind the scenes. On the other hand, even though the state sector might not be the dominant force in the economy, the country might still be able to progress by the use of state regulation of the private sector. This possibility of regulation being used to make the private sector serve the national interest became as integral to the Soviet conception of state capitalism as the theme of the private sector's separate and unbridled growth.

STATE CONTROL OF THE PRIVATE SECTOR

When state ownership of industrial enterprise is advocated as the means for state control of the economy in the people's interests, the obvious and often stated corollary is that private enterprise is not subject to state control and does not respond to the national interest. When monopoly capitalism is depicted as following its own 'spontaneous' laws of development in the interests of the capitalist class, Soviet scholars posit the existence of a fundamental antagonism between the state's and the private sector's interests. As their analysis of the big business sector shows, this struggle of interests is particularly strong between the big Indian bourgeoisie, 'clearly interested in a definite limitation of state capitalism's further expansion,' and the state's policy of increasing governmental participation in the economy, if only by state capitalist means.[30] There is a permanent conflict of interest between the capitalist producer and the government. However, the contradictions between these two sectors, though sharp, are nevertheless judged to be 'non-antagonistic,' in other words not irreconcilable, when state capitalism is viewed in its totality.[31] Indeed not only is there no competition between the investments made in the two sectors, but the state's capital projects are seen to be aimed at facilitating the expansion of private capitalism, the monopolies included. Of the public sector's investments 82 per cent were spent on such infrastructural promotion as the development of transport, agriculture, electrical power, and port facilities: areas of investment where there is no desire at all for private capitalist operation and so no conflict of interest.[32]

Public industrial investments were for the most part devoted to heavy industry where the capital cost was too high for the relatively weak private capitalist to be seriously interested. As for the monopolies, the state's own industrial activity did not check their growing power at all. On the contrary, it released them from having to make the necessary but unproductive investments in infrastructure. Heavy industrial construction with government funds provided the energy and chemical base for the economy and the foreign exchange needed to pay for imports, while protectionist laws ensured hothouse conditions for the branches where the monopolies did establish their operations.[33] Far from restricting private enterprise, state capitalism opened new horizons for the expansion of the private sector: 'The construction of transport, irrigation, highways and power generation facilities which is going on throughout the country prepares new opportunities for investment and creates the necessary conditions for the penetration of private capital in light industry and food production as well as in other less developed branches of the economy.'[34] As we have already seen, the Soviet dialectic does not always regard state capitalism as being restricted to the public sector and therefore separate from the private sector. On the contrary – and here a serious source of ambiguity emerges in the Soviet argument – the concept of state capitalism does also embrace the whole economic system including both the very substantial private sector and governmental policy towards free enterprise. In actual fact, as the Soviets recognize, the Indian government has from the beginning followed a policy of actively encouraging private enterprise. So closely were the private and public sectors interwoven that 'it is impossible to conceive the development of private capitalist enterprise in modern India independently of the state sector since the latter provides its aid and co-operation to entrepreneurs by all possible means – granting credits, guaranteeing raw material supplies, giving orders, customs protection and so on.'[35] Ambiguity surfaces in the value judgment that the Soviet analysts make. While there is some implication of collusion between the state and the private sector in the interest of the big bourgeoisie, this governmental aid for private sector development is not seen as entirely or even mainly regressive. In fact its immediate consequence – accelerating the development of capitalism – is actually considered historically progressive in India's present situation. 'In these conditions state capitalist development is the most important means of abbreviating the stage of primitive capitalist accumulation.'[36] If the state has succeeded in stimulating the expansion of private capitalism, this is certainly more in the national interest than having the economy stagnate at a stage of pre-capitalism.

That the state is promoting this activity also gives it some degree of control, though its control is, of course, far from being absolute. It was only after some delay that the Soviets began to take seriously the state's regulatory powers over the private sector. Once dismissed as being impotent to control the anarchic private sector, these economic levers were then regarded with considerably greater respect. N.G. Lozovaya, for instance, made a partial inventory of the Indian government's instruments of indirect action typical of modern mixed economies. By law or regulation the government could exercise some control over the supply of raw materials, fuel, and energy; it could affect the situation in different branches by licensing imports and controlling foreign exchange; it could aid industry through its financial and credit policy. Through such fiscal measures as lowering the tax on undistributed profits while raising taxes on dividends paid out, it could induce capital to reinvest savings or switch them into new branches of industry. It could create favourable conditions for key or export industries by such devices as amortization privileges allowing profits to grow without tax penalty.[37]

A noticeable feature of the general reassessment of the Indian polity made in 1967 by the scholars of the Indian Section of the Institute of Asian Peoples was the space devoted to the state's regulatory control over the private sector. Indirect control and state aid was judged effective in directing investment in desired directions. The aims of governmental regulation of industry were described as twofold, to channel the flow of investments, directing them into new branches while limiting them in existing branches, and to make the most efficient use of operating production facilities. This assessment considered the first objective to have been more successfully achieved than the second. The means used to promote greater industrial efficiency have had the desired impact to a limited degree only. For one thing, state regulations do not control small-scale industry, whose large expansion has created a serious problem of unused capacity. Licensing, for instance, is not a foolproof way to increase production: more licences are issued than are necessary to achieve the planned increase because entrepreneurs try to obtain more licenses than they really need. The regulation of internal trade has consisted of restrictions on traditional entrepreneurs by price controls. The partial control of the distribution system and the more effective state regulation of the banks have both been unsuccessful in controlling speculation and inflation. As for price fixing, these controls have only been imposed on wholesale commodities, whereas the price rise has been faster in retail goods. In any case, prices are fixed to ensure monopoly profits, and so only in a limited way promote the efficient use of capital. The government controls of external trade and foreign currency have limited imports, although they have not been able to prevent speculation in scarce imports that produces Rs 1.2 billion of profits. In the Soviet reassessment these relatively strong regulations are recognized as having had a definite influence on the private sector, showing that the anarchic processes of capitalist accumulation and the free market can be used by the state for the nation's development during its transition from a colonial to an independent economy.[38] With this acceptance of at least the partial effectiveness of the state's regulatory powers over the spontaneous workings of the private sector, the battle of the sectors appears in quite a different light. If the state can exert fairly effective control over the private sector through indirect regulation, if power is held by progressive groups pursuing the national interest, then state capitalism can indeed still pursue developmental goals even with a strong private sector. When the national bourgeoisie is described as not having realized its full potentialities (indicated by the big rise in the accumulated part of national income from 5.4 per cent in 1948-9 to 13.8 per cent in 1960-1), state capitalism is still credited as progressive.[39]

In a subsequent, definitive assessment of India's industrialization problems, G.K. Shirokov made a detailed review of the various state control mechanisms, which he found to have been largely inadequate. Although state control was 'intended essentially to limit the influence of market laws and adapt them to the needs of economic development,' the objectives could not be achieved 'because of the specific nature of India's backward economy, the shortcomings and restricted character of the control itself, and the concessions made to the monopolies.' Asking whether the spontaneous law of the free market would not have produced 'better results than a purposeful policy implemented by the government,' he concluded – surprisingly for a marxist – that 'in the case of a large-scale private sector in industry, the spontaneous market laws probably ensure a greater harmony between supply and demand and can clear the way to the improvement of the principal indices characterising the operation of large-scale private enterprises.'[40] He went on to explain: 'Control is possible only in structures governed by the laws of commodity-money and capitalist production. But in India the economy is as yet dominated by the small-commodity and semi-natural structures where the operation of the laws of capitalist production is distorted.'[41]

Shirokov did not go on to argue for a relaxation of all controls, since 'when the small-scale capitalist and small-scale commodity structures retain their position in industry, the laws of capitalist production act only in a modified way.' Indeed, if Shirokov had one overriding concern about the Indian economy it was far less the growth of large-scale capitalist industry than the proliferation of the traditional 'small-scale commodity structures' which have impeded the growth of domestic demand for the output of manufacturing capacity, the increase of domestic capital accumulation, and the integration of the economy as a whole. Whether state capitalism plays an equally positive role in the more primitive small-scale sector of the economy is quite another question.

SMALL-SCALE PRE-CAPITALIST ENTERPRISE

The growth of the private sector, particularly of the monopolies, and the reconciliation of state regulation with an autonomous private capitalism indicate that in the Soviet view, capitalism is winning the political-historical struggle in India at the expense of the non-capitalist path. But this relative strength of straight capitalism over socialist tendencies does not necessarily mean that capitalism is the dominant form of economic production compared to pre-capitalist forms.[42] For when Soviet scholars analyse third world capitalism they are generally talking about the modern part of the economy. The struggle between the two paths of development that they consider to be the major tension in Afro-Asia is a choice between two routes of industrialization, the one emphasizing industrialization within the state sector, the other growth via free enterprise development. By implication, third world development will be by modern industrial means whether capitalist or socialist. Increasingly over the years there have been references in the Soviet writings to another type of economy quite distinct from that of industrialization, whether capitalist or socialist. This is 'small production' (*mel'koe proizvodstvo*) which is seen as a deeply entrenched mode of production that is an obstacle to necessary technological modernization. T.S. Pokataeva referred impatiently to this small enterprise for having conserved the old technology from colonial and pre-colonial times,[43] making it clear that the modern way is using large-scale, capital-intensive enterprise with modern technology, whether by the capitalist or socialist paths.

Other writers too are concerned that pre-capitalist forms of production are frustrating the proper blossoming of capitalism. L.R. Gordon-Polonskaya has described how straight capitalism has been slowed down and distorted in Pakistan by what she has called the 'survivals of feudalism.' Because of 'the tight cohesion of capitalist and feudal forms of exploitation,' she noted, 'it is sometimes very difficult to distinguish the handicraft worker from the hired worker.'[44] This complaint is revealing. The marxist-leninists' impatience with the persistence of feudal elements in the Asian economy is but part of their general problem of accounting satisfactorily for the general predominance of small-scale producers in the third world economies. In some cases, small-scale production is considered as a secondary trend in the development of modern capitalism. While big and middle capital represent the development of capitalism 'in depth,' then the 'strikingly rapid growth of small manufacturing enterprises' represent the accompanying development of capitalism 'in breadth.' In India these small 'manufactory' type of establishments, along with non-registered, non-household manufacturing units, increased in the five-year period 1956-61 by 300 per cent and 250 per cent respectively.[45]

Other Soviet authors do not consider this small-scale production to be capitalist, since the operators themselves take part in the production process even if they also employ a little manual labour.[46] The analytical problem of how to classify small-scale production entails a further policy question. If these handicraft and artisanal producers are pre-capitalist and constitute obstacles to capitalist development, then government policy should not encourage their survival and still less their expansion. Rather, they should be overcome by the forced development of capitalism under a bourgeois regime or by skipping a historical stage and turning them into socialist forms of enterprise under a non-capitalist system. In India the issue is more complex still. In discussing the relationship between what they describe as two separate trends of Indian capitalist development, L.I. Reisner and G.K. Shirokov observed that the monopolies have actually formed close links of control and co-operation with the lower sections of the capitalist class. 'Thus each big business house is becoming now an apex of a huge pyramid, the foundation of which is made up of a great number of smaller partners, associates and quasi-independent entrepreneurs.'[47] In the 1967 review of the Indian economy by the Institute of Asian Peoples the small-scale producers were described as a pre-capitalist economy that has been conserved because of the peculiar conditions obtaining in the colonial and post-colonial situation. This petty factory industry represents the lowest forms of capital, independent of productive capital.[48] In the same volume governmental regulation was described as incapable of controlling these small enterprises.[49]

One Soviet scholar, S.A. Kuzmin, has broken through the ideological indecisiveness of his colleagues by tackling small-scale production as a policy problem. Since 'between one-third and one-half of the industrial output of these (developing) countries is accounted for by small-scale commodity production,' they constitute a policy problem of the greatest magnitude.[50] Kuzmin was interested in small-scale production not just because it was widespread but also because it could be found in different economic modes of production. Village handicrafts, originally the main industrial form of the primitive self-sufficient village economy, had become involved in the process of commodity exchange because commodity-monetary relations had drawn the once remote villages into the capitalist market. The preservation of large rural regions almost untouched by the capitalist market maintained handicrafts as an important form of production. Artisanal production was not confined to the remote village. Small-scale urban production included the following forms: the craftsman who still owned his capital – the implements and means of production – and had at least formal independence; the handicraft worker who has been partially expropriated by merchant-moneylender capital; the producer who has become a hired worker and fills others' orders using others' tools, while still working at home; and the manufactory, with some obsolescent equipment of low productivity using predominantly manual labour. Thus the basic traits of small-scale commodity production are the small number of persons employed, the limited size of fixed capital, the predominance of manual over mechanized labour, and the unpaid labour by the owner and members of his family.

Kuzmin was not interested in traditional handicraft production as a policy problem since the amount of public investment needed for its development depended on such external factors as the ability to create a demand in the foreign market for its handmade luxury products. However, two groups of small-scale industry have real industrial potential as alternatives to capital-intensive factory production. The first is cottage production of consumer goods mainly by manual labour, that is, handicraft production of the same goods produced also by factory industry. As raw materials some use semi-finished goods produced by factories and so become part of the factory production process; others use their own raw material and so compete directly with the factories. The second small-scale group are the more modern enterprises that use some, though not the latest, machinery producing goods that correspond to factory standards but use considerable amounts of manual labour with the obsolescent equipment. Because of the shortage of large-scale capital and the internal market's growing demand for consumer and producer goods that factory industry cannot satisfy, these manufactories use equipment discarded by large-scale industry. The market requires their production to have the same standard and quality as factory-produced products. In some cases a number of manufactories perform separate operations in the total production process.

These millions of small-scale producers are only nominally independent in a personal sense and as a group are linked inextricably with the over-all factory system. They are exploited by the parasitic network of moneylenders and merchant middlemen who supply them credit at exorbitant rates for the purchase of their raw materials and who control the sale of the products. The integration of small-scale production in the economy is expressed by the former buying its raw materials such as yarn from the factories and by the craftsmen taking on specific operations in the factory production processes.

The heart of Kuzmin's analysis was his comparison of small-scale and factory industry using a number of indicators applied from marxist economics.

Fixed capital. Kuzmin measured the gap between the amounts of fixed capital used per worker in factory industry compared with small-scale industry by country and by industry. He found fixed capital to vary in India from 2.2 times greater in factory industry for electoral goods to 8.2 times in pharmaceutical to 14 times in soap-making and 48.6 times in metallurgy.

Working capital. In India the gap in the amounts of working capital per worker in factory and small-scale industry was less than in the case of fixed capital, ranging from 2 to 4 times, the ratio of working capital to fixed capital being higher in small-scale production which, even if it has little machinery and other fixed investment, has relatively large amounts of raw material stocks, finished output in stock, unfinished production, and liquid assets.

Working capital / output. The amount of working capital is no indicator of the effectiveness of an enterprise, but the ratio of working capital to the volume of production does indicate efficiency: the lower the ratio the more advantageous the operation. In all Indian industries but flour milling, small-scale industry had a more favourable working capital/output ratio than factory industry since small enterprises could economize on capital tied up in stocks of raw materials and often produce goods directly for customers' orders. Producing goods from the customer's material allows small-scale industry to economize on working capital and so hold its ground against factory competition.

Labour productivity. Kuzmin compared labour productivity in South Asia and Japan measured by two sets of indices: on one hand the value of processed raw material per worker and gross output per worker and on the other the same indices per unit of wages paid. In India the superiority of factories over small-scale production was largest where small-scale production was most dispersed and factories most modern. For the majority of the industrial branches, however, the gap was much smaller, and a higher labour productivity in small-scale industry was even found when measured per unit of wages paid: in Indian electrical engineering and light machine-building, gross output per unit of wages paid out was smaller in factories than in small-scale industry. In Japan the levelling out of productivity levels was still more pronounced. The levelling of the differences in productivity when combined with other factors like lower capital/output ratios encourages not just the preservation but also the development of small-scale production. The gap in the index of productivity tends to narrow in countries with a vast unemployment problem since the earnings of factory workers rise slightly with the demand for skilled and semi-skilled cadres and the improving organization of the proletariat, while the dispersion and lack of organization of cottage workers keeps their wages at minimal levels. Kuzmin was unwilling to predict whether a growth in the absolute productivity per worker as a result of technical progress in factory industry will offset this advantage. In any case it was clear that until such time as the surplus labour force was absorbed by large-scale industry and conditions of a normally functioning developed economic system applied, there would be a continuing *raison d'être* for small-scale industry by virtue of its productivity per unit of wages.

Gross output / capital ratio. For the weak economies the coefficient of gross output per unit of capital is one of the most important for comparing the effectiveness of small-scale and factory industry since it gives an indicator for the least burdensome capital outlays to achieve the basic physical production targets needed to assure social reproduction – producing enough to meet the basic needs of the economy. In India small-scale production's gross output/capital ratio exceeded large-scale industry's by 2.5 times in soapmaking, 1.7 times in the chemical industry, 2.3 times in electrical commodities, 3.3 times in metallurgy, and 1.8 times in machine-building, although it was inferior in flour milling. Kuzmin pointed out that the output/capital ratio of new factory-scale industries in the developing economies must be expected to suffer during the transitional period when the equipment is being brought into operation and up to full capacity and the capital is being depreciated, whereas investments in small-scale production have a much shorter initial period of inefficiency.

Value added / capital ratio. The value added/capital ratio is a more refined output/capital indicator, the magnitude of the transferred value being eliminated, leaving the actual productivity of the factory. Here too Kuzmin reported that small-scale industry in India had a very considerable advantage in the net output per unit of capital. This was partially because low labour productivity in factory enterprises resulted from the failure of gross output or even net output per worker to grow proportionally with the growth of the factories' technical base. In part the low cost of manpower in small-scale industry made the enterprise's variable capital artificially understated: where a considerable part of the labour force is made up of the entrepreneur and his family 'the share of variable capital in all of the enterprise's capital altogether tends toward zero.' Nevertheless this does mean that in many cases small-scale industry produces higher income per unit of capital invested or more employment for the given level of capital investment.

Surplus value / variable capital. The amount of surplus value created per worker (the 'exploitation norm') was much higher in factory industry in India than in cottage industry.

The surplus value / capital ratio. The amount of surplus value created per unit of capital, the 'profit norm,' tended to be higher in factory industry, although the differences are not very great. In some cases small-scale industry's profit norm was higher again because of the very low wages of workers and owners' families in small-scale industry.

Summarizing his analysis, Kuzmin put the industrial branches into three categories:

1 Branches in which small-scale industry has higher indicators both for gross output and value added and for the profit norm. Cottage industry then has all the advantages and 'every right to priority capital investments' in that branch.

2 Branches where factory industry has higher coefficients for these indicators.

Large-scale industry equally has 'an undivided claim to the entire possible investment sum' for these branches.

3 It is the third category which provides the policy dilemma, those branches where small-scale production has higher indicators of gross output and value added per unit of capital but a lower profit norm. This also is the most common situation in small-scale industry.

Kuzmin went on to argue that the time factor is a critical consideration in making an investment policy decision. Using an example based on coefficients from India's light machine-building industry, he showed that, assuming the entire surplus product is reinvested and assuming no time lag in putting investments into operation, small-scale industry has the initial advantage. After five years factory industry produces more net product, although for gross product small-scale industry is still in the lead. By the fourteenth year factory industry begins to outstrip small-scale operations in gross output as well. Introducing time lags in putting investment into operation considerably changes the picture in favour of small-scale industry.

There are further complicating factors to introduce. The basic coefficients can be seriously affected by technical progress increasing labour productivity and affecting the capital/output ratio per worker. Changes in the market that affect prices will also have an impact on the profitability and the surplus product or accumulation rate which planners will have to consider. Social measures of national importance like nationalization could affect capital values and thus the coefficients of output/capital ratios. Another important question determining the choice between large- and small-scale industrial development is their respective impacts on the balance of payments, for example by increasing the purchase of machines and raw materials abroad or replacing imports. Changes in the size of the export or import surplus or inflationary financing may themselves have a multiplier effect on consumption and further imports. The point that Kuzmin was leading up to was that 'the selection of the criteria for capital investments in various technological modes of production is determined first and foremost by the complex of those economic and, in some cases, social conditions under which the decision must be made.'[51] Kuzmin had no specific formula to answer every hypothetical situation, but was arguing for a careful consideration of all the relevant factors before deciding how to distribute limited capital resources between large- and small-scale technologies. If there were enough capital to achieve the necessary output with modern forms of production, there would obviously be no problem, but, in conditions of capital scarcity a combination of various technological modes can be used to attain any given level of gross production with the greatest possible surplus product. Using labour-intensive modes, however, will permit considerably increased employment and may save imports of capital goods and raw materials.

The surplus product is of interest, too, as a source of capital accumulation for economic growth. 'According to the most modest estimates, India's small-scale industry annually creates a potential accumulation fund in excess of 1 billion rupees.' Small-scale industrial commodity production 'has not as yet lost its significance as a potential source of initial capital accumulation.' How this source is used raises another matter, the problem of merchant-moneylender exploitation.

True, the scattered nature of small-scale production, the lowering of its productive efficiency as a result of poor raw material supply, etc., factory competition, the plunder of capital accumulated in it by numerous middlemen, and other negative factors sharply reduce the value of this source. However, these very same factors also suggest a way for the more effective use of the possibilities hidden in small-scale production: government management of its activities, higher efficiency through more rational organization and the concentration in government hands of that part of the surplus product that at the present time falls into the hands of the middlemen.[52]

Kuzmin's specialist message was far more sophisticated than that of the normal Soviet political economy generalist. The historical tendency may well be for large-scale industry to be more effective, but for the foreseeable future small-scale commodity production is a reality of continuing importance. Small-scale industry may be an analytically distinct mode of production, but this does not prevent Kuzmin from reporting the 'broad opportunities for co-operation between the factory and small-scale and handicraft enterprises, co-operation in which small-scale production will supplement the factory and not compete with it.'[53]

The powerful Indian bourgeoisie was striving to subordinate small-scale production completely, thereby bringing it fully into the sphere of capitalist exploitation. But this generally inevitable process of capitalist development continued to be impeded by such factors as the widespread dispersal of small-scale producers making factory control ineffectual, their dependence on moneylenders' capital which the large entrepreneurs could not control and the craftsmen's own powerful resistance to absorption by factory industry.

At this point Kuzmin came back to the role of the state. A solution to the investment question is only possible with a double approach 'if there exists a planning principle in the economy and government regulation and control over the distribution of the resources.'[54] The planning principle means investment decisions that are made in the over-all interest of the balanced development of the economy. Regulation means greater government activity in small-scale industry by the organization of industrial estates in the government sector where the possibilities of small-scale production can be best realized.

Although Kuzmin did not base his analysis on a state capitalist schema, he arrived at a state capitalist position as soon as he raised the question of the role of private capitalism in the evolution of small-scale industry. He noted that private capital had become aware of the potential of small-scale production and was interested in exploiting government aid for small-scale industry, not just to increase its own sphere of economic activity but to stimulate the development of capitalism and the strengthening of the private sector.

The forces of capitalism see the industrial estates being set up by the government as cradles to promote the growth of capable small entrepreneurs, but they are not interested in the needs of the national economy as a whole. Capitalists are interested in such indicators as the profit norm, want to expand small enterprises that consume manufactured goods, and so are attempting to put lightly mechanized production to their own service. They are not interested in the economic lot of the craftsmen and the artisanal worker whose low wages permit higher exploitation norms.

'Only the government can bring about a radical reorganization of small-scale production and guide its future development, observing the interests of society as a whole as well as of the small commodity producers themselves.' Kuzmin at this point had reached his conclusion. From close economic analysis based on his marxian categories he had passed to policy statements based on political faith. Private capitalism will prolong the agonizingly slow process. State capitalism, on the contrary, can bring to this modernizing, if anachronistic, sector the benefits of guidance and intelligently applied resources. It can liberate the craftsmen from their slavery to the merchants and moneylenders. Through setting up industrial estates where small-scale production can operate on an integrated basis with factory industry, it can decrease production and capital costs while improving the supply of raw materials and ensuring the sale of the products at fair prices beyond the reach of the merchant-usurers. In social terms this means that state capitalism could provide support for the entire urban petty bourgeoisie against large-scale monopoly capital in India. 'The organization of "industrial estates" under government control will expand the sphere of operation of the government sector and, accordingly, its planning base. Moreover, the "industrial estates," if they are organized on a wide enough scale, can become one of the most important tools of the government in planning economic development and in balancing various branches of the national economy.'[55] 'The very logic of development' will educate the small producers to the necessity for co-operation. Co-operation in supply and sales will allow the elimination of usurious indebtedness and the large losses caused by the middlemen's commercial operations. The

argument for state intervention rests on the need to achieve social-political transformations as a precondition for fully benefiting from the economic advantages
of small-scale production in an underemployed, undercapitalized economy. Only
the government can bring about the necessary radical reorganization.

Kuzmin, with his concern for optimizing the factors of production, prescribed state support for small-scale production. L.I. Reisner and G.K. Shirokov
accepted the petty production sector with less enthusiasm. While they drew
some satisfaction from the 'growing over' of cottage industries into small-scale
industry as evidence of capitalist development, they were obviously not delighted
that small-scale unorganized enterprise was growing so quickly, its number of
employed having jumped in five years from 1.7 million (11 per cent of the total
industrial work force) to 4.2 million (20 per cent of the total employed), while
large-scale industry's share of the workforce fell from 19 to 16 per cent from
1955 to 1961. That small-scale unorganized industry (with average incomes of
Rs 1,150) was growing much faster than small-scale organized industry (with Rs
1,900 per worker) indicated the 'uneven nature of development' in India. This
was explained in terms of the regulatory power of the state – or rather the limits
of the state's power to regulate the private sector. Unregulated small-scale industry had grown so surprisingly because cottage industry had not been prevented
from being transformed into the unorganized mechanized sector; in contrast, the
shift to the organized sector encountered burdensome formalities imposed on
each establishment. The small unorganized establishments benefited from a
'peculiar protectionism' resulting from the high taxes on the organized sector,
more rigid application of labour laws, and a longer procedure associated with
licensing and the importation of equipment.[56] This sector grew from two sources.
There was an accelerated transition from manual production to small-scale mechanized production in traditional sectors of industry catering to the consumer
markets. Secondly, industrialization itself stimulated the creation of small enterprises in new sectors like chemicals, metal products, and repairing equipment.
Owing largely to the 'protectionist measures of the government in favour of
home production' the number of small organized enterprises in India increased
by 368 per cent from 1947 to 1962 – much faster than the 61 per cent increase
of large establishments in India during the same period.

The Indian experience was anomalous in terms of the marxian model of capitalist development because the 'direct dislodging of the lower forms of production by the higher does not play a big part here,' thus ensuring 'a relatively pro-
longed coexistence of different types of industry.' What makes the perpetuation
of this parallel development highly probable is government policy: 'At the same
time the state evidently will continue to exercise a stabilizing influence, seeking
to prevent the excessive advance of individual groups of enterprises.'[57]

The more attention they devote to the pre-capitalist economy, the more serious Soviet observers take this problem to be. As Shirokov put it in 1975, there is in India a 'clear preponderance of pre-capitalist and early capitalist forms.' Furthermore, the 'traditional sectoral structure' with its 'extremely low labour productivity' constitutes 'a practically independent reproduction cycle.' Indeed the retention and expansion of small-scale commodity production as an integral part of India's industrialization strategy has resulted in 'the gap between the higher and lower structures [being] widened,' thus increasing the imbalance in the economy's development.[58]

The complexity of pre-capitalist modes of production in Africa offers the Soviet theorists both a challenge and an opportunity. 'The majority of African countries are still characterized by a significant diversity in conditions of socio-economic and political development of the transition period and the coexistence of the following systems: clan-tribal, patriarchal-feudal, petty-commodity-producing, national private entrepreneurial, enterprises associated with foreign capital, and state capitalist.'[59] Because 'capitalism was not a product of the internal development of the productive forces and production relations there,'[60] because the adoption of local large-scale capital 'is in fact a "superstructure" over an underdeveloped economy,'[61] and because of 'the absence of a prevalent mode of production which could subordinate all other modes of production to itself,' the bourgeoisie 'did not completely consolidate itself into a ruling class economically and politically.' This allows a 'state of the revolutionary-democratic dictatorship of the working people,' identified as 'the most progressive representatives of the intermediate and middle sections, mainly the intellectuals, civil servants, and, in some countries, army circles,' to place their country on a non-capitalist path.[62] And it still goes without saying for Soviet ideologues 'that the newly-free countries can make any real economic and social headway only if they adopt the socialist orientation.'[63] Although this rhetorical dogmatism still pervades Soviet writings, their actual treatment of social classes does show a strong empirical thrust.

7

The class struggle and the industrial revolution

Coming to intellectual grips with the dogged persistence of a 'multistructural' economy dominated by various pre-capitalist modes of production has been the prerequisite for adjusting the traditional Soviet class paradigm to the third world's peculiarities. Whereas Moscow's marxist-leninists once declaimed on the surging proletarian forces, they can now accept that 'the African working-class movement is still in its initial phase' since in Tropical Africa for example the number of industrial workers continues to be 'insignificant.'[1] Where the class structure is inadequately developed, Soviet analysis concentrates on the social nature of the groups that took power following decolonization. Since some 65 per cent of the urban population consists of 'the representatives of the interme- diate and middle sections (mainly intellectuals, civil servants, the military and the petty-bourgeoisie)' and since the latter are defined as the 'small traders, handicraftsmen, owners of small enterprises in the service sphere, and so on,' Soviet class analysis is less substantial in African countries than it is in the more capitalistically developed societies of Asia.[2]

STATE CAPITALISM AND THE CLASS STRUGGLE

The she-loves-me-she-loves-me-not duet that runs through the Soviet writings on state capitalism appears again in their analysis of the class struggle in Asia. As in its critique of monopoly capitalism, so in the analysis of the class struggle, Soviet analysts present classes in contradiction that somehow seem able to coexist satis- factorily.

'As is well known India's governmental power is in the hands of the national bourgeoisie whose interests define the character and specific features of Indian state capitalism, its lack of coherence and its contradiction.'[3] To say that, by definition, Indian state capitalism serves the interests of the national bourgeoisie does not prevent the affirmation that it is also in the best interest of the masses: 'To the extent that Indian state capitalism is aimed at liquidating economic backwardness and encourages the country's independent economic and political development, one must recognize that it is a progressive phenomenon which largely answers the interests of the broad popular masses.'[4] Having affirmed in this way that the Indian state can serve the interests of all classes, R.A. Ulyanovsky was quick to insist that this does not mean the class struggle loses its intensity; on the contrary this struggle is gaining in strength, although 'this may often not be noticeable, since state capitalism is not only a new form of bourgeois property but also a new form of class struggle in society.'[5] A. Levkovsky emphasized the acceleration of the process 'of class formation and crystallization, a process typical of capitalist society.'[6] At the same time the social antagonisms inherent in such a society deepen, and the 'front of the class struggle' broadens.

At the top of the social pyramid 'the reactionary features of the Indian bourgeoisie are sharpening,' while at the base the influence of the progressive organizations was growing. Official statistics of the strike movement proved the tense nature of the 'contradiction between labour and capital.' The Soviet proposition that the class struggle is growing constantly was hard to reconcile with the more detailed analysis of the interests of the various social strata in the Indian industrial sector. The bourgeoisie was rather more complex than it might at first appear, while the interests of the proletariat did not seem, on closer inspection, to be as exclusively fixed on social conflict as the impressive figures on man-days lost per annum might indicate.

THE BOURGEOISIE

As distinguished from the majority of the developing countries where there is little more than a 'bureaucratic bourgeoisie,' India's industrial bourgeoisie constituted a sufficiently strong social basis for capitalist development. As G. Mirsky put it, the national bourgeoisie is undeniably capable of 'scoring some success in industrialization and the acceleration of economic growth rates.'[7] This bourgeoisie was no instant elite drawn from the governmental bureaucracy but had roots going back two centuries to the period when India was already on the point of entering a capitalist stage of development.[8] As N.A. Savelev wrote, already in the eighteenth century India had a strong incipient commercial capitalism with active internal and external trade, and the economy showed all the signs of the impending birth of a capitalist mode of production. The imposition of colonialism's yoke slowed and deformed this process, with the upper class entering administration and trade. National capitalism developed irrepressibly, despite British control in the nineteenth century, forcing the emergence of an

Indian bourgeoisie. The Indian national bourgeoisie, at the highest level of gen-eralization in Soviet analysis, was in power, using state capitalism to further its own interests in developing an independent national economy – and by implica-tion was opposed both to the socializing pressure coming from the proletariat and to the colonizing tendencies of the big bourgeoisie who wanted to make deals with foreign capital and tie India politically as well as economically to the world capitalist market. It was this national bourgeoisie, developing its own capi-talist enterprise despite the restrictions imposed by the British imperialists, that had led the national liberation struggle under the leadership of Gandhi whose political instrument was the Indian National Congress. As in many other coun-tries, such as Burma, Indonesia, or the Philippines, the establishment of bour-geois power 'was the logical completion of a definite stage of the national-libera-tion fight.'[9]

This has been a fact of sustained progressive significance. As recently as 1976 Academician Rostislav Ulyanovsky could write that 'the anti-imperialist potential of the national bourgeoisie can hardly be said to have expended itself,' for 'it cannot be denied that many elements of this bourgeoisie are capable of fighting colonialism, racism, foreign aggression and feudal reaction, of accelerating the breakdown of patriarchal social structures that have outlived their time, of stimulating the development of national economies, working for national, state control over natural resources, restricting the field for the comprador bourgeoi-sie and foreign monopolies. Many of them are waging an active struggle for peace and international security.'[10] Along with the ruling groups in countries like Bra-zil and Mexico, the Indian bourgeoisie had enriched itself rapidly in the second world war, so that, once in power, it had a significant base which it was able to expand using state capitalism to reduce the extent of imperialist exploitation and government measures to protect and develop national industry. As a result the years since independence have seen a great expansion of bourgeois power as national capital grew first in areas not competitive with foreign monopolies and then in such citadels of foreign capital as the cotton, sugar, and coal industries.[11] With the development of economic activity from the most advanced steel mill to the most primitive handicraft production and with the adaptation to the mixed economy of 'historical vestiges' such as caste and pre-capitalist sharecropping, it is small wonder that the Indian national bourgeoisie is seen 'to be a complicated social complex, containing strata at different levels of socioeconomic evolu-tion.'[12] These strata and the boundary lines between them are the object of con-siderable scholarly debate among Soviet orientalists, for, while 'national bour-geoisie' is used loosely for the 'ruling circles' who control the workings of state capitalism, it is crucial for the marxist-leninist interested in the future shape of the class struggle to have an accurate appraisal of the economic interests of these social strata and the political alliances they are likely to form. Even though a class may have an objective homogeneity because of its relationship to the productive process, within it there may be strata in conflict with each other and allying with other classes to achieve their aims. The two basic criteria used by Savelev to define boundaries within the bourgeoisie were size of income and the number of hired workers employed. Drawing two lines at Rs 2.5 million and Rs 0.5 million he puts the owners of big capitalist concerns earning above the upper line in the big bourgeoisie, those with small enterprises earning under the lower line in small entrepreneur class, while those left in between were the middle bourgeoisie.[13]

THE BIG BOURGEOISIE

More important than a simple financial measuring rod is the social, economic, and political description of the big bourgeois. They were the most reactionary part of Indian society, the big industrialists linked financially to foreign monopolies and socially to the large landowners, trying simultaneously to limit the growth of the public sector and to increase their influence within the governmental machinery. The national monopolies, the economic instruments of this class, tried to 'strengthen their influence over the state and the public sector in order to subjugate them entirely.'[14] Supported by their international allies, the foreign monopolies, these national giants aimed to transform the state sector into a rampart of their own interests and asked for participation in the management of public corporations in order to transform them into a means for exploiting the people and to withdraw them from the control of the 'democratic bourgeoisie.' In the initial phase of this struggle, they did not press directly for the sale of the state firms but insisted that 'businessmen' be placed in their management and granted a share of their stock to create mixed public-private corporations. But the big bourgeoisie continues to demand more and more control until the state sector in industry becomes fully 'privatized.' However uniform their interests may appear, all the big bourgeois groups do not follow the same policies towards state capitalism. While the big bourgeoisie has a well-established tendency to take reactionary positions, as could be seen by the big Indian monopolists' setting up the Swatantra party to oppose the national bourgeoisie's Indian National Congress, there are differences among the monopolists. The Birla family, for instance, furiously resisted any development of the state sector, whereas other groups such as the Tata family supported the state capitalist policy of the government, trying to use it in their own interests.[15]

Savelev observed a 'new' monopoly bourgeoisie emerging in the more capitalist developing countries such as Mexico and the Philippines. In India this young industrial bourgeoisie did not have the same close links with large landowners and with the system of feudal merchant-usury exploitation in agriculture. Although it shared the class interests of big capital and had the same desire to strengthen exploitation, its views on economic policy were different. Oriented to production for the internal market, it supported forced industrialization. While willing to form joint companies with foreign capital, the new monopoly bourgeoisie insisted on keeping the controlling voice. With radical views approaching those of the national entrepreneurs, the new monopolists had not yet lost their revolutionary and anti-imperialist potential.[16]

THE NATIONAL BOURGEOISIE

The national bourgeoisie in India was even less homogeneous than the big bourgeois stratum. Soviet scholars speak of the 'national bourgeoisie' in general through such concepts as the 'ruling circles' (excluding the monopolistic corporations of the big bourgeoisie) or the 'governing classes' who direct state capitalism in the interests of national capital.[17] 'The ruling circles of India are rightly convinced ... that the strengthening of the country's political independence is directly related to industrial development, above all in heavy industry, and that the state must direct and force this development.'[18] 'The national bourgeoisie in general understands as a class that unprecedented opportunities for accumulation are opening up before it.'[19] Although by number this middle bourgeoisie was the most numerous stratum of its class, firms with a production of from Rs 0.5 million to Rs 2.5 million only account for 7 per cent of national production. These middle bourgeois, the owners of small trading firms and transportation and communal services, were in constant economic difficulties, chronically indebted to the big banks.[20] Medium-sized entrepreneurs approved of the public sector development in heavy industry because it answered their needs without threatening their interests. This 'industrial middle bourgeoisie,' the core of the national bourgeois class, continually felt the competitive threat of foreign and national monopolies. Not having the financial strength to raise itself to the economic level of the big capital which threatened it, it supported state capitalism, which at least was not a competitor. Although unhappy with strict governmental control and state interference in the private sector (afraid of losing its own independence), the middle bourgeoisie favoured giving priority to state enterprises over private or foreign monopolies.[21]

Anti-imperialist and anti-feudal, the middle bourgeois had not lost their progressive significance, supporting the democratization of the state and society. Although their economic and social base was contracting both relatively and absolutely, they were inconstant allies, tacking between one opponent and another, taking an inconsistent approach to foreign capital, and making insufficient use of nationalization. The proletariat was thus advised to aim at isolating the middle bourgeoisie from contact with imperialism and the forces of internal reaction.[22]

THE SMALL BOURGEOISIE

The small bourgeoisie, Savelev warned, was not to be confused with the artisans and small traders constituting the petty bourgeoisie. Actually Savelev considered that the lowest stratum of the local capitalist class should not be distinguished from the middle bourgeoisie. Only those producing Rs 50,000 annually were really receiving capitalist income, and only those commanding over twenty workers could really be said to be personally dissociated from the productive process.[23] Since they experience the same economic difficulties as the middle bourgeois, they often demonstrate a unity of views on economic, social, and foreign policy questions, making a united front against the domination of the monopolies, the big landlords, and big capital.

Though the differences in operation and interest between the big bourgeoisie on one hand and the middle and small bourgeoisie on the other led Savelev to imply that a serious conflict was imminent within the Indian bourgeoisie, two other scholars expressed a different view of the prospect of internal class conflict. In their large study of the modern Indian bourgeoisie L.I. Reisner and G.K. Shirokov identified two trends in the bourgeoisie's evolution. At the class summit the concentration of monopoly capital was proceeding, while at the bottom small-scale manufacturing was expanding enormously under the encouragement of the government's state capitalist policies. Although they noted disagreements and tensions between the bourgeoisie's summit and base, this potential for conflict had been reduced through some absorption of medium and small business by big business. A further factor reducing the danger of a middle bourgeois fight against the monopolistic bourgeoisie was Nehru's political tradition of keeping a balance between class strength by state regulation of big business expansion.[24]

THE PETTY BOURGEOISIE

The petty bourgeoisie has generally been looked upon by marxists as a vacillating social stratum. Artisans and small traders were a kind of sociohistorical reject, not obeying the capitalist development law calling for their polarization into one of the two leading classes of the capitalist stage of development, the bourgeoisie or the proletariat. Soviet analysts of the third world, however, have been paying increasing attention to what they grudgingly came to admit can often be the

the most decisive class, whether in economic terms or political, especially when the national bourgeoisie is not fully formed.

For one thing, the petty bourgeoisie is numerous. In India thirteen million (twenty to twenty-five million if families were included) were producing in the non-registered small-commodity sector of the economy. Nine-tenths of them were artisans. They produced 30 to 35 per cent of the nation's income and one-third of its industrial production. Yet this group was one of the most insecure in the population. Its income was very low: in Brazil $40 to $50 per annum, in India $45 to $50. Artisans experience all types of oppression from foreign and local exploiters. Traders and shopkeepers fall deeply into dependence on the usurious moneylenders. Although an artisan may possess his own means of production and may even employ hired labour in his small operation, he is not, in Savelev's view, engaged in real capitalist business. He works directly in the production process side by side with the hired worker. Furthermore, his revenue is too low to be considered capitalist. The artisan is in fact in direct competition with large- and medium-scale enterprise and is threatened to his very economic core by the developing capitalism that tries to take over and absorb cottage industry.

If the petty bourgeois is different socially and economically from the bourgeois, he is also different politically. Where antagonistic contradictions ripen within the capitalist class, the petty bourgeoisie has shown unexploited revolutionary potential. This tendency could be seen in India by the petty bourgeois support in Kerala for a coalition led by the Communist Party. Savelev concluded that if the urban petty bourgeoisie could be torn from the bourgeois influence of private property yearnings and armed with a progressive ideology, it would join the fight for democracy.[25]

To S.A. Kuzmin, the situation was not so simple and the conclusion not so optimistic. As Marx himself had observed, while the small-scale craftsman may be semi-proletarian in one dimension, he is a budding capitalist in another. 'In the capacity of owner of the means of production he is a capitalist. In the capacity of a worker he is his own hired worker. Thus as a capitalist, he pays himself wages and extracts profit from his capital, i.e. he exploits himself as a hired worker and, in the form of surplus value, pays himself that tribute that labour must pay to the capitalist.'[26]

The urban petty bourgeois are certainly hostile to the increasing production of consumer goods by big private capital which continues to threaten their ruin. In addition, they need state aid in the form of credits for the development of small-scale enterprise. Their preference for state capitalism is also due to the amount the state purchases from them and to the increased employment created by the construction of state sector projects.[27]

But the analytical problem goes well beyond the petty bourgeoisie's desire for support from government regulation and finance. The decisive question concerns the effect of state capitalist aid on this huge class. Will the industrial estates being set up to encourage small-scale production on as modern and efficient basis as possible turn out to be a 'cradle for fostering capitalists,' developing entrepreneurial talent for the continued expansion of the bourgeoisie? Or will they be a means to spread the message of co-operation and socialism? Kuzmin did not give an answer, but it was clear from his analysis that even if the small-scale producers were strong enough to resist absorption by big industry and even if their interests were sufficiently opposed to big capital for class tension to continue, it is doubtful whether petty bourgeois radicalism would go much beyond support for a progressive programme regulating the monopolies and providing long-term development for small-scale industry.

INTELLIGENTSIA

While the thrust of the marxist-leninist class analysis is directed at those classes involved in the capitalist production process, there is a growing awareness that the intermediate social groups cannot be ignored. Their numbers are huge – normally far greater than the proletariat – and growing. Furthermore, they often provide the bulk of the leadership and cadres of the revolutionary movement, especially where the industrial classes are too weak to dominate the political process.

In recognizing the importance of the intelligentsia G.I. Mirsky and T.S. Pokataeva adopted many positions generally accepted by non-marxist scholars, and have even acknowledged that class analysis may be of only limited use in explaining political behaviour. Analysing the third world intelligentsia by its social extraction, for instance, 'by itself cannot lead to any conclusions concerning its political orientation.'[28] Those from the same social milieu have become both marxist leaders and reactionary activists. Youth receiving modern education, torn from their traditional background, do not necessarily express the interests of their own class. Sons of rich bourgeois and landlords have often become revolutionary militants, especially when they compared their backward homeland with the ideals or realities of the metropolitan countries. The intelligentsia has a long history as the hearth of political movements and, with the broadening of the education system, have taken on a new political importance, being instantly mobilizable since politics gives them a 'way of life' allowing them to feel effective and expend their energy. The overproduction of students in the humanities, compared with the insufficient preparation of technicians, engineers, and economists, leads to discontent with the existing socioeconomic system and often attracts them into the fight for radical transformations. Despite the great importance of their precious support for progressive political forces, they are unstable. Although their general values are anti-business, bourgeois nationalism was the natural ideology for people seeing no prospect before them except in a modern industrialized society blocked by colonialism from independent economic development.

The civil service is similarly of increasing interest to Soviet theorists as a considerable economic and political force. Through the growth of the state sector, particularly by nationalizations, civil servants had come to form 20 per cent of Latin America's hired labour force. In India they numbered eight million. Although their social origins were not homogeneous, some coming from the upper bourgeoisie, the civil service in the Soviet view formed a petty bourgeois, semi-proletarian stratum that, in its material position, was coming close to that of the proletariat since civil servants do not own any means of production but sell their labour. Suffering from low salaries, they are increasingly active in politics and provide the active core of many parties. Such a many-sided stratum has difficulty in achieving full unity of political views. Like the students, the great mass are progressive, interested in the full eradication of colonial survivals and socio-economic progress. Like the intelligentsia, in whose ranks it is sometimes included, the civil service is ideologically unstable and liable to bourgeois nationalist influences.

Mirsky and Pokataeva define the intelligentsia much more broadly than 'intellectuals.' Besides 'mental workers' they include the representatives of the free professions, artists, those with higher education, including civil servants, and even students. However, once having shown in their description that class-economic explanation is not helpful in analysing the intellectual's behaviour, Soviet writers revert to the stock class formulas in their predictions: even though the intelligentsia is growing numerically, its leading role is limited and temporary. In India, for instance, the intelligentsia was not as important a class as in less developed countries. Its relative importance was declining as the proletariat's role grew.[29]

THE PROLETARIAT

Reading Soviet references to the proletariat requires considerable subtlety. From the number of claims that the proletariat is leading the fight against the monopolies and the struggle for the non-capitalist path, marxist-leninist analysis conjures up an initial impression of a powerful sociopolitical force on the point of becoming the dominant factor on the national scene. This may be misleading if the Soviet author has changed – particularly in his conclusion – from a statement of fact about the working class to a statement of faith in the ultimate victory of the proletariat. The problem is increased by the synonymous use of 'proletariat' and 'Communist Party.' 'The proletariat is struggling for the nationalization of foreign monopoly capital' may more likely mean that nationalization of foreign companies is on the programme of the Communist Party. Confusion is further generated by the Soviet tendency to make prescriptive statements in descriptive form. Soviet authors may write, for example, that the proletariat is supporting state capitalism when they mean that the Communist Party *ought* to support the government's whole range of economic policies.

As one reads more carefully, their confidence in the proletariat seems less than it first sounds. First of all the proletariat is numerically small and organizationally weak in most developing countries. In Africa, it is 'insignificant' in its share of the population.[30] Definite parts of what does exist are under the influence of bourgeois ideology and middle-class parties. In short, the working class in Asia and Africa is extremely heterogeneous, consisting 'in the main, of diverse non-proletarian elements, such as farmhands and day-labourers employed by landlords, the village rich and partly by other peasants, as well as wage workers in handicrafts and manufacture, where capitalist exploitation is combined with patriarchal-feudal methods of oppression and with the economic dependence of the producers on landowners, merchants, usurers and numerous intermediaries.'[31] Where it exists in recognizable form, most of the proletariat is in light industry – primarily food in countries where industry is only starting, though in more developed countries like India and Egypt textiles have employed most workers. The most significant change in the structure of the proletariat is its growth in heavy industry especially in the most advanced developing countries.[32] The heavy industry workers have won concessions from the bourgeoisie and so have improved their material position, which is better than workers outside heavy industry. The most literate and conscious workers, they play a vanguard role in the working class, as the growing strike statistics demonstrate. The transformation of the economy onto a modern technological base changes the composition of the proletariat by creating skilled, literate, and trained workers. The growth of the working class in the state sector is considerable, because of the creation of a state capitalist industry. For this reason the proletariat as a class also favours state capitalist development, which insures the public sector's industrialization, thanks to the co-operation of the Soviet Union.[33] The proletariat appears to have a long-range view of its best interests through the development of capitalism. 'The overthrow of imperialist domination and the arrival in power of the national bourgeoisie created the conditions for an accelerated development of capitalism and, as a result, for a rapid development of the gravedigger of the bourgeoisie, the working class.'[34]

But India's unique political situation placed the proletariat in a contradictory position, as L.A. Gordon explained. On the one hand the 'liquidation of the colonial dictatorship' should have facilitated the organization and struggle of the working class. Economic success should have established the material conditions for progress towards a state of national democracy and then socialism. On the other hand the peculiar economic role of the bourgeois state at the current stage of development made the 'propagation of the ideas of scientific socialism in the working-class movement' more difficult: the direct intervention by the state in economic life, often in ways that controlled and limited the capitalist activities of the bourgeoisie, 'obscures to some extent the opposition between the interests of labour and capital.' It is difficult to organize the proletariat to fight the bourgeois state if it is the government itself which is protecting the wage-earners in their struggles against their employers.

There were in the Indian working class situation as many positive as negative factors. On the favourable side, Gordon noted, it had grown significantly: from 4 to 5 million in 1939 to 7 to 8 million by 1950. It was also growing faster in heavy industry than in large industry. And there has been an 'extraordinary concentration' of the proletariat, 50 per cent of the working class being employed in factories with over one thousand workers, thus facilitating class organization.

On the negative side there had been a decline in the relative strength of hereditary proletarians in the working class because of the increasing mobility between village and city and a weakening of the proletariat's organization, thus facilitating the penetration of bourgeois influence in the workers' milieu. This bourgeois danger was itself a consequence of India's relatively successful independent capitalist development, progress which had acted 'favourably' on the material situation of the industrial proletariat.

The democratization of society, its cultural improvement, social legislation reforms (limitation of the working day, minimum wage law, paid holidays, social security), had raised the feeling of human dignity and of legal rights among the workers. But these improvements in the workers' condition also allowed the 'propagation of reformist illusions in the ranks of the working class.'[35]

Since these reforms had been accomplished by a bourgeois government and since the bourgeoisie influenced the workers' movement directly through its own trade unions, these improvements favoured 'bourgeois manœuvres.' Thus one analyst concluded that, to the extent that the proletariat is interested in achieving the nation's goals, and to the degree that the bourgeois state can resolve these problems, the working class struggle should not be 'limited' to 'traditional forms' such as strikes but should be extended to support certain acts of the bourgeois state. From a prediction of growing class struggle the analysis ends up as a tactical recommendation for proletarian support of capitalist development.

In this context the Communist Party of India was quoted as indicating its support for state capitalist development: 'The Communist Party of India, as the leading party of the working class, appreciates the country's undoubted progress and supports the society's democratic elements which aim at a more thorough development and strengthening of the state's economy. It points out that state capitalist property, the supreme form of bourgeois property, has shown itself capable of sufficient resistance against foreign capital and, in addition, prepares the material elements of socialism.[36]

The proletariat's fight in the developing countries is primarily a struggle to limit the activity of capitalist laws strengthening exploitation, in other words a fight for an improved standard of living. What is good for the proletariat is good for the nation: an improvement in the material position of the workers is the most important factor in broadening the internal market, a necessary condition for the growth of industry.[37]

The attentive reader is still left uncertain about how the marxist-leninists envisage the future evolution of the class struggle in India under state capitalism. According to Shirokov and Reisner the big monopoly bourgeoisie was not monolithic and had not succeeded in dominating the lower groups of the bourgeoisie, particularly because of Nehru's policy of maintaining a balance among the classes.[38] M.A. Aleksandrov and S.M. Melman assert on the contrary that the big bourgeoisie dominated the petty bourgeoisie just as much through its economic power as by its political organization.[39] They also noted that the middle bourgeoisie still played an important role despite the small expansion of its membership. Debate continued on the political significance of these class relationships. Savelev thought it better to consider the small and middle capitalists together since they faced the same economic difficulties. Agreeing in practice on the main political and social questions, these two strata could lead a common front against the domination of big capital.[40] But Shirokov and Reisner believed the significance of these differences inside the bourgeoisie should not be exaggerated; such conflicts could not transcend the main social contradiction, namely, the antagonism dividing the workers on one hand from all the groups of the exploiting class on the other.[41]

In this tolerant atmosphere, the Soviet bark on the class struggle sounds clearly worse than its bite. The marxist-leninist methodology leads logically to the identification of serious 'contradictions' between the classes of any society. In the case of their analysis of Indian state capitalism, the reader's problem is to determine exactly what is the significance of these contradictions. One can read that the proportion of strikes has risen, that the social classes have become consolidated, but still not be able to deduce how serious is the crisis depicted. The initial impression from the class analysis of India was that the social situation was ripe for a revolutionary explosion. But any difference of interests between social groups was labelled a 'contradiction,' and in the Soviet writings on India contradictions appeared between the different elements of the imperialist bourgeoisies, between the big bourgeoisie and the state sector, between the national bourgeoisie and the petty bourgeoisie, and so on. Either these contradictions were serious, and therefore signified that Indian society was on the point of major conflict, or they were simply diverging interests between the nation's different social groups. The key to unlock this problem lies in the unusual theoretical confession that a bourgeois state can achieve the major aims of the 'broad popular masses.' If this is so, then class contradictions are non-antagonistic in the same way that contradictions between social strata can exist in socialist societies without leading to revolutionary confrontation.[42]

WHICH REVOLUTION?

If there are divergences in the Soviet views on as basic a question as the industrial proletariat's role in the Indian economy, this is largely because two quite different positions concerning capitalism coexist in the Soviet writings.

Capitalism must be buried
Most prominent is the familiar line which presents every third world country as experiencing a struggle between capitalism and socialism. In this perspective it is clear that capitalism is a bad force, although it is now conventional for the Soviet analyst, with his perspective of three decades of Indian independent development experience, to concede that significant achievements have been made under the aegis of capitalism: 'Considerable headway has been made in overcoming economic backwardness, in industrialization, in uprooting the most odious forms of feudal and semi-feudal exploitation of the peasantry and in strengthening economic independence. Much too has been done to improve the health services and to deal with illiteracy. And on the international arena India has come to play an important role.'[43]

The marxist-leninist does not read defeat in signs of progress under capitalism; on the contrary he sees the prelude to its final decay. Quoting Lenin's statement that it would be a mistake to believe that this tendency to decay precludes the rapid growth of capitalism, the established Soviet authority on imperialism, V. Rymalov, insists that 'Marxist-leninist political economy maintains that it is the development of the productive forces of capitalism that undermines the foundations on which bourgeois society rests.'[44] Capitalism loses coming and going. Denounced for its failure to solve the basic problems of the developing countries, its successes nevertheless comprise its death warrant. 'In India, the tragic contradictions of the capitalist model of development for the emergent states have been more manifest than in any other country. We could cite impressive figures testifying to her economic achievements. But the contrast between wealth and poverty is no less striking; it is not only a legacy of colonialism but the result of capitalist relations in Indian society. As for the economic successes, India has scored them in spite of capitalism rather than thanks to it.'[45] Again, the successes of capitalism are overtaken by its failures.

The Soviet discussion of the policy questions raised by the fundamental problem of capital accumulation best illustrates the reasoning of the negative line on capitalism. Accumulation is a constant preoccupation of marxist-leninists concerned about growth, for it is only if sufficient savings are invested that the economy's capital can be increased and the process of expanded reproduction generated. It is an aspect of all the economic processes; it cannot be solved by itself in isolation from more concrete problems of agrarian reforms, the development of the state sector, planning, and the struggle against foreign capital. 'Accumulation as the broadening of social production is the synthesis of the solution to these more concrete problems.' Conversely the methods of solving the accumulation problem affect all prospects for development and industrialization as it is one of the most important aspects of accelerating the economy. For the generally low rates of accumulation which are far less than in the developed countries are not enough to liquidate backwardness or even double per capita income in 25 to 50 years.[46] In Y.V. Potemkin and V.A. Sandakov's analysis, to identify the factors limiting accumulation is to discover the general direction of the solution, the radical socioeconomic transformations that will break through capitalism's bottlenecks.

The impact of cyclical fluctuations in the world capitalist economy, in particular the declining prices for developing countries' raw material exports, and the exploitation of the third world by imperialist companies require a determined fight against foreign capital's positions in the economy. Internally, the existing system of production relations does not maintain the initial growth rates achieved with the initial intensification of capitalist development. Confronted with the vestiges of feudalism, capitalism is exhausting its own possibilities. But the insufficiency of financial resources reflects the undeveloped social and economic structure. The accumulation problem in Africa will only be solved, in the Soviet view, by solving the whole catalogue of that continent's development needs. 'Therefore at the present level of the national revolution, these countries may secure additional financial means by carrying out socioeconomic changes including radical agrarian reforms, by developing the cooperative and state sectors of the economy, by launching industrialization, by the gradual settlement of questions of national cadres, by firm measures to liquidate abuses and non-payment of taxes through restricting the positions of foreign monopolies and preventing leakage of capital from the country, through limiting consumption by parasitic classes with a view to their liquidation, and so forth.'[47] In other words the way to resolve the accumulation problem with a pre-capitalist economy is the programme for agricultural economic development in the country. While more thorough capitalism may be a remedy for backwardness in pre-capitalist agriculture, the route to faster accumulation in the industrial section of the economy is to shift to non-capitalist methods and away from capitalist accumulation whose burdens of increased indirect taxes and inflationary fiscal policies fall on the workers' shoulders. Potemkin and Sandakov took the Communist Party of India's economic programme as their accumulation remedy: high taxes on high incomes, state sector appropriation of profitable light industries, ending inflationary financial policy, control on transfer of foreign and national capital abroad, state monopoly or control of export-import trade, state control on internal wholesale and retail trade in major commodities, the nationalization of the credit and financial institutions. These measures, changing the main sources of accumulation from the coffers of the foreign and the rich to accumulation by the state, were a direct threat to the capitalist way. They too could not be implemented in isolation but must be part of a broad and radical programme of general democratic transformations.[48]

The industrial revolution is still to be made
Beneath the surface a diametrically opposite line can be read just as loud and just as clear. While Potemkin and Sandakov were urging radical socioeconomic transformations for India, Shirokov and Reisner were demonstrating that it is not the socialist but the industrial revolution that must be encouraged. Because of the 'extremely slow rate and different sequence of phases' of industrial development in India compared to the developed countries, because of the 'extreme weakness of the core of industrial production,' because there has been 'so far no direct ousting of the small-scale by large-scale production,' because 'large-scale industry has not yet taken a decisive place in the industrial structure,' yet because also 'capitalist forms of industry already prevail in the country,' and 'most of the output of industry (in value) is produced at mechanised enterprise,' this meant 'that the industrial revolution in India has entered the final stage.' The industrial revolution may be entering its final stage, but Shirokov and Reisner made it clear that it was doing this very gradually and without revolutionary upheavals. In fact their reading of the balancing role of the Indian state led them to predict that, despite a probable acceleration in the capitalist progress of the backward industrial structure 'the evolutionary nature of the changes is likely to be preserved.'[49] Shirokov restated this economist's view some years later: 'Though

industrialisation is conducive to the capitalist transformation and integration of [the] economy, it is not tantamount to an industrial revolution in the entire economy.'[50]

Intellectual support for this moderate view of capitalism's prospects came from Kuzmin, whose analysis demonstrated that modes of production corresponding to different stages of historical development can coexist in the same economy. Applying Marx's historical-analytical framework, Kuzmin showed why small-scale production, a transient mode of production in the classical model of European capitalist development, was not destroyed in the third world by the development of capitalism. Because of the exhaustion of the third world economies by imperialist exploitation, capital accumulation did not take place at the rate achieved in the industrialized west. Since the third world's capitalist structures were weaker, they were not able to bring small-scale modes of production under their control but have had to share the internal market with the small producers. The mass of 'surplus' population was a second important factor. The resulting low cost of manpower and the low effectiveness of using machines and modern technology deprive the capitalist sector in third world countries of one of its most powerful stimuli to expansion and reinforces the vitality of the small-scale commodity structure. Furthermore the unintegrated nature of these economies, which have some highly developed branches oriented towards the world market while others are completely missing, makes it easier for lower economic forms, which would be crushed by competition under other conditions, to coexist with the capitalist sector.[51]

Obvious political support came for this moderate line on capitalism from the Soviet publication *International Affairs*, which noted darkly that 'reactionary forces are exaggerating [India's] difficulties and deliberately ignoring the country's achievements.'[52] On balance it would seem that the second, moderate line has both the heaviest scholarly and the strongest political backing in the Soviet school.

The acknowledgement of an organic interconnection between the regulatory state, private enterprise, and even the pre-capitalist sector testifies to the increasing acceptance by Soviet political economy of the mixed economy in the third world. But by reintegrating the private sector into state capitalism and by approving state encouragement of private investment and small-scale production as a means of shortening the primitive capitalist accumulation stage, the Soviets do not resolve an important ambiguity in their analysis. If state capitalism, private capitalist enterprise, and pre-capitalism can work hand in glove, what is to prevent this relationship from continuing? By developing public sector activity, we were told in the 1950s, state capitalism was leading the Indian economy towards the 'non-capitalist path of development.' Now that this hope seems illusory (barring a radical shift in the Indian power structure) are there not grounds in Soviet testimony itself for positing a continued development of a mixed economy with active state and private sectors linked by deliberate co-ordinating measures?

Nevertheless, while the Soviet comprehension of the government's indirect controls of the economy may be increasing, this does not reflect an altered view of state capitalism as much as a feeling in the 1970s that the Indian system was regressing in its degree of state control. State capitalism was adapting to the mixed economy, not vice versa.[53] The dminished effectiveness of state control allowed a greater degree of freedom for the forces of the capitalist market. When the state intervened it was more to regulate a given activity of the private sector than to absorb that activity into the state sector at the expense of old-style capitalism.

'Capitalist relations are developing apace in India.'[54] In India 'capitalism has won out.'[55] 'This task is being solved along the capitalist path of development although the Indian National Congress calls for "socialist-type society."'[56] From being the model for the new transitional stage of state capitalist development, India had become the model of simple capitalist underdevelopment. This meant that the state was no longer seen as the increasingly dominant direct agent in the economy's industrialization, but rather as an important factor alongside the vigorous private economy. Did this mean that the Soviet attitude to the Indian system had changed dramatically? In balance it would seem not. Despite the obvious Soviet concern for the strength of the monopolies and the right-wing political pressures they generated, despite their unhappiness about the failure to solve basic economic and social problems, despite the shift of vocabulary from state capitalism to capitalism, the change was more of tone than of substance. Gone was the almost exuberant optimism that characterized their first reappraisal of Nehru's democratic socialism. In its place was the less expectant, more accepting attitude shared as much by *Time* magazine as the *New Times*.

What was common to the Soviet analysis of the third world in the mid-1970s and that in the mid-1950s was the centrality of India. That country remained pivotal to the Soviet analysis as a model for a particular type of development. It remained the country most often cited in discussions of state capitalism planning, accelerated industrialization, or class struggle. It also remained central in another sense – neither left nor right. Though not socialist or non-capitalist as were other countries that received their independence and Soviet attention more recently, neither was it monopoly-capitalist or feudal. The Soviet analysis remained as middle-of-the-road as India's position; India's praises were not sung inordinately, nor was it denounced with the venom reserved for the reactionary.

The Soviet analysis had matured. This did not mean it had become more homogeneous. On the contrary, it seemed to embrace a greater variety of apparently contradictory currents. Some scholars remained deeply sceptical: state capitalism has been unable to achieve its two basic aims of mobilizing inactive productive forces and increasing the rate of accumulation.[57] Others were uncritically enthusiastic: the achievements of the previous two decades testified to the correctness of the path India was taking in building an independent national economy through industrialization and expansion of the state sector.[58] It is left to the reader to choose which is the more appropriate of these differing positions. Whereas the integrated quality of Soviet political economy is one of its most striking characteristics, the extensive Soviet writings on state capitalism leave the outside reader with some sense of fragmentation. If it is up to the reader to choose which of the opposing lines to accept, then the analysis has ended up more contradictory than coherent.

PART THREE

FOREIGN AID AND TRADE

8

Independence and foreign investment

INDEPENDENCE, THE STARTING POINT

The best conceptual bridge for an outsider wanting to enter the Soviet view of the developing countries' position in the world – historically, politically, and economically – is their understanding of national independence. For marxist-leninist researchers the notion of independence links their analysis of a country's internal social and economic problems with their appraisal of its relationship to the outside world. The story of a nation's independence is the struggle to extricate itself from capitalism internally and imperialism externally: 'The achievement of independence requires pushing the anti-imperialist, anti-feudal revolution to its conclusion.'[1] The anti-feudal revolution is the complex of radical agrarian, economic, and social transformations necessary for building the industrialized basis without which the essential issue, dependence on imperialism, cannot be resolved. Internally, 'the struggle for strengthening national independence is indistinguishable from the struggle for social progress.'[2] Externally, the fight for economic independence is 'the main aim of the anti-imperialist struggle.'[3] The anti-imperialist revolution is the process of breaking the political, commercial, capitalist, technological, and ideological chains that have kept the colonies and ex-colonies in a position of political servitude and economic stagnation.

The discussion of independence does not only involve a merging of internal and external factors; it also requires in the Soviet analysis a meshing of political with economic considerations: independence, or rather dependence, is still the clue for breaking the riddle of underdevelopment. For the third world's economic backwardness is, in the Soviet view, a direct consequence of its original rape by western adventurers, its subsequent more systematic despoliation by the colonial system, and now by its continuing exploitation by dominating imperialism. While Soviet political economists refuse to dissociate the political from the economic aspects of the dependence complex, they do distinguish two consecutive but separate stages in the liberation process: the initial winning of political freedom and the subsequent struggle for economic autonomy.

POLITICAL INDEPENDENCE

The Soviet assessment of the formal independence acquired by the new states at the moment of decolonization shifted considerably after the Stalinist denunciation of political sovereignty as a mere façade for continued colonial status. The termination of colonial status by the national liberation movements became recognized as a major event, heralding the 'breakaway of more and more countries from capitalism' and the 'collapse of the colonial system of imperialism,' thereby precipitating the third stage of world capitalism's general crisis.[4] 'Under the present conditions of global struggle between two systems, the political independence won by the nations of Asia and Africa appears more and more prominently as a great revolutionary factor, as the decisive prerequisite for the further intensification of anti-imperialist revolutions.'[5]

Political independence does nothing to abolish the third world's painful economic heritage from colonialism, its technological backwardness, its low level of production, its archaic socioeconomic relations, or its widespread poverty. But it does put an end to 'non-economic compulsion,' the various types of controls exerted over the colony. The sovereign state now becomes free to decide how it will relate to the outside world, on what terms it will trade and on what conditions it will receive foreign capital in the future.[6] Not all third world countries have even attained political independence. Their formal sovereignty notwithstanding, the countries of Latin America are still dependent on imperialism. These semi-colonies' 'long-standing dependence on the imperialist power was concealed by an even more ancient form of sovereignty.'[7] But as every Soviet schoolboy knows, even political independence is but the first step on the long road towards the goal of true economic independence. Having achieved political independence, the national liberation movement in each new state must move into its second stage, the struggle for economic independence. For without this true independence there can be no real economic development.

ECONOMIC INDEPENDENCE

Political independence is the alpha but not the omega in the alphabet of the national liberation movement; it is the necessary but not sufficient condition for pursuing economic independence. The dialectical relationship between political and economic liberation is simple: political independence opens the way for a real development of the national economy; of itself, it is simply an empty form. Without transferring the fight for state sovereignty into a struggle for economic development, political independence will remain but an empty shell, as Latin American history has shown.[8]

While most Soviet analysts identify the struggle for economic development with the struggle for economic independence, the policy implications of their position depend on what precise meaning they give to 'economic independence.' In some cases independence is defined as complete freedom from imperialism. Here the problem is clear-cut: 'It is impossible to win economic independence from imperialism without breaking the stranglehold of foreign capital.'[9] If, as some writers maintain it is only in China, North Korea, and Cuba, which are already embarked on the road to socialist construction, where 'the question of liberation from imperialist exploitation has been fully solved,' it follows that independence requires joining the socialist camp and, by inference, breaking off economic relations with the capitalist system.[10] The struggle for economic independence is then a struggle against the entire system of world capitalist relations. In other cases Soviet analysts present independence as already possible for the politically sovereign Afro-Asian countries since the emergence of the socialist system, together with its political and economic support for the third world, has changed the international power situation. Already the developing countries can act as 'independent and equal partners with imperialism.'[11] This more moderate view corresponds with a reassessment of imperialism implying that it can 'to a certain extent exist economically without colonies.'[12] Achieving economic independence means in this view regulating, not breaking, relations with the world capitalist system. In his major book devoted to this question, L.V. Stepanov's starting point was a definition of economic independence in absolute terms as 'the full freedom to dispose of [the state's] national resources without limitations from any external forces whatsoever and without limitations coming from imperialism's policy or elements of its economic system.'[13] Stepanov observed a number of limitations that put the dependence of the less developed countries in quite a different category from that of the developed. A major limitation was the loss of national wealth flowing into foreign pockets. Considering the redistribution of wealth from the poor countries to the rich in accordance with the 'objective laws of world capitalism,' at an annual rate of $20 billion, the developing countries are seen to have lost the freedom to dispose of this amount of their own national resources in their own interests. 'They irrevocably lose control over the part of their national resources fallen under the command of the highly developed capitalist states.'

Stepanov found a second restriction on independence in the developing countries' weak control of those resources remaining under their own nominal control. Export economies are forced to adjust to the dictates of the world market, i.e. respond to the needs of the industrially developed states rather than to those of the nation. From his general definition of economic independence Stepanov proceeded to apply several specific criteria: one-sided agricultural or raw material specialization, extreme dependence in selling their products on foreign markets, great needs for financial and technical resources attracted from abroad, strengthening of foreign capital investment in the local economy, participation in the currency zone of former parent states, and special agreements with western markets like the European Common Market. Taken individually, some of these criteria do not necessarily spell dependence for all nations. New Zealand's exports of agricultural and raw material products form a greater percentage of its exports than do those for India and Turkey, but Stepanov does not consider New Zealand to be dependent. There has been more investment of foreign capital in the economies of Europe than in the developing countries, yet the former are more independent than the latter. Applied together, however, they describe the total situation of inequality that the developing countries find themselves in vis-à-vis the world capitalist economy. Inequality, indeed, is Stepanov's synonym for dependence. The two underlying factors determining the third world's inequality are its low labour productivity which is the economic basis for its backwardness, and its membership in the world capitalist system, which perpetuates its economic exploitation.

Having defined third world dependence in terms of economic backwardness and continued links with imperialist exploitation, Stepanov faces the policy question raised by his definition: which has priority – economic growth, to liquidate backwardness and raise national productivity thus establishing the basis for imperialist exploitation, or prior abolition of exploiting links with imperialism, thus creating a base for the free development of the national economy? The first view he identifies as that of bourgeois economists who reduce the inequality problem to backwardness without considering the question of exploitation or dependence. The other 'extreme view' is also unsatisfactory since it ignores the fact that economic backwardness is the basis for exploitation. Stepanov answers that economic growth and national liberation must proceed together: 'The efforts made by the peoples to develop their national economy and their fight to suppress imperialist exploitation are inseparable parts of a single process.'[14]

Stepanov's argument does not seem to have laid to rest the Soviet dilemma of whether to give economic growth priority over relations with imperialism or to advocate a political resolution of exploitative ties with imperialism as a prelude to genuine economic development. Some authoritative voices have spoken for the latter, more radical line arguing for the reorientation of the developing third world with the socialist bloc: 'the further strengthening of economic links with the countries of the socialist commonwealth opens before these young states real prospects of achieving economic independence.'[15] Others have put the major emphasis on internal industrial development. While the absence of industry compels the underdeveloped countries to remain agrarian and raw material appendages, 'a well-developed national industry is rightly called the backbone of independence.'[16] 'The transition of developing countries from one qualitative state (economic dependence on the imperialist monopolies) to another (economic independence) must necessarily be accompanied by their transition from [a] monovariant to [a] polyvariant situation.'[17] Commenting on the African struggle for economic independence, L. Alexandrovskaya spoke of the 'unquestionable progress' which she saw 'reflected in the nationalisation of foreign companies, in the absolute and relative growth of state revenue and expenditures, in the ... greater employment of the African population.'[18] This position leads to the moderate economists' line defining economic independence as self-sufficiency in the production of the means of production. They present independence as a relative category. In Kuzmin's words, the developing countries 'must stand *more firmly* on their own feet and *reduce* their dependence on the world market in providing the vital needs of reproduction.' In this view independence is established as an ideal towards which the policy-maker should be heading, a criterion that should be considered, though not to the exclusion of others, in deciding development policies. In countries that are large enough, with enough natural resources and a potentially strong economy, independence is a practical objective. It must be pursued with care and consistency. Each industrial sector must be supplied from the domestic economy; otherwise 'a lessening of dependence on the world market for some types of commodities will be offset by the intensification of this dependence for other types.' Kuzmin talked about a totality of production facilities, 'a complex, which while sufficiently broad is not *necessarily* all-encompassing.' He recognized that not all countries have an equal capacity for independence. The majority of the African nations can only create the production of means of production 'within an entire region or several regions.' However India is the prime example, along with Pakistan, Egypt, Indonesia, and certain others, of countries that 'can in full measure and with advantage for themselves develop the production of the means of production.'[19] The debate continues. It is not surprising that with opinions so opposed on the central problem of independence the Soviet analysis of the specific external economic relations between the third world and the capitalist and socialist worlds is similarly diverse.

THE NEED FOR EXTERNAL CAPITAL

There is no doubt, wrote two hard-line Soviet analysts on the problem of foreign aid, about the developing world's huge need for capital, modern technology, and specialists if it wants a quick liquidation of its economic backwardness and dependence.[20] The developing countries' economic and social backwardness sharply limits their own sources for internal accumulation of capital. Their internal market and their national production are too small to produce enough surplus to finance their own accelerated development. 'Economic backwardness, an archaic social system and a steady decline in raw commodity prices tend sharply to limit the sources for internal accumulation in the African countries. That is why the developing countries attach very great importance to recruiting financial resources from outside.'[21] The frank acceptance of the developing countries' huge needs for external resources is a relatively recent development for Soviet scholars, concerned as they have been with the priority of achieving independence by restricting ties with imperialism. An unresolved tension between recommending independence as the sine qua non of development and recognizing the need for external finance with its threat of greater dependence underlies the whole Soviet analysis of the foreign investment, aid, and even trade.

Of the three external sources of finance, aid from the international organizations is in their view too limited in size. The second, intergovernmental loans and aid, which had by 1967 risen to $8-9 billion, is 'a relatively small amount as compared with their requirements.' As all the developing countries want to stimulate their productive forces, they are 'therefore forced to invite foreign private capital,' the third but most onerous source, about whose position and future the Soviet analysts are extremely concerned.[22] Their concern is not just that private capital 'demands excessively high profits, which lead to a financial drain from the developing countries'; it is also that private capital spells the perpetuation of monopoly imperialist control of the third world. Foreign investment is the oldest, and in leninist thought the classical, expression of imperialism's inner compulsion to export capital in order to resolve its internal contradictions of declining profitability and to establish its own cheap agricultural-cum-raw-material sources abroad. Colonialism gave a political sanction and guarantee to this compulsive export of capital by the parent-state monopolies that reaped superprofits from exploiting the colonial labour force and selling manufactured goods back to the defenceless colonial market.

INDEPENDENCE: THE CHANGE OF THE GAME

While the Stalinist analysis maintained that formal independence had changed nothing in the nature of colonialist domination, the starting point for current Soviet analysis of the third world's international position is rather that, in establishing its political independence, the new state breaks the major colonial chains tying it to foreign exploitation. India's achievement of independence in 1947 furnishes a good example.

In the domain of international economic relations, India has stopped being the agricultural and raw material appendage of England. Although the position of foreign capital is still very strong in certain of the economy's branches, the monopoly of foreign capital inside the country and in India's relations with the world market has evolved considerably. With the loss of its governmental hegemony over India based on its military occupation of the country, English capital has lost its colonial monopoly in landed property, rail transport, the means of communication, military production, the largest irrigation systems, as well as in the field of state taxes, finances, bank credit and tariff policy. Its position in foreign trade has been abruptly weakened and, more important, its monopoly in the supply of the modern means of production has disappeared.[23]

Cracking the monopoly of imperialist capital did not mean, however, that foreign capital changed its objectives. On the contrary, according to two development scholars, foreign capital seeks to perpetuate the underdeveloped countries' economic backwardness and drain profits from them. The Soviet view of foreign private investment is in fact a highly hostile unmasking of the aims, features, and consequences of this traditional weapon of imperialist domination.[24]

AIMS OF FOREIGN INVESTMENT

In the opinion of those Soviet analysts who maintain that imperialism has not changed its character since decolonization, the export of capital remains an inherent characteristic of state monopoly capitalism in the third stage of its general crisis. Imperialism still seeks new spheres of application for its excess capital, new markets for its excess productive capacity, and new sources of raw materials and agricultural products for its own industries. While foreign capitalists have had to adapt to the new conditions of independence by adjusting the forms of their activity in the new states of the third world, they have not changed their aspirations in any significant way. Their positions were weakened by the achievement of political independence in the various colonies, but the foreign monopolies did not retreat. On the contrary, since their investments in the traditional colonial branches such as tea and jute plantations were no longer sufficient to dominate the new states, more capital was exported, but this time in order to gain a foothold where new economic action was growing. To achieve this it was necessary to establish an understanding with the new ruling circles. As V.I. Pavlov put it, 'for this reason, if they were to try to conserve their position in the country's economy, the monopolies had to take part in the creation of new industries both in the private and in the state sector.'[25]

While the foreign capitalists invest to defend their economic position, they do this with the support of the local big bourgeoisie and the qualified approval of the ruling circles. The new national bourgeoisie now in power did not at all intend to 'tolerate the former uncontrolled supremacy' of the foreign monopolists, but rather intended to extract 'the maximum benefit from its co-operation with them.' The reason for the national bourgeoisie's 'compromise' with foreign capital becomes clear when it is seen how the deals work in practice. The collaboration of an Indian firm with an international corporation for the construction of a new industrial branch is a 'particularly profitable affair' since the new enterprises benefit from a monopoly position within the country thanks to the policy of tariff protection for new industries. The notorious 'joint companies' based on both foreign and local capital participation are the product of these compromises which allow Indian capitalists 'to take root in new key industries even when they do not have the foreign currency necessary to purchase the equipment.' In the prevailing conditions of an acute balance of payments deficit, India's 'official circles' also look with favour on these joint companies as one of the channels for the entry of the equipment necessary for the country's industrialization. This explains the Soviet observers' dialectical evaluation of the joint companies: 'On the one hand they have facilitated the creation in India of some centres of the most modern heavy industry, but on the other hand they signify the expansion of foreign monopoly control in India's new industries.'[26]

Soviet scholars emphasize the extent of foreign capital penetration and control by quoting example after example of joint companies. Thus in the aluminium industry, 60 per cent of Indian aluminium in Uttar Pradesh belongs to a Canadian-American firm; another operation in Madhya Pradesh has been established with a Swedish firm, a third in Mysore in co-operation with the American company Reynolds, and Madras Aluminium was being set up with Italian capital. In the chemical industry most firms collaborate with English companies led by the most powerful, Imperial Chemical Industries, while on the Indian side the Tata monopoly plays the major role. In the rubber industry 'foreign capital threatens to establish absolute control.' Long lists of this type give a cumulative impression of an economy dominated by foreign capital. Despite the evident cooperation between foreign and local capital, Soviet analyses underline the deep contradictions between the aspirations of the foreign investor and the local government. R.A. Ulyanovsky maintained that the continued exploitation of the developing countries by the United States provided the objective basis for the aggravation of the contradictions between the third world and imperialism, contradictions that are fundamental and antagonistic, not temporary and transitory.[27]

In Africa, V.G. Solodovnikov argued, 'the very nature of foreign investments and the conditions under which foreign capital operates are contrary to the national interest of independent countries.'[28] For in Africa the legal forms of foreign investment established during the period of arbitrary imperialist rule are still virtually the same: enterprises, and often whole branches of industry, belonging to foreign capital are controlled from abroad. This makes it possible for the imperialists to interfere in the internal affairs of the sovereign countries, something they are prone to do since their aim is not just to pump out profits but to pursue a policy aimed at stifling the development of national industries. Even worse, they have 'a marked distrust of the long-term national programmes of economic development,' i.e. industrialization and planning. They very rarely seek genuinely to develop industry, preferring to control the local market, extract raw materials, or assemble commodities rather than develop heavy industry under national control. Despite the developing countries' effort to change the conditions for foreign investment, the monopolies have refused to revise their demands. As a result, 'there crystallizes more and more sharply an irreconcilable contradiction between the political and economic goals of young sovereign nation states striving for economic independence ... on the one hand and international imperialism on the other.' So long as this one-sided economic relationship persists, genuine independence 'will continue to be a long way off' because any country with foreign capital investments will never be secure against interference in its internal affairs.

In larger, more developed and stronger states such as India, there had been an evolution of the forms in which foreign capital operated. The creation of 'mixed enterprises' operating 'under the mask of national capital' was the most significant development.[29] In such companies, where part of the capital was provided by the foreign corporation in the form of imported equipment in return for part of the share capital, the contradictions between foreigner and national did not appear so strong. True, these companies represented a means of penetration and control of the national economy by the imperialist monopoly. There were conflicts between the national bourgeoisie and the foreign companies: the former pressed for the establishment of complete production cycle in, for instance, the automobile industry in India, a development resisted by the foreign partner.[30] The growing foreign control in India represented by the proliferating technical and commercial agreements between foreign and local capital was, in the Soviet view, not in the national interest. But the efforts made by the national government of India and the local bourgeoisie to encourage the establishment of mixed companies would indicate that the contradiction involved was more theoretical than operational. As for the government, the 'official circles' approved of this device as a means of importing foreign capital equipment without increasing the balance of payments problem. The mixed companies were indeed particularly profitable for local big business, allowing it to expand into undeveloped sectors requiring heavy capital investments and the latest technology, an expansion made possible by the co-operation of foreign partners. Y.I. Loshakov observed that foreign monopolies were encouraging local monopolies, implying that if there were contradictions they were between the monopoly and middle levels of the local bourgeoisie, not between imperialism and big Indian capital.[31] Contradictions between local and foreign capital were 'of course' still there, but Loshakov provided no evaluation of the relative weight of these contradictions as opposed to the common interests uniting the two. The reader gains the impression that the latter far outweighed the former.

The danger identified by Soviet writers was essentially a political one: by reinforcing the position of local monopolies the effect of foreign investment was to push India along the capitalist path of development and to pressure her towards abandoning her non-aligned foreign policy in favour of full support for western foreign policy. The contradictions are thus more between foreign investment and what the Soviets consider India's real, objective national interests than between foreign investment and India's national interests as conceived by her bourgeois government. A. Maslennikov considers that foreign capital in India is still reactionary and even more dangerous as a result of numerous concessions won in 1966.[32] It is precisely in this strengthening co-operation between foreign capital and national big capital that the Soviet analysts of India find the greatest cause for alarm: the political result is a strengthening of the forces of right reaction in their attack on the progressive aspects of Indian government policy – the development of the state sector through governmental planning. Backed up by their foreign partners, the big Indian capitalists have increased their attacks on government policy, penetrating seven out of the sixteen vital branches once officially reserved for state-controlled industry.[33] Through the increased strength of the Swatantra party and their control of the right wing of Congress, the big capitalists increased their pressure on the government's social and foreign policy.

While the political impact of continued foreign private investment is clearly negative in the Soviet view, even in a country like India which is relatively independent and progressive, the consequence of imperialist investment in the 'semi-colonies' of Latin America has been far worse. Here foreign corporations bring the local oligarchy under their direct influence, diverting the national bourgeoisie from its anti-imperialist leadership role. Even the impact on the proletariat is politically regressive, for in paying higher wages American-controlled firms are corrupting the 'labour aristocracy' with bourgeois illusions and so undermining the unity of the working class. It is only in the 'non-capitalist' states that the political harm done by the foreign capital investment is minimized. Under non-capitalism these foreign companies find themselves 'under effective financial and political control by the state.' Not able to rely on 'any extensive network of agents in the country such as reactionary classes' they have to operate timidly in a kind of social vacuum.[34]

THE ECONOMIC IMPACT OF FOREIGN INVESTMENT

While no Soviet writer questions the political danger of foreign investments, the impression conveyed of their economic consequences is less uniformly negative. It is true that the hard-line Soviet position still maintains sweepingly that 'the prerequisite for industrial progress is the elimination of foreign capital domination.'[35] The 'penetration' of foreign capital in the economy is painted in this approach only as an index of foreign control and the negation of economic development.[36] But when Soviet researchers were elaborating on the long lists of firms established in the various developing countries they were at the same time indicating the extent of industrial development taking place as a result of this investment. What was once implied is now openly accepted. Savelev acknowledges that the new form of mixed company co-operating with foreign capital helps force the pace of the economy's industrialization, and in the most desired form, with high capital intensity and modern technology.[37] Foreign capital also brings management cadres: Ghana gave the administration of a public textile factory to the United Africa Company.[38] However, the introduction of new techniques by foreign monopolies reduced employment in Tanzania's private sector from 307,000 in 1961 to 247,000 in 1964.[39] Although Savelev points out the disadvantages of foreign investment (payments of profits abroad in foreign currency, the import of spare parts, the maintenance of the third world as a raw material and agrarian appendage), he nevertheless considers that foreign private investment *increases* these countries' economic independence.[40] Others who look at foreign investment as a way of meeting the developing countries' need for external capital accept the view that the various forms of direct and indirect investment and technical agreements have led to economic development, especially in undeveloped branches of the third world economy.

While the Soviet economists have conceded the developmental impact of foreign private investment, they have not forgotten what marxists have always considered to be the main negative economic impact of foreign investment – exploitation. Very simply, the 'money drain,' the return flow of dividends and capital back to the investing country bleeds the underdeveloped world of its most precious resource, its painfully gathered internal capital accumulation. 'Any capitalist country exporting private capital abroad after a certain period begins to derive from its foreign investments profits exceeding its export of capital.'[41] In the twenty years from 1945 to 1965, V.G. Solodovnikov reported, the export of $26.2 billions of private US capital made $58.5 billion in direct profits of which $40.6 billion were transferred back to the United States. The drain of money resulting from foreign investment in Latin America was constantly increasing. From $415.6 million a year in the late 1940s it had risen to $815 million in the 1960s. Once the return of profits to the imperialist countries exceeded the export of new private capital, this drain 'nullifies all the efforts to help these countries along the lines of external aid and reduced interest on state credits.' For the imperialists the export of capital means the acquisition of enormous tributes and enrichment through exploitation of the people of other countries. This means that 'not only are the imperialist countries far from financing the economic advance of the underdeveloped nations, but on the contrary they get enriched at the expense of the latter.' If this very unfavourable trend is not checked and the sums transferred from the developing countries are not limited in size, the economies of these states will incur an ever-increasing damage which will 'negate all the efforts and measures to encourage their exports and improve conditions for obtaining loans.'

The impression created by this analysis is of the almost uncontrolled growth of foreign investment in the developing countries, as a result of the dual imperialist objectives of gaining control of the leading sectors of the developing countries' economies and maximizing their extraction of profits and dividends. Pavlov provided figures to underline the huge growth in the volume of foreign investment in India. After 1957 the expansion of this investment enjoyed a second wind, encouraged by concessions made by the government in tax arrangements, lowered restrictions against foreign participation in national companies, and the admission of mixed companies into new branches of industry. For instance, the agreements on double taxation made between India and the USA, West Germany, and Japan were largely responsible for the rise of foreign investment to Rs 330 million in 1959 compared to Rs 130 million for the two preceding years. As a result, during the second five-year plan foreign investment in private heavy industry alone was more than twice as high as the plan's target volume, amounting to Rs 2 billion, 23 per cent of all investments in this sector.[42] After receiving further concessions on foreign penetration of state sector branches, conditions governing the obtaining of the controlling packet, and guarantees against nationalization, foreign investment grew from a total of Rs 6.9 billion in 1961 to Rs 8 billion in 1964.[43]

Though Soviet observers gave the impression of inexorably growing foreign investment and control, they managed simultaneously to be surprised at the meagre volume of this capital flow. V.I. Pavlov observed that, for the third Indian five-year plan, the net influx of foreign capital was only to reach Rs 1,420 million, 'not more than 6 per cent of the currency deficit' forecast by the plan. Why, Pavlov asked, despite all the concessions made by the Indian government to attract foreign capital, did the latter not rush into India in a huge torrent, say, a billion rupees each year? He answered that foreign capital still felt there were too many risks posed by Indian nationalism: control of the re-export of profits and capital, control of the construction of new firms, control of the imports of raw materials and semi-finished products.[44] Ulyanovsky added that American balance of payments difficulties had imposed limitations on US investment in the developing countries.[45] Perhaps more significant was the growing perception, by those Soviets who felt imperialism had made significant changes, that investment in the developing countries was less attractive for western investors than the picture painted by their radical colleagues would suggest. Apart from certain still essential raw materials like oil, uranium, or aluminum, the West's demand for raw materials from the third world was declining. The development of western raw material resources and the changing import needs as a result of technical progress diminished the necessity for developing new projects outside western economies. Nor was the cheap labour available in the third world as powerful an attraction as it had once been. It may have allowed a high rate of exploitation, but the local markets were still too narrow. Monopoly capital generally preferred to invest in highly developed economies with advanced technologies, leaving it to governmental aid to develop unprofitable and politically unstable economies.[46]

POLICY RECOMMENDATIONS

If the Soviet scholars see foreign capital alternatively as restrictive or modernizing, small wonder that their policy conclusions vary widely. The same author, in fact, may make recommendations that appear contradictory at first glance. From the position that the nature of private investment is incompatible with national sovereignty, 'an inevitable conclusion arises that the process of nationalizing foreign property in the developing countries, including those of Africa, will in all probability be steadily mounting.' Solodovnikov made a more specific recommendation at the United Nations Economic Commission for Africa in January 1967. Placing the responsibility on the shoulders of the countries exploiting the third world, he moved that each developed nation whose capitalists made profits from the developing countries should set up an aid fund equal to the profits received from the third world and distribute these funds without interest for projects 'not liable to attract private foreign capital.' This would make the capital-exporting state responsible for 'the harmful influence of its foreign companies' activities on the economies of the developing nations. In turn, this would undoubtedly weaken the tendency for nationalizing foreign private property in the developing countries.' In this line of reasoning, the policy problem 'boils down to a struggle for modification of the conditions under which foreign capital is invested.'[47] Analysts conscious of the developing countries' need for foreign investment give 'this struggle for modification of the conditions' a very gradualist content: 'Naturally, it should not be forgotten that the struggle in the

African countries for economic liberation from imperialism can succeed not through the drastic rupture of existing links with capitalist countries but by using these and gradually directing them in the national interest in proportion to the development of production forces. The building up of the national economy of the African countries should start from existing relations and find support in them.'[48] But even this moderate control of foreign investment was not being followed by most countries. Rather the reverse was true. L. Aleksandrovskaya noted with dismay the attempts made by African countries to attract foreign capital to their countries: they were 'going begging to capitalist countries,' though their dependence on these countries was the basic reason for their backwardness. From this closed circle there was no hope of exit to economic independence.[49] Much more appropriate were the efforts by other countries to make 'an adamant stipulation' that investment should facilitate the implementation of national economic development programmes and should guarantee non-interference in internal affairs.[50]

For countries such as India that have chosen the path of accelerated development through the national bourgeoisie's compromise with foreign capital, the government's use of the public sector can reduce some of the negative internal effects of foreign investment. The public sector has incomparably superior capacities to those of the private sector for resisting the claims of foreign monopolies.[51] It can try to obtain the participation of foreign capital on a credit basis without permanent ownership of the projected enterprise's capital. It can buy back the capital belonging to the foreigners, thus transforming a mixed foreign/state capitalist firm into an entirely public company. Most important of all, it can use the co-operation offered by the socialist countries as a bargaining lever to force the participation of imperialists who are reluctant to let the state sector be built up entirely by socialist help.

Discussion of the imperialist monopolies as 'multinational corporations' only crept into the Soviet analysis in the mid-1970s. Writing in 1976 Rostislav Ulyanovsky identified them as an 'extraordinarily powerful lever for economic pressure on the developing countries [that] represents a qualitatively new form of neo-colonialist exploitation camouflaged as economic exchange.' Even if their form was new, their content was old: they impede 'the development of truly independent national economies,' because their 'purpose is to establish enterprises and branches of industry integrated into the reproduction of the national product of the industrial capitalist countries.'[52] Because of this, 'the developing countries' main demand in the exercise of sovereignty over their natural resources boils down to establishing full control over the multinationals' activity.'[53]

For those Soviet observers who consider the economic benefits of foreign investment as still outweighed by the liabilities, the answer must be much more radical. Though every country except Burma was creating favourable conditions to attract foreign investment, R.N. Andreasyan observed, the goal was for foreign capital to be finally thrown out of these countries. For him the 'real struggle to liquidate the domination of foreign capital implies, strategically, a policy aimed at eliminating its domination and at nationalization, and, tactically, a flexible policy aimed at making temporary use of the capital of the imperialist powers – provided there is strict limitation of its activities, liquidation of reactionary pro-imperialist forces at home, transition to the non-capitalist way of development and reliance on the world Socialist system.'[54] Though he noted that such non-capitalist countries as Algeria and Guinea continued to be 'in direct economic dependence on imperialism,' he saw a basic difference between them and the countries taking the capitalist path: the latter 'regard foreign capital as a natural and permanent factor, whereas the non-capitalist countries see it as an unavoidable but temporary measure.' They had wrested ever greater concessions from the foreign companies on revenues, control of operations, and independent exploitation of their own resources. The problem was to defeat reactionary pro-imperialist monopoly groups at home and to resist the demands of foreign capital for enslaving conditions abroad. 'With the all-round assistance of the world socialist system,' the leaders of countries taking the non-capitalist way used state and private foreign investment for economic development. In the final analysis this radical line reverted to the primacy of politics: 'A revolutionary political regime is the best guarantee that, given favourable conditions, foreign capital will eventually be thrown out.'[55]

We have come back to Stepanov's dilemma. The radical approach assumes that foreign investment entails dependence and that without prior economic independence there cannot be development. But an opposite assumption is accepted by the moderates: that despite the problems posed by foreign investment, there can be no meaningful progress towards independence without the development it causes. Other analysts look elsewhere, to governmental aid, as a superior type of external capital available in greater quantity and free of many of private foreign investment's inherent disadvantages.

9

Imperialist 'aid'

There are obvious parallels between the Soviet views of private foreign investment and imperialist governmental aid. Just as the Soviet interpretation of foreign investment concerns the motivations of the western monopolies as much as
the actual impact of the projects created by their capital, so the Soviet analysis
of western aid is even more concerned with the motivations of imperialism than
with the actual impact of the western credits. The same dichotomy between the
radical and moderate approaches carries through in the analysis of aid. The divergence is based on two differing assessments of imperialism: one is that it is as
bad as ever, the other is that it has modified.

Just as foreign investment is seen as the extension in the post-colonial period
of the colonial monopolies' domination, so western aid is seen as the continuation of the metropolitan governments' efforts to exert political and economic
power in their former colonial hunting grounds. Foreign investments are seen to
be an attempt to resolve state monopoly capitalism's internal contradictions;
western aid is a device to solve imperialism's contradictions in the third world.
Foreign capital flows are as much a part of the imperialist political economy as
governmental aid is an integral part of imperialist foreign policy. If aid is an
essential expression of imperialism, small wonder so much space is devoted by
development scholars to debates about whether the character of imperialism has
changed or not. At a seminar on neocolonialism held in the Institute of World
Economics and International Relations both the hard radical line and the moderate economists' lines were clearly presented.[1]

THE HARD LINE: NO CHANGE IN IMPERIALISM

According to L. Stepanov, changes in imperialism were merely of façade; its inherent exploitation of the third world remained unchanged: 'Regardless of the

external forms of economic relations, the imperialist exploitation of former colonies and semi-colonies remains.'[2] As long as the heritage of colonialism had not been removed, there could be no question of equality between developing and developed nations. The massive movement of wealth from the underdeveloped to the industrialized world by the return flow of profits, interest, and capital, amounting to a total annual deficit for the third world of $6.5 billion, did force neocolonialism to make some outlays of assistance to preserve its control. Still, this aid only led to growing economic dependence for the receiving countries.

Supporting this view another participant in the discussion, Y. Khavinson, attacked those 'bourgeois ideologists' who maintained that imperialism ends with the end of colonialism. On the contrary, 'the weakening of imperialism ... is attended by an intensification of its aggressive aspirations.' Imperialism may well undertake large-scale attempts at purchasing many states' allegiance, but it cannot renounce its social essence and basic principles, envisage a balanced reconstruction of the underdeveloped economies, or allow for the end of their subordinate status in the system of the international capitalist division of labour. 'Neocolonialism is the same old imperialism; though it may change its appearance, it retains its essence in full.' Far from being undermined, the economic positions of imperialism were even growing stronger, capitalist elements were entrenching themselves in many developing economies, and the monopolies still retained decisive advantages deriving from the heritage of colonialism. In other words, for Khavinson, the mechanism of imperialist exploitation had not undergone any fundamental changes.[3]

Hardliners readily agreed that certain important changes have taken place on the world scene. As V.L. Tyagunenko, director of the Institute of World Economy and International Relations, put it, imperialism no longer enjoys a territorial division of the world. The monopolies have completely lost control of the socialist developing countries. The imperialists have been forced to make concessions to the national liberation movements so that political relations between developing and developed cannot be based on their old lines. But for all these transformations, imperialism still has an aggressive nature, a tendency to enslave the underdeveloped, and it cannot exist without oppressing or exploiting the small and weak countries. The export of capital and aid is designed artificially to delay the decay of imperialism, acting as a fire extinguisher to stifle the flames of revolution. But this has nothing to do with real aid.[4] It has everything to do with imperialism's desperate efforts to hang on. As Tyagunenko wrote elsewhere: 'The imperialists are doing their utmost to retain the liberated countries within the capitalist orbit. They resort to subversion, open destruction of productive forces (as was the case in Guinea and Algeria), economic blockade, all manner of price and currency manipulations, intervention and the threat of intervention, sharpening of ethnic contradictions and territorial disputes and so forth.'[5]

MODERATE DEDOGMATIZED LINE

Whereas the hardliners' position is based on highly politicized propositions about the intentions of a diabolical imperialism, the moderates talk more coolly in economists' language. Their points are made by referring to what they see as simple facts calling into question the 'dogmas' of their radical colleagues. One of these facts is the surprisingly good health of the European metropolitan economies despite the breakup of the colonial systems. The loss of colonial superprofits has not after all undermined the economy of the former parent states as Lenin had predicted. Experience has shown that they can 'to a certain extent exist economically without colonies.'[6] Britain's loss of its colonial hegemony had even given an impulse to progressive economic change: 'The breakup of the colonial system has induced structural developments in Britain's economy dictated by modern scientific and technical progress and leading towards the establishment of new, progressive branches.'[7] For the Netherlands, too, decolonization gave an impetus to progress. Since 'the availability of a good raw-material source and a wide commodity market in Indonesia weakened the stimulus towards improving and developing progressive industries and methods of industrial production in the Netherlands,' the loss of the colonial sources of accumulation forced the monopolies to intensify their production on a higher technological level.[8]

The technological revolution has been a shock absorber for the effects of decolonization and acts as a break on further imperialist expansion. Britain could not afford the capital export required for neocolonial expansion if it wanted to modernize its home industrial base.[9]

Along with this far less aggressive, far more self-sufficient picture of imperialism at home goes a revised appraisal of imperialism's interest in the third world. Imperialism no longer controls the course of events. The imperialists have lost, for example, such profits of political rule as the colonies' direct contributions to the parent-states' budgets. The new states now levy their own taxes and make their own laws. As a result of nationalizations of foreign property and reductions of profits transferable to the metropolis, the rate of imperialist profit is declining, the flow of funds to the imperialist countries from the underdeveloped world is diminishing, and imperialism is having to pay much more, in the form of $5 to $6 billions of assistance, to retain its position in the third world.[10] As a result, imperialism's objective has changed from guaranteeing economic exploitation of the colonies by non-economic methods to cultivating capitalist relations in the developing countries and including them in the sphere of 'ordinary' capi-

talist exploitation.[11] Far from wanting to prevent economic progress, the imperialists are aware of the need to clear away feudal structures and are 'striving to
develop capitalism through reforms from above.' An example of 'the capacity
of the imperialist bourgeoisie to resort to reform' is the land reform abolishing
landlord property which the Americans imposed on Japan.[12] Similarly, in the
industrial sectors it is not true, in V. Pavlov's opinion, that imperialism prevents
development in the third world. It is in imperialism's interest to promote industrial development,[13] or as G. Mirsky put it, imperialism must 'pull' the underdeveloped economies to a modern level so as to extend the possibilities for
capital investment.[14]

AIMS OF IMPERIALIST 'AID'

Despite the critical differences of opinion over the definition of imperialism
there is nevertheless a Soviet consensus on the objectives of western aid as the
foreign policy and economic expression of imperialism in the third world. V.
Rymalov quoted an American government official as saying that aid was 'the
most effective economic means for the attainment of American foreign policy
objectives in the underdeveloped countries.'[15]

Soviet value judgments on the quality of American foreign policy differ considerably from the State Department's interpretation. Governmental aid, as the
long arm of its imperial foreign policy, is regarded as the United States' principal
means of increasing its influence in the new countries that used to be the political monopolies of the European powers. Though imperialism's objectives are
numerous, O.V. Maev summarized the neocolonialist aims of western aid to Asia,
Africa and Latin America under the following heads: 1/ To support the imperialist economy by subsidizing the expansion of its own monopolies; 2/ Ideologically
to fight socialism by forcing the developing countries to limit the state sector, to
give free rein to private enterprise and to concentrate on preparing the necessary
conditions for private capitalism; 3/ To try to maintain capitalism in the developing countries and tie them firmly to the imperialist camp and to support
[local] big business, its most trusted colleague, in achieving these ends.[16] In the
unmasking of the motivations behind imperialist aid it is the hard line which dominates the discussion.

No Soviet scholar will question the indissoluble link between state aid and
private investment under state monopoly capitalism, a system run by and for the
monopolies. The inextricable connection between the private and governmental
instruments imperialism uses to achieve its aims are summed up in one sentence:
'The essence of the reciprocal action of government credits and private investments is the fact that the former clear the road for the latter and the latter in

turn facilitates the achievement of the aims of the former.'[17] For its home economy, imperialist aid fulfils the traditional, self-serving function of capital export: creating markets for the metropolitan industries. Thus 65 per cent of French subsidies came back as orders for equipment. Similarly, British aid for the construction of Nigerian railways created export orders for British heavy industry.[18] Aid thus helps solve capitalism's own internal problems. Without granting 'aid,' the United States would not be able to ensure a supply of the raw materials it needs from the third world. At the same time the export orders created by its own tied aid maintain American exports of equipment and bolster the level of employment at home.[19]

With the decline of private investment in the developing countries, state aid has taken over the basic imperialist activity of capital export. It assumes the function of guaranteeing the inviolability and high profitability of private investments,[20] while putting pressure on the developing countries to keep them on a capitalist path of development and so in the world capitalist system. French aid, for instance, maintained the old colonial practice of investing in infrastructure as a continuing policy of creating a favourable climate for the further development of monopoly capital. While its investment in ex-colonial infrastructure still made up 60 per cent of all expenditures there, France gave loans to monopolies for the extraction of mineral and agricultural materials and also participated in the capital of these firms. The hand-in-glove relationship of aid and foreign investment could be seen in US loans to the local governments. The construction of hydroelectric projects through this aid would create the infrastructure necessary for American business to set up plants in the area. The granting of loans also allowed western cadres to penetrate the governmental services as experts to supervise particular construction projects. Because imperialist 'aid' is designed to solve the economic problems of the imperialist countries rather than to answer the needs of the recipients it is generally printed between quotation marks in Soviet texts.

While there is no question among Soviet analysts that aid is self-serving in economic terms, there is considerable disagreement about just what ideological ends the aid serves. Measuring the ideological element of imperialist aid policy produces the greatest divergence of views among Soviet writers. The implication of the hard line is that American-dominated imperialism uses aid as 'a major instrument in the hands of the imperialist powers for continuing their colonialist policy in the underdeveloped countries.'[21] While imperialism has had to resign itself to the independent status of these countries, it is utterly unwilling to accept their economic independence since this would prevent it from exploiting their immense natural wealth. In order to keep the developing countries within the capitalist system, therefore, imperialism is building relations with the former colonies on the Latin American pattern, 'according to the principle of combining formal independence with continued economic oppression and exploitation.'[22] Thus, for instance, US aid to Ceylon was 'aimed solely at supporting the plantation economy as a result of which Ceylon's economic system was extremely one-sided.'[23]

Put very bluntly, 'the principal task of imperialist "aid" is to block the process of national and social liberation which is in progress in the countries of Asia, Africa and Latin America.'[24] Far from allowing this national liberation to proceed in India, the imperialists aimed to transform that country into an 'oriental support for the world capitalist economy.' Foreign loans, too, served the ideological aims of resisting the growth of the socialized state sector and increasing the development of private enterprise in that country. It is true that much imperialist aid did go to the state sector – $225 millions of American aid even financed the six-year plan in Nigeria – but this simply reflected the 'new flexibility' introduced by the Kennedy regime in the policy of using American aid to fight socialist tendencies and strengthen private enterprise in the third world.[25] That the export by the United States of 'state capital' was thirty-three times the volume of American private capital inflow into India indicated to R.A. Ulyanovsky how strong has been the American urge to prevent India's transition to the socialist road.[26]

Aid for industry is given not to the state sector but rather to private enterprise. Even the World Bank, which Soviet observers consider to be under the direct control of the US State Department, gave loans to the Indian government only for the construction of infrastructure projects, whereas its loans for industrial enterprises went to the private sector. Most of the American loans for the purchase of industrial equipment went to the local private sector, which as a general rule meant the local monopolies. Analysing the American credits of 1958 from the presidential development fund, V.I. Pavlov showed that, of the $175 million granted to India, the Indian private sector received $72 million, the public sector $63 million, and public and private transport $40 million. Breaking down this aid by industrial branch, he concluded that the state sector did not receive a single dollar for manufacturing industries, whereas $72 million went to industrial development in the private sector, 'especially the branches where Indian monopolies allied with foreign capital are dominant.'[27] The loans of the Export-Import Bank followed the same pattern. In a three-year period Indian private industry received $250 million credit for the purchase of equipment, while the state sector did not receive more than $40 to $50 million, apart from the loans for hydroelectric stations. Governmental loans to the developing countries 'to a significant degree have the character of state-monopoly export of capital.'[28]

Ideological and geopolitical motivations reinforce imperialism's economic interests. The economic aims of imperialism do not alone suffice to explain why aid in the form of credits to the underdeveloped countries was the means increasingly used to achieve its foreign policy. The history of American aid shows that imperialism resorted to granting aid to the non-aligned countries 'only to the extent that the failure of their attempts at political and military intervention in these countries became evident.' In its first period, American 'aid' consisted almost exclusively of wheat loans and grants. 'Since 1955 when the failure of the American plans to draw India into its aggressive camp became clear, the USA began to finance their agreement principally by credits.'[29] While the Western powers had been very little concerned with India's economic development before 1958 they finally came to the point of granting large credits after the failure of their direct aggression in the Middle East and as a reaction to the favourable results of India's economic co-operation with the Soviet Union. The increase of American aid that characterized the second period of imperialist assistance was thus motivated primarily by a desire to impede India's co-operation with the socialist camp.

Worse still is imperialism's non-economic assistance, which serves purely cold war ends. American military aid is singled out for particular criticism. Rymalov asserted that 85 per cent of the aid Thailand had received had gone to pay for military materials and services of military advisers, while it spent itself on its military establishment seven times more than it had received from the US. As for Pakistan, because of its participation in SEATO and CENTO, 70 per cent of the state's revenue went for the military. Its per capita revenue had been falling since 1954 when it joined SEATO. Western economic projects were 'insignificant in comparison with the military aid.'[30]

Imperialism may be, at heart, the enemy of industrialization for the developing countries' economies, as L.I. Aleksandrovskaya still maintained,[31] but Soviet analysts no longer asserted that the vastly increased flow of imperialist state funds to the third world prevented any industrial development. The hardliners maintain, however, that imperialist participation in industrialization is designed either to take control of the economy or to divert it away from heavy industry. The change that Rymalov noted in imperialism's approach to industrialization in the third world is that while in the old days it did everything to prevent industrialization, now it is trying to seize the commanding heights in the new leading branches.[32] Baskin's view of the relationship between imperialist aid and development is slightly less restrictive. Citing the French *Jeanneney Report* of 1963 he noted that there was no word on heavy industry, proving that France too wanted to limit economic development to agriculture and light industries. The Americans also tried to convince the new states not to push industrialization.[33]

Imperialism's reactionary aims in the developing countries show its aid to be 'forced' by the internal compulsions of the world capitalist system, the external imperatives created by the existence of the socialist camp, and the growing independence of the developing countries themselves. What, then, is the character of western aid? Does it achieve its objectives?

ECONOMIC EFFECTS OF IMPERIALIST AID

Apart from the objection that the form of foreign aid is ideologically dangerous, encouraging industrial development only in the private capitalist sector, Soviet analysts also consider the economic consequences of imperialist aid to be undesirable.

There is, to start with, the high cost of imperialist aid. V.S. Baskin argued that such high interest rates as 5 or 6 per cent on World Bank and Export-Import Bank loans could not be called 'anything but enslaving conditions.'[34] Loans do not resolve the developing countries' shortage of foreign currency; they simply increase their liabilities. V.G. Solodovnikov noted that the growing state debt of ninety-seven developing countries had reached the huge total of $36.4 billion by the end of 1965, having grown at the yearly rate of 13.8 per cent for ten years. 'The huge and swiftly mounting foreign debts is a heavy burden for "Third World" countries. In 1962, it amounted to $22,000 million and at the beginning of 1971 reached $66,700 million, growing 12-14 per cent annually on the average. In 1970, foreign debt and interest payments by these countries totalled $6,000 million.[35] One consequence of this was that amortization payments on these debts had been increasing even more rapidly: from 1956 to 1965 from $0.7 billion to $3.5 billion.[36] Foreign aid makes up an increasing proportion of state sector investments. In India, from Rs 1,880 million (10 per cent of the investments of India's first five-year plan) to Rs 10,900 million (24 per cent of the second plan's investments), foreign aid was to reach Rs 15,200 million or 25 per cent of the third plan's total investments. The associated increase in debt would require India to pay Rs 5,921 million in interest and repayments during the third five-year plan. With the growing indebtedness, more new loans would be required to pay back the old. Another cost disadvantage comes from aid being tied by donor countries to their own industry's output. The lack of competition among potential suppliers tends to increase the price of goods purchased on such state credits, which 'deepens the non-equivalent character of the exchange.'[37]

The tying of American credits to the purchase of goods coming from the United States reduced the real value of these loans to India by 25 per cent to 30 per cent because of the higher American prices for equipment equally available from Japan or Europe. Another factor further reducing the efficacy of aid is the large proportion spent on importing consumer goods. Of all the loans granted India up to September 1956 54.4 per cent, or Rs 4,037 million, went to buy agricultural produce. By the same date India had received from the United States only Rs 1,000-1,100 million for 'production needs,' and these were directed towards small-scale projects, not large projects in heavy industry. In the last two years of the second five-year plan the USA gave Rs 700 million of aid annually directed towards industry and the relief of social problems. But since India was receiving food grain aid of Rs 1,150 million annually from the United States, V.I. Pavlov concluded that the widening of American loans for productive aims had not caused a radical change in the structure of the aid.[38]

Of the aid spent for industrial development, most was for food processing and light industries producing consumer goods, rather than for capital goods: they augmented India's capacity for 'simple reproduction' but not for 'expanded' reproduction. By not establishing branches with complete cycles of reproduction, this aid, in Soviet eyes, did not lead to genuine independence.[39] With rare exceptions, the repayment of American loans had to be made in dollars, so that the new American aid still forced its beneficiaries to depend on selling their own products on the American market for several decades.[40]

FOOD AID

As the United States was the animating force of modern imperialism, Soviet analysis of western aid centred on American programmes. Chief among these was the shipment of food grain as aid, an archetype for Soviet observers of harmful imperialist aid. While Soviet analysts did not deny the increasing need of many developing countries for imported food or the useful role that American food aid thus played in 'extreme circumstances,'[41] they insist that supplying huge quantities of food cereals neither eliminates nor even affects the basic causes for this need to import. The food grain shipments which form the bulk of American aid to India under Public Law 480 failed to solve India's agricultural problems and did not in themselves increase India's agricultural output. On the contrary, the aid was responsible for the stagnation of agriculture in India, since, with an assured external supply, the government refrained from carrying out the radical agrarian reforms required to achieve a major increase of food production at home.[42] Furthermore, the selling of American cereals at prices set by the developed countries with their high productivity of labour further depressed local agrarian production because these prices were too low to stimulate Indian producers to increase production for the market.[43] While these food imports could mainly be paid for in local currency, some had to be purchased for dollars repaid at 3 to 4 per cent interest; the drain on the balance of payments was increased by the requirement to transport the grain in American ships at high rates, also payable in hard currency, that had to be earned by exports to the west.[44]

The Soviet analyst looked beyond the direct economic impact. He saw American food aid as a strategy for strengthening the USA's trade expansion on the world's agrarian market while disposing of its home surpluses. Food aid also facilitated the expansion of American monopolies because 25 per cent of the local funds accumulating in the US account were used to make loans to American firms operating in the receiving country.[45] The huge wheat shipments were paid for in rupees and deposited in a US account in New Delhi, which presented 'a menace to the country's economic independence' because this colossal and growing fund remained under American control. According to the terms of the August 1956 agreement all the receipts from the sale of the American wheat, together with half the cost of its transport by sea, were to fatten the account of the American government in India. With this money it financed its embassy's propaganda activity in that country, specifically the vast programme of the US Information Agency, the education of Indians in the USA and of young Americans in India and the publication and distribution at low prices of publications praising the American way of life.

The American government also used this money to grant rupee loans to India, mainly for hydroelectric projects in the state sector and industrial construction in the private sector. While their structure is not criticized, their interest rate is high. In any case, they 'in no way solve the problem of searching for foreign currency to buy equipment' abroad. Furthermore these rupee funds did not diminish the concentration of enormous quantities of national currency in the hands of the Americans, giving them an instrument of influence over the economic and ideological life of the country. Already by the middle of 1958 the Indian wheat loan debt had almost reached Rs 5 billion, only an insignificant part of which had been used for the development of industrial productive forces.[46]

I.M. Shatalov observed that 'food deliveries have become an important instrument of policy for the imperialist circles of the west' and quoted with sympathy the declaration of the Egyptian minister of agriculture: 'We are faced with the complicated task of increasing agricultural production in order to guarantee our national security.'[47] The Soviet scholar cannot discuss the economics of aid for long without returning to his basic concern: aid spells greater political influence for imperialism.

POLITICAL CONSEQUENCES OF IMPERIALIST AID

Apart from the direct impact of its aid, imperialism realized other political benefits from government largesse. In the French case aid was 'an important weapon for undermining political independence.' The French government aimed to establish client elites by balancing the chronic deficits in underdeveloped states' budgets. In addition, France maintained military bases and French soldiers in its former empire and kept these semi-colonies in its currency zone.[48] Foreign aid led to direct interference in the recipient's foreign policy: in the Indo-Pakistan conflict of 1965, the west withheld its aid as blackmail to pressure the Indian government into ceasing hostilities.[49]

There are political costs involved in technical aid as well. Although technical assistance does supply needed specialists for local enterprises and state administration, it also spreads bourgeois ideological influence in the developing countries.[50] The two sides of the coin come out more clearly in a discussion reprinted in *International Affairs*, Shatalov noted that 'engineers and technicians in the third world countries have an exceptional part to play in transplanting the achievements of science and technology.' V.G. Solodovnikov, however, observed that 'Today Africa is overrun by specialists from the imperialist countries who are influencing not only economic development, but also politics, ideology, and education in the African countries. France alone has almost 40,000 specialists there, most of them university, high school and secondary school teachers.'[51] The price of World Bank aid is imperialist economic advice to pursue a path of continued dependence. Thailand was advised in the 1959 report of the World Bank to close its state-owned enterprises because they were unprofitable and not to develop heavy industry but to expand the production of raw materials and light industry by the private sector. This was the imperialist ideological line in a nutshell.[52]

Further political consequences of imperialist aid can be seen in the activity of the 'Aid Club,' the consortium organized by the World Bank with the western donor countries. The major characteristic of this aid was its great increase after 1958. In the first three years of its second five-year plan, India received Rs 4,850 million in aid, or 19 per cent of its annual expenses. Soviet observers, however, were ambiguous about this increase, which they condemned as both too big and too small. At one moment the increase of aid was expected to raise the level of India's debt and so her dependence. V.I. Pavlov found an indication of this dependence in the western insistence that India spend more of its own precious foreign currency reserves to achieve its plan targets. In the next breath he attacked this aid as too niggardly: 'despite its increase, the volume of credits has remained insufficient' to cover India's deficit.[53]

The politics of the Aid Club was seen as a western effort to frustrate and pressure India in its planning process. The western powers 'postponed as long as possible their decision on the financing of the third five-year plan programme.' The third meeting of the Aid Club held in Paris in September 1960 was put off to the month of May 1961. As a result, by the beginning of 1961 India had already received Rs 2.4 billion in Soviet credits for the third plan, compared with Rs 240 million promised by the USA up to that date. Nor did the May meeting produce any concrete results, though one month later India received the promise of Rs 10.2 billion for the first two years of the plan. Even counting the $250 million loan made by the World Bank, India received $810 million less than she had asked for. Again in 1962 India received promises of credits amounting to $2,200 million, which was $400 million less than the amount requested. The delays, the procrastination, and the inability to cover the Indian deficit signified to Soviet observers that the western powers had not renounced their policy of using 'aid' to put pressure on India.[54]

The fact that the aid provided by international financial institutions seemed no different either in aim or character from bilateral imperialist credits explains why the International Bank for Reconstruction and Development (the World Bank) is considered by all Soviet analysts to be under US domination. When giving statistics on American aid R.A. Ulyanovsky included those provided by the World Bank and its subsidiaries.[55] In the Soviet view the World Bank reflected its American control by giving loans for infrastructural development that did not lead to economic independence or provide competition with imperialism.[56] As an example, in the $784 million loan of the IBRD to India made on 31 October 1961 the state sector received $529 million, of which $377 million was for rail transport, $64 million for port construction, $74 million for the construction of hydroelectric stations, and $6 million for the national airlines. 'For its *industry* the state sector did not receive a single dollar.' On the other hand, the whole amount of the $255 million which went to the private sector went for industrial construction.[57] 'In the 1971-2 fiscal year the IBRD allocated 52.6 per cent of all loan commitments for the construction of infrastructure projects, as against 17.4 per cent for industry and 6.2 per cent for agriculture.'[58]

The activity of international financial organizations is seen as one of the most characteristic manifestations of 'collective colonialism.' Lumping together American private and governmental investment with that of the World Bank, Pavlov estimated that over $600 million had been spent to strengthen the Indian private sector up to the inauguration of the third five-year plan in the attempt to resist industrial growth in the public sector. This policy of interfering in the developing countries' policy-making by providing advice hostile to the development of industry in the state sector has continued. The World Bank used its participation in the Indus River project to intervene as a mediator in Indo-Pakistan relations. It recommended that India devalue the rupee and change its policy to attract more foreign capital. It even refused in 1966 to provide further aid till it had approved a detailed version of the fourth five-year plan.[59]

However negative the cumulative Soviet assessment of the nature and impact of imperialist aid may be, the Soviet conclusion is not the negative one the reader has been prepared to expect. On closer inspection a number of hints can be found that give the moderates' view of imperialism greater, even decisive weight. V.I. Pavlov conceded that western credits helping to construct such infrastructural components as railroads, communications, and power generation were not simply second best but necessary for the economy's development: 'Without the development of these branches, the economic self-sufficiency of any country is unthinkable.'[60] Without the point being emphasized, it is also clear from Soviet texts that this infrastructural development, largely financed by imperialist aid, takes place mainly in the public sector. Though the impression is mostly given that imperialist aid floods in to gain control of the commanding heights in the developing countries' economy, other remarks show that western aid is too small, not too great: India did not get all the aid from the World Bank that it needed for the third plan.

Though the high rate of interest demanded by the donor countries is presented as extortionate, aid is also presented by Soviet economists as a kind of compensation for the losses suffered by the developing countries in the 'nonequivalent exchange' from which their exports suffer. In Rymalov's terms aid is 'ordinarily a fraction of the billion-dollar profits reaped by the monopolies'[61] and less than the losses incurred from the unequal terms of trade. The implication of such remarks is that western aid is positive, if insufficient. Soviet analysts of India's problems more recently have considered western aid to be necessary and no longer feel the need to write the word between quotation marks.[62] That they consider western aid to be ultimately more productive than the reverse is implied by their statements that if it were not for socialist aid the developing countries would not get any aid from imperialism. The Soviet Union is surely not taking credit for providing the third world with harmful goods. The classic example of this position is the assertion that western (British and German) aid to India's public sector steel industry came only after the Soviet Union had signed an agreement to build the famous Bhilai works for India. Rymalov cited Khrushchev as saying that capitalist aid is 'a kind of assistance rendered by the Soviet Union to these states.'[63] 'This aid which the capitalist countries are planning to extend to the states which have recently won their independence should also be viewed as a particular kind of Soviet aid to these states. If the Soviet Union did not exist, is it likely that the monopolies of the imperialist powers would aid the underdeveloped countries? Of course, not.'[64] Even the World Bank, 'which is controlled by the United States,' was forced by Soviet competition to make concessions in the field of aid to the public sector.[65]

Soviet authors continue to maintain that imperialism is responsible for causing the foreign financing problems of the developing countries. Since it is
through the extraction of super profits and non-equivalent exchange that the imperialist powers exploit the developing countries,[66] they have an obligation to
recompense the damage done to their former colonies.[67] The implication is clear.
Imperialism should give aid, which can after all contribute to development in the
third world.

Should the developing countries then resist western aid? Pavlov asks this question in relation to India's case and, as an answer, quotes Ajoy Ghosh, the late
Indian communist party leader, as saying that foreign aid should by no means be
terminated: 'We have never considered and we still do not consider that India
should not receive loans coming from countries outside the socialist camp. On
the other hand the Indian people have the right to insist that the loans India
receives from any country are given under conditions as favourable as those
received from the socialist countries.'[68]

V.S. Baskin referred to Lenin's approval of the application of foreign capital
and, considering aid to be in addition a legitimate compensation for damages suffered, asserted that the developing countries 'have every reason to demand of
western countries a significant broadening of financial and technical aid at low
rates (less than 3 per cent), long periods of amortization and repayment by
national production.'[69] But there is a limit. Looking at Africa, Solodovnikov disapproved of the high portion (50 to 60 per cent) of the local development programmes that are financed from foreign sources. The developing nations of
Africa, he felt, should first and foremost concentrate on mobilizing their internal
resources: 'The major role should be played by the home sources of economic
development with the external ones being just an additional factor that can
sometimes boost or facilitate development.'[70]

Yet the insufficiency of exports and of internal sources of accumulation restricts economic development, making the dependence on foreign aid 'unavoidable.'[71] If the developing countries need more aid, but only on 'as favourable
terms as those we get from socialist countries,' what are the qualities that aid
must have to be fully acceptable to the Soviet economists? Their exposition of
the merits of socialist aid provides their answer.

10

Socialist aid

Soviet aid has indeed an excellent image in the Soviet press. Whether it be the feat of taming the Nile at the Aswan dam or breaking the American embargo on Cuba's sugar market, the USSR has, in the writings of Soviet commentators, captured the imagination of the world in its own efforts to meet the capital needs of the developing countries. Reading their analysis of their own aid is like looking at imperialist aid through a glass, but brightly. Whatever was negative and suspect in their assessment of imperialist activities becomes positive and magnanimous in their report of their own system's performance. In presenting their interpretation they follow the same pattern used to analyse imperialist aid: they present socialist aid as an integral part of socialist foreign policy, then examine its effects, both economic and political, in order to draw their final conclusions.

SOVIET AID, INTEGRAL TO SOVIET FOREIGN POLICY

The Soviet self-image on the international scene is that of vanguard of the world revolutionary process, having an impact on the continuing revolution in the colonial and ex-colonial world far out of proportion to its material contribution. In summary form the main points are as follows:
- Prior to 1917 the colonies and semi-colonies of the underdeveloped world could look to no foreign government for support.
- With the great October Revolution, the Soviet Union announced the new principles of its foreign policy as an expression of the international policy of the working class and its communist vanguards. The renunciation of annexations and the revolutionary appeal to the toiling masses of Russia and the Far East showed that this policy accorded with the interests of all nations, including the most backward and exploited.

- 'Great October' was integrally linked to the breakdown of the colonial system. By showing that independence from imperialist domination was possible, the Soviet Union infused the colonial peoples with new faith in their own strength.
- The USSR's powerful example of rapid progress from backwardness showed what socialism could achieve by industrialization in underdeveloped countries.
- The Soviet Union has always given open and firm support for the national liberation struggle since it is the internationalist duty of the victorious working class to help the people of the third world break all their oppressive fetters.
- While this support was mainly moral and political up to the Second World War, since then the USSR has provided technical and economic assistance to eliminate all survivals of colonialism.
- Marxism repudiates the export of revolution ('any attempt to use assistance to backward nations as a means of imposing the new social and political system can only undermine friendship').
- The Soviet Union's victory in the second world war and the emergence of the world socialist system in Europe and Asia were decisive factors stimulating the national liberation movement.
- The world socialist system's support subsequently created favourable international prerequisites for the rapid victory of the national liberation movement. Imperialism was thus unable to repress the national liberation movement after the second world war since it now had to bear in mind that the newly sovereign states can rely on the immense economic and military potential of the world socialist system shielding the independence of the ex-colonies.
- The aim of the Soviet Union is the development of good-neighbourly relations with all countries without exception; Soviet policy toward a particular country is independent of the latter's social state system but depends on the country's government's desire to establish friendly ties with the Soviet Union on the basis of equality and reciprocity. Hence Socialist aid is different in basic principle from imperialist 'aid.'

THE NATURE OF SOVIET AID

Just as Soviet foreign policy is different in principle, so Soviet aid is 'not motivated by temporary, tactical or egoistic considerations; it is intrinsic to the very nature of the socialist system and the humanistic ideas of marxism-leninism.' Disinterested in its humanitarian motivation, the aim of Soviet aid is 'to strengthen the positions of underdeveloped countries in their struggle against monopoly capital.'[1] Or, as defined by Andreasyan and Kondratev, the aims of Soviet aid are to liquidate imperialist exploitation, create genuinely equal and friendly co-operation, develop the national economy, strengthen the state sector, reinforce its planned base, realize industrialization and diversification, and suppress backwardness.[2] In short, its aims are to answer the third world's urgent development needs: create the preconditions for rapid economic and cultural advance in the less privileged countries.

The difference in aims is further expressed in the claimed difference in nature between Soviet aid and western aid. While the latter represents 'the product of unrestrained exploitation by monopoly capital of their own people .. including the underdeveloped countries' and serves in turn 'in open or masked form as instruments of further exploitation,' Soviet credits on the contrary 'represent a portion of the material wealth created by the Soviet people and constitute their own property. Consequently they cannot serve the aims of enslavement and exploitation of other nations.'[3] Or, in Baskin's words, being part of the material wealth produced by labour free of exploitation, this aid logically cannot be a means of exploiting others.[4]

Nor do Soviet credits constitute an 'export of capital.' Soviet aid in their view is free from any shade of exploitation: not keeping any equity in the projects it helps construct, Soviet aid does not extract superprofits or take root in the economy as does private foreign investment. Rather, loans from socialist countries to the state sector acquire the character of state capital in the developing countries' own capitalist paths of development; they help fight for economic independence from imperialism by reinforcing the positions of national capital. Socialist aid is provided magnanimously; unlike western aid it is not the expiation of a moral debt since it is not compensation for damages caused by imperialist exploitation.[5] Furthermore, socialist aid is not a surplus that has to be forced on a reluctant third world. In a planned socialist economy there is no overproduction of commodities and no financial surplus for which some outlet must be found abroad.

This uniqueness is seen both in the political and economic characteristics of socialist aid. Once completed, the projects created with socialist aid come under the full legal control of the host country, directed by national cadres. No concessions are asked, no share is given in the future profits of the enterprise, and no demands are made for a right to control the plant once constructed.[6] The arrangements under which aid projects are worked out guarantee the full equality of both sides and the mutual respect of each country's sovereignty.[7] There are no conditions leading to intervention in the internal affairs of the recipient countries. And there are no demands for repayments in the form of military or political commitments.[8]

ECONOMIC EFFECTS

The economic characteristics of socialist aid are equally designed to maximize the independence of the receiving countries. Repayments are spread over twelve years, start after the delivery of equipment, and bear a low rate of interest. Payments are arranged on barter terms using the receiving country's own products. This conserves the recipient's foreign currency and increases its foreign market. India may indeed be the most capitalist of the third world countries, but the Soviets have no hesitation in representing their aid to India not just as one of the most important constant factors of third world development 'whose significance has been vividly demonstrated by the twenty-year history of the Indian Republic' but as an example of 'co-operation of the emergent countries with the Soviet Union and other socialist countries.' Furthermore, Soviet aid continues to have a significance far beyond its economic developmental impact and far beyond India's own boundaries. 'It is difficult indeed to overestimate the role played by Soviet-Indian ties in promoting security in Asia and helping the nations freeing themselves from colonialism to advance to prosperity and progress.'[9]

The Soviet writers' description of the conditions for the construction of the big iron and steel complex at Bhilai, the first showpiece of Soviet aid outside the communist bloc, illustrates their view of their own aid: Soviet industry undertook the technical control of the construction and was to deliver the equipment for the plant, in addition, the USSR guaranteed sending the necessary specialists to India as well as training the requisite Indian personnel. A maximum utilization of Indian industry was foreseen in the production at Bhilai of the necessary materials for the steel mill. As Rymalov put it, 'contrary to the USA, the Soviet Union showed in practice its good will to lend assistance in offering its credit at advantageous conditions for the construction of heavy industrial enterprises in the underdeveloped countries.' The economic consequences of this aid are equally exemplary. The construction at Bhilai, in this regard also, was of the greatest importance for India's economic development. Its production target of a million tons of steel for 1960 was to be one-third of the country's production capacity at that time; when expanded to its planned full capacity of 2.5 million tons by the end of the third five-year plan it would be producing one-quarter of the entire steel production projected for 1965. 'By this token, the production of this complex will reduce at one blow the dependence of the country on importing metal from abroad.' To this basic contribution must be added the fact that the unit cost of production is considerably lower than the price of imported metal, allowing India to economize $150 of its foreign exchange for every ton of steel produced at Bhilai. Compared to the German and British steel mills put up at Rourkela and Durgapur, it was constructed more quickly and produced more output of higher quality and with a greater rate of profit. In 1960-1 it made a profit of Rs 15.3 million for the state's budget while the other two plants made losses of Rs 7.1 million and Rs 15.6 million respectively. In 1974-5 Bhilai's profits were Rs 390 million.[10] Little wonder that Khrushchev referred to the success of this enterprise as 'not just representing a step in India's industrial development but also a symbol of the co-operation of Soviet and Indian specialists.'[11]

A whole-hearted commitment to industrial construction is a continuing theme of Soviet statements on aid which, according to one source, had by 1973 been allocated as follows: 'roughly 90 per cent of the means envisaged in the Soviet Union's agreements on economic and technical cooperation with the developing states are channelled into the buildup of production branches, with over 75 per cent going into the manufacturing and power industries. Over 50 per cent are earmarked for the building of heavy industries.'[12] In India Soviet credits have also gone to build a long list of key installations producing the means of production in heavy industry: a factory for heavy machinery able to equip a steel plant with the capacity of a million tons in Ranchi, Bihar; a mining equipment plant at Durgapur, West Bengal, to produce forty thousand tons of mechanical equipment per year or mechanize annually the extraction of a million tons of coal.

It is not enough to construct heavy industrial projects in the state sector; they have to be operated efficiently and profitably at their designed capacity, and they have to find a market for their products. Towards the end of the 1960s, as the first generation of the Soviet heavy industry projects were completed, they developed serious problems at both the supply and the marketing ends of the production process. Supplies of raw materials and fuel for the plants were in some cases insufficient, preventing full operation and demonstrating the need for a more integrated economic base. Even when the plants were able to produce they could not find a sufficient market to keep them operating at capacity. This requires the solution of a whole range of new problems: the organization of planning and management, efficiency and profitability of operation, training of personnel and swift growth in labour productivity, questions of supply and the sale of finished goods, and so on.[13]

The protocol India signed on 19 December 1968 with the Russians incorporated measures 'designed to raise the economic efficiency of industrial enterprises built in India's state sector under the Soviet-Indian agreements.' The Soviets were to send specialists as consultants on these problems and, more concretely, to help develop markets for their own aid flagships. They were to help the Ranchi heavy-machine-building plant in filling orders for complete machinery and equipment for the first stage of the Bokaro steel works, thus demonstrating the viability of the national production of the means of production. They were to help adapt the mining equipment plant at Durgapur to manufacture new products in demand on Indian and foreign markets. In general they were to help design enterprises that could place orders for complete machines at the machine-building plants (Ranchi, Hardwar, and Durgapur) and at the precision instruments factory (Kota). The message of this new stage of Soviet aid was that Soviet-Indian economic relations must be practical. They must 'take into account the structural changes in the Indian economy during the years of its independent development, its export potentialities and import needs.' The new protocol thus foresaw India's exporting of more non-traditional items and importing machine tools and needed geological equipment.[14]

Summing up two decades of Soviet aid to India, a 1976 report stated: 'In that great Asian country more than 90 large industrial projects have been or are being built or designed with Soviet assistance. The projects now in operation produce 30 per cent of India's steel, 50 per cent of her oil, 30 per cent of refined oil, and 80 per cent of metallurgical equipment.'[15]

The Soviets also deliver equipment and provide technical assistance for projects in the infrastructure: hydroelectric power stations in India, the colossal Aswan Dam in Egypt, port and road facilities in Yemen. One assessment noted the following figures: of 3.5 billion rubles in credits, 70 per cent were for industrial construction and would increase steel production by 5.5 million tons, iron ore production by 4.3 million tons, the generation of electricity by 4.7 million kilowatt hours, coal production by 2.7 million tons, and refined oil by 8.6 million tons. The Aswan Dam in Egypt was to increase the cultivated land of Egypt by one-third and would have an electrical generating capacity of 2.1 million kilowatt hours.[16] Another assessment put the total socialist bloc aid figure at 5 billion rubles in credits, of which 4 billion from the USSR had gone to thirty countries.[17]

It is not just in heavy industry or the complementary infrastructure that Soviet credits finds application. However much Soviet economists may bemoan elsewhere the one-sided dependence of economies exporting agricultural raw materials, Soviet aid also goes to developing the traditional export branches. 'Large tracts of jungle have been cleared for sugar-cane and cotton cultivation with the aid of Soviet specialists and machines.'[18] Apart from its aid to industry the Soviet Union has provided assistance in the development of the medical industry and agriculture, notably by creating a model mechanized farm as the property of the Indian state.[19]

Since economic and social progress in the third world directly hinges on a solution to the 'problem of national personnel, on the scale and rate at which these countries are able to train their own specialists who will serve the interests of their peoples,' helping to train personnel is part of the anti-imperialist struggle for national liberation.[20] Besides contributing to the development of most of the important productive sectors in the Indian economy – and the other socialist countries co-operate in this international effort – the Soviet Union provides technical assistance, training cadres, and specialists to use modern techniques. Specialists are trained in the Soviet Union while workers learn new jobs on the actual construction site. Eight hundred engineers and technicians received training in Soviet establishments for the construction of Bhilai. As a result, all the operations in Bhilai are currently carried on 'exclusively by Indian specialists.'[21] The establishment of the Bombay Technological Institute for twelve hundred students and five hundred post-graduates was the most spectacular Soviet capital project in university training. Another was the Conakry institute in Guinea. More selectively, Soviet economic missions give advice on specific problems such as setting up the mechanism for long-term planning. 'By 1974 Soviet figures showed that 15,000 students from the third world had studied in higher educational institutions of the USSR, of which 53 per cent had trained in the engineering and technical professions, 25 per cent in pedagogy, 12 per cent in medicine and 10 per cent in agriculture.'[22]

THE POLITICAL EFFECTS

The political impact of this aid derives from its economic consequences. Soviet aid for industrial development has broken the imperialists' monopoly on the supply of industrial equipment and advanced technological knowhow. The existence of an alternative supply of aid has itself increased the ex-colonies' margin of independent political manœuvre. While imperialist aid entails the maintenance of economic and therefore political dependence, Soviet credits facilitate the creation of an independent national economy. There is no doubt in any marxist-leninist's writings that Soviet aid accords with the underdeveloped countries' best vital interests.[23] The Soviets assert non-interference to be a basic feature of their aid. They also claim that socialist aid in itself has a progressive impact on the entire political system. It stimulates an interest in socialism, engendering a desire to use such socialist methods as planning and state-operated industrial production. It offers moral support to the progressive forces in the country, promoting their unity and encouraging – through the development of heavy industry – the physical growth and consolidation of the working class.[24] By sharing in the gains of the socialist system, aid orients the underdeveloped country toward economic and technical co-operation with the socialist camp. Even if it is the bourgeoisie that is in power, aid 'is nevertheless of assistance to the people.' Its prime purpose is to build up the state economic sector which is, after all, the potential basis for non-capitalist development. The rapid growth of the working class re-adjusts the balance of socioeconomic forces to the detriment of the private capitalist sector.[25] Supporting the nation as a whole, rather than 'any particular group within the country,' Soviet aid applies the principle of peaceful coexistence helping different social systems with widely different ideologies – the parliamentary republic of India, the monarchy of Afghanistan, the feudal state of Yemen – strengthening their fight for genuine independence,[26] and demolishing the artificial barriers erected by imperialism to prevent equal co-operation between nations.

THE CREDIBILITY GAP

The Soviets' description of their own aid programme is painted in such glowing red that the spectre of a credibility gap confronts the reader: is it not all too good to be true? It is here that a careless, hyperbolic style damages what is a very strong case. But the material is presented without the detail and balanced qualifications that would make the analysis rise above the level of propaganda. For Soviet aid clearly does offer very significant advantages. It does extend the range of choice for countries shopping for external capital sources and does therefore increase their independence. Where they are having difficulties selling their traditional exports on the western markets, the repayment of their Soviet loans in traditional goods does provide a net gain. The fact that Soviet loans were provided at a much lower interest rate must certainly have been a stimulus to improving western aid conditions. There is no doubt that the introduction of peaceful competition into the international politics of aid giving significantly increased the flow of aid, at least to those countries strategically enough placed to be able to play this cold war game. For the would-be non-aligned country to receive both western and eastern aid gave neutralism a practical content. Ideologically too, the concentration of Soviet aid on heavy industry constructed as nationalized enterprises with no residual foreign participation in the management of these firms coincided with the socialistic aspirations of government leaders wanting to increase these states' active participation in the economy and so reduce the often overpowering influence of foreign corporations in their own economic affairs. Furthermore, in actual practice the Soviets' aid has turned out to be exceptionally effective. In neighbouring Afghanistan the Soviet Union by 1964 had given $375 million worth of industrial, infrastructural, and agricultural assistance with great flexibility and without political interference. Afghanistan is an example of the scrupulousness with which the Soviet has provided aid to non-communist countries without attempts at political subversion or undue ideological pressure. Guinea, Egypt, and Cuba can all testify to the essential political help provided at moments of crisis. When Guinea was cut off by de Gaulle upon accepting his offer of independence, the Soviet Union responded immediately with what was needed to affirm her independence: rifles for its troops, the necessary imports and markets for Guinea's exports.[27]

The picture is not, however, entirely to be painted in luminous pink. Socialist aid has known its defeats and difficulties as well as its triumphs. Even in the spectacular and successful Bhilai, there has been major trouble with the forced blast furnace in the second stage of its expansion. According to Goldman, the Russians have refused to turn over design and control decisions to the Indians, contrary to their claims in theory and contrary also to the Germans' practice at Durgapur. While the Soviets accuse the imperialists of tying their aid, all Soviet aid projects have to be fully supplied from the USSR, even when superior western equipment may be needed. The Soviets, too, have had their white elephants: a luxury hotel in Afghanistan that is barely used and a third sports stadium in Mali; and of course in Indonesia, that land of disappearing aid projects, their own disasters rival the most catastrophic of the western donations.[28] While Soviet writers will admit in conversations that their aid sometimes falls short of perfection, there is no hint of self-critical awareness in their publications. This is unfortunate, for, were they able to write in a more balanced and comprehensive perspective, noting the shortcomings as well as the advantages of their own aid, their readers would not find it necessary to check with western research to corroborate their judgments.

A second shortcoming in the Soviet self-analysis of aid is the surprisingly superficial treatment they give it, when in fact their case is so strong. As a rule, they will simply outline the advantages in general of their aid and give as illustrations journalistic, sketchy paeans on the spectacular progress of, say, the Aswan Dam in its harnessing the forces of nature. One exception to this superficiality is the book written by Yershov on the socialist states' participation in the construction of a state oil industry for India.

THE YERSHOV STORY

In the colonial period the international oil monopolies had already cornered the Indian oil market in all its spheres from import to distribution. The British company Burma-Shell virtually ran the oil department of the colonial administration. Come independence, the national bourgeoisie's plan to accelerate Indian development and strengthen her economic independence required a major expansion of petroleum production. The huge burden of importing increased quantities of oil products, aggravated by the shortage of foreign exchange in a country with a chronic deficit in its balance of payments, made the creation of a national oil industry an urgent priority. The imperialist oil monopolies, however, were not interested in investing capital in India when they already had a stranglehold on the local market and could make huge profits from importing oil from their own low-cost Middle East refineries. They accordingly spread the idea that India had no oil deposits of her own. Only reluctantly did they accede to the government's request to set up refineries on Indian soil, a concession that was conditioned partially by the extortionary privileges extracted from the government, partially from the country's penury in foreign exchange which restricted the amount of crude oil it could in any case import. While their refineries were an improvement for India (at Rs 35 per ton, this meant a foreign exchange saving of Rs 12 million per annum from 1955 to 1961), the benefit was largely offset by the repatriation of the oil companies' profits. Even so, the three foreign oil refineries did not satisfy India's growing demand and only further deepened her dependence on the monopolies' supplies. Worse, the oil companies actively undermined Indian independence: they operated a de facto cartel, fixing prices at the arbitrary and exorbitant level of the cost of oil in the Texan gulf, dividing up the local oil market, maintaining a united front against the national bourgeoisie's attempt to break their monopoly, and waging a concerted campaign against the construction of a public sector in the oil industry.[29]

All, however, was not lost, since to slay, or at least contain, the imperialist dragon and rescue the developing damsel India possessed two weapons: internally its state capitalist sector, and externally genuine aid from the socialist camp. With the petty and middle bourgeoisie too weak to undertake the costly project of oil exploration and refining and with the big bourgeoisie reluctant to do battle with the foreign companies, it was clearly only by implementing the government's 1948 policy of developing key industries in the public sector that India could satisfy its urgent need for expanded oil production. The creation of the Oil and Natural Gas Commission (ONGC) in 1955 was a necessary, but not sufficient, condition for establishing a state oil industry. Without technical expertise and extensive capital, the ONGC could neither seek oil nor exploit the discoveries, as the foreign oil companies did not hesitate to remind it. It was at this point that the socialist camp came to the rescue, first in the form of a team of Soviet geologists making a five-month geological survey and submitting an optimistic exploration project which the government incorporated in its second five-year plan; second, with prospecting and drilling equipment supplied by the Soviet and Rumanian governments under easy credit terms (Rs 850 million repayable in twelve years at 2.5 per cent); third, by training five thousand oil specialists and workers at Baku and Krasnoda. The triumphal discovery of oil at Cambay and other sites exploded the myth of Indian oil poverty, reduced India's dependence on the oil monopolies and provided the basis for consolidating this part of the public sector.

Having helped in the location of its petroleum resources, the socialist camp proceeded to help the Indian public sector construct the refineries that both the World Bank and the foreign oil cartels had opposed. The Rumanian government agreed to build a refinery at Gulati and the Soviet Union to construct refineries at Barauni and Koyali. The advantages of these new additions to the public sector were legion. Not only was India's productive capacity to be increased by 7.25 million tons per year by the end of the third plan but the public sector was to make a significant inroad into what had been an exclusive reserve of foreign capital, gaining 40 per cent of the Indian market. This meant both that the state could benefit from the high profit rate of oil refining (recouping its initial outlay within two or three years) and that, in learning to build its own refineries, India could progressively lower the foreign exchange costs of such public sector plant construction.

The saga of socialist support for national petrochemical development does not end here. In pursuing the logic of an integrated public oil industry, India set up the corporation Indian Oil to market the products of the nationalized refineries, to supply other public enterprises with oil products, in short to share in the responsibility and profits of oil distribution at the same time as it ended the foreign monopoly in this field. As little could be done without a reliable source of kerosene and diesel oil greater than the low capacity of Indian wells, and as the foreign companies still resisted supplying any oil that they were not going to distribute themselves, a contract signed in 1960 with the USSR solved this problem also. Soyuznefteksport agreed to supply India with kerosene and diesel oil to end her shortage and save the foreign exchange at the same time: payment was to be in rupees at prices lower than the American and British companies were asking. The 18.4 per cent profit made in 1962-3 vindicated the policy of expanding the public industrial sector as a means for accelerating the rate of internal accumulation and taking India a step nearer true independence from the foreign monopolies.

The final by-product of this growing public sector has been the reaction of imperialism. Having frustrated in vain the state's successful venture in oil development, the oil companies reluctantly capitulated on a series of points. They signed new agreements incorporating their Indian operations as national rupee companies, lowered their prices in the face of Soviet competition, and, in the case of the American Phillips Petroleum Company, even agreed to participate in the construction of a nationalized refinery with the government holding 51 per cent of the share capital. Though modifying their line considerably, the imperialists did not change their basic strategy of maintaining control of the Indian oil market and extracting maximum profits: they forced the government to accept some agreements that perpetuated the monopolies' long list of special advantages in importing equipment and exporting profits.[30]

Devoted to showing how correct the state capitalist path of development is, how good are the socialists and how bad are the capitalists in this particular branch of India's industrial development, Yershov's story has the immediate strength of consistency and conviction. What makes this Soviet version of the first decade of India's oil development more persuasive is the large extent to which it is substantiated by non-Soviet observers in India. If one compares Yershov's thesis with three non-communist statements on the same subject – an official statement by P.R. Nayak, chairman of the ONGC, a more radical view by R.N. Gupta published in the *Economic Review*, and a more dispassionate study by M. Subhan – one can see that, despite the variations in tone between the discussion of an administrator-politician, a socialist with no patience for the private sector and a scholar with less obvious axes to grind, the story is essentially the same.[31]

All versions agree on the large measure of progress achieved in a relatively short period in the governmental sector. All, too, verify that this had been progress made in the face of deliberate resistance by the western oil companies. Nayak contents himself with noting that the search for oil had not received any significant attention 'for various reasons' which he does not spell out 'despite the *known* fact that India contained very large sedimentary areas normally regarded as favourable for oil deposits.'[32] Less inclined to mince his words, Gupta declares that the oil companies 'alleged' (i.e. falsely) that 'India was almost a dry region for oil reserves' even though this view was 'given the lie' by the geologist D.N. Wadia in the 1940s.[33] Pointing out that the oil exploration would nevertheless have been a risky venture, Subhan, for his part, notes with more indulgence the economic factors that restrained the oil companies: the small, scattered consumption of petroleum products which, even in 1953, was only 3.3 per cent of the total energy consumed in India.[34] On the subsequent resistance by the west to state-sector oil development, one can find a verification in Nayak's reporting of the 'much cautionary advice' that the government received about the risks and inexpediency of such a large state operation. Of the many countries that the government approached for assistance in developing refineries for the state sector, responses only came from the Soviet Union and Rumania.[35] Subhan corroborates that the World Bank questioned the economics of these refineries condemning the Indian policy as 'ideological.'[36]

On the positive side of the Soviet story there seems little room for scepticism. In Subhan's judgment the discovery of a number of oil fields where none were thought to exist was 'helped immeasurably by the Soviet and Rumanian technicians.' The second decisive factor in the development of the government's oil policy was the substantial technical and financial help given India by the Russians and Rumanians. Nayak records that of the 675 foreign specialists the great majority came from the USSR and many from Rumania, that the Soviet Union was the main country whose facilities were used for training technicians abroad, that the socialist governments provided exemplary collaboration in building the first state sector refineries, especially in affording 'the maximum possible facilities, including the provisions for our use of Soviet norms and standards for refinery designs, a sphere of information which is often regarded as a jealously guarded secret.'[37] As for the acrimonious question of oil prices, it is, according to Subhan, 'one field in which Russian help has proved invaluable to the Indian government: the Soviet offer of crude oil had to be declined when the British and American companies refused to refine it, but the latter reduced their price to the Russian quotation of 97/6 per ton from 112 shillings.

It is interesting to note that the tension existing between the oil companies and the Indian government appears much sharper from the Indian than from the Soviet writings. While in the Soviet view the compromise between the big bourgeoisie and imperialism prevents any great hostility between the two parties, Subhan, writing in 1962, felt that the breach seemed to be complete: 'All recent evidence suggests that the Indian government is determined to establish the supremacy of the public sector in the industrial development of the country.'[38] An otherwise colourless and sober article, mentioning the difficulties arising from the distribution by the public sector of Soviet kerosene and diesel oil, states that the private oil companies had substantially reduced their supplies to certain areas (in apparent retaliation). The government assumed 'massive powers' to ensure against a possible breakdown of distribution. That the problem was solved by mutual discussion making it unnecessary to use these prerogatives implies the existence of considerable tension, as does his conclusion that 'the Indian Oil Corporation has done exceedingly well in the recent crisis.'[39]

On one point of substance, however, the Soviet analysis is seriously deficient: the acknowledgement of aid provided the same sector but by western governments. From reading Yershov one would conclude that it was only the socialist countries that had taken any part at all in aiding India's oil industry. But Nayak makes it clear that assistance came from many quarters: the UN special fund assisted the ONGC to set up a research and training institute; the Institut Français du Petrole helped set up the Indian Institute of Petroleum in a 'shining example of foreign collaboration in a vital field;' the Italian State Oil Corporation (ENI) helped lay 2,000 miles of pipeline and train Indian engineers; India has also benefited from the UN Technical Assistance Program, the Colombo Plan, and even the USA.[40] This co-operation may only have come with the proven success of the government's capacity to develop its own oil industry, but it came nevertheless. There is no indication in the Soviet story of how western competition forced a reduction in the prices charged the Indians by Soviets in building new refineries. This information substantially undermines the simplistic manicheism which leads one to believe that whatever the west promotes is basically harmful whereas all socialist co-operation has the Midas touch. Even in such an area where Soviet aid has been the most helpful, and the west, represented by the international petroleum giants, has in fact been the most unco-operatively hostile, the persuasive power of the Soviet analysis would be increased by recognizing what positive elements there are on the side of both western aid and of foreign private investment. Even K.D. Malaviya, the former oil minister reputed for his intransigence against the foreign companies, wrote in 1956 that 'what the foreign oil companies are doing for us is in many ways a distinct contribution to our expanding economy.'[41]

THE NEED FOR FACTS

What the Soviet assessments of their own aid programmes need to be useful, apart from a more self-critical approach in the treatment, is more detailed and complete information. They claim that Soviet aid is cheaper because the rate of interest is lower. But the interest rate is not the only factor involved in the calculation of cost: if the project's price is higher than an equivalent western package, the lower interest loses its significance. If the prices paid for the receiving country's reimbursing exports are below world prices, the claimed financial superiority of Soviet aid will be greatly reduced. Once again it is to western sources that one has to turn to find out this information. In actual fact, the Aswan Dam quotation by the Soviets was lower than the German bid,[42] though it would seem that a new refinery projected for the Indian state sector was to be priced higher than a western rival. Information on Soviet pricing is, of course, not fully revealing, because of the arbitrary exchange rates fixed for the unconvertible ruble, but when measured against the amount of products that must be exported to pay the price, the local government can calculate whether or not an aid proposal is advantageous.

A similarly vital area that the Soviets leave undiscussed is the problem of capital intensity. In Goldman's view, Soviet projects tend to be too big: the polytechnical institute constructed in Guinea has a capacity for fourteen hundred students yet an enrolment of only one hundred.[43] What kind of planning goes on in deciding on the viability of a project? What kind of criteria are used to choose between alternatives? What efforts do Soviet consultants make to relate a project's size to the needs of the local economy? These critical questions are not asked, let alone answered, by the Soviet analyst.

PROSPECTS OF SOVIET AID

There is a final and even more crucial problem that one would hope the Soviet writers could discuss with greater frankness: the prospects for the expansion of

Soviet aid programmes in the future. The reader of Soviet specialists' writings on aid can only gather that there are definite limits beyond which Soviet aid will not be expanded. One indication of this is the vociferous rejection of moral responsibility for the problems of the developing countries.

A firm indication of Soviet intentions could be seen in their response to the pressure put by UNCTAD on the developed countries to increase their aid to 1 per cent of their national income. The Soviet response was blunt: 'It goes without saying that this demand should not and cannot apply to the socialist countries, which have never plundered and do not plunder the developing countries and cannot therefore be in any way responsible for the consequences of the colonial and imperialist domination which has brought these countries to such a dire economic plight.'[44] The ideological imperative is clear: as Stepanov wrote, the socialist countries cannot allow themselves 'to be put on the same plane as the imperialist states.' A second defence has been an updated version of 'socialism in one country.' Since the socialist countries are performing great historical tasks in founding a new society, they consider the creation of socialism as 'fulfilment of their international duty.'[45] The implication is that the third world benefits indirectly from the construction of socialism and that, by spending their capital on home construction, the socialist bloc countries are in effect aiding the developing countries.

Whatever the justification employed, it is in any case made clear that the Afro-Asian and Latin American countries cannot count on the socialist states satisfying all their aid needs.[46] Soviet commentators of course protest that they will rush to the side of any country transferring to the socialist path of development, but they do not make clear how much aid can be relied on. The impression given is that the Soviet Union will not count the cost in aiding a state on the socialist path. Whether a radical leadership deciding to break its neocolonial bonds would be able to secure an adequate alternative source of capital from the Soviet Union cannot be learned from these writings. It was clear that the flow of capital from the Soviet Union to the developing countries was not likely to increase significantly. Hence the emphasis by Soviet writers on the need for the developing countries to rely first of all on their internal sources of accumulation. Hence too their insistence that trade - especially with the socialist countries - is tantamount to aid, and in the long run healthier.

SOVIET TRADE

The role of the socialist system as principal guarantor of the independence of the underdeveloped countries is claimed as much in the commercial as in the aid relationship. Trade with the socialist system offers the young nations a chance to profit from the successes of socialism 'on the basis of entire equality and recipro-cal advantage.'[47]

Association with the socialist bloc allows the third world to benefit from the 'international socialist division of labour.' This means that, by trading in the world socialist market, they can use the products of advanced socialist indus-tries. As a result they will not need to construct simultaneously all the branches of their economy but can concentrate their attention on the ones essential for the acquisition of their economic independence. For while the 'objective laws' of the world capitalist system offer the developing nations no hope for an im-provement of their plight of overproduction of raw materials and falling prices, the world socialist market offers, in Kodachenko's words, 'the most favourable conditions for mutually advantageous commerce.' Trade with the socialist coun-tries tends to equalize the levels of these countries' development and provides a market sheltered from the price fluctuations characteristic of imperialist com-merce even though based on world prices. It is for this reason that socialist trade with the developing countries should be considered as 'aid allowing them to achieve economic independence.'[48] The proof of the pudding is in the growing dimensions of socialist third world trade. Third world trade with socialist coun-tries multiplied by 6.2 times from 1960 to 1974, from 1,660 million to 10,300 million rubles.[49] 'In Asia this process has embraced almost all the underdeve-loped countries, especially the foreign trade of India.'[50]

India is indeed the star example to which the Soviets point. When speaking of Soviet-Indian trade Russian authors emphasize both its rapid increase since the acquisition of the country's independence and the favourable conditions which characterize these commercial exchanges. Their discussion of this relation pro-vides the best example of their commercial analysis.

The first commercial five-year agreement made on 2 February 1953 estab-lished the ground rules for favourable relations, including payment for India's purchases in rupees, transport of produce exchanged in both Soviet and Indian boats, and the establishment of reciprocal trading accounts. For a country in the midst of balance-of-payments crises the clause ensuring all payments in rupees was especially advantageous in Rymalov's analysis. Of 'particularly great signifi-cance for India's economic development are the deliveries to this country of Soviet industrial equipment which the developing countries cannot procure on the capitalist market.' In addition, India could sell its traditional export pro-ducts at fair prices. By a new agreement signed in December 1955 the Soviet Union was to deliver 'goods of prime necessity for India's economic develop-ment,' such as a million tons of ferrous metal ingots, mining, oil, and other heavy industrial equipment. The receipts from these sales would permit the Soviet Union to buy new raw materials and industrial articles in India, improving by this means the latter's commercial balance. By 1958 the Soviet Union was buying 50 per cent of India's pepper exports, 20 per cent of its raw wool. In addition, 'wanting to encourage the development of Indian industry, the USSR began to buy growing quantities of jute sacks, leather shoes, wool cloth ... and artisanal products.'[51] By 1974, 45 per cent of the USSR's imports from India were manufactured and semi-manufactured products.[52]

The experience of these first years resulted in the signing of a long-term commercial agreement in November 1958, in which both partners granted each other the 'most favoured nation' clause and founded a system of clearing accounts which 'answered India's wish to carry on this trade on a balanced basis without spending any foreign currency.'[53] The agreement of June 1963, which was to double the 1962 volume of exchange by 1966, 'prove[d] the reciprocal interest which both countries have in multiplying their commercial contacts.'[54] This multiplication can be seen in the figures reported for Soviet-Indian trade which went from Rs 127 million in the early 1950s to Rs 4,120 million in the early 1970s to Rs 7,000 million in 1975.[55]

By its long-term agreements, by its fixed prices, by the absence of the profit motive, by Soviet purchases of traditional exports plus industrial products, 'trade with the socialist countries convincingly shows that, as opposed to robbing, exploiting methods of [imperialist] trade, there exist democratic, just methods of trade based on the principles of equality and mutual profit of the trading partners.'[56]

While qualitatively excellent, socialist third world trade is quantitatively still insufficient. It has grown by unprecedented rates and has very favourable prospects of future similar expansion; from a volume of 0.27 billion rubles in 1955, Soviet trade with the developing countries had grown to 1.4 billion rubles by 1964 (from 4.6 per cent to 10.3 per cent of Soviet foreign trade), and by 1980 should reach 11 billion rubles. This trade is growing five times as fast as world trade in general. Nevertheless the socialist position in third world trade is still 'very modest,' making up only 4.8-5.1 per cent of the developing countries' foreign trade (1976).[57] 'In the light of the objective conditions, the world socialist system and its individual participants at the present time are not in a position to take on themselves all or the greater part of the economic trade links of the developing countries and replace the west's markets for them.'[58] They cannot become the principal market for third world exports. This is true of the majority of the types of tropical agriculture and mineral raw materials. Cuba's sales of sugar to the world socialist system cannot be considered typical. So while in some places the size of socialist trade is presented as colossal – Ghanaian-socialist bloc trade increased from 1957 to 1964 from 4.5 per cent to 40 per cent of Ghana's total commerce – the prospect for socialist trade is not presented as an ultimate cure for these countries' problems any more than is socialist aid.

But if it leaves something to be desired in terms of quantity, Soviet analysts claim a second qualitative advantage for their trade with the developing countries: of itself it improves the latter's trading position on the world capitalist market. For the steady expansion of economic ties with the socialist world 'has also deprived imperialism of monopoly positions in the sphere of consumption of the key export products coming from the third world.' It has helped transform the developing countries 'into equal partners in international trade and to eliminate such iniquitous imperialist devices as artificially low prices on the products of the underdeveloped countries and inflated prices on their own exports.'[59] Thus Soviet trade does not mean breaking ties with the west any more than does receiving socialist aid. Rather, it 'increases the possibilities for trade with other countries, including the industrial capitalist countries,'[60] but on the basis of mutual advantage and complete equality.

As in their discussion of aid, the Soviet discussion of their trade with the developing countries is a case of good material inadequately exploited – at least for the sceptical reader wanting proof for propositions that are presented as self-evident truths. And again it is from non-Soviet sources, both western and Indian, that one must verify the Soviet claims. A monograph written by Sumitra Chishti for the Indian Institute of Foreign Trade has reviewed India's trade with East Europe and approved it on all counts: its composition, export and import prices, terms of trade, whether trade has been diverted, its impact on increasing imports through expanding exports, its influence on the quality of Indian production, and the prospects of further trade expansion.[61] Goldman maintains that the stability both of prices and of volume of the developing countries' trade with the Soviet Union is less than in their trade with the west. For India, which is the Soviet Union's largest non-communist partner, he reports that the fluctuation in volume of trade is generally greater than with the west and that prices are at best equal to world prices. He points out other problems not considered in the Soviet writings: that some countries, e.g. Brazil and Ghana, were in some difficulty as to how to use the ruble credits they accumulated from their sales to the Soviet Union. If there is a good world demand for a country's exports, selling them for unconvertible rubles can be a liability. Furthermore, if the Soviets resell their purchases on the world market, this will redound to the disadvantage of the original exporter who will have lost the chance to earn that amount of foreign currency.[62] For countries like India, faced by insufficient markets for their products, the advantages far outweigh the disadvantages. The opening of new markets does not prevent the satisfaction of old; in fact, they may provide an experimental launching pad for penetrating the old western markets with new products: India's exports of manufactured goods to the Soviet Union that would face stiff competition in the west (footwear, vacuum flasks, refrigerators) provide an opportunity to gain experience and improve quality that may eventually allow her to penetrate western markets with these products. Since Soviet imports of consumer goods are growing and the Soviet Union is likely to continue to suffer from major shortages in its own supplies of hard foreign currency, the projections of vastly increased imports by the Soviet Union of consumer products from the developing countries seem realistic and obviously advantageous for those countries with whom it nourishes good commercial relations.

11

Both truck and trade with the imperialists

While the quality of the third world's trade with the socialist bloc outweighs its quantity, the opposite is true of third world trade with the imperialist bloc. Since the meaning of economic independence is liberation from an exploited, unequal position in the world capitalist system, release from one-sided colonial trading relationships is a *sine qua non* of genuine statehood. Yet inequality and exploitation persist as the defining characteristics of the economic relationships between the third and the imperialist worlds.

THE INEQUALITY OF ONE-SIDEDNESS

L. Stepanov pointed out the seriousness of the trade gap from which the underdeveloped countries suffer, a gap which prevents them from satisfying their needs in foreign currency and obtaining the supplementary external sources of accumulation needed to pay back their huge foreign debts. Quoting UN projections, he noted that by 1975 the underdeveloped world would need $97.7 billion worth of imports but would have an export market only for $73.5 billion, leaving a gap of $24.2 billion. But there was more wrong with these trade figures even than met the eye. Their overriding characteristic was the unequal realtionship between rich and poor, dominating and dominated, summed up by the notion 'one-sidedness'; one-sidedness geographically and one-sidedness structurally.

One-sidedness is a direct survival of the colonial period when the metropolitan monopolies owned and controlled the flow of goods from colony to mother state. The maintenance of this control is a major handicap limiting the economic role of the developing country in the international capitalist division of labour to that of an 'agricultural and raw material appendage' of imperialism. Quite apart from the restraining impact that foreign trading firms have on third world trade with the socialist bloc, the control of external trade by foreign capital is an obstacle to its autonomous development as it keeps the trade pattern fixed in the colonial mould. British monopolies control 80 per cent of Pakistan's jute exports; two-thirds of Malaya's foreign trade is controlled by foreigners; 63 per cent of Equatorial Africa's foreign trade is under French control. American monopolies' participation in Latin American foreign trade has 'huge dimensions.' Without the liquidation or limitation of the control of these trading monopolies, the developing countries' foreign trade cannot serve genuinely national aims.

One consequence of this continued neocolonialist control of the actual trading operations is to perpetuate the one-sided nature of the developing country's exports – normally raw materials shipped to the western markets. In many cases a country may have only one or two significant export products and so depend dangerously on the world market's fluctuating demand for these products. How vulnerable some economies are needs no explanation beyond a simple statistic: bananas form 71 per cent of Panama's exports; coffee accounts for 73 per cent of Colombia's foreign earnings. Paradoxically, countries heavily dependent on food exports also turn out to need food imports. 'Agricultural and raw material appendage' takes on meaning when a country exports in raw material form but imports it as a consumer good: Mozambique exports sugar cane and imports refined sugar; Indonesia exports rubber and imports rubber products; Nigeria exports cocoa and imports chocolate.[1] Although Latin America is an area producing agrarian products, only Mexico is self-sufficient in food production.

The one-sided structural nature of foreign trade is reinforced by the geographical one-sidedness resulting from ex-colonies whose major market is still the former mother country This is a state of affairs that has increased, not decreased, with time: L. Aleksandrovskaya noted that the majority of the African countries are trying to conserve and even increase their trade with the old developed countries[2]; 70 to 75 per cent of their foreign trade is still with capitalist countries, mainly the former parent states; 20 per cent is among African countries themselves; and only 5 per cent is with the socialist bloc.[3] While the utilization of these old economic links is necessary to the extent that it allows the ex-colonies to ease their difficulties, this is not in Aleksandrovskaya's view a satisfactory situation. For the prospect of exporting products to the western world is paradoxically gloomy. On the one hand the international capitalist division of labour continually strengthens the third world's agricultural and raw materials specialization; on the other the increasing agricultural production in the west and the introduction of synthetic replacements for raw materials threatens a further decrease of trade, creating an increasingly perilous situation. As if this were not enough, artificial barriers to the developing country's exports exist and are even increasing: tariffs, quotas, and other forms of discrimination continue, along with the establishment of regional groups of imperialist countries like the European Common Market aimed at 'increasing the exploitation of developing countries.'[4] Furthermore, the foreign corporations' control of a country's trade inhibits the development of commercial links with socialist countries, thus preventing its attempts to increase its economic independence. In Sri Lanka, for instance, the domination of foreign capital in external trade 'continued to be an obstacle to extensive Soviet-Ceylonese trade.'[5]

EXPLOITATION BY NON-EQUIVALENT EXCHANGE

Continuing inequality of the developing countries in world commerce is the basis for their continuing exploitation by the mechanisms of the international capitalist market. Exploitation is inherent in the foreign monopolies' activity in third world trade, for when they act as traders they make profits at the expense of the new states. The developmental effectiveness of foreign trade is forfeited by the liberated countries since profits made in this commerce accrue to the foreign firms. The new state is deprived of the fruits of its labour – and an important source of capital accumulation.[6]

Trade with the imperialist countries brings on exploitation of another kind: 'non-equivalent exchange' in which the backward countries lose out whether exporting or importing from the industrialized world. In the language of liberal economics, the developing countries suffer from deteriorating terms of trade: the prices they receive for their raw materials and unprocessed agricultural products are low and have declined with the increased supply and decreased demand. On the other hand the products they most need to import, equipment and other manufactured goods, keep rising in price as they become technologically more sophisticated. The price scissors in which they are caught means that, even though they may expand the physical volume of their exports, their actual export revenue may decline. While African exports doubled in quantity, they brought in only 10 per cent more revenue.[7] Senegal's exports to Europe grew by 30 per cent in five years but her net receipts of foreign currency only grew by 3 per cent.[8]

The developing countries' loss by the price scissors is their developed partners' gain. V.S. Baskin estimated that one-half of Africa's exports have been taken free by the imperialists, a figure he put at $6.5 billion. The loss caused by the worsening terms of trade (assuming the same volume of trade over the years) is equivalent to 40 per cent of the credits and aid the developing countries have received from the west. Two-fifths of the aid received from the west is thus only compensation for damage inflicted on the developing countries by the world capitalist market.[9] Not only do the imperialist countries profit from these price movements; they are responsible for them. The monopolies put definite pressure on the more independent countries by manipulating the world market price. Ghana, for instance, doubled its cocoa production, but its receipts dropped 'since the British and American trusts contrived to reduce prices on cocoa beans to less than half the previous figure.' This price policy had a definite goal: the overthrow of Nkrumah. The same economic sabotage has been carried out against Guinea, Mali, Zambia, and other states. The Union Minière cut the price of copper by 40 per cent to undermine Congo (Kinshasa) that had been acting against the Belgian monopoly's interests.[10]

Nor is it a coincidence that the goods produced by the west for export have risen in price, while the price of products imported by the west have declined. It is no accident that exported foodstuffs produced and exported by the imperialist countries, such as wheat, have maintained their prices, whereas raw materials produced in developing countries have not. Practically, Soviet analysts consider this to result from the power of the imperialist monopolies to manipulate prices to their own advantage; they also provide a theoretical explanation in the labour theory of value. On the assumption that the price of a commodity should reflect the labour content put into its production, its price should differ depending whether 'simple' (i.e. cheap, unskilled) labour is used to produce Ghanaian cocoa or 'complex' (i.e. technologically based and expensive) labour is used to produce a western tractor. Non-equivalent exchange thus means 'the exchange of different quantities of materialized labour corresponding to an unequal level of productivity in contractor countries.' It is an expression of the fact that 'different countries do not have the same labour productivity.'[11] According to Stepanov, then, the roots of the developing countries' problems lie 'in the sphere of production and not in the sphere of circulation.' Stepanov was rephrasing his basic theme: the way out of backwardness is through raising labour productivity in the third world, not through changing the relationships of supply and demand for their products on the world capitalist market. As long as this gap in productivity between the underdeveloped and the developed countries persists, exploitation by unequal exchange will continue.[12] For even when they sell the same product at the same price as western economies, the less developed economies are exploited by non-equivalency. Through the mechanism of the world market, Egyptian cotton sells for the same price as American cotton even though US productivity is fifty times greater than the Egyptian. This shows how prices are 'foisted' on the newly developing countries who are pillaged even without military occupation.[13]

POLICY RECOMMENDATIONS

Deliverance from this exploitation through world trade can only come to the developing countries by transforming foreign trade from an instrument of robbery to a lever of development. On these countries' foreign trade depend the reconstruction of the national economy, the character and dynamics of their internal change and the measures and rates of their economic development. When foreign trade stops being a supplier to the imperialist economies and an appendage in the international capitalist division of labour, it can become a component part of the national economy of the independent state, one of the most important factors suppressing its colonial backwardness, raising its productive forces and overthrowing its former dependence on imperialism. The change that Soviet writers envisage – the transformation of foreign trade into part of the fight for economic independence – requires a fundamental reconstruction of foreign trade. How this is done depends both on the international situation, that is, the country's relations with the socialist and capitalist countries, and on how thoroughly and radically each state rebuilds these links with the world markets and solves its internal problems of development. This internal prerequisite is industrialization. According to Kondratev, only the radical path 'to liquidate the narrowness and one-sided commodity structure of foreign trade and to rationally transform it' can succeed. But this complete reconstruction of foreign trade does not necessarily mean a full break from the world capitalist market, a full transfer into the world socialist market or even complete isolation and autarchy. Much more moderately it can mean that, with the support of the world socialist economy, the developing country breaks the unequal character of international trade, affirms its sovereignty on the world market, and to a maximal degree gets equivalent exchange. Kondratev quoted the Communist Party of India as affirming that the more India weakens its links with the world capitalist market and the more it strengthens its ties with the world socialist market, the more its economy will profit. 'Not a break of trade relations, but their complete reorientation for the independent development of the national economy: this is what the progressive forces are fighting for.'[14]

But what is this 'complete reorientation?' Kondratev talked of the robbing intermediaries of the foreign trade firms but recognized that they may be the only source of markets for certain countries and certain products. The alternative depends on the size of the socialist market, but as we learned elsewhere this is only 10 per cent of the world market with no promise of growing spectacularly. While countries must diversify to reduce their dependence on the western markets, it is also pointed out that to increase their exports they must increase their specialization. The full liquidation of the positions of foreign capital is recommended, but it is reaffirmed that these countries do not need to get out of the world capitalist market. Such contradictory views constantly assault the reader in even the best Soviet writing.

The policy conclusions are thus equally confused for trade as for aid. The preference for radical solutions dominates, but a gradualist realism keeps pushing to the surface, either through the juxtaposition of unresolved contradictions (diversify but specialize) or by such frank acknowledgement as 'these countries can work out an optimal national economic plan only by taking into strict account the possibilities of going into the world market and the possibilities offered by the international division of labour.'[15] In essence Soviet observers support and prefer 'radical solutions' that will transform a backward to an advanced economy, but recognize with increasing openness the practical difficulties faced by the very weak developing countries.

Much can be done by state capitalist devices inside the country. The control of foreign and domestic trade by a state agency is a basic form of which they generally approve. The most radical solution is to nationalize the firms controlling foreign trade and bring all internal trade under government ownership and control. The least progressive is regulations to achieve some government control over pricing and tariffs or quotas to limit indiscriminate importing of non-essential consumer goods. In between come such institutions as India's State Trading Corporation (STC) which stimulate exports and mobilize internal resources for the growing imports needed by the five-year plans. The monopoly accorded the STC for the import and export of certain goods allowed a more judicious utilization of the world capitalist market and a stronger resistance to the pressure of foreign monopoly competition. With the strength of the government behind it, it could counteract the harmful pressures of non-equivalent exchange.[16] Even though the State Training Corporation is designed to serve the interests of the ruling bourgeoisie and so does not combat the private commercial firms by nationalizing them, it nevertheless reinforces state capitalism in foreign trade and concentrates in state control commercial relations with trading firms of other countries, notably those of the socialist bloc. 'The reinforcement of the state's role in the organization and operation of foreign trade by the creation of a powerful state export-import corporation ... answers the country's needs.'[17]

Another recommended line of action is the international co-operation of developing countries to resist imperialist exploitation. With chronic overproduction of most export products in the developing countries and their declining role in world markets, these countries have been faced with 'the real danger of boycott and blockade by the imperialist powers.' These can only be overcome by 'establishing an effective solidarity front of all exporters with political support from the socialist states.'[18] Since many small economies which were mere cogs in the colonial empires have had their development deformed and so remain completely dependent, regional economic organizations are needed to compensate for their shortage of natural wealth or economic potential. In Africa particularly, the regional organizations have a considerable role to play in strengthening inter-African economic and cultural relations and in the struggle against the monopolies. They can do a great deal towards an equitable distribution of economic potential, thereby creating prospects for growth and development for the small independent countries. 'But all this is possible only if the regional organizations are anti-imperialist and anti-monopolist in orientation ... Otherwise, regional organizations will become an evil because neo-colonialism will inevitably use them as a new form of its own.' Some regional organizations set up by the colonialists such as the Customs and Economic Union of Central Africa (Gabon, the Central African Republic, Cameroun, and Congo [Brazzaville]) can be useful for economic development, since, if they cannot resist the monopolies singly, they can oppose them together. But this union is in fact a 'Trojan horse for the French monopolies.' Federations set up under colonialism enabling monopolies to exploit whole regions as a bloc must now unite their members to eradicate monopoly domination.[19]

Soviet commentators strongly suspect special arrangements between developing and developed countries. The Commonwealth's system of preferential tariffs are not considered a boon: they bear the stamp of neocolonialism, retarding these economies by preserving their one-sided export structure of raw materials.[20] It is not clear, however, whether the have-not members of the Commonwealth should try to break out of its chief financial instrument, the sterling bloc. The disadvantages (the great influence exerted by British banks on the less developed countries' currency and financial policies) seem to be at least balanced by the advantages (the influx of British capital as long as they need it, British governmental aid 'which most newly independent countries still cannot afford to be without,' using their British credits to purchase needed industrial goods).[21]

The French currency zone gives the French monopolies tariff protection against foreign goods and the African states preferential terms on the French market. The ex-colonies are kept in the French orbit by 'assistance' covering their budget deficits and unfavourable balance of payments. Their objective should be to break down this system since 'economic co-operation within the framework of an area dominated by France can only emphasize the subordinate status of the newly independent states within the system of the world capitalist division of labour.'[22] Similar suspicion is directed at the association of African and other underdeveloped countries with the European Common Market whose 'short-term and illusory advantages ... are fraught with great danger for the countries' economic development.'[23] However the danger is seen less in the ECM's imperialism than in its failure to act as imperialists. After all the ECM is the chief market for third world exports of raw materials. The Common Market's programme of achieving agricultural self-sufficiency would be 'a severe blow at the interests of the developing states and could seriously interfere with their economic development if they failed to find markets for their goods.'[24]

For some of the more moderate analysts the problem has nothing to do with the breakup of colonialism. It is a question of the processes involved in the present scientific and technical revolution causing trade among developed countries to grow faster than trade between the developed and less developed. European industry's structural and technological developments in industry and agriculture explain how the 'colonies have also lost much of their importance to their former parent-states as suppliers of agricultural raw materials.' The further development of their own raw material production will lessen their dependence on the developing countries. Nor with their backward economic structure can they provide 'an adequate market for the leading branches of modern industry.'[25] The changing structure of world capitalist production and foreign trade was the main reason for the deterioration of the third world's terms of trade.[26]

The conclusion to be drawn from this non-ideological, more technical view is that the fate of the third world's foreign trade will depend on the growth of its productive efficiency relative to the rise of its real wages.[27] Where the parent-states still spend on some third world raw materials such as oil or uranium, then the developing countries must take advantage of the contradictions between monopoly capitalists to get the lion's share of the oil profits.[28] Dependence here is recognized as a two-way street. The underdeveloped can profit from their dependent position when the imperialists themselves need them as a 'raw material appendage.' Moderate Soviet counsellors warn against throwing out the baby (western markets) with the bathwater (foreign monopoly domination). It is not, after all, a question of no truck or trade with the imperialists. Perhaps no truck, but by all means trade.

THE DECOLONIZATION THEORY BY THE BACK DOOR

With the acceptance, whether reluctant or frank, by the Soviet analysts of the economic importance and moral necessity of imperialist aid to all developing countries, the Soviet theory of imperialism has itself undergone an implicit transformation, despite claims to the contrary by defenders of the radical line that nothing in the nature of imperialism has changed. For if western aid is now perceived as genuinely assisting economic development when suitably directed and controlled by the host country, the marxist-leninist vision of the developmental role of imperialism in the third world has come full circle back to Marx's optimism about the British historical impact on the East.

Marx had been very enthusiastic about the regenerative role of British colonialism in India which was to succeed the British destruction of the Asiatic economy. Not only had colonialism imposed political unity on India but it had given her 'a native army organized and trained by the British drill-sergeant,' a free press 'introduced for the first time into Asiatic society,' and a native class 'endowed with the requirements for government.' In addition, the British had introduced the railroad, a necessary condition for bringing India out of stagnation and making her enter the path of industrialization: 'You cannot maintain a net of railways over an immense country without introducing all those industrial processes necessary to meet the immediate and current wants of railway locomotion, and out of which there must grow the application of machinery to those branches of industry not immediately connected with railways. The railway system will therefore become, in India, truly the forerunner of modern industry.'[29]

Thus the English bourgeoisie 'will not fail' to create the material conditions necessary to start 'the development of the productive powers' in India. This optimistic view of imperialism's capacity to save India from the Asiatic mode of production had a definite influence on the first Communist notions about the role of British imperialism in Indian economic development. M.N. Roy had early declared India to be ripe for the bourgeois democratic revolution. Adding Lenin's theory to Marx's optimism, R. Palme Dutt, the famous Anglo-Indian communist, in 1927 wrote in his important book on India that the growing export of British capital to the colonies was 'an economic necessity of imperialism,' and concluded that in India 'industrial development constitutes today the keystone of the British government's policy.' According to Dutt the lightning development of modern industry had placed India in the ranks of the 'eight first industrialized countries of the world.'[30]

It is important to draw special attention to this first communist thesis to emphasize that the anti-development theory of imperialism was originated only in the stalinist period. In fact it was only after the stalinization of the Comintern and the condemnation of M.N. Roy's 'decolonization theory'* at the sixth Comintern Congress in 1929 that marxism-leninism-stalinism made imperialism's resistance to economic development in the colonies an official dogma.

The new stalinist analysis admitted this to be a change from Marx's projections. In a footnote to his 1953 volume E. Varga frankly stated that imperialism had failed to accomplish the historical mission which Marx had assigned it. Great Britain had, for example, destroyed the old Indian society but in the period of its colonial rule had then resisted the development of India's productive forces out of competition with and fear of the growing national bourgeoisie. It is this imperialist resistance to industrialization which explained why India still suffered

---

* Roy maintained that Britain's economic problems forced it to develop India's industrial economy as a market for British capital goods. This process would establish the basis for an increasingly self-sufficient bourgeoisie which would gain independence.

in 1947 from 'an insufficient development of capitalism.'[31] What is crucial to an understanding of the current contradictions in the Soviet analysis of aid is that destalinization has not brought any formal change in this thesis.[32] In the destalinized 1957 edition of the same book Varga retains the same footnote criticizing Marx's fallacious prediction. Thus Soviet ideology keeps its very negative assessment of imperialism both in the colonial phase and currently. Although the Soviet texts state that nothing has changed in malevolent imperialism as Lenin described it, they in no way give the impression that imperialism remains all-powerful on the world scene, freely exploiting the colonial countries. On the contrary, one of the main themes of the Soviet view is precisely the decline of imperialism in the face of the socialist camp's ineluctable progress.

To the extent that 'aid' is considered to be forced on imperialism by the national liberation movement and by competition with the socialist camp, the existence of 'aid' is a sign of how imperialism is on the defensive. Thus the power of the socialist camp has forced imperialism to beat a retreat, and aid is the only means of maintaining its presence in the liberated countries. Similarly when discussing the motivations of imperialist aid the Soviet analysts find it necessary to deny any change in the character of imperialism 'which continues to be aimed at maintaining and extending the imperialist exploitation of the young states, at preventing them from achieving economic independence; it is aimed, in particular, at preventing the nationalization of foreign property and the transition, in the final analysis, to non-capitalist development and cooperation with the socialist countries.'[33]

Soviet authors still insist that such motivations as the search for strategic raw materials and the need to export capital are fundamental to imperialism.[34] But the moderate line recognizes that the revolutionary development of synthetics has drastically reduced the strategic importance of the colonial world as a supplier of raw materials for the west. With the technological revolution the capitalist countries no longer have to export capital to compensate for a fall in aggregate demand.

As has been more recently observed, the foreign monopolies invest abroad to create markets and are in fact wanting to see an expansion of the developing countries' internal markets for the very products that their branch plants will produce. As for the imperialist governments, they have a similar interest in promoting general world prosperity so that their own exports will have a market, from wheat to iron and steel plants. Hence

the policy of holding back industrial development in the Third World has been replaced by the neocolonialist conception of industrialisation which provides for the transfer to the newly-free countries of industries which are not dynamic, that is, industries with a low organic composition of capital, low productivity and poor capacity for accumulation and the utilisation of mostly simple living labour. The purpose of the said conception is to secure the intensified exploitation of cheap labour and the concentration of the dynamic industries in the home countries ... Whereas only recently the neocolonialists sought to prevent the industrialisation of the Third World, now they try to keep it in scientific and technological dependence.[35]

The basic radical line remains officially unamended, since the theory of decolonization has not been formally rehabilitated. That two such diametrically opposed lines can coexist uncomfortably over the years gives an indication of the strains within the Soviet development school and helps to explain many of its continuing glaring contradictions and inconsistencies.

ASSESSMENT

The reader of Soviet political economy gets used to a regular measure of inconsistencies and unresolved contradictions. With the Soviet analysis of the external economic relations of the developing countries, he has to absorb logical difficulties of an exceptional order.

There are first of all the straight contradictions that have been noted in the preceding pages: imperialism has/has not changed since decolonization; foreign investment does/does not contribute to the third world's development; western aid is/is not old-style colonial export of capital; trade with the west can/cannot be on equal terms; socialist aid is/is not qualitatively different from western aid; and so on. These are not simply cases of incompleted arguments that can be resolved by providing a synthesis to the thesis and antithesis. They are fundamental disagreements between the radical and the moderate assessments of the various aspects of aid and trade problems.

Another group of inconsistencies springs from the inherent manicheism of the radical line which insists on the absolute, qualitative difference between what is socialist and what is imperialist. The crude they-are-bad-we-are-good approach leads to a whole series of positions unacceptable to the non-believer.
- Soviet observers accuse imperialists of exploiting the third world through the mechanism of the world price system, which pillages the less developed economies through the mechanism of non-equivalent exchange. Yet they admit that Soviet commerce with the underdeveloped countries is based on the same world prices. It follows, as Che Guevara once heatedly pointed out, that the Soviets are accomplices of imperialist exploitation of the third world.
- Soviet analysts take western donors to task for partially tying their aid, but

do not admit that their own aid is totally tied by the inconvertibility of the ruble and the system of joint clearing accounts.

- The international capitalist division of labour maintains the ex-colonies as raw material appendages, yet the international socialist division of labour allows them to concentrate on industrial essentials to develop their industries while importing their other needs from the socialist bloc. How such a position can be defended when, according to the labour theory of value, the differing levels of labour productivity are what distinguish the developed from the undeveloped is never made clear. It is simply a statement of faith that the imperialist and the socialist cannot ever be put in the same analytical category.

- Soviet writers cry 'Dependence!' when observing India's imports of specialized equipment from the west, but shout 'Liberation!' when they report the supply of capital goods from the socialist bloc. Yet Soviet projects need follow-up supervisory personnel and spare parts just as western ones do.

- Although western aid for infrastructural development is considered inferior to Soviet aid for heavy industry, Soviet observers credit themselves for giving non-productive aid for the construction of hydroelectric projects. While they criticize French aid to India for *merely* covering India's export deficit with France, this defect becomes another virtue in socialist aid to India, which allows the country to import from the socialist bloc more than she exports.[36]

It is of course possible for readers to make their own syntheses of the contradictions and inconsistencies resulting from the Soviet double standard. By extracting from the Soviet description of socialist aid the positive criteria to be encouraged and from the main criticisms of imperialist aid the negative attributes to be avoided, one can construct a simple model of the ideal foreign participation in the economic development of a given Afro-Asian nation. Aid would be not so much overabundant as of high quality: directed economically at the creation or expansion of the most needed industries (heavy industry producing the means of production, producer-goods production, infra-structure, and agriculture, in that order); it would not put undue burdens on the country's balance of payments by arranging for barter deals allowing the receiver to pay for the goods in its own traditional exports; the interest rate would not be high, and the terms of repayment would allow each project to amortize itself. Politically the aid would not be tied to the purchase of goods in the donor country; there would be no foreign equity or management or technical participation in the project once completed; it would maximize the use of local skilled and unskilled labour; the aid projects would be integrated in the long-term planning and would contribute towards the expansion of the state's industrial sector, thus facilitating the progress of state capitalism towards the non-capitalist path of development via the restriction of the activity of private capital, foreign and national. By making such a synthesis of the analysis of imperialist and socialist aid, we would have a coherent and acceptable model of the general outlines of 'good' aid.

The important point is not that this would be the right selection in any absolute sense; rather there is such a large range of facts and views in the Soviet analysis that each reader can select the set that corresponds to his or her own predilections. The party *apparatchik* can find the hard ideological line for internal use of agitprop and for demonstrations of intraparty fraternal solidarity. The diplomat can find ample soothing and encouraging passages to maintain good relations with his third world counterparts. The researcher can concentrate on the non-ideological analysis that surfaces in the scholarly press or academic debates. While this incoherence may be politically necessary in an ideological state, it has a real danger: instead of being all things to all men, the Soviet analysis of the third world's aid and trade problems may mean nothing much to anyone.

PART FOUR

AGRICULTURE

12

Agrarian reforms

A reader unversed in Soviet writings might wonder what solutions marxism-leninism can contribute to the agrarian dilemmas of the third world. Was not marxism an economic response to the nineteenth-century crisis of European industrial development in which agricultural considerations were given remarkably short shrift? Furthermore, if agriculture is in fact the Achilles' heel of the USSR's own socialization process, what relevance can the Soviet writings have for agricultural problems outside the socialist bloc? Even if it is conceded that marxist-leninist movements have been most successful in areas with a backward agriculture and an impoverished peasantry, the sceptic can retort that this success was due more to pre-revolutionary tactics than to post-revolutionary policy. While communists begin as revolutionaries, the dubious might point out with David Mitrany that with a 'minimum programme' supporting the poor peasants' demand for an equal share of private property, they end up as oppressors by attacking the peasants' desire for their own land and imposing the exploitation of the peasantry by the proletarian state through forced collectivization.[1]

It might be pointed out that communism has only gained and retained power without outside military support in underdeveloped, predominantly agricultural countries.[2] While collectivization may not appear to western eyes as an ideal formula for agricultural development, it had clear attractions for the post-revolutionary Soviet leadership, not to mention for the Chinese, the North Koreans, and the North Vietnamese. Although one would have expected the Soviet orientalists to apply to the third world their own country's experience of forced development through 'primitive socialist accumulation,'[3] it is striking how little of the Soviet analysis is actually based on the Soviet historical experience of collectivization. Of all Soviet development writing, agricultural analysis has in fact the most coherent theoretical model and is the least affected by the ideology of cold war realpolitik.

THE SOVIET AGRARIAN SOCIOLOGY

Distinct from the internal political economy of state capitalism and international economics, agrarian relations constitute the third major focal point for the Soviet analysis of the developing countries' problems. Although integrated into the Soviet political economy opus on the third world, agricultural research has its own specialists, its own books and articles, its own scholarly tradition, and indeed its own theory of the developing situation. This constitutes a sociology of rural agrarian development distinguished both by its analytical rigour and by its faithfulness to the spirit of Lenin's own theoretical position. The reasons for devoting considerable research and analytical resources to the third world's agriculture are clear: since the peasantry makes up 90 per cent of the third world population, no revolutionary theory can be credible without taking its unique problems into serious account, and since agriculture provides most of the national product in the Afro-Asian world even economics cannot let the rural scene fall by the analytical wayside. In many ways the most radical area of Soviet analysis, agrarian sociology concentrates first of all on the dual question of agrarian reforms and capitalist development, reaching its revolutionary conclusions through its view of capitalism's failure to develop.

AGRARIAN REFORMS

To raise the agrarian question in vast subcontinents where the overwhelming majority of the population lives off the land is to raise all the major problems of a society undergoing the trauma of modernization. While Soviet theorists are interested in the totality of each socioeconomic situation, their concern is primarily focused on structural transformation in a historical perspective. The general marxist-leninist concern is for the transformation of an agrarian economy from a 'feudal' to a 'capitalist' – and ultimately a socialist – stage of development. The great emphasis placed on agrarian reforms by the ruling elites of all the newly independent Afro-Asian states made the content and results of these reforms the specific focus for the first Soviet rural studies in the third world. Indeed the studies of agrarian reform provide a forum for examining their thinking on such related problems as the nature of the agrarian heritage left by colonialism and the possibility for capitalist development in third world agriculture, the transformation taking place in the rural class structure and technical problems facing agricultural growth.

The general Soviet assessment of the state of agriculture in the third world is gloomy. The technical basis of production and production methods are not being modernized significantly. Agricultural production on the exhausted land deteriorates, so that the working masses go hungry, the rate of economic development is slowed down, and the developing countries' position in the anti-imperialist fight for independence is weakened.[4]

THE FETTERS OF THE COLONIAL PAST

The chains of the past clank heavily in the marxist-leninist consciousness. Whether these shackles are the old social relationships of the traditional Afro-Asian system or the fetters clapped on by the colonial powers, they are almost all seen as obstacles to progress condemning the working people to poverty.[5] The instinctive reaction of the Soviet analyst is a fear of historical 'survivals' and a faith that the old can be destroyed. The corollary of the social engineer's confidence that he can replace one class with another as easily as a surgeon transplants hearts is the fear that, unless drastic social surgery is carried out, the elements of the old will survive, adapt, and rise to dominate again. If the feudal elements learn new tricks and entrench themselves in the evolving order, they will be increasingly difficult to revolutionize. To destroy the old may be the secret wish of every Soviet third world analyst, but to live with the past is a burden he has to bear.

In tropical Africa, for instance, after toying with the Afro-Socialists' claims that the peasant communes could be a starting point for socialism,[6] Soviet theorists decided that the primitive community structure was a definite obstacle to development. Economic efficiency, in particular labour productivity, is extremely low, and the communal structure obstructs the development of national consciousness. As the traditional sector is stagnant, it 'no longer accumulates the capital needed to improve the means of production on a modern scientific and technological basis.' 'We are firmly convinced that the African community has outlived itself and is no longer in keeping with the modern level of social organization of production.'[7] Therefore it must be radically transformed. In any case communes are only collective economies in a formal sense: because the surplus product goes to the chiefs, they are really disguised feudal systems.[8] It follows that they must necessarily break up into capitalist, not socialist, forms. The condemnation of the commune illustrates a recurring characteristic of the Soviet analysis: a combination of marxian scorn of what is outmoded by the modern with an un-marxian rejection of what does not fit easily into the standard development categories of feudalism, capitalism, or socialism. It is un-marxian, since Karl Marx himself had devoted considerable thought to the distinctive features of traditional village society and had rejected the notion that, especially in Asia, it could be considered feudal.

If one goes back to Marx's writings, and most especially his articles of 1853 on India published by the New York *Daily Tribune*, it is clear that he distinguished feudalism from what he called the Asiatic mode of production. On 2 June 1853 Marx wrote to Engels: 'Bernier rightly considered the basis of all phenomena in the East – he refers to Turkey, Persia, Hindustan – to be the *absence of private property in land*.'[9] And Engels replied on 6 June: 'The absence of property in land is indeed the key to the whole of the East. Herein lies its political and religious history. But how does it come about that the Orientals did not arrive at landed property, even in its feudal form?'[10]

In an article written for the New York *Daily Tribune* of 25 June 1853, Marx summarized his views on the Indian social system, which he saw as characterized not by feudalism but by a dual system of central governmental control and village self-sufficiency:

These two circumstances – the Hindu, on the one hand, leaving, like all Oriental peoples, to the Central Government the care of the great public works, the prime condition of his agriculture and commerce, dispersed, on the other hand, over the surface of the country, and agglomerated in small centres by the domestic union of agricultural and manufacturing pursuits – these two circumstances had brought about, since the remotest times, a social system of particular features – the so-called *village system*, which gave to each of these small unions their independent organization and distinct life.[11]

It appears well established in Marx's texts and in the opinion of both marxist[12] and non-marxist[13] specialists that he considered feudalism did not exist in Asia. On the contrary, village self-sufficiency and central government responsibility for irrigation systems comprised what for Marx was a sufficiently distinct economic structure to qualify as a historically and analytically separate stage of development – the Asiatic mode of production.

Soviet orientalists, however, have doggedly refused to come to grips with the Asiatic mode of production since 1931 when those who used this concept were condemned as Trotskyists. Up to the early 1960s Soviet analysts 'systematically abstained from any reference to Marx's texts on the Asiatic mode of production.'[14] Though the revival of interest in this concept by western marxists has led to its formal rehabilitation in the Soviet scholarly press,[15] there has been no revision of the position which defines the colonial economy as feudal. The Soviets thus reject Marx's paradigm of a distinctive Asiatic mode of production for precolonial and colonial agricultural society in favour of Lenin's analysis of the Afro-Asian situation in terms of its deviation from classical European feudalism. In their view the colonial regime retarded an already established feudal system and prevented it from developing into its next, capitalist, stage.

There are good reasons to concentrate on India for the Soviet analysis of agrarian relations. For one thing, the rejection of Marx's Asiatic model in favour of Lenin's European paradigm is explicit:

Indeed, with the usual run of things, as soon as the peasant's destitution had grown to a point where a large proportion of them would have been forced to part with their landholding and sell their manpower rather than their produce, i.e., to join the proletariat, trade and money-lending capital and the landlords would have to embark on organising agriculture along capitalist lines ... This failed to happen in the Indian countryside on a scale at least partly comparable to Europe's.[16]

Secondly, Soviet observers themselves consider India to be a laboratory for the study of all Asian agrarian problems: 'Practically any variant of agricultural development in the Asian countries ... can find a parallel in India's agricultural development.'[17] As a result, it is on Indian agriculture that the Soviet academy has exerted most effort and so developed the most authoritative experts.

INDIA'S AGRARIAN HERITAGE

The Soviet account of the state of agriculture inherited from the colonial period by independent India is a duet of harsh judgments and forgiving statements in which the blame for the disastrous conditions of the Indian village is laid at the feet of the British colonizers and the positive features credited to the painfully slow evolution of a native Indian agrarian capitalism.

Such Soviet writers as A.L. Batalov and R.P. Gurvich show little restraint when they spell out the calamitous state of Indian agriculture under British rule. 'Misery, famine and disease, this was the destiny of the vast masses of colonial India.' There is in their view no doubt about the origin of India's evil: the cause of India's agricultural decline is simply the 'colonial situation of the country and its pitiless exploitation by the English monopolies.'

The colonial system sinned both in commission and in omission. As exploiter, colonialism first of all pillaged India of its prodigious riches. Then 'the competition by English merchandise caused massive havoc among millions of Indian artisans.' Finally colonialism transformed the country's agriculture into a 'raw material and agricultural appendage' to provide for the economic needs of the mother country. At the same time it wreaked more damage in failing to construct anything in the place of what it destroyed. 'The concentration of the large irrigation network and the bulk of the land in the hands of the colonial rulers, the dominant position of British export companies in the Indian raw material markets, the tax pressure, the complicated system of impositions by water taxes and other non-economic constraints: all this insured an increase of food stuff and raw material production which the English imperialists needed.'[18]

The imperialist pillage which took her huge riches and ruined her economy, turned India from a potentially wealthy country at the point of autonomous capitalist development into one of the most miserable of the backward nations. 'In India a population of several millions went hungry while foodstuffs and agricultural raw materials were exported at low monopoly prices to the mother country.' While the exploiters became rich, the standard of living of the native population fell to the level of chronic famine which between 1901 and 1944 accounted for 30 million deaths.[19]

In Marx's analysis the necessarily destructive action of English colonialism played a historically progressive role which made possible its subsequent but equally inevitable constructive activity: 'England has a double mission to fulfill in India, the one destructive, the other regenerative: the annihilation of the old Asiatic society and the foundation of the basis of western society in Asia.'[20] Soviet theorists, however, no longer endorse this optimistic historical judgment. They neither consider that the destruction wreaked by the English was objectively positive nor find any constructive activity to praise on its own merits. Their principal reproach against English colonialism is that, having wrecked the native economy by imposing free trade, it constructed on the debris a 'zamindari' and 'rayatwari' system, which they label as a feudal and semi-feudal system of agricultural exploitation.

In the zamindari system which covered half the country 'landed proprietors of a feudal type' dominated the countryside. The zamindars, 'one of the main ramparts of colonial power,' had concentrated in their hands the 'largest part of the cultivated lands, though as a general rule they did not themselves run their own agricultural operation, renting out their land instead.' By contrast in the rayatwari regions, the moneylenders and traders became landowners by expropriating the lands belonging to the peasants.

By the time of independence from 55 per cent to 60 per cent of all the private land belonged to large landowners, and 75 per cent of all cultivated land in British India was rented. 'On the one hand a process of concentration of property in the hands of a small number of zamindars, jagidars and other landowners of a semi-feudal type was taking place; on the other hand the cultivation of the soil was carried out mainly on very small areas of parcelled land.' In the United Provinces, 55 per cent of all farms had less than 0.8 hectares; the vast majority of the peasantry cultivated areas of less than two hectares.

Between these two extremes of the agrarian pyramid was a 'huge parasitic stratum of rent collectors.' These intermediaries lived not from the fruit of their labour but from their capacity to find a role in the game of extorting more from their tenants than they had to pay their own landlords. The pressure of this exploitation on the cultivator was accompanied by declining productivity and a reduction of the area cultivated per capita, so that finally 'more than 60 per cent of the population of colonial India was in a constant state of famine or semi-famine.'[21] Crushed from above by this pressure extracting high rents, the peasantry was also squeezed from below by the 'relative agrarian overpopulation' which helped keep land rents at an extremely high, or feudal, level.[22] Dominated by large land holdings, undermined by fragmented land cultivation, India's semi-feudal agriculture was blighted thirdly by the predominance of commercial and usury capital interested more in extracting interest payments than in promoting production.[23]

The main explanation of India's state of near-famine is thus not to be found in such natural factors as droughts or floods, in its primitive technology, nor even in the Malthusian theory of overpopulation,[24] but rather in its colonial exploitation and, 'in the countryside, by the reign of feudal survivals which are responsible for the extremely backward state of Indian agriculture.'[25]

At the same time as G.G. Kotovsky denounced imperialism for restraining agricultural development, he observed that the latter was nevertheless evolving along capitalist lines: 'The agrarian policy of the British colonizers was directed towards the maintenance of semi-feudal production relations in the Indian country-side. Nevertheless the transformation of India into an agricultural and raw material appendage of England stimulated the development of monetary relations in the Indian countryside as well as the growth of commercialized agriculture.'[26]

Given the restrictive role ascribed to British rule, the emphasis placed in the Soviet analysis on the development of rural capitalism is particularly striking. Despite a repressive imperialist policy designed to restrict colonial economic progress, capitalism was maturing ineluctably out of the feudal economic structure. Many capitalist signs of agrarian capitalism were already detected at the colonial period. In production relations capitalist-type firms were being established. Quite apart from such traditional exports as tea and jute a large part of agricultural production was sold commercially on the internal market. Taking rice as a typical example of foodgrains, M.A. Maksimov and V.G. Rastyannikov have estimated that, when India gained independence, 28 per cent of the total rice crop was surplus sold on the internal market and 20 per cent was used as workers' salary. 'It is clear that at least half the rice produced in India went into the sphere of exchange relations.'[27]

There were also technical indices of a growing agrarian capitalism. Kotovsky saw them in the growing specialization of the various geographical regions as well as in the cultivation of crops to supply local industry for export markets. Social indices of growing capitalism were no harder to find. There was an increasing material inequality among the different social strata, in the countryside, a sure sign of the transformation of the old seigneurial and peasant classes into two new antagonistic classes, the bourgeoisie and the proletariat.[28]

The decline and fall of local manufacturing based on agriculture, the general development of a commercial and money economy in the country, the creation of private semi-feudal, semi-bourgeois landed property and its entry into commercial exchange, the organization of a capitalistic plantation structure, the efforts to start up capitalist farming by large landowners, the differentiation of the peasantry, the formation of a class of agricultural workers: such were the signs of capitalist relations which were developing in India, coexisting and intermingling with the surviving elements of the precapitalist rural structure.[29]

Feudal production relations still had a sufficiently strong hold as the dominant economic structure for their elimination by capitalism to be seen by the Soviets as a historically progressive process.

While the marxist-leninists noted some positive traits in the production system and the class situation of rural India on the eve of its independence, they observed nonetheless that agriculture was in a state of alarming stagnation and suffering from a growing crisis. Parallel to the acute structural contradiction between 'the land monopoly of the semi-feudal proprietors and the peasant economy of small production trying to develop its agricultural productive forces,'[30] were the growing social contradictions between the classes threatening to explode in agrarian revolution. The combined force of these critical pressures made agrarian reform by the newly independent Congress government of urgent priority. 'Thus the impetuous growth of the peasantry's struggle and the objective needs for capitalist development forced the national bourgeoisie which came to power in 1947 under the cover of the Indian National Congress to declare [a programme of] agrarian reforms.'[31] Overthrowing the old by radical reforms is the alpha and omega of the Soviet agrarian analysis. The feudal agrarian structure must be cleared away if accelerated growth of the agricultural forces is to be achieved. Without radical progress in agriculture there can be no general progress, since agriculture dominates the third world economy: 'The solution of the main problem, i.e. the abolition of feudal type agrarian structure and hence clearing the way for an accelerated growth of productive forces in agriculture, is one of the most important prerequisites for an economic, social, political and cultural development of the newly sovereign Asian and North African states.'[32]

THE POLITICS OF AGRARIAN REFORM

Agrarian reform may be in the objective economic interests of the bourgeois-national state, but it is only when the peasantry become actively engaged in the class struggle that reforms get implemented. The strong peasant movement to throw off the feudal yoke was 'not the least of the causes' of land reform in Iran. Otherwise the class nature of state power will determine such an important result of the reforms as the extent to which large-scale landownership is preserved. That the nationalization of foreign landownership took place in Algeria, Tunisia, Egypt, Burma, and Indonesia but not in Morocco, Malaysia, Ceylon, or India was due to the more progressive class composition of the former countries' ruling groups. Success, furthermore, breeds success: 'the deepening of revolutionary transformations in the countries of the East leads to further radicalization of agrarian reforms.'[33] On the other hand failure engenders failure. Repression and retrenchment may stifle the social forces best able to lead the struggle for reform. The Indian example falls between these extremes. Although the revolutionary agrarian movement was repressed, the general social pressure was still strong enough to break through the landlords' initial resistance and force the implementation of a first round of bourgeois democratic reforms.

While the contradictions forcing agrarian reforms in India were economic and social, what decided their policy content and the way they were implemented was the class character of the new country's political leadership. The fact that the transfer of power was not to the proletariat led by its communist party but to the national bourgeoisie under aegis of its party, the Indian National Congress, determined not just the general direction the economy was to take but in particular the whole thrust of its agricultural development. Since, in the Soviet view, there are only two possible ways to solve the agrarian question in any country, the class structure of the government determines which path is chosen. The first and radical road 'is the revolutionary abolition of landed property carried out in the interests of all the peasantry by the complete liquidation of the large landowner class.'[34] 'Truly revolutionary was the nature of the land reform in Cuba, which was started in 1959 and reached its peak after 1963. It ultimately resulted in the complete abolition of big landownership. Within a' short time most of the former estates had been turned into big agricultural enterprises of a socialist type which now account for 70 per cent of the agricultural lands and contribute most of the agricultural output.'[35] Having adequate financial resources is an important factor, to be sure. 'The biggest bourgeois-reformist agrarian changes in Latin America are effected in Venezuela. Landed property is alienated for redemption equal to its market value, while the peasants receive allotments within the set minimum level (17-20 hectares) free of charge. Such a land reform was made possible by the revenue the state received from foreign oil and mining corporations.'[36] But in Africa even the dominance of revolutionary democrats in the state machine is not enough to guarantee success. 'The socialism-oriented countries have found it very difficult to carry out agrarian transformations against the odds of the extremely backward countryside, the shortage of material and financial resources and specialists, the resistance put up by reactionaries, and the conservative attitudes of the bulk of the peasants.'[37] Because a national bourgeoisie achieved independence for India in 1947, this signified that 'the class which had taken the lead in the mass anti-imperialist national liberation movement and which had now reached power, could not effect a radical, anti-feudal agrarian revolution.'[38]

However, once in power the bourgeoisie found itself politically obliged 'to tackle the agrarian question in order to maintain its leadership of the national movement during its new stage.' Put bluntly, the second and moderate path of bourgeois agrarian reform was required to distract the peasantry from the insurrectionary movement which had already erupted in such areas as Telengana and which threatened to break out elsewhere if no reforms were made. Despite this political impetus for bourgeois reforms, the period from 1947 to 1953 was almost a complete failure. Although the legislatures enacted agrarian reforms, the landed proprietors led a bitter and effective resistance against their implementation by challenging their constitutionality in the courts and by putting pressure on the civil servants. Soviet commentators conclude from this that the national bourgeoisie did not really want to sacrifice the political support of the landed proprietors, to which it was in any case closely tied both by family and financial connections.[39] Such an implicit compromise with the reactionary agrarian class could not last against the growing menace of the peasant movement which had reached the point of an armed insurrection under communist direction in the Telengana region. After 1953 the bourgeoisie determined to extend its rural political support by implementing its programme of 'bourgeois-landlord agrarian reforms.'[40] This was designed to provoke a split in the peasantry's class ranks, rallying to the government's side the well-to-do peasants while sacrificing the poor peasants, but keeping the sympathies of those large landowners who were willing to transform their holdings into capitalist-type farms able to stimulate agricultural production.

The agrarian reforms answered a political need first of all, but they were also necessary for economic reasons. As we have seen, Indian agriculture was in a state of full crisis, which in Soviet terminology meant 'the contradiction between the national needs for independent development and the obstacles which were in its path.'[41] Structural roadblocks preventing the desperately needed expansion of agricultural production formed the main obstacle to developing the capitalist mode of production in the economy as a whole. Driven by its own economic imperatives, the bourgeoisie was obliged to attack the archaic agrarian structure, hoping to replace it by a new and more efficient mode of production relations. Thus the Indian National Congress was forced to adopt in the years following independence a broad programme launched under the slogan of 'the land to the tiller.' This political platform included abolition of the zamindari system, elimination of the intermediaries between the peasant producers and the government, establishment of an acreage ceiling on land holding, the guarantee of tenants' rights, and reducing rents and granting tenants the opportunity to buy the land they had been cultivating.[42]

While the programme was a step forward, it was by no means radical. It did not spell the annihilation of the large landlord class but only its gradual transformation. This was in fact the class meaning of the moderate, bourgeois-landlord path for solving the agrarian question. 'The bourgeois landlord agrarian reforms are accomplished by strengthening the kulaks and partially limiting the large landholdings which get progressively transformed into capitalist farms. This whole process was accompanied by the ruin and proletarization of the overwhelming majority of the peasantry.'[43]

Indian agricultural policy was thus not aimed at a complete destruction of the survivals of the feudal structure but rather at the gradual achievement, with the co-operation of the large landowners, of certain definite changes in the agrarian structure encouraging some modernization and a more rapid development of the agrarian economy along capitalist lines.

THE DEVELOPMENT OF AGRARIAN CAPITALISM

The Soviet story of agricultural evolution in the third world is the story of a capitalism that couldn't. The analytical schema is universal and clear. Commercial agriculture grows, and class differentiation takes place. All this is accompanied by the increase of agrarian overpopulation, the pauperization of most of the peasantry, and the destruction of the traditional forms of production. Consequently sharecropping as the main method of pre-capitalist exploitation of the peasantry is pushed out by the exploitation of hired labour. The peasantry divides into two capitalist classes: the agrarian bourgeoisie and the agrarian proletariat, now working as hired labour.[44] Soviet third world agricultural analysis reads like an over-willing theory in search of an evasive, unobliging reality. For although the theory is based on the hypothesis that capitalism must develop, the complex reality continually challenges this axiom with indications of flourishing pre-capitalist forms.

To say that agriculture is developing along the capitalist path under a bourgeois regime is little more than a tautology for marxist-leninists. What interests them is a precise catalogue of what capitalist phenomena have developed, and to what extent, so that they can then identify the exact stage reached in the process of the destruction of feudalism and its replacement by capitalism. The criteria of capitalist development used by marxist-leninists vary slightly from author to author, but they generally fall into three main groups: the signs of the elimination of feudalism, the various indicators of capitalist production relations, and the material indices of the expansion of the agrarian economy.

Decline of feudalism
Question number one in the evaluation of the effects of agrarian reform is the extent to which feudal exploitation has been reduced. The prime criterion for measuring feudalism is the nature of landlord-tenant relations. Despite the failure of statistical data to distinguish between feudal-type petty tenancy and entrepreneur-type capitalist tenancy, it is an 'obvious' conclusion in most countries with agrarian reforms that 'petty tenancy' has ceased to be the principal form of peasant land-holding. This means that the feudal exploitation of the peasantry has diminished – 'the most important result of the agrarian reforms.'[45]

As far as the decline of feudalism in India is concerned, Soviet experts observe that the agrarian reforms have liquidated the social and economic privileges based both on custom and law traditionally enjoyed by the rent-collecting strata which dominated the countryside.[46] 'For all the limitations of the agrarian reforms, their historically progressive and objective significance rests without any shadow of doubt in having restricted the extent of the peasantry's feudal and semi-feudal exploitation.'[47] This has principally been achieved by the government's purchase of a major part of the larger landholdings.[48] The landed class, as the carrier of the feudal mode of exploitation, had to give up part of its property. The large landholders did not suffer as much as this may imply, since the basic principle of India's agrarian legislation is 'a concentration of land in the hands of [those members of] the well-off rural classes who are capable of generating capitalist production.'[49]

Structural transformation
Among the indices of capitalist growth, Soviet analysts are above all interested in positive indications of structural transformation. Soviet specialists agree that capitalist farming is replacing the feudal operations in the large landholdings.[50]

'The large landholders could not survive ... except as bearers of capitalist relations.'[51] In other words the proprietors have begun to farm their own land directly instead of living solely off the rent of their land leased to tenants or sharecroppers. The well-off peasants also show signs of capitalist enterprise by taking on 'more and more' salaried labour. Also in the lower agrarian strata the worsening of the sharecroppers' plight shows another painful step being taken along the capitalist road. The sharecroppers are continually ceding the ownership of their permanent capital (tools and livestock) to the larger landholders and taking on the labourer's role as agrarian proletarians.[52]

In the rural property structure there are several indications that the conditions for capitalist farming are being achieved: a massive expulsion of the poor tenants from the landlords' property,[53] the consolidation of fragmented land parcels by the better-off peasants, and the purchase by the more privileged tenants of title to the land they had traditionally worked and could now enjoy as their own property.[54]

Commercialization

Among the quantifiable indicators of capitalist development in agriculture are those showing its commercialization. More and more farmers produce mainly for the market. Areas of commercial farming and livestock breeding take shape, even where the monetization of agriculture is lowest (Afghanistan, Yemen). Where the capitalist structure is most developed (Egypt, Turkey, Syria, Tunisia, and India) 5 to 10 per cent of the largest owners control up to one-half of all operated land areas and have a still higher share of the marketable produce. At the other end of the social ladder, the widening of the small-scale peasant producers' sector means a gradual strengthening of agrarian capitalism. The general trend may be clear, but the degree of change varies widely depending on the initial level of socio-economic development at the time of the reform, the changes undergone by the landownership and tenure systems, and the general direction or rate of economic development.[55] Looking at India's agrarian market, Soviet analysts see a growing commercialization in the increased sales of agricultural produce to industry and in the growing monetary expenditures of the rural population. This broadening of the agrarian market in turn stimulates the accumulation of capital, permitting some peasant investment in technical improvements which indicate an 'intensified development of agricultural production.'[56]

Increased production

Finally, Soviet observers see signs of a strengthening agricultural capitalism in the indices of production. A. Maslennikov, for instance, used as proof of capitalist development both the increase of agricultural production by 31 per cent between 1949-50 and 1958-9 and the factors which contributed to this growth, such as the expanded area of irrigated and seeded land plus the increased use of fertilizers and modern equipment.[57]

Although Soviet indologists declare in unison that the capitalist agrarian structure is developing in absolute terms, they nevertheless have great difficulty in pinpointing exactly where Indian agriculture is situated between the stages of feudalism and capitalism. No Soviet analyst ventures to affirm that capitalism has been established in India in all its western splendour, for they all recognize that many feudal 'survivals' persist even within the new capitalist farms themselves. The precise identification of just how feudal or how capitalist was Indian agriculture became the subject of a continuing debate among Soviet agronomists. The controversy revolved around the relative importance of the feudal vestiges as compared with the capitalist indices. One line of argument, represented by Maksimov and Rastyannikov in the late 1950s, did not appear to doubt that capitalism was, in the final analysis, winning out. Kotovsky on the other hand had more doubts, denying that the feudal-type farms had become capitalist, although they had created a favourable basis for capitalist operation.[58] In an article which apparently reflected the general Soviet scholarly consensus, R.A. Ulyanovsky stated that 'one can no longer speak of the overall domination of feudal survivals in the Indian countryside even in the regions of former large landholding.'[59] But the question of how far capitalism has advanced in the countryside had not been solved.

Some scholars have satisfied themselves that capitalism is now the dominant tendency in Indian agrarian development. Rastyannikov and Maksimov started their major book with the phrase, 'In studying the development of capitalism in agriculture,' thus making it clear that they had no doubt that the question was how far capitalism had gone, not whether capitalist development was taking place.[60] Ulyanovsky referred to the 'green revolution' as a case of 'accelerated capitalist development of agriculture in India.'[61] Nevertheless Soviet publications indicated that the degree of capitalist development remained an open question. Articles have pointed out how persistent are the 'semi-feudal survivals' in Indian agriculture, even in those areas already considered to be capitalist. One written by an Indian but published in the learned journal of the Institute of Asian Peoples in Moscow maintained, for example, that 'semi-feudal relations predominate up to the present [1963] in Indian agriculture.' This strong statement was supported by numerous observations which cast doubt on the validity of some Soviet criteria indicating the capitalist nature of Indian agriculture: 'Even the employment of salaried labour in agriculture has elements of feudal exploitation. The workers are still tied down by permanent debts contracted with their masters.'[62] In one revealing paragraph L. Stepanov summarized the tantalizing complexity of the Indian rural economy:

The two most prominent features of India's agrarian system today are the survival of pronounced feudal relics and a somewhat accelerated development of capitalist relations in the rural areas. A factor apart is the existence of large tea, coffee and rubber-tree plantations, many of them organised on the lines of capitalist big business, producing for export, and maintained by harsh exploitation of hired labour. Foreign capital is strongly entrenched in this sector of Indian agriculture. In certain areas, on the other hand, where tribal social relations have persisted, the cutting and grass-fallow system of land tenure prevails, based on community cultivation of the land. This is simply subsistence farming, in which whatever is produced is consumed by the farmers, and there is no barter trade with outsiders. The great majority of small peasant holdings (around 80 per cent) are also run, essentially, on a subsistence basis, with crops barely able to ensure the peasants' food supply, leaving nothing for sale.[63]

Having pointed out how far capitalism has progressed, Soviet indologists put greater emphasis on the pre-capitalist sector which still produced the bulk of the national revenue. K.M. Varentsov and M.A Maksimov pointed out that in India 'kulaks' only made up 3.7 per cent of all farmers and that even the kulak was unable to farm fully as a capitalist, having to rent much of his land at enslaving sharecropping rates because of the high rate of interest he had to pay the usurer.[64] Rastyannikov himself reported that, while there had been a gradual increase in the delivery of commodity products to the market by the entrepreneurial stratum, on the whole the agrarian bourgeoisie was not the main supplier of commercialized grain.[65] Only 40 to 45 per cent of the national revenue came from capitalist types of agrarian enterprise.[66] According to R.P. Gurvich, capitalist forms were growing at a slower rate than that at which small commodity production was breaking up.[67] Capitalism may be a growing force but it was not the principal producer.

According to Rastyannikov and Maksimov this petty commodity production sector was less a precursor than an obstacle in the way of the bourgeoisie's development toward capitalism. The nature of primitive accumulation does not encourage capitalist development; it restrains its progress.[68] The system of state taxes and the longevity of transitional property forms were preventing the agrarian bourgeoisie as a class from separating from the small peasantry even though the latter remained ready for the transition to capitalism. The agrarian capitalists that appeared were forced to choose between the two conflicting paths of capitalist development: the radical (peasant) direction and the conservative (landlord) path. The conservative tendency was dominant thanks to the close ties linking big urban capital with the large landowners.[69] The government's conservative agricultural policy was thus responsible for the failure of rural capitalism to develop. By maintaining in place the large landlords and abandoning radical agrarian reforms, pre-capitalist vestiges had been allowed to survive.

But this was not a unanimous point of view in Moscow. L. Rudin considered that capitalist development was prevented less by such subjective factors as the government's policy than by the objective problem of relative overpopulation. In his view no radical reform could produce a de facto transformation in the village economy as long as the colossal reserve supply of labour ready to work at any price kept growing.[70]

WHAT PRICE CAPITALISM?

To understand the Soviet preoccupation with capitalism in third world agriculture one must start from their position that feudalism is the dominant mode of production under the colonial regime. We have seen that Marx himself had rejected feudalism as the right concept to describe the Asiatic economy. While it is not the business of a non-believer to cry 'heresy,' it is important for an appreciation of Soviet development theory to know that a fundamental dispute involving its whole theoretical foundation lurks below the intellectual surface.

Whatever the orthodoxy within the marxist tradition of the Soviet use of the concept of feudalism, a more important problem is its usefulness as an analytical concept. An American specialist on Indian agriculture, Daniel Thorner, questioned the existence of a 'feudal' system in a country which had 'neither seigneury nor serfs. But India has not either what is essential to this system: neither the feudal contract nor real vassals nor fiefs ... A feudal regime without castle, without serfs, without feudal contract, without vassals, and without fiefs, is not a feudal regime. The expression is useless, in any case for rural India.'[71] This has become a largely semantic question. The Soviet claim is not that the agrarian system of colonial India has been feudal in the sense that it demonstrated the defining characteristics of European land relations in the middle ages. Rather it is 'feudal' in the sense that it is pre-modern or, more precisely, pre-capitalist. A relationship appears to them 'feudal' if it prevents the development of capitalist relations, if it allows a level of exploitation which is excessive, if it diverts capital resources to wasteful, non-productive uses. It is feudal, in other words, if it does not encourage the historically necessary and desirable evolution of capitalist – or under revolutionary leadership, socialist – forms and structures of production. 'Feudal' in the marxist-leninist vocabulary applied to the third world has *changed* rather than *lost* its analytical content.

While the Soviet conception of feudalism represents a theoretical innovation dating from the stalinist period, their idea of agrarian capitalism remains more strictly leninist. Marx's analysis of the development of agrarian capitalism was concerned with the independent peasant of the countries in western Europe at a period when socialists were interested in the technical transformation of the countryside under the dual process of the concentration of landholdings and the mechanization of agriculture in larger-scale cultivation. Marx fitted the problems of the peasantry into the same conceptual system of capital, labour, and surplus value that he had used to explain industrial problems: the peasant, owning his means of production, is a capitalist; but as a worker he is his own wage-earner.[72]

Though agriculture was not the centre of interest for Marx in industrializing western Europe, the 'agrarian question' was a more crucial social, economic, and political issue in underdeveloped Russia, but one difficult to analyze in Marx's rather schematic and derivative terms. It was George Plekhanov, the 'father of Russian marxism,' who set himself to adapt marxism to a Russia dominated by quite a different system of agrarian relations.[73] The conceptual tools that Lenin used to investigate Russian agriculture were based on Plekhanov's agrarian theory.

Given the backwardness of Russia's economy in the process of rapid development at the end of the nineteenth century, and given too the Russian marxist's ideological need in their polemic with the Populists to insist on the profoundly capitalist nature of their economy's transformation, it is quite understandable that Lenin should have been pushed into exaggerating the signs of capitalist development in the countryside where his revolutionary rivals were most strongly entrenched. In his own major scholarly work, *The Development of Capitalism in Russia*, written in Siberian exile where he had good access to existing data gathered by the village zemstvo organizations, Lenin assembled a long list of criteria of agrarian capitalism that described a village-based peasant agriculture just starting on a process of genuine expansion under the impact of the urban economy's industrialization.[74]

The parallels between the emergent agriculture of 1890s Russia and the development problems of the non-communist ex-colonies is sufficient for the Soviet orientalists to apply Lenin's paradigm of agrarian capitalist evolution to the village economy in India or Ghana. In their view Lenin has already articulated all the theory necessary for the study of contemporary third world agriculture. When pressed in interviews whether any aspects of the leninist analysis of the disintegration of the Russian village economy are not applicable to Indian agriculture, Soviet scholars reply that the distinctive features of the Indian situation – whether the caste system, the different type of moneylenders' domination, or the greater agrarian overpopulation – are only differences in degree and not in kind from the Russian situation of 1900. Hence the complete relevance of Lenin's analysis for their purposes.

Although one can readily see why Soviet theorists should be prone to analyse Indian agriculture in terms of its capitalist development, it is quite another matter whether this preoccupation with capitalism is analytically significant and whether it leads to valid policy recommendations. The major heuristic weakness of the Soviet concept of agricultural capitalism is its all-embracing character in application. We have seen that their criteria of capitalist development include technical factors promoting an increase of agricultural production and productivity. Evidence for a development of capitalism is found in the expansion of the area under irrigation or the use of improved insecticides. Thus it would appear that any development of the productive forces in a non-communist country must for a Soviet observer constitute capitalist development. Yet such technological improvements could theoretically be made with no change of the production relations: a feudal agriculture using fertilizers could increase its yields without becoming ipso facto more capitalist.

A further difficulty with these criteria of capitalist development is that they would apply just as much to agrarian developments in a socialist system. All the signs of a modernizing agriculture – from the specialization of production in the various regions through technical improvements, to the trend to large-scale enterprises – would characterize equally well a socialist as a capitalist agricultural development.

While no Soviet scholar asserts that any single criterion would alone suffice to establish the presence of capitalism, some of their economic indices are open to criticism on the grounds of insufficient precision. The employment of salaried workers, for example, is one of the most fundamental of indicators of capitalism. In their discussions Soviet analysts do not define precisely how many salaried workers a farmer must hire, or for what proportion of the year, for him to be considered a capitalist. In their current view a peasant could be non-capitalist for the major part of the year, but capitalist at seed and harvest time when he takes on some helpers. Making their criteria more rigorously defined would make the existence of capitalist relations more empirically measurable. Daniel Thorner proposed for example that for a peasant to be considered a capitalist farmer he would have to hire salaried agricultural workers for a total number of hours greater than those provided by the peasant's own family.

The vagueness of the application by Soviet scholars of their criteria of capitalist development to Indian agriculture brings us back to the assessment of whether capitalism is the dominant economic structure. It is clear that in applying their own criteria they find capitalism in regions where a large number of non-capitalist or feudal characteristics abound. They consider, for example, that farms run personally by the large landowners are capitalist. However their technological base is often at the same primitive level as that of the oppressed peasants and their productivity is as low. Furthermore the 'kulaks,' the rich peasants who act as carriers of the capitalist mode of production, by possessing their own land

and enough acreage to produce for the market are themselves using their profits for 'usury' lending and their lands for subletting to poorer peasants. The champions of capitalism are practising feudalism literally in their backyard. If agrarian capitalism can exist without capital or even a modern technological base and if its carriers can still perpetuate pre-capitalist relations, it becomes difficult for the reader to judge whether the Soviet interpretation of the evidence justifies the conclusion that capitalism is dominant. Thorner for one felt that 'up to the present in any case capitalism has not been a dominant economic form in the country; it is premature to affirm or deny that it is today the principal tendency.'[75]

It is also difficult to assess the policy implications of the dominance of capitalism. For some revolutionaries if capitalism is dominant they must push forward for the second, socialist phase of the two-stage revolution. Soviet agrarian analysis, however, is not the most revolutionary part of marxist-leninist development theory. The dominance of capitalism simply seems to mean that capitalism is developing relatively faster than any other production mode, even if it is not absolutely the dominating sector of agriculture. The Soviets can be accused of using 'capitalism' so broadly and vaguely that they blur whatever clear conclusions their methodology could have been expected to produce. While this charge is better grounded in the Soviet analysis of other newly independent countries where their research is more superficial, it is less correct for India where the Soviet expertise is impressive. It would be more accurate to say that in applying a very blunt conceptual tool to an extremely complex situation the consistency of their argument and the clarity of their over-all judgments often suffer heavy losses.

For if the description is clear – and the best Soviet indologists handle their crude analytical tools with great subtlety, so that their discussion of the pre-capitalist capitalists and the post-feudal feudals does take account of the nuances of the real situation – one then has to ask whether this elaborate exercise is worth the effort. Is it merely the translation into marxist-leninist vocabulary of information produced by scholars in a liberal-bourgeois language? Does it not detract from the original picture as painted in local colours and concepts? Certainly for the non-marxist reader something is lost in the translation: a feeling for how the rural village really is seen and lived in by the various resident actors. The endless complexity of the Indian traditional scene is undercut by the broad categories of the marxist schema. The purists are offended, and local experts protest that things just do not look the way the Soviets describe it.

For all its conceptual vagueness, the picture painted is comprehensible: an agricultural system in the process of a laborious historical transition from one mode of production to another. 'Feudal' and 'capitalist' are ideal types for the analyst that allow him to place the complex observed phenomena into categories that are basically simple and lead to simple policy conclusions. Are they *too* simple? When asked this question the Soviet scholars' first answer is that they are writing for the Soviet public, who understand the marxist-leninist language and logic. This readership is accustomed to the application of a highly categorical and dialectical intellectual system. There may be more immediate comprehension by the Soviet reader of the Russian indologists' articles than of Russian translations of western monographs. Will there be more true understanding? The understanding will be different certainly, since thinking in historical-economic terms is not as central a preoccupation for the liberal as for the marxist-leninist, for whom it is the basic point of departure. As an epistemological problem, the debate can ultimately only end in a final standoff: some will find the marxist-leninist framework indispensable to their thought and writing; others will find it incompatible with their frame of mind.

Among the Soviet indologists, the convinced marxist-leninist agronomists strongly swear to the superiority of their method and its results: they can better comprehend the minutiae of the liberal's case study by placing such empirical microanalysis in their macro-historical perspective. Yet some marxists among the Soviet orientalists express genuine doubts about the adequacy of their conceptual equipment to deal with the distinctive and unique aspects especially in the traditional economic forms e.g. Mirsky and Varga. And still other Soviet writers will confide that in their view the marxist-leninst apparatus is but a sham, a ritual formulation tacked on to the introductory and concluding chapters in obeisance to the CPSU. Marxists outside the Soviet Union have a different type of critical independence, mixed with a greater disinclination to give Soviet theorists the benefit of the doubt. We have referred above to the unhappiness particularly of the French marxists with the Soviet reluctance to re-examine their concepts of feudal and capitalist historical stages in favour of the culturally specific Asiatic mode of production. More important, Indian Communists have complained to their Soviet confrères that the English translations of Russian books have not appeared relevant to their own party workers or political concerns. The non-marxist is likely to respond that, beyond a certain point, one would expect diminishing intellectual returns from imposing a foreign conceptual structure on a particular socioeconomic reality. For such non-marxists as Daniel Thorner the Soviet attempt to conceptualize the problems of Indian agriculture capitalism is not adequate to characterize the dominant features of the Indian countryside even if it is appropriate for some types of agriculture.

There is a further objection to which the Soviet use of 'capitalism' as a historical stage of development is liable: the basic hypotheses do not permit any alternative other than to identify the stage of development of India's agriculture as capitalist. Consider the logic: if the choice facing Indian agriculture is between two paths, the socialist and the capitalist, and if the socialist option is excluded because the proletariat led by its Communist Party does not hold power, then Indian agriculture must be on a capitalist path. There is no third way. Any idea of a third road between capitalism and socialism is dismissed as only a myth propagated by the bourgeois ideologues to mislead the people. Those who proclaim the co-operative movement as a third path of development are at best fooling themselves, at worst deliberately duping the masses: for under capitalist production relations 'agrarian co-operatives are a manifestation of the capitalist development in agriculture.' The only alternative is co-operatives in the socialist countries, where they constitute 'one of the forms of socialist transition in agriculture.'[76] The historical development paradigm is clear. Indian agriculture progresses along a road which begins with Feudalism and will neatly end up in the stage of full Capitalism.

In the hands of the less sophisticated writers this is indeed the undifferentiated, simplistic view, as analytically useless as the equally ethnocentric western dogmatism which maintains that only private property farming with Massey-Ferguson tractors can solve the food production problem in the third world. The careful Soviet analyst does make some distinctions in the type and degree of capitalism. Lenin himself distinguished between two kinds of capitalist development – the American (peasant) or the Prussian (landlord) paths. The American road was based on the individual small farmer's property, while Prussian capitalism was an outgrowth of large landed estates coming to produce for the market. Agrarian reforms that genuinely abolish latifundia can inaugurate peasant-capitalist development; India's agrarian capitalism has been the less progressive landlord version.

Field exposure to the multiplicity of agrarian relationships in the new nations of Afro-Asia has precipitated a further refinement of categories. At least in regimes with 'revolutionary democratic' leaderships seen as more progressive from the Soviet viewpoint, variations of feudal and even pre-feudal property relations can be seen evolving in ways that might bypass the capitalist stage. What is interesting in the more recent years is that, with the increasing number of conceptual options open to them, Soviet indologists have increasingly identified India as the archetype of landlord-capitalist development in the third world. Archetype, not stereotype. The more familiar one becomes with Soviet analysis, the less tempted one is to dismiss out of hand this continual action of fitting local reality into an outside frame of reference, an operation that is in principle no different from that of a structural-functionalist or systems analyst fitting the Indian system into his categories of articulation and aggregation or inputs and outputs.

Why then is there such a consuming interest in the capitalism of third world agriculture? It is possible that there are factors other than the theoretical and the conceptual which impel Soviet orientalists to concentrate so strongly on the capitalist mode. One clue comes from Soviet scholars' generally benign view of capitalism as a historically progressive stage of development compared with the feudalism from which it emerges. If Soviet analysts have any reason to support a country's government – and there is ample proof of their over-all support for New Delhi – then they would be encouraged to insist on the positive role that capitalism and hence the bourgeoisie, play there. This ideological motivation is strengthened by the marxist-leninists' dialectical moral attitude towards capitalism. While they like to underline the evils of capitalist society in order the better to show how scientific socialists champion the interests of the exploited, they can also salute capitalism's achievements, which historically prepare the material conditions necessary for the transition to socialism. If the analysts show, for example, that the bourgeoisie has made great progress but that the peasantry's situation has deteriorated, they can both deplore the unjust consequences of the capitalist system and rejoice that the class struggle will inevitably be further aggravated.

This equivocal ethical approach toward capitalism is reinforced by a still more fundamental need of the marxist-leninist to define the historical stage attained by a given economic system. As a doctrine at least officially directed towards revolutionary action, marxism-leninism aims above all at analysing a socioeconomic situation in order to determine what point class relations have reached and what class tactics should be deduced for the proletariat. The more developed that capitalism appears, relative to the preceding mode of production, the more optimistic can the analyst be in his tactical recommendations for his local comrades and in his general conclusions about the ultimate result of the struggle for the socialist path.

What is striking in the Soviet approach to capitalism is the favourable attitude to it. If the kulaks' situation leaves something to be desired it is that their relative strength is too weak and their chance to improve their technology insufficient. Kulak farms are criticized because they are not capitalist enough.[77] Thus, although they periodically maintain that India can only solve its problems by choosing the socialist path, Soviet observers appear so enthusiastic about capitalism that the non-marxist may be forgiven for wondering why the progress already achieved by so slight a capitalist development will not continue indefinitely as capitalism consolidates itself. For a marxist-leninist, of course, it is doctrinally given that the more capitalism develops the more its internal contradictions will destroy it. For a good leninist, too, the socialist path can begin at any stage of historical development. Moscow's indologists certainly subscribe to the thesis that socialist development could begin in India as soon as the Communist Party takes power. But even if the marxist-leninists are only interested in the seizure of power, their class tactics to reach this goal will still depend on their analysis of the current stage of development. Non-maoist marxist-leninists with an increasing disposition towards peaceful access to power will be more comfortable discussing class tactics under a familiar capitalism where the inevitable historical forces can look after themselves than at an earlier stage when more voluntarist political intervention would be required. The strong Soviet commitment to analysing Indian agriculture in terms of capitalism can be further understood by pursuing the class analysis of the countryside.

13

Rural class relations

The Soviet analysis of the third world's rural classes is theoretically inseparable from their explanation of how agrarian capitalism emerges from feudalism. In the countryside the two classes supporting the feudal mode of production are the landlords and the peasantry. The class dynamic provoking the changeover from a feudal into a capitalist mode of agrarian production occurs when both these classes break up. Some landlords become a feudal remnant that is pushed out of existence but others become a new entrepreneurial bourgeoisie; while some peasants work up into bourgeois farmers, others fall into the category of rural proletarians. The new rural bourgeoisie and the agrarian proletariat 'carry' the capitalist mode of production. Although this paradigm is simple, analytical hairs are split so finely in its application that the clarity of the Soviet presentation is put into some jeopardy for the unwary reader.

THE LANDLORDS

The impact of agrarian reforms on the feudal landlord class has varied widely from country to country. As a rule the influence wielded by the landlords and the plantation-owners on governments has been largely responsible for the failure of the agrarian reforms to undermine the economic interests of the large-scale landholders. This is especially graphic in countries like Morocco, Thailand, and Malaysia, where agrarian reforms have made no headway, or Nepal and Sri Lanka, where they are still at a preliminary stage of implementation, but less true of Iraq or Egypt. Except for Burma, the abolition of large landownership is incomplete. It has proceeded by setting a ceiling on ownership and by transferring, with due compensation, part of the landlords' property to former tenants. Because this appropriation of landlord holdings tended to be implemented by administrators closely associated with the feudal elements, and because the tenant beneficiaries had a minimal consciousness of or participation in the reforms, there was ample chance for vested interests to manœuvre and preserve their position. Even where the economic and political positions of feudal elements have been dealt the biggest blows, as in Egypt, Iraq, Syria, and the ex-zamindari areas of India, the landlords have retained holdings many times greater than the peasants. This is because the land reforms were aimed not at the abolition of feudal landownership but its gradual replacement by large and medium bourgeois property.[1]

Landlordism is not the major rural class issue in all areas of the third world. It is not a problem in tropical Africa where uncultivated land is still abundant. Nor is the dominance of landlord property generally the principal constraint in Southeast Asia where the peasantry is not forced to lease land on enslaving terms. 'On the contrary, with the exception of the Philippines, some regions of Vietnam and contemporary Burma, landlord property did not occupy a dominating position in Southeast Asia in the mid-twentieth century as was the case in the Near and Middle East or India.'[2]

In India, the landlord was dominant as the carrier of feudalism and remained central even as capitalism emerged. Indeed, the Soviet analysis of the large landholders gives a good example of the marxist dialectic which discovers opposing tendencies in every phenomenon. For Soviet marxists the landlords form a clearly defined social class which incarnates both the reactionary maintenance of the old feudal barriers and the potential for a progressive change of the agrarian structure towards capitalism.[3] Their thesis is that the feudal landlord class has not been fully transformed by India's reforms. It remains dominant in the countryside and quasi-feudal in its production relations. The legislated abolition of the zamindar system has not, in actual fact, led to the liquidation of this feudal landlord class. For even if the zamindars have been weakened by the expropriation of a large part of the land that they used to rent out, the size of their financial compensation by the state has nevertheless left them amongst the richest landowners. In addition they have retained very large properties because of the incomplete nature of the expropriations. They have not only kept their equipment and houses but also the *sirs*, those parts of their properties which were said to be under their own direct cultivation. Thanks to their dominant position in the villages and to their consequent corruption of the local administrators who registered landholdings, and thanks as well to the ruthless expulsion of the tenants from the land claimed by the zamindars to be their *sirs*, these 'liquidated' zamindars have remained an integral part of the proprietor class in the Indian countryside.[4]

Not only do the large landholdings survive; so do semi-feudal relations under their aegis. Having expelled the peasants supposedly to enlarge the lands kept under their personal capitalist farming, the large property owners proceeded to re-lease their land at even higher rents than before.[5] They use the liquid capital acquired from compensation not on technical improvements to their properties but on merchant-usury exploitation of their tenants. They increase their control of the peasantry by lending money at enslaving rates; they speculate by buying the right to the peasants' crops at low prices and selling them when market prices are high. Through such activity not only do they fail to contribute to agrarian development but they also block it by reinforcing the feudal forms of exploiting and throttling the poor.[6] Seeing Indian agriculture from this perspective, some Soviet analysts feel that feudalism still predominates in India. The antithesis in the Soviet argument is that the reforms are after all succeeding in transforming feudal into capitalist agriculture by turning the former feudal landlords into bourgeois farmers.[7] The standard illustration for this opposite proposition is the transformation of the proprietors, who until then had lived as parasites off the rents received from their tenants, into entrepreneurs running agricultural operations on their own *sirs*. Some of the phenomena that indicated the maintenance of feudalism are also seen to stimulate capitalist development. Financial compensation for the land expropriated from the zamindars, for instance, permits them to invest in modern, mechanized means of production for use on the land they retain under their direct cultivation.[8] Owning their own means of production, they become capitalist farmers.

Even the reinforcing of certain types of sharecropping can be a historically progressive step towards capitalism. The legal legitimization of sharecropping, for example, constitutes in the judgment of Maksimov and Rastyannikov, not stagnation as one might have expected, but on the contrary 'a definite stage in the disintegration of the feudal and the establishment of the capitalist mode of production.'[9] For sharecropping further separates the producers from the means of production by transforming these once feudal peasants into a class of salaried agricultural labourers. Sharecropping is an 'intermediate structure which performs the mission of depeasantization, of clearing the land for capitalism.[10] At the same time the former landlords who now appropriate the sharecroppers' agricultural instruments become a class of rural employers using the workers as their labour force.[11] The change of various types of feudal rent into sharecropping signifies a further approach of the big landowners to the capitalist mode by facilitating this form of primitive accumulation.[12]

The transformation of feudal-type properties into capitalist enterprise is deduced from the considerable reduction of the area rented out. A parallel growth of direct cultivation by the owners of their own 'cleaned' land has been observed.[13] According to R.A. Ulyanovsky, from 75 to 80 per cent of the large landowners cultivated their farms themselves.[14] Numerous intermediaries, well-to-do peasants, and even privileged tenants have been able to obtain their own land, if not by grant at least by purchase. All this does not imply that Soviet observers believed the reforms have revolutionized India's agrarian production relations. G.G. Kotovsky insisted that 'the implementation of the agrarian reforms has produced no new distribution of land' and that 'for the great mass of tenants, the change in their legal status has only had very little significance in economic terms.'[15] All emphasize that it is the class of landed proprietors becoming the new agrarian bourgeoisie which has benefited most from the governmental programmes of agricultural promotion in credits, in irrigation and in agro-technical aid; they are enriching themselves as they develop their capitalist operations.[16] Thus the conservation by the ex-feudal landowners of large quantities of land (which would have indicated the partial failure of radical reforms from the peasantry's point of view) is the indicator of success for moderate reforms aimed at putting Indian agriculture on the 'landlord' path of conservative capitalist development.[17]

The 'synthesis' in the Soviet discussion of the landlords is confusing. V.G. Rastyannikov and M.A. Maksimov maintained in their definitive work that the large landowners becoming capitalists were the chief class support of what they called 'summit capitalism' in Indian agriculture. While conserving the main bases of the old agrarian structure and property they were transforming themselves into an entrepreneurial stratum by applying methods of primitive capital accumulation.[18] They were further consolidating their position by strengthening their links with the summit of the urban and monopolistic bourgeoisie: they used state capitalist measures for their enrichment and transferred a large part of their surplus capital into commercial-industrial capital.[19]

This analysis did not go unchallenged in the Soviet school. L. Rudin, in reviewing the Rastyannikov-Maksimov book, questioned their concept of 'large landowner' for including princes, large zamindars, middle and small landowners, and well-off peasants, and so exaggerating the power of the big landlords.[20] They included among the landowners those earning Rs 2,000, yet they admitted in a footnote that Rs 2,000 was only considered enough for a plot to be economically self-sufficient.[21] If Indian agriculturalists could belong to the summit class of landowners even when barely self-sufficient, where did that leave the class at the other end of the social ladder?

One can understand very well that the large landowners obtain their revenue from rents coming from the exploitation of the peasants. What is less clear is the frontier delimiting the reactionary class of large landowners from the progressive class of bourgeois farmers. Size of property does not seem to be the principal criterion, for Kotovsky maintained that large landowners existed even in Kashmir, where the most radical reforms have been effected and the smallest land maxima imposed. To a large extent the act of giving land for rent, an aspect of semi-feudalism, appears to be the fundamental criterion determining membership in the feudal class. Still, this index does not designate exclusively the agrarian rich, for the peasants show signs of the same semi-feudalism. One must perhaps be content with the general idea that, as feudalism stands for pre-capitalism, so is 'large land-owner' a relative classification for the better-off and privileged of the country who still dominate village life. One wonders, nevertheless, whether this does not make the proprietors seem richer than they really are. For Soviet scholars sometimes note that even the country rich cannot afford to invest in modern equipment or buy the fertilizer necessary for the scientific cultivation of their land. Kotovsky reported for example that the annual investment of the richest farms (26 acres average) was only 336 rupees per year, whereas a tractor cost 10,000 rupees.[22]

THE RURAL BOURGEOISIE

As a new class, a product of the very process of capitalist development, one might have thought that the rural bourgeoisie would not present any analytical ambiguity to the marxist-leninist. Yet complexity is built into the Soviet model of agrarian class formation, which shows the bourgeoisie recruiting its cadres both 'from above' and 'from below.' On the one hand it emerges from the land-lords who are turning to capitalist farming on their own lands and from the trading and usury strata that have penetrated into land ownership as in Iraq, Syria, or Lebanon. Where this new bourgeoisie is defined as operating large-scale capitalist agriculture, as in Turkey, there is less problem in identifying it, but the point at which farmers stop being feudal landlords and start being rural bourgeois is not clear. Nor does this analysis define at what point the other recruiting source of rural bourgeois, the stratum of rich peasant farmers evolving out of the peasantry, becomes fused into a new bourgeois class. The Soviet experts themselves confess to some difficulty in drawing these lines. In Southeast Asia, for instance, where the size of large properties has appreciably diminished and where there never had been a large feudal landlord domination, Soviet theorists resolve the difficulty by labelling the elements emerging from the feudal and from the peasant classes as a single 'rural elite.'

A further difficulty in the Soviet category of the rural bourgeoisie is that it employs both capitalist and pre-capitalist methods of exploitation. While the rural bourgeois are capitalist to the extent that they employ hired labour on their farms and invest their surplus in urban real estate and industrial shares, they also lease their land on shackling feudal terms and engage in usurious money-lending and commercial speculation. Their income from the latter is often very substantial and sometimes the principal source of their revenue.[23]

At first glance these confusions seem not to apply in the Indian case, where the label 'kulak' is introduced to describe the richer farmers who have enough property to employ salaried labour.[24] Comprising only 3.7 per cent of all farmers, Indian kulaks often operate capitalist enterprise only on part of their land, renting out the rest at feudal sharecropping rates. Having to borrow at high interest rates from usurers and able to save only low amounts for capital investment, the kulak is unable to farm fully as a capitalist.[25] Moreover, India's agrarian bourgeoisie turns out to be less homogeneous than the concept kulak indicated, for its members have come both from higher and lower social strata.

The rural bourgeoisie has found recruits first of all in higher castes because to acquire property one needed not just enough capital but in addition the social privileges enjoyed only by those at the top of the caste ladder. According to the Soviet observers' own testimony, this big bourgeoisie could hardly be distinguished from the landlord class. For it too used feudal methods of exploitation, letting land out for rent, participating in moneylending and speculative market operations, and even continuing to receive revenue from inherited caste privileges.[26] Although Maksimov and Rastyannikov claimed that the new bourgeoisie as a class was in contradiction with the 'renovated old classes' whose yoke restrained the bourgeoisie's progress,[27] they also indicated that these big bourgeois holding the key positions in the countryside were intimately connected with large landed property.[28]

While writing of the big bourgeoisie as a distinct social layer, Soviet scholars also refer to a peasant bourgeoisie pushing up from the middle layers of the peasantry. These are the former privileged tenants who were able to purchase the land they had rented and become independent farmers, freed from the arbitrary control exercised by feudal village forces. Having appropriated part of the lands of the feudal aristocracy, these new bourgeois were also able to take advantage of government programmes promoting agricultural development. Although the class which benefits from the assistance of a bourgeois government is itself the carrier of the capitalist mode of production, semi-feudal relations exist even in this, the more progressive part of the rural entrepreneurial class. Nevertheless the social situation of these former middle peasants has improved so much because of the distribution to them of some of the zamindars' lands and the purchase of their own land,[29] that in the Soviet view they are an element of the new peasant bourgeoisie. They come from the small-commodity economy, the farms of under 15 acres into which capitalist features have been slowly penetrating. Half of the farms between 15 and 2.5 acres in size hire labour, thus demonstrating their maturity for a transition to capitalism. It was the increase in the size of peasant landownership that led to an entrepreneurial stratum forming among these direct producers.[30]

The growth of this rural bourgeois element is very slow because the small-commodity economy continues to present difficult obstacles to capitalist development. Transitional forms of landownership and the domination of large urban capital, combined with merchant-usury exploitation and heavy state taxation, hinder the separation of an agrarian bourgeoisie from the small-commodity economy. Another indicator of the slow progress of capitalism among this large section of the rural bourgeoisie is the stagnation of the ratio of marketed production to total output, a ratio that was no higher after twenty years of independence than in the colonial period.[31] In fact an increase in agricultural output or even a rise in prices received by these small producers does not lead to an increase in the amount marketed, but rather to a higher home consumption.[32]

The major analytical problem for the Soviets is to explain the strength of these pre-capitalist processes in the allegedly capitalist rural elites. Rudin criticized Rastyannikov and Maksimov for failing to explain satisfactorily why the processes of primitive accumulation hinder rather than encourage capitalist development. He pointed out that earlier Soviet dogma had an easy answer to this problem: the colonialists had conserved feudal survivals as an act of policy. But the national bourgeois government has actively encouraged both their destruction and capitalist development. Yet while the conditions have decisively changed, the old pre-capitalist methods still infuse the economy; it is not good enough to blame the government for maintaining conservative capitalism and large landownership. Thus even in the analysis of the agrarian bourgeoisie, the Soviet description of the rural capitalist class development remains too contradictory for their dialectics. In one paragraph the agrarian bourgeoisie seems well matured; in another its capitalist façade hides a lurking feudal or peasant order. It would seem that the Soviets are hoping to identify an agrarian bourgeoisie as part of the effort to uncover the traces of capitalism. Starting from Lenin's hypothesis that with the development of capitalism there must be a polarization of the old seigneurial and peasant classes, they have a strong impulse to find a new agrarian bourgeoisie evolving as a distinct rural class.

In a more recent (1974) reformulation of his analysis, Rastyannikov has defined the upper stratum in Indian agriculture not as the landowner class as a whole, but as a separate 'upper exploiting stratum of rural society: the groups of landowners who under the two-tier structure of the former feudal class made up its lower tier and representatives of the moneyed classes (merchants and usurers).' What accounts in his view for the rural elite's ability to thwart the new round of agrarian reforms in the 1970s was 'the tendency to integrate the trading, speculating and money-lending interests of the rural topmost groups of exploiters.' With their links into the army, the police, the legislative assemblies, and the rural self-government bodies, the large landowners who reside in the countryside have become an independent political force – a phenomenon that is true throughout Asia: the 'rural oligarchy which is gaining in strength possesses ever greater freedom of independent action within the framework of the social patterns in the developing Asian countries.'[33]

THE PEASANTRY

The peasantry presents an equally stubborn problem for Soviet analysts. In the marxist-leninist historical schema the peasants constitute the central feudal class from whose ranks should crystallize the two hostile groups in fully fledged capitalist agriculture, the bourgeoisie and the proletariat. Yet the peasantry is still the main class in the third world, making up, along with the semi-proletarian and proletarian strata, from 90 to 95 per cent of the agrarian population. For those interested in radical socioeconomic transformations it is this feudal stratum whose class struggle is the main determinant of the revolution. Since the solution of these countries' main revolutionary or democratic objectives is impossible without the peasants' active participation, the tactics of the working class (i.e. of the Communist Party) require forming a united front with the peasantry as the main ally. For those more interested in achieving immediate reforms, the peasantry as the main direct producers are also the motive power forcing the needed agrarian transformations.[34] 'The peasantry can provide the basis for non-capitalist development if the agrarian policy pursued by the national-democratic state is understandable to the peasants and helps immediately to improve their material conditions and opens up before them real prospects for a fundamental change in their living conditions in the future.'[35]

As Burma's experience showed, the active participation of the tenants in carrying out agrarian reforms is the best guarantee of a genuine implementation of tenancy legislation.[36] R. Ulyanovsky described the process:

One of the most difficult tasks was to reorganize semi-feudal agrarian relations. The problem was to eliminate the three-fold exploitation of small peasant farms by the landowners and the commercial money-lenders who operated via precapitalist land tenure, credit on usurer's terms, and trade.

It became necessary to rid millions of small farmers of the harmful effects of the semi-feudal, semi-capitalist system of relations of production, which was the archaic agrarian system left as a legacy by the colonialists. With that end in view, usury has been outlawed and is now a criminal offence, state agricultural credit has been substantially extended, and a state monopoly has been established on the purchases of an ever-growing range of farm produce. Multi-purpose agricultural cooperatives are developing, and among the new laws adopted are those providing protection for the rights of farmers, for the non-prosecution of tenants failing to pay rent, and for the abolition of land rent ...

Fairly strict rules regulating private land ownership and land tenure have been introduced. This has given rise, for the first time in the East, to a type of national-democratic state ownership of the land designed to help agriculture gradually join the general stream of non-capitalist development.

Of course this does not rule out the differentiation of the peasantry and growing class polarisation. But the countryside has in the main been cleared of pre-capitalist relations, while capitalist relations have been undermined.[37]

In the main, peasants are in a terrible situation throughout the third world. A large percentage have no land or very little; overpopulation leads to competition for the privilege even of share-cropping at high rents; parcelling reduces the size of the plots that they do cultivate; there is no employment for those losing their land.[38] The results of the agrarian tenancy acts have been contradictory. They have strengthened their legal status, giving the right of occupancy to tenants, prohibiting various feudal exactions and limiting the rise of rents, 'thus promoting a switchover from the most extortionate payments in kind to cash rents.' The substitution of petty peasant proprietors for landless tenants has meant the widening of the small-peasant sector. But since the political situation in the rural areas generally did not help them gain their rights, the reforms to a large extent 'served to conserve the archaic forms of production relations in agriculture,' leaving many tenants still suffering indebtedness and rack-renting under feudal exploitation.[39]

Although Soviet observers have noticed some progressive developments at the summit of the agrarian class pyramid, they are far from satisfied with the condition of the lower strata, particularly the peasantry. In the Indian case the landed class has greatly profited from the agrarian reforms while the principal producers have suffered.[40] Indeed, the dominant Soviet impression of the agrarian reforms' impact on the peasantry is continued stagnation, if not deterioration, in the condition of the rural masses. Reform of the old agrarian structure has not changed the onerous exploitation of the peasantry, nor has it solved its principal problem, land hunger.[41]

The peasant remains oppressed by a triple burden of feudal, moneylending, and commercial exploitation. Feudal exploitation survives not just because of the unchanged landholding system (as we shall see below), but because the poor and illiterate peasants are powerless before the domination of the large landowners who continue to be masters in the villages. Since the civil servants themselves fall under this seigneurial influence, governmental efforts to limit the degree of arbitrary power exercised by the village aristocracy have failed. The inferior position of the poor peasant is compounded by oppression at the hands of the moneylender, who commands the major share of agrarian credit, despite the creation of credit co-operatives by the various state governments. Having pitifully small resources, the peasant finds himself obliged to turn for help to the usurer to whom his debt increases inexorably.[42] With his crops pledged in advance, he loses in commercial exploitation the chance to receive the market price for the fruit of his labour. These difficulties would not perhaps be so serious if his land situation had improved.

That there can be no solution to the agrarian crisis without a prior solution to the land question among the peasantry is a common theme of the Soviet analysis: 'the main question, the land problem, remains unsolved.'[43] Indeed the massive expulsion of the tenants by the large landowners wanting to increase their *sirs* – a process Soviet observers describe in detail – seriously aggravated the already deplorable condition of the subtenants and agricultural workers, reducing their share of the supply of land still further.[44] The conditions for the purchase of land were too onerous (being several times the annual rent) for most peasants to be able to enjoy the security symbolized by this acquisition of private property.[45] The ceiling set for the size of large properties has led to no real redistribution of property among the landless peasants. The limitation of rents has only been instituted as the exception, not the rule.[46] Even when the landlords have been expropriated, the peasant must continue to pay rent to the 'total proprietor, the state.'[47] On the land which is still given out to rent the great pressure of 'relative agrarian overpopulation is so intense that the high level of rent remains the major problem for the poor peasantry.'[48] 'Rents have remained unchanged, except where they have gone up.'[49]

In their reports Soviet experts have pointed out certain improvements in the peasant's lot. But what he has gained by the official liquidation of the zamindars he has lost because of the increase in direct and indirect taxation,[50] a burden which doubled in a two-year period.[51] Legislation meant to defend tenant rights has not prevented the expulsion of 42 per cent of the 'protected tenants' and their pauperization – though not proletarization.[52] 'As a result, despite the changed situation, the contradictions between the landlords and the peasants remained as acute as before.'[53]

The peasantry does not seem to be as historically mobile as the Soviet hypotheses would have led them to expect. Proletarization of the lower layers, the corollary of the embourgeoisement of the well-to-do groups, should be the normal consequence of agrarian capitalist development. The thesis on the differentiation of the peasantry into bourgeois and proletarian classes goes back to Marx himself: 'For it is also a law that economic development divides out functions among different persons and the artisan or peasant who produces with his own means of production will either gradually be transformed into a small capitalist who also exploits the labour of others or he will suffer the loss of this means of production ... and be transformed into a wage worker.'[54] Lenin retained the same idea about the transitory nature of the peasant class in his analysis of Russian conditions. The problem in the Soviet analysis is not that it claims a non-existent class differentiation to have taken place. Kotovsky did not close his eyes to the evidence which shows that, however poor, the landless peasant still tries to cultivate some land; this is a 'non-proletarian pauperization of the peasantry in which the poor peasants still remain cultivators.'[55] Rather, this situation is treated as historically pathological: proper agricultural development is being frustrated. Soviet marxism-leninism thus appears unable to conceive that a peasant economy can continue to flourish – despite the historical persistence and widespread existence of this form of social organization.[56]

THE AGRARIAN PROLETARIAT

Although the formal status of the expelled tenants has been transformed from tenant to worker, they have not become real proletarians, for they often re-rent the land they used to cultivate.[57] They may not be genuine proletarians, but they are considered by the Soviet experts to be one of the major components of the agrarian proletariat. In fact Rastyannikov and Maksimov attacked bourgeois sociologists for trying to obscure the phenomenon of agrarian proletarization: 'Bourgeois sociologists hide the nature of the Indian process, namely capitalism developing in the country since the end of the past century, throwing the large masses of peasants out of their caste dependence into the ranks of the agrarian proletariat.'[58] Even for those bourgeois sociologists who are willing to be convinced, it may not be immediately evident why the land poor are considered proletarian. By Rastyannikov and Maksimov's own testimony the strata out of which this new socioeconomic class is being formed make up what they also call a permanent reserve army of unemployed. Elsewhere they call the agrarian proletariat the most numerous division of the exploited working mass in agriculture, which, united by their general interests, becomes the nearest ally of the industrial proletariat.[59] It is possible that ideological optimism may be pushing Soviet scholars to exaggerate the extent of the agrarian proletariat's formation, just as enthusiasm for capitalism may have impelled them to exaggerate the development of the kulak class.

Kotovsky has provided a more sober, qualified view of the agrarian proletariat. Examining the employment breakdown of hired labour in rural India, he found the 'main part' to be used in 'big farms of a capitalist type,' 64 per cent of all agrarian labourers being employed in farms based on hired labour, 36 per cent in the small-commodity sector. However the average size of these 'big farms' is only 'several tens of acres,' and they employ one or two labourers, rarely more. The group that Kotovsky considered most like the industrial proletariat are the plantation labour force; these made up only 1.3 to 1.5 million of the 40 to 50 million agrarian labourers in the 1950s. More interesting are the 'semi-proletarian' elements, the agricultural labourers with plots that they either own or rent. From 1947 to 1965 their number doubled, while the average size of their plots declined from 3 to 2.6 hectares, showing the pauperization and proletarization of the peasant masses. Although in an economic sense they are fully workers, hiring out their labour, they remain small-commodity producers in their social psychology.

Kotovsky concluded from this large percentage of rural workers holding plots that the formation of a hired labour class was taking place 'in breadth, not in depth.'[60] His reader might draw another conclusion from this evidence. Noting the increase in the ratio of payments in kind to payments in money for 'proletarian' labour reported by Kotovsky, noting that Rastyannikov and Maksimov considered the majority of the 'proletariat and semi-proletariat' to be surplus population, unable to find 'application' as a freed labour in an industry developing too slowly to employ them, and observing too that these expropriated peasant producers are still exploited by pre-capitalist methods,[61] the reader might be forgiven for thinking that rather less progress in the formation of capitalist agrarian classes has been made than Kotovsky implied – especially when he himself pointed out elsewhere in the same monograph that the process of class formation is proceeding very slowly and is just as far from completion for the agrarian workers as for the national bourgeoisie.[62] If this 'proletariat' is a class without self-consciousness and without organization, if it is still being exploited by pre-capitalist production relationships, if its members suffer from feudal survivals in their consciousness and political backwardness owing to 'lower forms' of anarchic caste movements and inner-village conflicts,[63] then the rural proletariat seems to be remaining stubbornly non-proletarian.

WHITHER THE CLASS STRUGGLE?

The general political conclusions drawn by Soviet observers from their observations of agriculture in the third world are extraordinarily diverse, ranging from optimistic revolutionary slogans to sad pessimism. K.M. Varentsov and M.A. Maksimov, for instance, found the basis for a broad united front of the democratic forces in the 'abyss' between the handful of semi-feudal exploiters and capitalist elements on the one hand, and on the other the whole class gamut of the agrarian proletariat and semi-proletariat, the army of sharecroppers without rights, the peasantry, and small and middle manufacturers. Denying the importance of the contradictory interests of different peasant groups, they maintain that the fight against imperialist exploitation is the major factor uniting not just the poor peasantry but also the better-off with the proletariat. This enthusiasm for a broad united front is qualified by the recognition that 'these favourable possibilities are still to a large degree potential.'[64] More sceptical Soviet voices have warned against imagining the peasantry to be a revolutionary force. In discussing the political potential of the third world armies, Mirsky, for instance, wrote that 'the mass of soldiers are in the majority of cases politically just as undeveloped and passive as the peasantry from which they come.'[65]

Whatever the conceptual difficulties encountered by Soviet analysts in applying the leninist grid to the Afro-Asian rural scene – and the reader may find it difficult to follow their use of evidence in their search for the correct interpretation of the facts – these problems are openly and honestly confronted. The same can unfortunately not be said for their prescriptions for the class struggle. In jumping from the 'is' to the 'ought,' Soviet writers leave analysis and turn to ideology. The starting point for class tactical analysis is the rural classes' composition and objectives. Whatever the Soviet analytical confusions, there is less doubt about the implications of the Indian agrarian reforms' failure to improve the peasant masses' condition. From the failures to achieve agricultural development Rastyannikov concluded that there are growing class contradictions.[66] 'The incomplete liquidation of the semi-feudal relations of production, the lack of solutions to the land question, the reinforcement of the contradictions within the agrarian economy, combined with the development of agrarian capitalism: all this forms the basis for a further aggravation of the social contradictions and the class struggle in India's countryside.'[67]

But what exactly are the prospects for this agrarian class struggle? While Rastyannikov and Maksimov wrote of the classical anti-feudal unity of the peasantry, a colleague cautioned that there is a general decline of the peasant movement in the third world and that the Indian peasantry is typical of this reduced revolutionary potential. The class has been split; the kulaks are no longer revolutionary; its organizations have declined since successfully forcing the governments to implement anti-feudal reforms.[68]

The dual social composition of the bourgeoisie, the contradictory analysis of the proletariat, and the uncertain description of the peasantry have led to very different recommendations for tactics in the future class struggle. Those who, like Kotovsky, emphasized the landlord aspect of the bourgeoisie have observed that the rich peasants have themselves become small semi-feudal proprietors

Like the large landowners, they are struggling to transform their domains into capitalist farms and use state capitalism to achieve this aim. As the 'peasant summit' and the kulaks strengthen their position, their interests join those of the large landowners, so that they tend to form a single class of 'entrepreneurs.' Kotovsky concluded that, because of the identity of interest between these new agrarian bourgeois and the large landowners, they end up by opposing the peasant movement.[69]

Maksimov and Rastyannikov on the other hand underlined that even the rich peasants have difficulties with the large landowners. The kulaks have less chance to improve their technical base, to receive state credits, or to liberate themselves from feudal survivals than do the dominating landowners, who are the principal beneficiaries of governmental aid to agriculture.[70] Although these authors agreed that a part of the big bourgeoisie has already become reactionary, they maintained that this part is of minor importance compared with the other section of the bourgeoisie, which is in direct conflict with the big landlords from whom they claim a share of their landholdings. Thus they concluded that between the bourgeoisie and the peasantry there is still the basis for an alliance aimed at the definitive liquidation of feudal vestiges and the abolition of commercial and moneylending exploitation.[71] The same experts have since apparently become more radical, at least as far as their class strategy was concerned. Rather than advise bourgeois-peasant alliances for further capitalist development, they subsequently prescribed the need for the working class to make a union with the most massive force of the people, the peasantry, with the aim of completing the national-democratic stage of the revolutionary process.[72]

Whether the rural workers have enough unity to make the talk of working class strategy meaningful is not entirely clear in the Soviet analysis. As N.I. Semenova showed, the organization of agrarian workers by caste produces contradictory results: caste organization helps politicize the poorest strata of the countryside but slogans of class peace weaken their revolutionary force.[73] Kotovsky's analysis showed the low objective concentration of rural workers (very few farms outside the plantations employ more than one or two), and the subjective fragmentation of caste and of religion (30 per cent of agrarian workers are untouchables or belong to a classified tribe). He concluded nonetheless that they are now a 'class by itself' whose entry into an 'active class struggle will inevitably provoke a decisive change in the distribution of the country's political forces.'[74]

Ambiguity persists. Those who emphasize the lack of capitalist development imply that an increased progress of capitalism would entail the definitive expulsion of the poor peasants from the land and their entry into the proletarian ranks seeking employment in industry. A second recommendation advocates solving the land question by granting to all the peasants enough land to ensure their subsistence. But 'the land to the peasants' is a petty bourgeois programme par excellence. Its realization could well lead to the perpetuation of the peasant economy whose possibility and efficacity the Soviets deny.

Thus it is not very clear what should be the aim of the class struggle in the countryside. In a general way the Soviets give the impression that the peasantry is fighting for land and security against exploitation. There are two possible conclusions: either the Soviets do not want to admit that success in this struggle would consolidate the peasant economy or they support this struggle simply as a minimum programme which would be politically necessary to obtain the tactical alliance of the peasantry if the proletariat is to take power. Soviet experts do not confront this fundamental question. Nor do they give any concrete proof that this programme of equal distribution of land to all the poor peasants is practicable.

Given the huge size of what they call 'relative agrarian overpopulation,' – and Kotovsky reported that in 1952-3 there were 28.2 million workers in the country who worked for less than five days per month[75] – there would have to be a gigantic fund of land to give each poor home the minimum, say eight acres, necessary for the subsistence of an Indian family. In fact Soviet indologists have had a chronic tendency to exaggerate the 'enormous resources' and 'limitless possibilities' for the increase of agricultural production.[76]

Soviet analysts have observed that the large landowners and kulaks profit from the size of their farms to achieve technical improvements offered by large-scale production. By supporting the slogan 'the land to the tiller' are they not contradicting their advocacy of large-scale production? It is this failure to tie down loose ends in their arguments which gives Soviet analysis much of its air of inconsistency or incompleteness.

The Soviet dialectic of the rural class struggle thus turns out to be as equivocal, but less credible, than the analysis of the transformations that have occurred within these classes. While one current in this analysis finds that the peasantry and proletariat fight against a united front of the bourgeois and the large landowners, the other feels on the contrary that the peasantry and proletariat should unite all the democratic patriotic forces in an alliance against the large landowners.

These divergences in interpretation find their logical consequence in two differing views about the future solution to agrarian problem. The bourgeois-as-enemy line would advise a peasant struggle for a radical non-capitalist transformation of Indian agriculture, while the bourgeois-as-ally line promotes a political alliance aimed at further capitalist development. This ambiguity underlies the Soviet view of the agrarian reforms' impact on the growth of agricultural production.

TECHNICAL FACTORS IN AGRICULTURE

Although marxist-leninists firmly maintain that agro-technical improvements can have no real impact without prior radical socioeconomic transformations of the whole agricultural structure, they are nevertheless very optimistic about the productive potential of the third world. Y. Guzevaty went so far as to claim that the third world has eight to ten times more land available for agriculture than is presently used, so that the land could support three to four times the present population. The price tag: $20,000 million for fertilizer alone, and more for pesticides, farm implements, and so on. Though he concluded polemically that capitalism has 'no intention' of financing these measures, the interesting point is his faith that technology could produce the output.[77]

Despite a decidedly pessimistic view of the condition of India's peasant masses, Russian authors have recognized that a definite improvement of the agrarian production situation has taken place when judged by purely quantitative criteria. Agrarian production increased considerably during the 1950s. In accounting for this growing productivity, Kotovsky noted the influence of such factors as the expansion of the area under cultivation by 10 million acres, the increase of productivity by the intensified use of machines, chemical fertilizers, and improved seeds. In other words, 'the strengthened development of agrarian capitalism in India is, without any doubt, the principal reason for the well-established increase in the country's agricultural production.'[78] Although the agrarian reforms are given some credit for this agricultural production, these reforms are nevertheless criticized for not having solved Indian agriculture's critical economic problems.

Thus, despite the progress realized during past years, Soviet experts emphasize that the expansion is insufficient to satisfy the state's economic needs, whether to feed the population or to supply industry with agrarian raw materials.[79] As a result India has been obliged to import at high cost huge quantities of foodstuffs from the United States. Soviet analysts place heavy emphasis on the pernicious consequences of these imports, which in their view put the country still further at the mercy of the American monopolies and have an adverse effect on the balance of payments.[80] The diversion of funds for the purchase of food limits the extent of productive economic investments, in turn restricting the enlargement of the internal market and thus the expansion of Indian industry.

In strictly economic terms, therefore, the situation created by the agrarian reforms is far from bright. 'The agrarian reforms have thus not solved the agrarian question in India. While slightly accelerating the development of capitalism, they have nevertheless not established the conditions necessary for the growth of the productive forces, for broadening the internal market and for increasing capital accumulation sufficiently to bring an end to the country's economic backwardness or dramatically to raise the people's standard of living.'[81]

Though the agrarian situation leaves much to be desired, this is not for lack of natural potential or technical possibilities for an eventual increase of agricultural production. Soviet scholars provide a fairly elaborate exposition of India's vast agricultural potential. To begin with, there are 'enormous reserves' of land which are very incompletely used. 'If one only counts the uncultivated lands, the land under fallow and the unplowed land, the sown area could be increased by a minimum of 30 to 40 million hectares which would insure a harvest increase of between 20 and 30 million tons of food crops and which would help substantially to solve the food crisis.'[82] Batalov and Gurvich affirmed that millions of hectares of uncultivated land could be brought under cultivation, but western experts found this misleading. In the opinion of the agricultural geographer B.H. Farmer, this evaluation enormously overestimated the real potential of arable land in India: 'There is with the area already cultivated a very small area of land available for development in the Republic of India, in spite of the much larger area classed as "culturable waste," the figures for which have misled many ... In fact no one knows how much waste land in India *could* be cultivated under given technological and economic conditions, but recent preliminary studies suggest that it varies from about 20,000 hectares in crowded Kerala to 100,000 hectares in East Punjab and perhaps rather more in Assam.'[83] Batalov and Gurvich's image of a major solution to the Indian agrarian question thanks to a Soviet-type virgin-land campaign thus appears highly questionable.

In addition they spoke of a whole series of agricultural improvements which would increase the extremely low productivity of the cultivated land. Thus India must increase its system of irrigation and use it more fully, extend the use of mechanical equipment, which is currently very insufficient, improve the quality of its livestock and fodder, increase the production and utilization of fertilizers, use its natural manure fertilizer and its selected seeds more rationally, struggle against weeds and parasites which devastate harvests, and so on. While the Soviet authors used to refer to the 'inexhaustible reserves and possibilities for increasing agricultural productivity,' they concluded nevertheless that all these recommended measures could only be effective after a radical resolution of the agrarian question. For in the marxist-leninist vision the improvement of the technical factors will produce no results if it is not preceded by a preliminary and revolutionary reform of property and production relations. Without this preliminary solution, 'hybrid measures cannot solve any agrarian crisis.'[84]

This problem is far from resolved in the Soviet school of agrarian analysis. Two books published in 1970 maintained opposite positions on this point. In one, Stepanov still maintained that technical measures were futile without a preliminary radical change: 'With the Indian village what it is today, in the grip of the relics of feudalism and most of its population landless or land-poor, the vast funds invested in agricultural development are as good as scattered to the winds ... And the reason why, in India, all the measures which had been taken to catch up in this sphere have been of little effect is that they have gone beyond organisational and technological improvement and never helped, as much as they should have, solve the agrarian problem.'[85] In the other Academician Ulyanovsky recognized the fact that the 'green revolution' had made an impact without the prerequisite social transformations: 'With the assistance of the authorities, extensive agro-technical measures are being carried out ... And though use of these measures has mostly been made by the proprietors in the countryside – capitalist landlords, kulaks and a part of affluent middle peasants – these reforms promoted a certain growth of production of cereals (over 100 million tons per 540 million people in 1970). As a result it was possible to cut the chronic imports of grain from the USA.'[86] In 1974 the Soviet journal *International Affairs* noted that India had doubled her grain production from 60 million tons in 1947 to 115 million tons. 'Such an increase in agricultural output has been attained chiefly by carrying out a series of agricultural measures known as the "green revolution" [which] includes extension and improvement of the irrigation system, utilisation of high-yield seed, fertilisers and pesticides, electrification and greater mechanisation of agricultural production.'[87]

With this evidence before them, Soviet scholars now grant that technological change can produce economic progress without radical social transformations being a necessary prerequisite. 'Without undermining the economic strength of the feudal elements,' the green revolution 'creates in countries like India, Pakistan and a number of Latin American states the possibility of the capitalist evolution of landowner farming without radical changes in the agrarian system.' The modified Soviet position is that the economic impact of technological progress will be greater if there is a prior land reform. 'A case in point is Mexico, where a relatively radical land reform has stimulated a substantial increase in agricultural output. The Green Revolution which is predicated on essential agrarian changes and proceeds parallel with industrialisation yields the biggest effect.'[88] The corollary of this would appear to be that technological progress can produce social regress. In India, where advanced agricultural practices did not 'improve the position of the mass of the toiling people' the result has been to strengthen the position of the big landowners and rural bourgeoisie.[89]

STATE CAPITALISM IN AGRICULTURE

Even though structural changes may be the necessary condition for solving the land problem and so for pulling the third world's agriculture out of its secular stagnation, they are not sufficient. What is also required is a whole series of governmental measures ranging from investments in infrastructure to control of agricultural markets. In a word, Soviet experts also take seriously the role of state capitalism in agriculture, which goes well beyond the legislation and implementation of agrarian reforms.

In West Africa, which has never suffered from landowners' dominance or even a shortage of land, since there is plenty of unoccupied land, a main reason for stagnation in agriculture is the absence of a rationally organized, all-embracing, and democratically controlled network of state-owned purchasing organizations. 'If the farmer is not protected by the state from parasitic dealers, he is bound to lose all interest in increasing his produce. But the absence of incentives on the part of the producers means in the final analysis stagnation of agriculture and the national economy as a whole.'[90] When the farmers are unaware of the market situation they are robbed by speculators buying at low prices. In this situation the creation of a surplus product for investment remains very doubtful. The actual master of the land is the one on whom the sale of the crop depends. When dealers dictate prices, collective land ownership is illusory, but pauperization and migration of the farmer are the natural consequence. Without a radical democratization of the sale system, the private dealer will profit from any results of technological modernization. State capitalism becomes crucial at this point. In Senegal an Agricultural Marketing Board was set up in 1960 as the sole organization to buy peanuts from co-operatives, and private dealers and hold a monopoly for the export of peanuts. In Mali and Guinea the state made large-scale purchases of export crops. In Mali it had a similar monopoly in the purchase and export of peanuts as well as buying a number of other staple agricultural products. In Guinea the private dealers have been ousted entirely from the field of bananas and other fruits which a state organization buys from co-operatives. Thus along with the creation of more progressive forms of labour, such as democratically organized production co-operatives, a major function of state capitalist intervention in agriculture can be to oust the parasitic stratum of trade dealers from marketing.[91]

Even though the national bourgeoisie is continually berated for failing to undertake radical and all-encompassing agrarian transformations, Indian state capitalism is still kept under heavy pressure from Soviet authors to intervene at specific points of the agrarian scene where governmental regulations could cure a specific abuse. As in West Africa, the conditions of the Indian market are a Soviet concern. The attempt to bring the market under state control takes place amidst a sharp class struggle, since the merchants, wholesalers, and landowners defend their vested interests from mass attack. In actual fact, in order to conserve the positions of the ruling class as a whole, the state has made some infringements on the interests of some of its own ruling strata, nationalizing reserves, establishing price controls, setting up food zones, building warehouses for stocks, and reducing bank credits for speculative activity.[92] Governmental controls such as the fixing of minimum purchase prices and the regulation of stocks in major commodities like jute and cotton have had only a limited impact on the market.[93] What was needed, according to E.I. Mironova, was an implementation of the Gadgil plan, which included the nationalization of wholesale trade in food, the limitation of big trading capital, and the government penetration of grain supply. Because of the resistance of the trader class and the states, half measures such as the State Food Corporation are too limited to be effective.[94]

Another critical market role for the state is protecting national agriculture from the impact of international factors. Less progressive developing countries than India have had a more effective policy in this area. The establishment in Turkey of state purchase prices on foodgrains well above the world market level had a dynamic impact on the growth of foodgrain production which increased at an annual rate of 7.3 per cent from 1946-8 to 1953-5. When the policy was abandoned in the mid-1950s, this growth rate dropped to 2.5 per cent, and, from being an exporter of foodgrains, Turkey became an importer. In Japan the state's procurement prices on rice were kept at from 50 to 200 per cent above world prices from 1953 to 1963 to increase the economic efficiency and volume of grain production – at the cost of rice production of farms with below-average productivity. This kept a considerable part of the income produced within the village, expanding the agricultural savings fund. Without this stimulant, the large farmers would not have been able to renovate their technical base. In Ceylon in 1956-66 the price of rice was $17.80 per quintal, compared to $14.50 to $13.50 in Calcutta, but the growth rate of agricultural production was 3.5 per cent from 1960-1 to 1964-5, compared to an average of 2.4 per cent for Asia and the Far East as a whole.[95]

India, on the other hand has suffered from the increased integration of the national foodgrain market in the world capitalist market, importing from 1961 to 1965 18 per cent of the country's requirements in marketable grain and, from 1964 to 1966, 60 per cent of the country's total supply of marketable wheat. These enormous quantities of wheat thrown onto the Indian market and sold at world prices have upset the natural process of price formation which would have responded to national factors of labour productivity and production costs. According to the labour theory of value, the 'gulf between the corresponding values' has widened between the industrialized and the developing worlds. In the west, labour productivity has sharply increased, dropping the cost of production. Whereas in the United States it takes 4.4 man-hours to produce a ton of wheat and 30 man-hours to produce a ton of rice (1960-3), in India it took 492 man-hours to produce a ton of wheat (Punjab, 1955-7) and 947 man-hours to produce a ton of rice (Bengal, 1955-7). It is 'quite natural' that grain prices should be higher in India than world prices, which are regulated by the cost of production and the profit of grain production in the United States and Canada. The artificial depression of wheat prices has meant that wheat prices stagnated around an index mark of 88 to 89 from the period 1956-7 to 1964-5 (index 1952-3 = 100) while the price index for industrial goods reached 131 by 1963-4. This kept down the prices for other cereals, depriving the agricultural sector of a substantial part of its income and causing cereal production to stagnate. The need to protect Indian food markets from destructive world influences was also supported by Rastyannikov, who recommended a stabilized, government supported agricultural food price. This would improve the conditions of reproduction in the grain economy by increasing the savings fund and giving an impetus to expanding the area under foodgrain cultivation. While it might lower the sale of grain on the market by the petty producer, whose consumption would increase, the supply of grain would increase from the commercial farms. The consumer would benefit from prices lower than those created by speculation which 'rob the working population of a substantial part of their wages' and only put money into the pockets of the large traders who monopolize the markets and make huge profits amounting in the Punjab to 28-30 per cent (1964-5).

The government's failure to intervene effectively reinforces the Soviet argument that state capitalism in agriculture is designed to enrich the upper strata. The community development programme aimed at the technical improvement of agriculture has increased capital accumulation but has not given the expected results. The programme of state-supported co-operatives has been a direct aid to agrarian capitalism, enriching the well-to-do. As for the large state investments increasing the acreage under cultivation and irrigation, the area under cultivation did increase by 40 per cent from 1948-9 to 1961-2, as did the area under irrigation. While much of the former was divided among the poor, it was decided in 1965 to leave the irrigated land for big capitalist farms.[96]

The increased emphasis on the role of state capitalism in the Soviet analysis of Indian agriculture can be seen by the relatively tardy recognition of the importance of state planning in agriculture. In her general monograph on Indian planning, N.G. Lozovaya pointed out how the decline of agricultural production and its inability to satisfy the most minimal needs of the population in food or of industry in raw materials was the basic obstacle in the path of independent India's economic development. The expenditures on imports of grain in the ten-year period 1948-59 of Rs 14.4 billion were more than the $10 billion state investments for industrial development put out in 1951-61. The ruling circles understood that to raise agricultural production the state's planned activity was needed over more than one five-year period. Once launched into a discussion of agrarian planning, Lozovaya showed the same concern for its state capitalist base as Soviet analysts do for industrial planning. In agriculture the material bases of planning are first of all state property in agriculture, then the state financial and credit institutions, and finally the state budget. The limits of the direct planned action are drawn by the narrow confines of the public agricultural sector: the few state farms are lost in the sea of private farms; the production of fertilizer in state factories only satisfies part of the demand; the large state irrigation system is poorly developed.

As for the state-organized co-operatives, they are economically weak, have practically no production, and exert a negligible influence on the markets, where commercial-usury capital still dominates. For their part, the credit co-ops play a major role in encouraging capitalist relations as the landlords and rich peasants get the most credit, the poor peasants the least. Through the mechanism of the state's finances, planning consists of large capital investment in the distribution of improved seeds, fertilizers, and so on. Though these measures serve the land-owners and kulak elements before all else, they 'without doubt are linked to the rise of industrial agriculture and its productivity.'[97] Agricultural planning is thus seen as giving a nudge to the anarchic but natural process of capitalist development. From 1966 to 1973 the number of irrigation wells increased from 93,000 to 680,000 and electrical irrigation pumps from 500,000 to 2,100,000.[98]

While not impressive, the regulatory role of the state is growing. The increases in material indices – land cultivated and irrigated (increased by 40 per cent each), yields per acre, use of fertilizers, number of tractors (from 5,000 to 30,000 from 1945 to 1961) – show, according to Lozovaya, 'that the achievement of the measures foreseen by the five-year plans and the realization of the agrarian reforms helped bring agriculture out of its condition of disintegration.'[99] But the state's planning control in agriculture is far from perfect. Even the possibilities for directing capitalism are not fully exploited. Lozovaya returned to the recommendation of guaranteed prices as a way to achieve plan targets. The successful fulfilment of planned sugar production in South India was linked to guaranteed prices, since companies using a system of contracts, credits, and agro-technical services were able to influence the cane production even of the small peasants. Although the apparatus works so that the fruits of planning are picked first of all by landlords and rich peasants, this state capitalist function is real and has a practical significance in achieving capitalist development from above. Where it has failed, its weaknesses are due to the class nature of state power. Lozovaya quoted Gadgil's judgment that the premeditated indecisiveness in realizing a food policy can only be explained by the desire to defend the interests of the merchant usurers and wholesale dealers who make up a significant part of the capitalists' class base.

RADICAL SOCIOECONOMIC TRANSFORMATIONS NEEDED

The increasing prominence given by Soviet indologists to specific policy recommendations makes their analyses more accessible to the non-marxist reader. Such advice given within the context of the existing political and economic situation does not preclude their reaffirmation of the more grandiose solutions consistent with Soviet marxism-leninism. 'Whatever the significance of measures aimed at improving the agrotechnical standards of agriculture and developing state or co-operative enterprises and/or services in the fields of agricultural credit, supplies, marketing, extension of modern farm practices and research, etc., their successful implementation with a view to encompass a large section of the rural population requires ... the abolition of a system under which large-scale land ownership of feudal-type landlords (absentee as a rule) is combined with small-scale tenancy cultivation.[100] Soviet theorists are quite clear about the objective: a drastic increase in the rates of saving and capital formation in agriculture by the full liquidation of the feudal-landlord class. The preferred models are explicitly identified as those non-capitalist countries (Algeria or Burma) which have liquidated foreign landownership, parasitical forms of feudal-landlord ownership, and usurer or merchant exploitation while encouraging co-operative forms of production and aiding the peasantry with means of production, credits, and firm market prices controlled by state trading. All the peasantry, even the well-off, benefit from these radical bourgeois-democratic transformations.[101]

There is general Soviet agreement that the Indian agrarian reforms cannot solve the basic problems because they follow the worse of the two possible capitalist paths of development. 'The bourgeois transformations in agriculture,' as V.I. Lenin teaches, 'can be effected either in the interest of the landowners at the peasantry's expense or in the interests of the peasantry at the landowners' expense.'[102] Since Indian reforms favour the landowners, their consequence is the coexistence of feudal and capitalist exploitation rather than the elimination of the old agrarian relations. If the bourgeoisie's reforms are not genuinely directed towards the development of capitalism, the solution which would lead to a growth of agrarian production would involve an 'elimination of semi-feudal relations simultaneously with the country's industrialization,'[103] in other words, more genuine and thorough reforms that would properly install capitalist agrarian relations.

Maksimov and Rastyannikov gave the impression that the failures are more the result of an incomplete implementation of the agrarian reforms than of their incorrect nature. The fundamental problem in pre-reform Indian agriculture – 'the contradiction between the capitalist mode of production which is developing and the old agrarian structure' – has not lost its relevance. Is it therefore necessary to develop capitalism in India even further? This is the conclusion that follows if, in Marx's formula, the lower strata of the peasantry suffer 'less from the development of capitalism than from the insufficiency of its development.'[104]

India's agricultural problems – the continuing failure of agricultural production to develop fast enough, the still unresolved food problem, the industrial revolution hardly started in agriculture – cannot be overcome, the Soviet experts agree, within the existing agrarian structure. A second stage of agrarian reforms is needed that would liquidate pre-capitalist sharecropping, redistribute land, democratize the co-operatives, and liquidate the power of the landowners and kulaks in all spheres.[105] The national-democratic revolution still has to be achieved in agriculture. Its name is capitalism.

PART FIVE

CONCLUSION

14

Assessments and reflections

Having examined the three specific foci of Soviet writings on third world development problems, the reader should have little doubt that the output has been substantial. It is now time to make a general assessment of this opus and place it in its political and international context.

SOVIET WRITINGS AS A DEVELOPMENT SCHOOL

One overriding dilemma confronting the reader of the Soviet school is its deceptive distinctiveness. The marxist-leninist vocabulary itself imparts a specific flavour. To some extent this is a product of a revolutionary rhetoric extolling 'heroic struggles' of the 'toiling masses' led by their 'vanguard party.' What makes marxism-leninism really separate is its dual system of concepts, one applying to the capitalist world, the other to the socialist. For the Russian marxist-leninist, 'imperialism' only refers to the international dominance of the western powers, never to relations of domination within the socialist bloc (except as a device for attacking the heretical fraternal state of China). 'Non-equivalent exchange' refers to the unfair price differential between raw materials sold cheaply by the less developed economies in return for the expensive finished products sold by the developed western countries. Even though the Soviet Union may pay India the world prices for its tea and demand the going rate for a steel mill, they would bitterly reject the application to their commercial dealings with India of the notion of non-equivalency. There can be, by definition, no exploitation of labour contained in the value of socialist exports.

The simplicity and stability of Soviet concepts also sets them apart from non-communist scholarship. The use of jargon is quite rare, and the rate of formation of neologisms is low. Soviet writings are, presumably, comprehensible by all readers, academic or popular, in a way that would not be true of the more esoteric academic disciplines in the west. If conceptual innovation is necessary for the refinement of social science, then what Soviet analysis may gain in marketability of their academic products they may lose in the obtuseness of their analysis. As we have seen, the breadth of some concepts does in fact produce some obscuring vagueness. The Soviets tend to talk almost interchangeably about the 'ruling circles,' 'ruling class,' 'bourgeoisie,' 'middle bourgeoisie,' or 'national bourgeoisie' without making clear the significance for their analysis of these terms.

What reinforces the duality within the marxist-leninist conceptual framework is the strong value load carried by many of its key concepts. 'Imperialism' has a special meaning in marxism-leninism not just because it is the empirical shorthand for the international dynamic of the western industrialized nations, but also because it is endowed with a strongly pejorative content as the force that opposes economic and social progress in its ex-colonies. Similarly 'socialism' has both an empirical connotation as the socioeconomic system of the Soviet bloc countries and the positive normative content of being historically necessary and socially superior. The resulting manicheism has both benefits and costs. On the credit side there is a frankness some may find refreshing in this rejection of relativism: development is defined squarely in terms of desired social, economic, and political progress towards socialism and away from capitalism. On the debit side are the confusions which start as soon as a good quality is admitted in an allegedly bad force or when qualifications are made about a virtuous power's performance. Soviet scholars agree that the developing countries require external sources of capital accumulation, admit that the socialist countries cannot alone provide all the third world's needs, reject a quota of 1 per cent of GNP for socialist countries' aid, but maintain that the imperialist states should give more aid than this. While defending the virtues of socialist aid they recognize its 'tied character' – tied in rubles and tied to specific projects. When criticizing private foreign investment they recognize its positive economic consequences without always feeling the need to impugn its bad motivations.[1] The manicheism becomes muddled: the bad guys are needed for the good they are doing, while the good guys are operating just like the bad.

These qualifications in turn undermine the credibility of the subsequent use of a black and white language. Thus when Academican Ulyanovsky wrote in 1970 that 'everybody realizes that foreign imperialism, though deprived of political power ... is directly responsible for all the hardships of the people [of India], and no one can hide this fact,' the power of his statement has already been vitiated.[2]

The problem is not that an avowed ideological commitment is necessarily incompatible with sound analysis. All scholarship is based on a normative system whether explicit or implicit. One can argue that the explicit statement of the Soviet analysts' values allows the reader to discount judgments that appear more the result of arbitrary interpretation than of empirical analysis. In actual print the impact of imperialism on, say, India is analysed in a remarkably neutral fashion in the better Soviet writings, which accept many of the positive contributions of western aid. This is sometimes the case even where the author goes so far as to declare unashamedly in his introduction that the volume's purpose is 'to uncover the reactionary nature of the American leading circles' policy.'[3]

The more serious weakness that results from the Soviet scholars' normative position is their tendency to exaggerate and oversimplify their evaluation of particular phenomena. They have had difficulty, for instance, in qualifying their assessment of Indian foreign policy. Once they had decided that Nehru's over-all role in the world was progressive and anti-imperialist, the Soviet support for Nehru's Kashmir policy was far more unquestioning than almost all Indian opinion on the matter.

Maintaining the distinctiveness of the Soviet scholarly system keeps Soviet scholars in a state of continual tension. On the one hand authors like L. Reusner make efforts to bridge the conceptual gulf between liberal and marxist writings, showing how 'economic growth' and 'reproduction on an extended scale' are used synonymously.[4] Personal conversations with Soviet scholars in interviews or in seminars reveal how they can think and talk in a completely 'western' intellectual mode. On the other hand the political imperative to maintain if not intensify the ideological struggle with bourgeois scholarship dominates the whole Soviet opus. Thus the senior africanist V. Solodovnikov could write in 1974 that 'as the world revolutionary process becomes more profound, the ideological confrontation between capitalism and socialism is being intensified ... [by] the extension of the struggle between the two irreconcilable ideologies, capitalist and socialist, to the study of the history of the former colonies.'[5] The tension is unresolved. Even as Soviet experts make greater efforts to distribute their scholarly writings in translation throughout the world, they isolate their work from the potential non-communist readership by a vocabulary and style of writing that makes their output as distinctive as it is dismissable.

AMBIGUOUS ANALYSIS

Even if readers manage to filter out of their perception the unfortunate ideological tone that militates against effective communication of clear thought, more basic obstacles obstruct the easy acceptance of the Soviet development analysis. Most obdurate are the unresolved contradictions which we have seen running throughout the texts: there can be no development under capitalism vs there must be more capitalist development; the proletariat is weak and lacks class consciousness vs the proletariat must lead an alliance with the peasantry; imperialism resists third world industrialization vs imperialist aid facilitates important industrial development; independence can only be achieved by breaking ex colonial ties with imperialism vs independence is relative and will grow while maintaining trading relations with the West; the rural bourgeoisie is the enemy of agrarian development vs the rural bourgeoisie is leading capitalist development in the countryside. In the final analysis, unresolved contradictions are self-contradictions. Unless readers have insider information or have some external standard for judging, they have no way to determine whether there is a real Soviet position which is radical or moderate or whether a series of self-contradicting positions is not indeed *the* Soviet view of every major development problem.

Asking what policy recommendations are put forward by these writers provides no help in dealing with this enigma, for they contradict themselves even on the question of the policy question itself. Academician Ulyanovsky has recently (1975) maintained that 'Soviet scientists have never given specific recommendations for restructuring the socio-economic systems of other nations,'[6] even though he had earlier claimed, as we saw, that only communists are able to offer 'constructive ideas about the shortest roads and successful methods for eliminating their age-old backwardness.'[7] As we have also seen, Soviet writers both claimed and denied the relevance of the Soviet experience as a model for the third world's problems. Where their positions are not self-contradictory they tend, as we have seen in detail, to be fence-sitting, in their prescription of a balance to be struck between, for instance, infrastructural and heavy industrial development or between small and large-scale technology.[8] Readers wanting to know the final Soviet policy stance must either accept that it is both radical and moderate or make their own synthesis by extrapolating an unradical radicalism of the type expressed by Vladimir Kollontai, who places a radical position, such as 'in the present age the economic lag can be rapidly removed only if these countries introduce radical socio-economic reforms, eliminate foreign monopoly domination, put the social and political life on a thoroughly democratic basis, increase the economic intervention of the state, introduce effective economic planning on a national scale, and draw the bulk of the people into the process of social development,' side by side with the qualification that 'certainly the third world countries which have embarked on the non-capitalist path can hardly expect these measures to provide an instant remedy.'[9] One must simply accept as an article of faith that India's entry upon the non-capitalist path would mark the true start in solving India's problems, from agricultural production to the caste system.[10]

Even the 'minimum programmes' are scarcely buttressed by adequate reasoning. Yu.V. Potemkin and V.A. Sandakov supported without comment the electoral programme of the Indian Communist Party, recommending general democratic transformations to divert the big bourgeoisie's sources of accumulation into the state's coffers.[11] In recommending an increase of taxes on the rich they gave the impression that the state could collect huge amounts, even though, according to I.M Shatalov, there is very little to hope for on this road: 'the country has only a million taxable people; the others are too poor to pay anything.'[12]

The same absence of substantiation is true of their counsel on class tactics. Thus when Rastyannikov and Maksimov drew class conclusions from their study of India's agrarian capitalism, they wrote facilely of the need for a strategy of 'anti-feudal unity' of the working class and the peasantry, 'the most massive force of the people.' These old slogans of class strategy were presented without any evident relationship with the preceding analysis, which on the contrary emphasized the absence of class consciousness, the difficulties in organizing the country, and the lack of ideological rapport between the industrial proletariat and the poor people in the country. Soviet authors recommend favouring continued capitalist development in agriculture while simultaneously endorsing radical land reforms that would make capitalist farming difficult or impossible. Although the rhetoric of a revolutionary solution has never been entirely dropped from the Soviet analysis, the call for 'fundamental socioeconomic transformations' appears more and more ritualized and increasingly divorced from the concrete analysis produced by Moscow specialists.

Another problem derives from the incomplete absorption of modifications made in the Soviet analysis. For example, one of the most remarkable changes in the Soviet agrarian analysis during the 1960s was the re-evaluation of the role played by traditional elements in the countryside. In his introduction to *Castes in India*, G.G. Kotovsky broke with the old Soviet view that caste is only disguised class. He underlined the historic persistence of the caste system and its increased importance in modern social and political conflict.[13] S.F. Levin provided a penetrating discussion of the role of caste in the formation of bourgeois groups.[14] Though the caste problem was given prominence by these leading authors, this new awareness of the modernizing importance of the traditional social elements was not absorbed by their colleagues, many of whom continued to dismiss the traditional as anachronistic.

Even the three-dimensional paradigm of development turned out to be less impressive than it promised. We have already noted that the Soviet taxonomy of development models does have an internal dynamic. It is possible for a country to progress or regress along the model line – India could go from state capitalism to a national democratic state or monopoly state capitalism. Countries can also skip stages, going straight to national democracy if the proletariat gains access to state power, or to socialism if the 'vanguard of the proletariat' should seize power outright. However the large role played by the 'progressiveness' of a nation's foreign policy in the determination of its classification does insert an element of fundamental instability into the paradigm.

That all the elements of the Soviet view are integrally linked to each other in theory does not mean that all are well developed in actuality. The best elements of their output are the analysis of agrarian sociology and capitalism. The worst is the study of the political system, for, ironically enough, even though the Soviet analysis is highly political, it has no analysis of politics. There is no analysis of parties or interest groups or state politics for its own sake. It would be more accurate to say there is only reporting. The reporting is fitted into a simple framework that puts all political activity into one of the two camps that are seen to be fighting it out: either the progressive or the reactionary.

In India, for example, all the progressive forces are placed on the left, including the left wing of the Indian National Congress. The camp of right reaction is a many-headed hydra composed of different parties and organizations which are sometimes in conflict with each other but are united by general aims. Reaction is not seen in narrowly political terms of parties and politicians. It is a social-economic-political totality. Its economic base in India is the landlord class plus the Indian monopolies that want to push India onto a western type capitalist path. Its social base is varied. Communalism, blamed on colonialism as a direct consequence of the British divide-and-rule policy which heated up Hindu-Moslem hatred, is now seen by the Indian monopolies as a social base for spreading their influence among the masses. The middle class, heated by chauvinistic ideology, is also a potential and dangerous base for the right. Together with the 'ignorant masses burdened with social backwardness and religious prejudice, this middle class is becoming a significant force' and a potential support for fascism.[15]

The Soviet analysis of politics is weak partially because in marxism-leninism political science does not exist as an independent discipline. In the analysis of parties there is a virtual void. While half the propaganda brochure *Contemporary India: The Distribution of Class and Political Forces* is devoted to Indian communism, this booklet in no way reduces the need for a serious study of India's political parties, including the communist parties. Another reason for this political lacuna is itself political. When asked about the low quality of their political analysis, one of the leading personalities of the India Department at Moscow's Institute of Asian Peoples admitted the situation was unfortunate but explained that they could not after all write an analysis of the Indian political situation which would criticize their communist comrades, and any serious analysis would have to come to grips with the existence of the three mutually antagonistic communist parties in India and the reasons for their failures.

Two aspects of politics in India – the nationality question[16] and the social and intellectual content of political ideologies[17] – have been the object of some attention. Otherwise one must glean the Soviet view of political life in India from their sociological analysis of class contradictions and from discussions of the linkages between the corporate sector and the national bourgeois leadership. While it is asserted that the national bourgeoisie is acting in the interests of the people as a whole, there is no explanation of what political mechanics make this possible, especially when it is claimed elsewhere that the communist party is the real instrument for expressing the public's interests and that the proletariat should take over. However, the analysis is so inadequate that this prescription has to be taken on faith. The direct reports of election results in the pages of the *New Times* and *International Affairs* are the only other sources of political information in the Soviet press, but these articles are bereft of any serious analytical substance.

SOVIET WRITINGS AS DEVELOPMENT THEORY

The apparent strength of the marxist-leninist approach may actually explain the weakness of the Soviet opus. In theory, the interrelated integration of a multidimensional political economy appears attractive, for analysis of any issue is seen to be interdependently linked to the analysis of the whole situation of which it forms but a part. As S.A. Kuzmin wrote:

The process of industrialization in the developing countries is inseparably linked to profound social and economic transformations, in particular to a change in the existing agrarian relations, to the elimination of the dominance of money-lenders in agriculture and in handicraft work, to the liquidation of the predominance of foreign monopolies in the most important spheres of the national economy, to the democratization of social life, etc. Undoubtedly, industrialization will only be successful in these countries if technical and social progress go hand in hand. For the developing countries, with their agricultural and raw material specialization, the problem of industrialization means not only the creation of the key branches of industry but also the radical reorganization of the entire economy as a whole and profound changes in its very structure.[18]

The analysis of external problems as an integral part of the explanation of the internal dynamic of a country's economy, the linking of the discussion of agrarian and industrial development problems, the inseparability of state policy from class analysis: these are all attractive traits for readers sated by one-dimensional monographs with no general perspective. Unfortunately the a priori coherence of the Soviet approach ends up in incoherence in the actual writing.

When the tone, the style, and the content of the analysis becomes indistinguishable from the latest Party statement made by the political guardians of Soviet marxism-leninism, then analysis has become ideology. Take for example the words of Leonid Brezhnev: 'One need merely recall, for instance, events like the recent nationalization of the big banks in India and the impressive victory scored over the Right-wing forces at the last elections to the House of the People of the Indian Parliament. This is evidence that the masses of people in that country resolutely oppose the reactionary pro-imperialist forces and stand for the implementation of a land reform and other socio-economic transformations and for a policy of peace and friendship in international affairs.'[19] If a significant part of the Soviet analysis is no more than official ideological material, the integrated nature of the Soviet political economy becomes a liability rather than an asset. For if the analysis of each part is integrally related to the analysis of all the others, then a highly unscholarly but political component such as the Soviet analysis of a country's foreign policy and internal politics must be assumed to have an impact on the other parts of the analysis. Indeed one of the most plausible hypotheses to explain the surprising extent of the self-contradictory positions throughout the Soviet opus is the overlay of ideological positions coming from the Communist Party's political directorate upon the analytical results of the Soviet scholars' research and reflection. If, for instance, the national interests of the Soviet Union, as assessed by its Communist Party leaders, dictated close relations with India, including strong support for the Janata successors to Indira Gandhi's Congress government, it is understandable that the analytical consequences would be to find the national bourgeoisie in power to be progressive and so its policies of stimulating capitalist development necessary at that historical stage. At the same time Soviet scholars, proceeding with their work based on marxian and leninist paradigms, could find the ties of the ruling party with big capital and the rural elite so strong that there is no chance for breaking out of the vicious circles holding back the development of a self-sustaining internal market without genuinely radical socioeconomic transformations. Soviet publications have a monlithic, homogeneous aura, however many conflicting inputs – ideological and analytical, propagandistic and scholarly – they may contain. As a result the integration on which marxism-leninism prides itself leads in practice to its opposite: incoherence.

This assessment is confirmed by marxist critiques of Soviet work. In a relatively sympathetic review of Ulyanovsky, Pavlov, and Shirokov's work, Ranjit Sau took the Soviet authors to task for asserting that the national bourgeoisie held power in India as if this were an axiom 'without adequate supportive evidence.' 'But in fact there are objective indicators to the contrary: the "middle" bourgeoisie in India is extremely weak, and is constantly losing ground to the monopolies. The process of differentiation is on; but the middle bourgeoisie is falling more and more into the hands of the foreign monopolies for shelter and protection.'[20] To read non-Soviet marxists does suggest that, were the political and ideological constraints over Soviet scholars to be lifted, their writings not only might have more conceptual variety but could also be both more consistent and more radical. In western marxist writings on the concept of dependency, for example, one finds a view of the interrelationship of underdevelopment with imperialism leaving no room for the hesitant Soviet middle ground. Underdevelopment was caused by the integration of the third world in imperialism's economic sphere, foreign investment deepens exploitation, foreign aid perpetuates it, and import-substitution strategies reinforce dependence.[21] Industrialization prescriptions, using a western or a Soviet model, are dangerous: 'Attempts to analyse the reality of these countries as a result of backwardness in assimilating more advanced models of production or in modernizing themselves are nothing more than ideology disguised as science.'[22] Development, according to these marxists, can now occur only independently of world capitalist relations.[23]

Thus while one can certainly find evidence of improvements in Soviet scholarly writings over the past two decades, including a greater degree of independence from political directives and a more critical attitude toward doctrinal formulations on the nature of state capitalism and non-capitalism, it is difficult to avoid the final assessment that, whatever the merits of individual contributions to the vast Soviet opus, the total product is worth considerably less than the sum of its parts. A school without a theory, it is an approach leading in divergent directions.

SOVIET DEVELOPMENT ANALYSIS
IN ITS POLITICAL CONTEXT

That Soviet writings on the third world have only limited significance in their own right does not mean they are without significance. Kremlinologists have long had to rely on far less substantial writings in their speculations about the inner workings of the Soviet political system. Before dismissing this major library as so much low-quality paper, we must examine its political significance within the country of its origin, not to mention its geopolitical import outside the Soviet frontiers. Three propositions must be examined.

258 The Soviet Theory of Development

1. Soviet development writing is an index of Soviet foreign policy
At the highest ideological level of official statements at party CPSU functions or
obviously authoritative articles signed by academicians who hold senior Party
posts, Soviet publications can legitimately be taken as evidence for analysing
Soviet foreign policy directions. The Kremlin's hesitations in granting Castro's
Cuba full protection as a member of the socialist camp can be read in the docu
ments – and the delay in publishing them – confirming Castro's claim to be a full
marxist-leninist.[24] In the main, however, making inferences concerning foreign
policy from Russian publications is a highly speculative endeavour. It is probable
as we have noted, that some of the contradictions between the radical and the
moderate lines within the Soviet analysis stem from the USSR's geopolitical need
to support bourgeois third world regimes. The inaccessibility to foreign research
ers of the foreign policy process in the Soviet Union condemns such a proposi
tion to remaining permanently hypothetical. It makes even more tenuous the
reverse argument, namely that the contradictions in the analysis indicate the
existence of serious conflicts within the Soviet political establishment. Thus the
recently published statement that, 'since the Central Committee of the CPSU
exercises tremendous ideological control over the writings of Soviet analysts, any
noticeable contradiction in their writings should be viewed as a reflection of the
different trends within the CPSU ideological hierarchy'[25] is virtually meaningless
The simple fact is that outsiders do not know in most cases whether contradic
tions in print have significance for understanding Soviet foreign policy, interna
policy, ideology, or merely the ongoing scholarly debate. As Jerry Hough ha
written, 'there is no inherent reason to insist upon a united elite' in the Sovie
Union.[26] It is as plausible to deduce from the known explicit Party control ove
publications in the Soviet Union that the apparently monolithic medium has in
fact a multifaceted message. Soviet publications have ideological, propagandistic
educational, and scholarly functions. Although there is some differentiation be
tween propagandistic and scholarly organs, the very considerable overlap in both
authorship and content necessarily produces the contradictions that plague the
Soviet development writings.

Given the difficulty of knowing which, if any, of two differing statements re
presents the 'real' thinking of the Soviet foreign policy leadership, non-commu
nist scholars have clearly shown that they can adequately analyse Soviet policy
towards India, for instance, by studying Soviet policy outputs[27] or by using ideo
logical statements merely as a subsidiary body of evidence.[28] Such prudence to
wards the Soviet printed output shown by foreign policy analysts is further justi
fied by the 'growing divergence between the theory and practice of Soviet policy
towards India' which already in the 1960s allowed critical works on the India
economy to be published despite the strong diplomatic and economic suppor
given India by the Soviet Union.[29]

2. Soviet development writings are an index of intercommunist relations
It can be argued that the low quality of Soviet writings on third world politics is explicable in terms of their function as an esoteric means of communication between the CPSU and the communist parties in the third world. Certainly Soviet propaganda organs such as *New Times* were used for this purpose within the Cominform.[30] Applying this line of reasoning to present-day India, one might hypothesize that, if the article is emphasizing the dangers of the right-wing opponents of reform – 'large numbers of [rightist] Congress Organization followers are returning to the National Congress camp' (June 1971) – then the message for the CPI is to support the progressive elements in Congress against its right wing.[31] If the article reports positively about the CPI's actions – 'the intrigues of the Right were foiled by the Left and democratic, national patriotic forces, including the progressives in the Indian National Congress led by Prime Minister Indira Gandhi. The Communist Party of India took a firm stand against the calling of a Constituent Assembly (November 1976)'[32] – then it is clear to the pro-Soviet Indian communists that the Soviet Union would like them to continue along their long-standing route of supporting Congress.

Research indicates that, whatever may be the intent of the Soviet reporters, their influence on Indian communists' thinking is low. The level of information among Indian communists about Soviet writings on India is not perceptibly higher than the little knowledge displayed by other intellectuals. None of the CPI's leading intellects reads Russian, so the informational sources are as restricted for them as they are for others – and no Indian is intellectually satisfied by the crumbs that fall occasionally from the weekly *New Times* and monthly *International Affairs*. As for translations of other Soviet writings, the party's organs are unable to handle such a task. The weekly paper *New Age* has no space for reprints because of its limited resources. In any case the low rate of literacy in English and the few intellectual resources in the Party makes it practically impossible to have a serious ideological and theoretical CPI publication. Even the monthly *Mainstream*, known as a CPI-inspired magazine which can afford good design and long articles, only devoted 3 per cent of its columns to reprinting Soviet articles in 1971. Were more Soviet indology to be available in English it is doubtful how much impact it would have on CPI thinking. As Mohit Sen, the Party's leading theoretician, put it in an interview, Indian communists have been misled too many times by the errors of judgment and analysis made by Moscow observers such as A.M. Dyakov and V.V. Balabushevich for Soviet writing to enjoy the authority it did in the decade 1945-55.[33] Once analytically bitten, twice ideologically shy. What is more, he complained that Soviet indology is not relevant to the party's day-to-day concerns, since they are academic rather than political writings. More important, according to Sen, was the desire by the CPI to be intellectually independent of Moscow. Since the concepts and the methodology of marxism-leninism are universal, it feels no need for instruction in how to use the basic intellectual tools. These should better be applied by local communists to analysing the Indian scene than by foreigners working abroad, however superior their research resources might be.

3. Soviet writings are an input into Soviet foreign-policy-making

It is likely that some Soviet scholars, most obviously those entrusted with the direction of the major research institutes such as Tyagunenko and Kotovsky, and those who hold high political as well as academic posts, such as Ulyanovsky, provide an input into deliberations on Soviet policy towards third world countries. One leading Soviet scholar told me in 1968 that he and some of his colleagues had drafted the section on the national liberation movement for the CPSU's theses at the twenty-second Party congress. A disaffected Soviet development scholar confided in another interview that some of the more trusted scholars in his institute who were Party members were asked to write private papers for the party secretariat. These assessments of the political situation in specific countries were not formulated in ideological language, but they were not circulated either in manuscript or printed form. The reasonable assumption that politically trustworthy individual third world experts give foreign policy advice does not make reasonable the hypothesis that Soviet development writings as a whole have a significant impact on Soviet policy-making. As Richard Remnek admitted, the 'method of correlating scholarly analyses with Soviet policy offers, at best, an imprecise approximation of the degree of scholarly influence in the foreign policy-making process.'[34] The growing autonomy of Soviet writings from the ups and downs of Soviet third world relations indicates that, as a general rule, it is as dangerous for non-Soviet observers as for Soviet policy-makers to deduce Soviet policy from Soviet publications. The concept of non-capitalism would have given officials concerned with Soviet-Ghanaian relations in the early 1960s little predictive security: critical discussions of Nkrumah's dictatorial rule were only made after his fall from power. One has to assume, as does Albert Weeks, that 'Soviet foreign policy still uses communism as its compass, if not its blueprint' to blame the failure of Soviet-Ghanaian policy towards Nkrumah on their 'incomplete, unobjective studies.'[35] Even those who maintain that considerations of ideology, as distinct from national interest, determine Soviet foreign policy would have an extremely difficult task in trying to prove that the Soviet writing on developing countries were more the cause than the effect of the ideology - and policy-making process. It would seem more reasonable to conclude that, just as, on balance, 'the Soviet Union has sought to adjust its aid program to India's urgent needs,'[36] so Soviet development analysis has adjusted to the Soviet perception of third world development needs. The evidence that Soviet writings are a significant input into Soviet third world policy-making has yet to be produced.

THE GEOPOLITICAL IMPORTANCE OF SOVIET DEVELOPMENT WRITINGS

Our judgment that Soviet third world analysis is of only questionable political importance within the Soviet political system does not imply that it is without geopolitical significance beyond Soviet borders. Quite the contrary, in the struggle waged by the superpowers for the 'hearts and minds' of the third world it has been assumed that the ideological combat was not just a rationalization of the great power conflict but also a direct appeal to the uncommitted nations for them to adopt socialist or capitalist models for their own development. Politicians justified aid programmes as the means to buttress recipient countries from the subversive dangers of capitalism (or communism) and academics devoted monographs to assess whether countries x, y, or z were being drawn into the orbit of the imperialist bloc (or the socialist camp). As this was the era of social science model-building in the western academies and nation-building by the mostly intellectual new leaderships in the third world, it was not unreasonable to believe that ideologies would have a formative impact on the political, economic, and even social systems of these 'emerging' societies. Indeed the events that captured the headlines and dominated the book catalogues on third world problems concerned radical changes in these new states, whether the erection of Castro's marxism-leninism or the downfall of Nkrumah's socialism. By inference, the leaderships, including the elites in the civil service, the economy, the press, and the universities, could be shifted from one development path to another as if they were sitting on some huge teeter-totter, needing just an ideological impulse to push them one way or the other.

Recent political science research has, however, addressed little effort to assessing what impact superpower theories have actually had. To take India, the most thoroughly documented of third world countries, as an example, we have studies on Indian public opinion concerning the USA and USSR,[37] estimations of the relative political influence of the USSR and China,[38] comparative research on Soviet and American aid to India,[39] studies on the Soviet ideological line for Indian communism,[40] a sensitive analysis of the internal dynamics of Indian communism,[41] and anti-communist descriptions of the extent of Soviet propaganda distribution in India.[42] No work has been published on the influence of either the USSR or the USA on the thinking or policy-making of Indians.

Since an analysis of Soviet development theory would be incomplete without an assessment of its impact in the third world, the final research for this monograph was a case study to determine the influence of Soviet thinking on the elite of a single developing country. Given the primacy of India in Soviet diplomatic and economic support, and given its dominance in Soviet writings, India was the obvious site for the field work. One hundred interviews were carried out during

March and April 1972, just after the liberation of East Pakistan by the Indian army under the umbrella of the 1971 Indo-Soviet treaty and immediately following the March state elections in which Indira Gandhi's Congress Party had elicited a second sweeping mandate of public confidence. This was a period of national confidence vis-à-vis the outside world and, as far as the Soviet Union was concerned, a period when feelings towards the USSR were as friendly and unapprehensive as they had ever been. If the timing of the research biased the results towards favourable responses concerning the Soviet Union, so too was the selection of interviewees weighted in favour of their knowledge of Soviet thinking and its possible impact on the policy process within the Indian government.[43] In fact the research revealed that neither in theory nor in practice have the Soviets had any noticeable impact on Indian elites' ways of thinking or acting.

THE JOURNALISTS

Because the Indian intellectual world is effectively so small, the role of the journalist as intellectual pace-setter is very important. In what is a largely conformist intellectual milieu ideas circulate rapidly. Interviews with leading journalists revealed a set of attitudes that turned out to be widely held by all the academic interviewees: a blend of national self-confidence and remoteness from foreign thought. It was not from animosity towards the Soviet Union that the journalists expressed low interest in Soviet writing. During the course of interviews it became clear that this reluctance concerning Soviet thought had nothing to do with attitudes towards the Soviet Union, which were warm when they were not enthusiastic. That the Russians had proven themselves in action as India's best friends was a point repeatedly made by these editorial writers who expressed no fear of the Soviets nor any concern that India's military dependence would lead to improper behaviour by the USSR. Politically, pro-Soviet attitudes coexisted with ideologically anti-marxist-leninist views. Explaining why the Indian press carries virtually no Soviet material, most journalists evinced a great distrust for the political bias of Soviet scholars and what they consider the resulting low quality of their publications. Just as friendliness towards the Soviet Union accompanied apprehension concerning Soviet writings, so did a distrust of marxist-leninist writings coexist with a much greater interest in Soviet national interests than in Soviet ideological formulations.

THE INTELLECTUALS

Equally impressive was the consensus concerning Soviet writings revealed by interviews with Indian academics from the moderate centre to the far left of the

ideological spectrum. While the amount of knowledge of and the level of interest in Soviet writings vary among different academics depending on their area of
specialization, the attitudes of those Indian intellectuals who could a priori be
expected to be most familiar with Soviet thinking can best be presented in three
dimensions: little information, low credibility, and poor personal contact. The
most striking aspect of the intellectual relationship between India and the Soviet
Union was the extremely low level of information among Indian academics concerning Soviet development theory. Even at such a respected establishment as
the graduate School of International Studies at Jawaharlal Nehru University in
New Delhi, which has specialized in foreign affairs and area studies, the level of
knowledge about the Soviet Union in general and Soviet thinking in particular
was also low. Only one professor gave courses on Soviet politics. While there was
some interest in communist political theory, this was restricted to a knowledge
of Marx learned through western, anti-marxist texts. In fact, notwithstanding
the School's interest in area studies, including the Soviet Union, Central Asia,
and East Europe, the official curriculum for all courses given there included only
nine Soviet books. The lack of knowledge about Soviet writings on India did not
reflect disinterest in Soviet relations with India. On the contrary, discussion of
the Indo-Soviet Treaty and of the new power balance in Asia resulting from the
liberation of Bangladesh indicated a lively interest in Soviet performance and
intentions. Economists were interested in the efficiency of Soviet aid projects
compared to western project performance. Liberal political scientists were interested in the kind of relations the Indian communist parties, particularly the re-
putedly pro-soviet CPI, had with Moscow. But the question whether the Soviet
academic researchers had anything relevant to say about India was a non-starter
to Indian intellectuals.

The crux of the problem was reiterated in interview after interview: Soviet
scholarship suffers from an extraordinary credibility gap among Indians. What
little material Indian scholars have read is called by them 'turgid,' 'monotonous,'
'unreadable.' Worse than the style is the perceived poor quality of the writing,
dismissed time after time as 'only propaganda,' 'jargon,' or 'rhetoric.' The Soviet
intellectual is considered not to be free to write what he considers the truth, undertaking research only to refute accusations made by the Chinese or 'bourgeois
ideologists.' Where they are not being defensive, Soviet scholars are considered
to be 'political' academics, so constrained by party directives that they could
only present the official view of any particular topic. Underlying all these stereotypes of Soviet writing is the feeling that there is a double contradiction in
Soviet social science work on developing countries. One contrasts those Soviet
writings on the third world which are revolutionary in conclusions with Soviet
foreign policy towards third world countries, which is accommodating if not

supporting reactionary regimes. The other contradiction, between marxist-leninst theory, which is hostile to bourgeois capitalist systems, and actual Soviet analysis of India, which is presented as a progressive country, further discredits the Soviet school among the more critical thinkers.

It might be thought that this set of unambiguously scornful attitudes is bred of ignorance and could be corrected by better personal contact between Indian scholars and their Soviet colleagues. This is not the case. Contempt for Soviet writings may not be bred on familiarity, but it is certainly nourished by contact with the Soviet academic establishment. This contact takes two forms, meeting Soviet scholars visiting India and dealing with the Soviet Ministry of Education about research matters. When questioned about Soviet academics visiting India, Indian intellectuals have a number of responses, none favourable. The general view as summarized by one political scientist is that they 'come as academics but talk like diplomats.' Even those political economists whose better quality books are translated into English have disappointed their Indian interlocutors. Gordon-Polonskaya, author of an important study on Pakistan, gave a seminar at the School of International Studies but appeared 'doctrinaire,' unwilling to discuss questions in the seminar. This inhibition against frank and open discussions is compared with the more freewheeling, self-confident behaviour of western professors, who, while their bias is equally identifiable, are found more stimulating because of their readiness to engage in intellectual battle. Thus, whether the Soviet writings are dismissed for being determined more by ideology or foreign policy than by scientific considerations, whether the attitudes are based on direct knowledge of working conditions in the Soviet Union, or whether the scepticism is based on a knowledge more of Soviet English-language propaganda than the best Soviet scholarship, the views of liberal intellectuals in India are strikingly similar to those of their western colleagues, despite the unusually good relations of India with the Soviet Union and the pro-Soviet attitudes of the Indian elite.

There was as little informed knowledge about Soviet writings among radical as among moderate scholars. Whether formally members of one of the communist parties, ex-communists, or independent marxists, these intellectuals are less fellow travellers than parallel travellers: they are working with similar hypotheses, using similar concepts, but not particularly interested in what their Soviet counterparts have produced. Even a well-known young radical economist like Nirmal Chandra, working on the definition of rural classes in East Pakistan, who does refer in his writing to a Soviet book on this subject by Gankovsky and Gordon-Polanskaya, reported no intellectual contact of any kind with these authors apart from reading and citing their book.[44] Whether Paresh Chattopadhyay writing on state capitalism or Ranjit Sau trying to formulate the laws of development of the Indian economy, whether Ashwami Saith working on the peasant economy or Stephen Ganguli analysing Indian capitalism, the academics of the radical left appeared intellectually impervious to Soviet writings.[45]

Among Indian marxist scholars this absence of Soviet intellectual output is less a result of ignorance than a series of individual rejections of Soviet work seen at first hand to be inadequate. While liberal intellectuals ignore Soviet writing out of disinterest, Indian marxists reject Soviet 'hacks' with the contempt of jilted lovers. Whereas the younger academics at the doctoral level are completely ignorant of Soviet work, their more senior colleagues who have passed through the communist party in one or other of its former incarnations have come to a very similar, though more passionate, scorn of Soviet scholarship than liberal intellectuals. Soviet intellectuals are not searching for the truth, they say; their work is politically controlled, so that it is futile to study what they write; they are dogmatic, sterilely using pre-formed analytical frameworks; their scholarship is poor, using random footnotes to pretend it is serious.

This rejection of Soviet thought is not restricted to political economists. Marxist historians assume an attitude of amused tolerance in discussing Soviet historical work on India. While they appreciate and use some of the English translations of Soviet works on the Indian national movement, since these do accept colonialism as a reality and do not try to explain it away as do western historians, they show no real interest in Soviet historiography. For instance, they did not think recent Soviet thinking on the relevance to India of the concept of 'Asiatic mode of production' was useful enough to translate into English.

If intellectuals left, right, and centre show the same pattern of little knowledge, low credibility, and poor personal contact with Soviet intellectual sources, the prospects for increasing Soviet intellectual influence in India can hardly be considered rosy. A trend visible throughout the academic establishment is to reject foreign models and standards in favour of local approaches. On India's intellectual left, for instance, an indigenous school of marxist scholars is crystallizing. Although it is weakened by ideological and political cleavages, this collection of individuals is finding a collective identity through occasional seminars held on specific issues and an intellectual forum in the *Economic and Political Weekly* of Bombay which keeps the left open to non-marxists and communicates new thinking to a wide public of government and political leaders. What makes this emerging Indian marxist school congenitally unresponsive to Russian intellectual production is the perceived conservatism of Soviet marxism-leninism. Whatever its state of intellectual disarray, radical Indian thinking is not fossilized and would greatly resent the conservative orientation of Soviet writing, which, it is felt, uncritically accepts the virtues of state capitalism for India.

A further obstacle in the way of any Soviet impact is the fundamentally western orientation of all Indian intellectuals, radicals very much included. Indeed, if any new ideas are to fertilize the indigenous marxist schools, it seems, as Edward Shils has suggested, that they will have to come from the west. 'The USSR doesn't attract Indian intellectuals very much. Practically no one reads books about the USSR and certainly practically no one studies it in a scholarly way. Even though he claims that it represents the model for India, the leftist Indian intellectual does not care to learn about it in intimate detail. Even the leftists feel closer to Britain – not least when they deny what they think it stands for.'[46]

THE POLICY-MAKERS

The low impact of Soviet writings on Indian intellectuals does not preclude the possibility that the Soviet Union has influenced Indian policy-makers in their conceptualization of the state's role in planning.

After all Nehru never hid his admiration for the socialist (as opposed to the repressive) features of the Soviet system. Before coming to power he often referred in his speeches and writings to the Soviet experience as a model for India: 'So far as I am personally concerned,' he said in a speech given in London on 4 February 1936, 'I very largely approve of the Russian system of government and I hope some such thing will extend to India.' After almost ten years in power, when the basic structure of the Indian political and economic system had been assembled, he told Frank Moraes that 'the influence of the Soviet revolution ... [gave] a powerful economic turn to our thoughts.'[47]

Interviews with present-day planners and architects of Indian planning indicate that Nehru's 1930s image of Soviet industrialization and planning may have been the most important channel through which the Soviet model had its limited influence on policy formulation in independent India. Talking on the debates on the heavy-industry approach taken by the famous second-five year plan (1956–61), former Finance Minister C.D. Deshmukh recalled that there was not much Soviet input in their policy thinking in the late 1940s. The pro-Soviet thinking of Nehru was vague and ill-defined. A commitment to a major role for the public sector in infrastructure and heavy industry development had already been made by the Tata-Birla plan produced for the Indian National Congress in 1944 by the big capitalist wing of the party. The acceleration of industrial development through an interventionist state investment and planning activity was thus conventional wisdom for the new leadership of independent India.

This does not mean that Soviet experts did not participate in the background thinking for Indian planning. One Soviet economist, M.I. Rubinshtein, was invited by P.C. Mahalanobis to join the group of renowned foreign economists that he had assembled at the Indian Statistical Institute (ISI) of Calcutta to provide a brains trust in conceptualizing the planning system. Reports vary about

Rubinshtein's effectiveness in this assembly of world experts. Those favourably impressed by his contribution still rate it lower than that of Oskar Lange from Poland or Charles Bettelheim from France, both marxists who were stronger in intellect and more respected in their policy advice. According to C.D. Deshmukh, Joan Robinson was the most influential foreign economist with her left-leaning sympathies and theoretical rigour. The most generous assessment of Soviet policy influence came from P.C. Mahalanobis himself, who went to Moscow as early as 1952 to consult Soviet planning experts. Such economists as Strumilin and Varga gave him strong advice – but in the direction of not going too far with forced industrialization. Recalling the Soviet scissors crisis of the late 1920s, they advised against too much nationalization, against too large a steel target for the second five-year plan, and even supported Mahalanobis's inclination to support small-scale cottage industry at the same time as heavy industrialization was proceeding. Asked whether the second five-year plan would have been different without this Soviet participation, Mahalanobis replied that it was helpful to have their sympathy at a top level, 'like airforce cover for the army.' Thus, rather than pushing the Indians into radical action, Soviet influence on the Indian planning system was first to popularize the general idea of planning among Nehru's colleagues, second to restrain Indian policy-planners from over-enthusiasm, and third to provide both internal political support through their private conversations with Indian leaders and external ideological assistance through their public writings in the Soviet press.

This supportive participation in the Indian plan formulation was the high point of the Soviet involvement in the Indian policy process. It is true that Rubinshtein was followed by a number of Soviet statisticians who visited the ISI. Their contribution, however, was academic: they gave papers on Soviet statistical theory, not advice on Indian planning practice.[48] Rubinshtein thus remains the sole Soviet economist who had any personal involvement in the planning of Indian planning – a participation that must be contrasted with the Ford Foundation team of American economists that still have official status as members of the Planning Commission despite the officially cool relations between the United States and India. It is, in fact, only with some difficulty that there can be found in the Planning Commission economists even interested either in what the Soviets write about India or in what the relevance of the Soviet industrialization debate of the 1920s might be to India's industrialization problems. Whether from a feeling that Indian planners are highly sophisticated economists themselves or a belief that modern Soviet problems are quite different from those of India, P.C. Mahalanobis himself expressed no desire for further Soviet intellectual participation since the formulation of the second five-year plan.

Lack of interest and expectations concerning Soviet thinking is not just a linguistic problem. Wolf Ladejinsky, a prominent authority on Indian agrarian problems whose mother tongue is Russian and who works for an international organization in New Delhi, evinced no knowledge of Soviet writings, no interest in finding out about them, and no concern with what their recommendations might be. Underlying this dismissal of Soviet thinking among senior policymakers is the perception that ideology is far less important than national interests in determining whether the relations between the Soviet Union and India prosper, and that whenever problems arise between the two countries they can be resolved by direct negotiations.

The complete divorce of government thinking from Soviet marxism-leninism was best expressed by Mohan Kumaramangalam, then minister of steel and a member of Indira Gandhi's inner cabinet circle. Although a member of the communist party from 1935 to 1956, he did not read Soviet writings or have direct knowledge of Soviet thinking about Indian economics. While grappling in 1972 with the problems of increasing the efficiency and productivity of both public and private sectors in the steel industry by creating a new holding company that could exert complete control over the whole process of production from mine to ingot, he had no inkling of what the Soviets might be thinking of such a new venture.[49] Still expressing a strong interest in socialist goals, he was more concerned with raising the standard of living of the mass of Indians than expanding the state sector for the sake of ideological purity.

There is no decisive evidence suggesting that the negligible intellectual and political impact of Soviet indology in India is not the case throughout the third world. That marxist vocabulary has found its way into the speeches and writings of many African leaders does not indicate they have fallen under the influence of the Soviet, Chinese, or any foreign authority.[50] That Fidel Castro declared himself a communist and was admitted to the socialist camp had far more to do with *raison d'état* than with *raison idéologique*. Others, such as Nasser, practised the non-capitalist path preached by the Soviets but invoked Allah rather than Lenin. Chile was an example of a country with an autonomous marxist tradition, independent of the marxist-leninist school. In Latin American countries that have enjoyed political, if not economic, independence for generations, there are national intelligentsias that consider themselves best suited to work out the solutions to their own problems.

Soviet development writings continue to burgeon and to circulate in dramatically increasing volume around the world. Until quality prevails over quantity in the research institutes of the USSR, however, they will be more likely to serve as an uncertain guidebook for watchers of the Kremlin than as an alternative paradigm for students of the third world.

NOTES AND INDEX

Notes

ONE / QUESTIONS AND METHODS

1 V.I. Lenin, 'Better fewer but better,' *Collected Works* 33 (Moscow, 1965)
   500
2 'Almost overnight Communism in Africa has become an international problem of the first magnitude ... Now, in 1961, Africa has replaced the Middle
   East as the world's chief trouble centre, and it is likely to remain the main
   area of contest between West and East for many years to come.' Walter Z.
   Laqueur, 'Communism and nationalism in Africa,' *Foreign Affairs*, 39
   (1961) 610
      In the words of W.W. Kulski the developing countries are the principal
   battlefield of peaceful competition, Soviet style, whose aim is 'to change,
   piecemeal and without an all-out war, preferably by political, economic,
   and ideological means, the status quo in the non-Communist world to the
   detriment of the West in order to reach, eventually, the ultimate goal, the
   burial of all capitalist (non-Communist) systems.' W.W. Kulski, *Peaceful
   Coexistence, an Analysis of Soviet Foreign Policy* (Chicago, 1959) xx.
   The dominant concern for Soviet or Chinese infiltration, penetration, or
   influence can be seen in numerous publications through the mid-1960s.
   See, for instance, Zbigniew Brzezinski, ed., *Africa and the Communist
   World* (Stanford, 1963); Cyril E. Black and Thomas P. Thorton, eds, *Communism and Revolution: The Strategic Uses of Political Violence* (Princeton,
   1964); Fritz Schatten, *Communism in Africa* (London, 1966); Uri Ra'anan,
   'Tactics in the third world; contradictions and dangers,' *Survey* 57 (October
   1965) 26: 'Moscow believes that the particular stage now reached is highly
   propitious for a major breakthrough, changing the balance of forces.'
3 'The economic aid program appears, then, to be a prominent component of

a broader tactical shift in foreign policy designed to extend Soviet influence in the underdeveloped countries ... weakening the influence of the West, and of the United States in particular.' Joseph S. Berliner, *Soviet Economic Aid: The New Aid and Trade Policy in Underdeveloped Countries* (New York, 1958) 17

4 'It must be expected that the evolution of Mainland China will bear even more heavily upon these Indian decisions. China, the largest and most populous underdeveloped country in the world, has been lost to the West; it is now a communist country seeking to achieve economic expansion along a totalitarian path. To many people, it provides the only relevant alternative model to that of India ... Lessons from China may be adopted, whatever the nature of the costs.' Wilfred Malenbaum, *East and West in India's Development* (Washington, 1959) 9-10

5 Wolfgang H. Kraus, 'Notes on democracy and leadership in the new Afro-Asian states,' and Klaus Mehnert, 'The social and political role of the intelligentsia in the new countries,' in Kurt London, ed., *New Nations in a Divided World: The International Relations of the Afro-Asian States* (New York, 1963) 101-20, 121-33

6 'La doctrine et la méthode marxistes-léninistes du développement économique comportent le risque le plus grand: la perte de l'homme.' Henri Chambre, 'Le modèle marxiste de développement économique,' *Revue de l'Action populaire* 150 (juillet-août 1961) 857

7 'The Soviet form of Communist dictatorship has, among other things, been a means of industrializing a relatively backward country.' Alec Nove, 'The Soviet model and under-developed countries,' *International Affairs* 37 (1961) 29. See also E. Domar, 'A Soviet model of growth,' in *Essays in the Theory of Economic Growth* (Baltimore, 1957), and Francis Seton, 'Asia, Africa and the Soviet model,' *Survey* 31 (Jan.-March 1960) 38-44. The best treatment by an economist free of cold war ideology is Charles K. Wilber, *The Soviet Model and Underdeveloped Countries* (Chapel Hill NC, 1969).

8 Richard Lowenthal, 'China,' in Brzezinski, *Africa and the Communist World* 142-203

9 Alexander Erlich, *The Soviet Industrialization Debate 1924-1928* (Cambridge, Mass., 1960)

10 Wilber *The Soviet Model*, 'Part Two: An application of the Soviet model: Soviet Central Asia,' 137-215

11 For a good summary see Z. Brzezinski, 'Communism and the emerging nations,' in J.R. Pennock, eds., *Self-Government in Modernizing Nations* (New York, 1964)

12 Jawaharlal Nehru, *The Discovery of India* (New York, 1946) 376: 'But most of all we had the example of the Soviet Union which in two brief decades, full of war and civil strife and in the face of what appeared to be insurmountable difficulties had made tremendous progress.'

13 As Peter Wiles put it, 'His one-party system was of a different and more attractive kind than the communist, since it was supposed to embrace most of the adult population and to allow discussion.' 'Power without influence: the economic impact,' in *The Impact of the Russian Revolution 1917-1967, The Influence of Bolshevism on the World outside Russia* (London, 1967) 239

14 Ibid. 248: 'what Touré did was a perfectly logical extension of what Lenin did.'

15 The literature on the Sino-Soviet conflict is so vast and so meshed with third world politics that a footnote can hardly do more than refer to some landmarks. Donald S. Zagoria, *The Sino-Soviet Conflict 1956-1961* (Princeton, 1962) chap. 10, gives the basic background on the national liberation movement. Later assessments can be found in William E. Griffith, 'Communist polycentrism and the underdeveloped areas,' in London, *New Nations in a Divided World* 274-86; Brian Crozier, 'The struggle for the third world,' *International Affairs* 40 (1964) 440-52. An assessment of the impact of the dispute on Soviet policy in Africa is made by Robert Legvold, *Soviet Policy in West Africa* (Cambridge, Mass., 1970) 336-7. A more comprehensive and insightful treatment of the geopolitical, economic, ideological, and intracommunist impact of the Sino-Soviet struggle on the South Asian subcontinent can be found in Bhabani Sen Gupta, *The Fulcrum of Asia: Relations among China, India, Pakistan and the USSR* (New York, 1970). Provocative hypotheses proliferate in I.L. Horowitz, 'Brazil and the Sino-Soviet dispute,' in *Revolution in Brazil* (New York, 1964) 379: 'The Sino-Soviet split will further encourage in Latin America an independent and large-scale socialist movement at the expense of both Soviet and Chinese varieties of communism.' Compare: 'Indeed, the recent successes which the USSR has scored over China in Africa and Asia are due in a large measure to the fact that the non-Communist countries of both continents find the Soviet concept of a 'revolutionary democracy' infinitely more attractive than the Chinese doctrine that the establishment of a distatorship of the proletariat is an indispensable step toward the building of socialism.' Georg A. von Stackelberg, 'The Soviet concept of the revolutionary democratic state and its political significance,' *Bulletin of the Institute for the Study of the USSR* 13 (1966) 13

16 For a summary of the Khrushchevian reformulations see Leopold Labedz,

'Introduction,' *Survey* 43 (August 1962) 3-9. Donald S. Carlisle, 'Stalin's postwar foreign policy and the national liberation movement,' *Review of Politics* 27 (1965) 334-63, shows how the post-stalinist third world policy has roots in a foreign policy review that was under way before Stalin died. An overview of the post-Stalin approach is found in Thomas P. Thornton, 'Communist attitudes toward Asia, Africa and Latin America,' in Black and Thornton, *Communism and Revolution* 245-69.

17 The official party directive to the Institute of Eastern Studies, 'xx S'yezd Kommunisticheskoi Partii Sovetskogo Soyuza i zadachi izucheniya sovremennogo Vostoka' (The 20th Congress of the Communist Party of the Soviet Union and the Aims of Studying the Contemporary East), *Sovetskoe Vostokovedenie* 1 (1956) 3-12, is available as 'The 20th Congress of the CPSU and Problems of Studying the Contemporary East,' in Thomas P. Thornton, ed., *The Third World in Soviet Perspective: Studies by Soviet Writers on the Developing Areas* (Princeton, 1964) 79-87.

18 A historical background of Soviet eastern studies can be found in Walter Z. Laqueur, 'The shifting line in Soviet orientology,' *Problems of Communism* 5 (1956) 20-6. The same author gives an extended treatment of the Soviet thaw's influence on Russian orientology in chapter 6 of his *The Soviet Union and the Middle East* (New York, 1959) 159-86.

19 Alexander Dallin, 'The Soviet Union: political activity,' in Brzezinski, *Africa and the Communist World*, 20-1: 'the recent efforts have made the Soviet Union one of the world's leading countries in the study of Africa.'

20 V.V. Vol'skii, 'The Study of Latin America in the USSR,' in J. Gregory Oswald, ed., *The Soviet Image of Contemporary Latin America: A Documentary History, 1960-1968* (Austin, Texas, 1970) 19

21 From 1954 to 1963 some fifteen non-communist books on Indian economics and politics had been translated into Russian: Stephen Clarkson, *L'analyse soviétique des problèmes indiens du sous-développement (1955–1964)* (Paris, 1970) 234-6.

22 The most convenient bibliographical aid is the classified book and article catalogue in the Lenin Library in Moscow. The chief bibliographical guides produced area by area or country by country are Akademiya Nauk SSSR (ANSSSR) Institut Vostokovedeniya, *Bibliografiya Indii: Dorevolyutsionnaya i sovetskaya literatura na russkom yazyke i yazykakh narodov SSSR, original'naya i perevodnaya* (Bibliography of India: pre-revolutionary and Soviet literature in Russian and in the languages of the peoples of the USSR in the original and in translation) (Moscow, 1959, 1965); ANSSSR Institut Narodov Azii, *Bibliografiya Irana: Literatura na russkom yazyke 1917–1965gg.* (Bibliography of Iran: Russian language literature 1917-1965)

(Moscow, 1967); ANSSSR Institut Vostokovedeniya, *Bibliografiya Turtsii (1917-1958)* (Bibliography of Turkey 1917-1958) (Moscow, 1959); ANSSSR Institut Narodov Azii, *Bibliografiya Yugo-vostochnoi Azii: Dorevolyutsionnaya i sovetskaya literatura na russkom yazyke i yazykakh narodov SSSR, original'naya i perevodnaya* (Bibliography of Southeast Asia: pre-revolutionary and Soviet literature in Russian and in the languages of the peoples of the USSR in the original and in translation) (Moscow, 1960). Since 1964, yearly bibliographies covering all third world countries have appeared: ANSSSR Institut Narodov Azii, *Literature o stranakh Azii i Afriki. Ezhegodnik, 1961* (Literature on Asia and African countries. Yearbook for 1961) (Moscow, 1964); *1962* (Moscow, 1965); *1963* (Moscow, 1967); ANSSSR Institut Vostokovedeniya, *Literature o stranakh Azii, Afriki i Okeanii, 1964-1965gg.* (Literature on the countries of Asia, Africa and Oceana, 1964-5) (Moscow, 1972).

Various bibliographies of Soviet material have appeared in the west. See Leo Okinshevich, *Latin America in Soviet Writings: A Bibliography. Vol. II: 1959-1964* (Baltimore, 1966). See Mary Holdsworth, *Soviet African Studies 1918-59: An Annotated Bibliography* (London, 1961), for a helpful introduction to Soviet writings on Africa. Also of value were the publications of the Central Asian Research Centre in London; for example: *Bibliography of Recent Soviet Source Material on Soviet Central Asia and its Borderlands (including the Middle East)* (London, 1961-) semi-annual. For Asia, see Peter Berton and Alvin Z. Rubinstein, *Soviet Works on Southeast Asia. A Bibliography of Non-Periodical Literature, 1946-1965*, Far Eastern and Russian Research Series, No. 3, University of Southern California (Los Angeles, 1967). For a classified bibliography of Soviet writings on underdevelopment in general and India in particular see Clarkson, *L'analyse soviétique* 163-242.

23 Elizabeth K. Valkenier, 'Recent trends in Soviet research on the developing countries,' *World Politics* 20 (1968) 644-59
24 'The crudely manipulative nature of the Soviet official doctrine makes it an exasperating subject for analysis.' Alexander Erlich and Christian R. Sonne, 'The Soviet Union: economic activity,' in Brzezinski, *Africa and the Communist World* 49. Peter Wiles has said: 'Soviet social science is at an extremely low level of intellectual achievement and common honesty. Until very recently everything was decided at the top, by the political leaders. The task of the social scientist was to support the new top decisions, even if they reversed previous top decisions, and to criticize everybody at lower levels for not carrying them out. Since nearly all interesting questions were controversial, and controversy was dangerous, virtually no interesting research

was carried out. Moreover social science was under especially heavy censorship, and censors have to understand what they are reading. So they did not allow techniques to develop that they could not understand, and technique stagnated completely.' Wiles, *Impact of the Russian Revolution* 263.

25 'All attempts to account for Soviet foreign policy without clear regard to the ideological factor are ultimately sterile.' Laqueur, *The Soviet Union and the Middle East* viii.

26 Richard Lowenthal is the reigning master of interpreting Soviet ideological tea leaves to discern subtle shifts in interparty relations. See his 'Diplomacy and revolution: the dialectics of a dispute,' *China Quarterly* (Jan.-March 1961) 1-24, 'Has the revolution a future?' *Encounter* (Jan. 1965), or 'Duel with a shadow,' *Encounter* (Feb. 1962) 81-6.

27 Zbigniew K. Brzezinski, *The Soviet Bloc: Unity and Conflict*, Rev. ed. (New York, 1961) 367-8

28 'The new Soviet foreign-policy approach to the Asian and African nations brought forth innovations on the doctrinal plane ... However, it must be taken into account that the ideological precepts which themselves evolved in accord with Soviet policies and actual situations in the underdeveloped countries, had a pronounced effect upon later Soviet policies.' Arthur J. Klinghoffer, *Soviet Perspectives on African Socialism* (Rutherford NJ: 1969) 236

29 Thornton, *The Third World in Soviet Perspective* x

30 On problems of African socialism, see Klinghoffer, *Soviet Perspectives on African Socialism*. On the question of national integration in Africa, see Helen Desfosses Cohn, *Soviet Policy toward Black Africa: The Focus on National Integration* (New York, 1972). On India, see Vijay S. Budhraj, 'The Soviet Image of India.' Doctoral dissertation, Washington DC, American University, 1958; Leonard J. Kirsch, 'The Soviet view of the Indian economy,' in *Public Policy, Yearbook of the Graduate School of Public Administration* (Cambridge, Mass., 1959) 207-34; and Gene D. Overstreet, *The Soviet View of India 1945-1948*, Master's thesis, New York, Columbia University, 1953.

31 R.A. Ulyanovsky, *The Dollar and Asia: U.S. Neo-colonialist Policy in Action* (Moscow, 1965) 6

32 L. Delyusin, 'Socialism and the National Liberation Struggle,' in Y. Zhukov et al., *The Third World: Problems and Prospects* (Moscow, 1970) 251

33 Adam B. Ulam, *The Unfinished Revolution. An Essay on the Sources of Influence of Marxism and Communism* (New York, 1960) 10

34 Zbigniew Brzezinski, 'The African challenge,' in Brzezinski, *Africa and the Communist World* 206

35 For an expression of this discontent by an Indian political scientist see Rajni
   Kothari, 'State building in the third world: alternative strategies,' *Economic
   and Political Weekly* 7 (1972) 233-44.
36 Kulski, *Peaceful Coexistence* 121
37 Alexander Dallin 'The Soviet Union,' in Brzezinski, *Africa and the Communist World* 10: Soviet articles about Africa 'were characterized by an abund-
   ance of glosses and stereotypes.' Thornton *Third World in Soviet Perspective*
   88, remarked that 'Latin American studies have traditionally been among
   the weakest areas of Soviet 'orientology.' "
38 Kulski, *Peaceful Coexistence* 121
39 Thomas P. Thornton, 'Asia,' in Black and Thornton *Communism and
   Revolution* 282
40 Klinghoffer, *Soviet Perspectives on African Socialism* 49
41 Laqueur, *The Soviet Union and the Middle East* 1
42 Thornton, *Third World in Soviet Perspective* 88
43 S.A. Kuz'min, *The Developing Countries, Employment and Capital
   Investment* (New York, 1969) 7
44 The best monograph dealing with the reversals in the relations between the
   Soviet Union and the radical regimes of West Africa is Legvold, *Soviet Policy
   in West Africa*. See also Charles B. McLane, 'Soviet doctrine and the military
   coups in Africa,' *International Journal* 21 (1966). For a similar problem in
   Indonesia, see Uri Ra'anan, 'The coup that failed: a background analysis,'
   Problems of Communism 15 (1966).
45 For a brief survey of the Soviet-Indian relationship see Harish Kapur, *The
   Soviet Union and the Emerging Nations: A Case Study of Soviet Policy
   Towards India* (Geneva, 1972). The fullest analysis is in Arthur Stein's
   monograph, *India and the Soviet Union: The Nehru Era* (Chicago, 1969).
   For an Indian account see J.A. Naik, *Soviet Policy towards India: From
   Stalin to Brezhnev* (Delhi, 1970). More up to date is Robert H. Donaldson,
   Soviet Policy toward India: Ideology and Strategy (Cambridge, Mass., 1974).
46 During my two-month visit to Moscow in the summer of 1968 it took, for
   instance, two weeks of shunting from the officer in charge of Canadian exchange scholars, to the dean of the Economics Faculty of Moscow University,
   to a junior staff member detailed to look after me, to his contact with the
   Institute of Latin America, to the preliminary interview with its director,
   who finally set up my first meeting with two of his colleagues, who were to
   speak with me on one of the many subjects I had outlined as being of interest to me. The atmosphere created by such a method of selection was certainly not conducive to the richest intellectual exchange. Only on rare occa-
   sions was I able to interview a Soviet scholar alone. The norm was to have a

discussion with at least two scholars at a time. Whether this was a method of ideological control could not be known, but interviews à trois generally suffered a decline in intellectual rigour. Even these meetings were abruptly curtailed at the Institute of World Economics and International Relations when I was informed by its academic secretary that, since I had been working at the Research Institute on Communist Affairs, whose director, Zbigniew Brzezinski, was a notable cold war propagandist, they had no desire to facilitate my research, which, they deduced, must be motivated by similar cold war intentions.

47 For a study of Soviet academic politics at an earlier period, see Loren R. Graham, *The Soviet Academy of Sciences and the Communist Party 1927-1932* (New York, 1968).

48 The standard work on the relation between the USSR and the Indian communist movement is John H. Kautsky, *Moscow and the Communist Party of India: A Study in the Postwar Evolution of International Communist Strategy* (New York, 1956). See also David N. Druhe, *Soviet Russia and Indian Communism* (New York, 1959). The basic work on the post-war Communist Party of India with extensive background in the Soviet-Indian relationship through the Comintern is Gene D. Overstreet and Marshall Windmiller, *Communism in India* (Berkeley, 1959), though the best contemporary study of Indian communism – with far less concern with extra-party relations – is Bhabani Sen Gupta, *Communism in Indian Politics* (New York, 1972).

TWO / THE FIRST FOUR DECADES

1 Demetrius Boersner, *The Bolsheviks and the National and Colonial Question, 1917-1928* (Geneva, 1957) chap. 1

2 K. Marx and F. Engels, *On Colonialism* (Moscow, n.d.), provides the bulk of their articles on India and China, together with a selection of their correspondance on such issues as the absence of feudalism in Asia.

3 Hélène Carrère d'Encausse and Stuart Schram, *Le marxisme et l'Asie 1853-1964* (Paris, 1965) 17-20

4 Alexander Gerschenkron, 'The problem of economic development in Russian intellectual history of the nineteenth century,' in E.J. Simmons, ed., *Continuity and Change in Russian and Soviet Thought* (Cambridge, Mass., 1955) 11-39

5 S.M. Schwarz, 'Populism and early Russian marxism on ways of economic development of Russia,' in Simmons, *Continuity and Change*, 40-61

6 V. Lenin, *The Development of Capitalism in Russia, Collected Works* 3 (Moscow, 1964) 21-604

7 Carrère d'Encausse and Schram, *Le marxisme et l'Asie* 28-39
8 Herbert S. Dinerstein, 'Introduction,' in J. Gregory Oswald, *The Soviet Image of Latin America. A Documentary History, 1960-1968* (Austin, Texas, 1970) xiii
9 Richard Lowenthal, 'Russia, the one-party system and the third world,' *Survey* 58 (Jan. 1966) 46-57
10 John H. Kautsky, *Moscow and the Communist Party of India: A Study in the Postwar Evolution of International Communist Strategy* (New York, 1956)
11 Jaan Pennar, 'Moscow and socialism in Egypt,' *Problems of Communism* 15 (1966) 41-7
12 Bhabani Sen Gupta, *The Fulcrum of Asia* (New York, 1970) chap. 4, describes the complexities of international, intercommunist, and doctrinal issues of the Sino-Soviet-Indo-Pakistani imbroglio.
13 Boersner, *The Bolsheviks and the Colonial Question* chaps. 5 and 6
14 Laqueur, *The Soviet Union and the Middle East* 1
15 Chattar Singh Samra, *India and Anglo-Soviet Relations 1917-1947* (London, 1959) 1-19
16 Jane Degras, ed., *Soviet Documents on Foreign Policy* (London, 1951) 1, 15-17
17 K. Troyanovskii, *Vostok i revolyutsiya (The revolution and the East)* (Moscow, 1918) 40
18 Louis Fischer, *The Soviets in World Affairs. A History of the Relations between the Soviet Union and the Rest of the World 1917-1929* (New York, 1960) 207
19 G. Safarov, 'Predislovie' (Preface), in M.N. Roi, *Novaya Indiya* (New India) (Moscow and Petrograd, 1923) 4
20 A. Tivel', 'Vstupitel'naya stat'ya' (Introductory article), in D. Nagiev, *Indiya pod gnetom Anglii* (India under England's yoke) (Moscow, 1925) 5
21 Manabendra Nath Roy, *India in Transition* (Geneva, 1922) 17-84
22 R. Edyus, *Ocherki rabochego dvizheniya v stranakh vostoka* (Sketches of the workers' movement in the countries of the East) (Moscow, 1922) 49
23 Safarov, 'Preface,' in Roi, *Novaya Indiya* 3
24 L. Sunitsa, 'Predislovie' (Preface), in Roi, *Novaya Indiya* 5-6
25 Tivel', Introductory article, in Nagiev, *Indiya* 4
26 Nagiev, *Indiya* 23-4
27 Ibid. 42-6
28 Gene D. Overstreet and Marshall Windmiller, *Communism in India* (Berkeley, 1959) 122-222
29 J. Stalin, 'Des tâches politiques de l'Université des peuples d'Orient,' *Le marxisme et la question nationale et coloniale* (Paris, 1953) 242, 244

30 Allan and Anbor, *Mirutskii protsess i terror v Indii* (The Meerut trial and terror in India) (Moscow, 1934) 20

31 John P. Haithcox, *Communism and Nationalism in India: M.N. Roy and Comintern Policy 1920-1939* (Princeton NJ, 1971) chap. 6

32 'Ot izdatel'stva' (From the editors), in Dzhon Bosham, *Angliiskii imperializm v Indii* (English imperialism in India) (Moscow, 1935) 6

33 A. Pronin, *Indiya* (India) (Moscow, 1940) 79-80

34 S. Mel'man, *Indiya* (India) (Moscow, 1943) 114-22

35 E. Varga, 'Economies and economic policy in the fourth quarter of 1927,' *Inprecor* 8 (1928) 294, cited in Overstreet and Windmiller, *Communism in India* 107

36 E. Varga, *Izmeneniya v ekonomike kapitalizma v itoge vtoroi mirovoi voiny* (Changes in the economy of capitalism resulting from the second world war) (Moscow, 1946) 214-15

37 Ibid., 218-23

38 'Soviet views on the post-war world economy. An official critique of Eugene Varga's *Changes in the Economy of Capitalism Resulting from the Second World War*' mimeo. (Washington, 1948) 20-1

39 Richard B. Remnek, *Soviet Scholars and Soviet Foreign Policy* (Durham NC, 1975) 112

40 E. Varga, *Osnovnye voprosy ekonomiki i politiki imperializma posle vtoroi mirovoi voiny* (Basic problems in the economics and politics of imperialism after the second world war) (Moscow, 1953) 291

41 Ibid. 300-79

42 E. Varga, *Osnovnye voprosy ekonomiki i politiki imperializma posle vtoroi mirovoi voiny* (Basic problems in the economics and politics of imperialism after the second world war) 2d edn (Moscow, 1957) 1. As late as 1973 this volume was still cited by a Soviet author as a basic source on imperialism: V. Vakhrushev, *Neocolonialism: Methods and Manoeuvres* (Moscow, 1973) 13.

43 Ibid. 410-36

44 Ibid. 412-16

THREE / THE POLITICAL ECONOMY
OF STATE CAPITALISM

1 Y. Rozaliyov, 'Specificities of capitalist development in Asian and African countries,' *International Affairs* (Feb. 1976) 67

2 Jacques Lévesque, *L'URSS et la révolution cubaine* (Paris, 1976) 79-89

3 Rozaliyov, 'Specificities of capitalist development,' 67

4 V.V. Rymalov, 'Economic aspects of the current stage of the liberation revolution,' *International Affairs* (May 1967) 61

5 Anonymous introduction to Section 2, 'Rol' gosudarstva v ekonomike' (The state's role in the economy), in *Klassy i klassovaya bor'ba v razvivayushchikhsya stranakh* (Classes and the class struggle in the developing countries) I (Moscow, 1967) 78-9

6 A.S. Solonitskii and O.D. Ul'rikh, 'Gosudarstvennyi sektor v ekonomike razvivayushchikhsya stran' (The state sector in the economy of the developing countries), ibid. 81

7 V. Pavlovskii, *Ekonomika sovremennogo Tailanda* (Modern Thailand's Economy) (Moscow, 1961)

8 V.I. Iskol'dskii, 'Tailand' (Thailand), in *Plany-programmy ekonomicheskogo razvitiya stran Azii* (The economic development plans of the countries of Asia) (Moscow, 1966) 421

9 R.T. Akhramovich, *Concerning the Recent Stages in Afghanistan's Social History* (Moscow, 1967) 12

10 *Bol'shaya sovetskaya entsiklopediya* (Big Soviet encyclopedia), 2nd edn, 12 (Moscow, 1952) 317

11 A. Levkovsky, 'The state sector: its social content and development,' *Social Sciences* 5 (1974) 132-3

12 Rozaliyov, 'Specificities of capitalist development,' 70

13 N.G. Lozovaya, 'Indiya' (India), in *Plany-programmy ekonomicheskogo razvitiya stran Azii* (The economic development plans of the countries of Asia) (Moscow, 1966) 93

14 A. Levkovskii, 'Gosudarstvennyi kapitalizm v Indii – nekotorye osnovnye problemy' (State capitalism in India: some fundamental problems), *Sovremennyi Vostok* 5 (1958) 16

15 A.I. Levkovskii, 'Osnovnye problemy razvitiya gosudarstvennogo kapitalizma v sovremennoi Indii' (The main problems of state capitalism's development in modern India) in *Gosudarstvennyi kapitalizm v stranakh Vostoka* (State capitalism in eastern countries) (Moscow, 1960) 12

16 A.I. Levkovskii, 'Gosudarstvennyi kapitalizm i chastnokapitalisticheskoe predprinimatel'stvo v Indii' (State capitalism and private capitalist enterprise in India), in *Ekonomika sovremennoi Indii* (The economy of modern India) (Moscow, 1960) 177

17 Ibid. 178-9

18 Levkovskii, 'The main problems of state capitalism,' 16

19 R.A. Ul'yanovskii, 'Indiya v bor'be za ekenomicheskuyu nezavisimost'; o gosudarstvennom sektore v ekonomike Indii' (India's struggle for economic independence: concerning the public sector in the Indian economy), *Sovetskoe Vostokovedenie* 4 (1957) 11

20 R.A. Ul'yanovskii, 'Indiya v bor'be za ekonomicheskuyu nezavisimost' (voprosy goskapitalizma)' (India's struggle for economic independence: the problems of state capitalism), in *Nezavisimaya Indiya, 10 let nezavisimosti, 1947-1957, sbornik statei* (Independent India, 10 years of independence, 1947-1957. Collection of articles) (Moscow, 1958) 23

21 Ibid. 31-2

22 R.A. Ul'yanovskii, 'Ob osobennostyakh razvitiya i kharaktere gosudarstvennogo kapitalizma v nezavisimoi Indii' (On the specific characteristics of the development and nature of state capitalism in independent India), *Problemy Vostokovedeniya* 3 (1960) 27

23 Ul'yanovskii, 'India's struggle for economic independence,' 12-13

24 R.S. Gorchakov, 'Nekotorye voprosy razvitiya gosudarstvennogo kapitalizma v Indii v svyazi s tret'im pyatiletnim planom' (Some questions concerning the development of state capitalism in India in connection with the third five-year plan), *Vestnik Leningradskogo Universiteta* 23 (1961) 35

25 Ul'yanovskii, 'India's struggle for economic independence,' 32, 45

26 Ul'yanovskii, 'On the nature of state capitalism in India,' 37

27 Levkovskii, 'State capitalism in India,' 15

28 Gorchakov, 'Some questions on state capitalism in India,' 36

29 *Les principes du marxisme-léninisme. Manuel*, Editions en Langues Etrangères, 2nd edn (Moscow, n.d.) 417

30 Ibid. 257

31 A. Leonidov, 'Les dynasties ploutocratiques de l'Inde,' *Temps Nouveaux* 32 (4 Aug. 1948) 9-15; A. Diakov, 'L'activité du Congrès national indien,' ibid. 3 (12 Jan. 1949) 8-12; T. Erchov, 'Variété indienne de la pseudo-démocratie bourgeoise,' ibid. 11 (5 March 1950) 3-7

32 *Les principes du marxism-léninisme* 257-8

33 Ibid. 258-9

34 S.A. Bessonov, *Rol' gosudarstvennogo kapitalizma v ekonomicheskom razvitii Respubliki Indii* (State capitalism's role in the economic development of the Indian Republic) (Moscow, 1962) 17-18

35 A.L. Batalov et al., 'Itogi razvitiya narodnogo khozyaistva' (Balance sheet of the development of the national economy), in *Problemy ekonomicheskogo i sotsial'nogo razvitiya nezavisimoi Indii* (Problems of economic and social development of independent India) (Moscow, 1967) 9-16

36 Yu. I. Loshakov, 'Indiiskii monopolisticheskii kapital' (Indian monopoly capital), *Vestnik Moskovskogo Universiteta*, Series 7, No. 3 (1967) 64. See also his thesis summary *Kontsentratsiya proizvodstva i monopolii sovremennoi Indii* (The concentration of production and monopolies in modern India) (Moscow, 1967) 16.

37 O.V. Maev, 'Ekonomicheskaya programma indiiskikh monopolistov'
(The economic programme of the Indian monopolists), *Narody Azii i
Afriki* 5 (1964) 161. See also O.V. Maev, 'Indiiskii monopolisticheskii
kapital' (Indian monopoly capital), *Narody Azii i Afriki* 1 (1964) 21-36
38 O.V. Maev, 'Indiiskii monopolisticheskii kapital: zapadnoindiiskie gruppy'
(Indian monopoly capital: Western groups) and 'Indiiskii monopolisticheskii
kapital: vostochnoindiiskie gruppy (Indian monopoly capital: Eastern
groups), *Mirovaya Ekonomika i Mezhdunarodnye Otnosheniya* 8 (1966)
120-7, 3 (1967) 118-23
39 N. Savelyev, 'Monopoly drive in India,' *International Affairs* (April 1967) 35
40 I.I. Egorov, *Finansirovanie planov ekonomicheskogo razvitiya Indii* (The
financing of India's economic development plans) (Moscow, 1967) 214
41 Rozaliyov, 'Specificities of capitalist development,' 70-1

FOUR / THE STATE SECTOR

1 V.G. Solodovnikov, *Some Problems of Economic and Social Development
of Independent African Nations* (Moscow, 1967) 16
2 V. Solodovnikov and N. Gavrilov, 'Africa: tendencies of non-capitalist
development,' *International Affairs* 3 (March 1976) 37
3 Y.V. Gankovsky and L.R. Gordon-Polonskaya, *A History of Pakistan,
1947-1958* (Moscow, 1964) 245
4 A.K. Levkovskii, 'Gosudarstvennyi kapitalizm i chastnokapitalisticheskoe
predprinimatel'stvo v Indii' (State capitalism and private capitalist enterprise in India), in *Ekonomika sovremennoi Indii* (The economy of modern
India) (Moscow, 1960) 185
5 V.A. Kondrat'ev, 'Gosudarstvennyi kapitalizm i promyshlennoe razvitie
sovremennoi Indii' (State capitalism and modern India's industrial development), *Kratkie Soobshcheniya Instituta Narodov Azii* 51 (1962) 19
6 Levkovskii, 'State capitalism and private capitalist enterprise,' 183
7 Kondrat'ev, 'State capitalism and India's industrial development,' 19
8 Ibid. 20
9 Levkovskii, 'State capitalism and private capitalist enterprise,' 185
10 R.S. Gorchakov, 'Nekotorye voprosy razvitiya gosudarstvennogo kapitalizma
v Indii v svyazi s tret'im pyatiletnim planom' (Some questions concerning the
development of state capitalism in India in connection with the third five-year
plan), *Vestnik Leningradskogo Universiteta* 23 (1961) 37
11 Kondrat'ev, 'State capitalism and India's industrial development,' 22-4
12 O. Maev, 'Monopolii, banki i politika' (Monopolies, the banks and politics),
Mirovaya Ekonomika i Mezhdunarodnye Otnosheniya 11 (1969) 60

13 A. Maslennikov, 'Indiya: bor'ba vokrug ekonomicheskoi politiki' (India: the struggle over economic policy), ibid. 11 (1966) 105-6

14 Maev, 'Monopolies, the banks and politics,' 60

15 I. Egorov, 'Independent India's public sector,' *Social Sciences* 5 (1974) 157

16 A.I. Levkovskii, *Osobennosti razvitiya kapitalizma v Indii* (The special characteristics of the development of capitalism in India) (Moscow, 1963) 457

17 A.S. Solonitskii and O.D. Ul'rikh, 'Gosudarstvennyi sektor v ekonomike razvivayushchikhsya stran' (The state sector in the economy of the developing countries), in *Klassy i klassovaya bor'ba v razvivayushchikhsya stranakh* (Classes and the class struggle in the developing countries) II (Moscow, 1967) 95

18 Kondrat'ev, 'State capitalism and India's industrial development,' 28

19 R.A. Ul'yanovskii, 'Ob osobennostyakh razvitiya i kharaktere gosudarstven-nogo kapitalizma v nezavisimoi Indii' (On the specific characteristics of the development and nature of state capitalism in independent India), *Problemy Vostokovedeniya* 3 (1960) 29

20 Ibid. 25

21 Solonitskii and Ul'rikh, 'The state sector,' 96-9

22 R.N. Andreasyan, 'Developing countries and foreign capital,' *International Affairs* 5 (May 1967) 72

23 E. Bragina, 'Razvitie gosudarstvennogo sektora v promyshlennosti Indii' (The development of the state sector in India's industry), *Sovremennyi Vostok* 5 (1957) 7

24 Solonitskii and Ul'rikh, 'The state sector,' 98

25 Egorov, 'Independent India's public sector,' 157

26 Y. Kozlov and V. Kostin, 'The monopolies and "black gold" of Venezuela,' *International Affairs* 4 (March 1976) 123-4

27 V.L. Tyagunenko, ed., *Industrialisation of Developing Countries* (Moscow, 1973) 82-4

28 Andreasyan, 'Developing countries and foreign capital,' 72

29 Ibid. 70

30 Solonitskii and Ul'rikh, 'The state sector,' 98

31 Kondrat'ev, 'State capitalism and India's industrial development,' 29-30

32 Ul'yanovskii, 'On the nature of state capitalism in India,' 25

33 Kondrat'ev, 'State capitalism and India's industrial development,' 30

34 R.A. Ul'yanovskii, 'Indiya v bor'be za ekonomicheskiyu nezavisimost' (voprosy goskapitalizma)' (India's sturggle for economic independence: the problems of state capitalism), in *Nezavisimaya Indiya, 10 let nezavisi-mosti, 1947-1957, sbornik statei* (Independent India, 10 years of independence, 1947-1957. Collection of articles) (Moscow, 1958) 36

35 Kondrat'ev, 'State capitalism and India's industrial development,' 33
36 V. Shurygin, 'India: on the road to democracy and social progress,' *International Affairs* 5 (May 1974) 47
37 Bragina, 'The state sector in India's industry,' 7
38 Tyagunenko, *Industrialisation* 81
39 L.I. Aleksandrovskaya, 'Industrializatsiya razvivayushchikhsya stran i otnoshenie k nei razlichnykh klassov i sotsial'nykh sil' (The industrialization of the developing countries and the relationship to it of their various classes and social forces) *Classes and class struggle* II, 251-75
40 'Editorial Comment,' *New Times* 13 (31 March 1965) 8
41 Aleksandrovskaya, 'Industrialization of the developing countries,' 252-3
42 M.A. Aleksandrov and S.M. Mel'man, 'Privlechenie resursov iz-za rubezha' (Attracting resources from abroad) in *Problems of independent India* (Moscow, 1967) 118
43 Aleksandrovskaya, 'Industrialization of the developing countries,' 252-3
44 R.A. Ul'yanovskii, 'Indiya v bor'be za ekonomicheskuyu nezavisimost'; o gosudarstvennom sektore v ekonomike Indii' (India's struggle for economic independence: concerning the public sector in the Indian economy), *Sovet-skoe Vostokovedenie* 4 (1957) 11
45 Solonitskii and Ul'rikh, 'The state sector,' 103
46 M.A. Sidorov, review of S.K. Bose's *Some Aspects of Indian Economic Development, Narody Azii i Afriki* 2 (1964) 185
47 E.A. Bragina, Review of Charles Bettelheim, *Independent India, Narody Azii i Afriki* 3 (1965) 225
48 Ul'yanovskii, 'India's struggle for economic independence,' 11
49 N. Savelyev, 'Monopoly drive in India,' *International Affairs* (April, 1967) 35
50 Solonitskii and Ul'rikh, 'The state sector,' 113
51 Solodovnikov, *Some Problems of Independent African Nations* 16
52 Kondrat'ev, 'State capitalism and India's industrial development,' 35
53 G.K. Shirokov, Review of V.V. Ramanadham, *The Finances of Public Enterprises, Narody Azii i Afriki* 3 (1965) 224
54 Solonitskii and Ul'rikh, 'The state sector,' 107
55 Solodovnikov, *Some Problems of Independent African Nations* 17
56 Solonitskii and Ul'rikh, 'The state sector,' 89-93
57 E. Gryaznov, 'India: Main Tendencies of Socio-Economic Development,' *International Affairs* 12 (Dec. 1971) 55
58 Ul'yanovskii, 'India's struggle for economic independence,' 42
59 O.D. Ul'rikh, 'Pozitsii gosudarstvennogo i chastnogo sektorov v ekonomike razvivayushchikhsya stran' (The position of the state and private sectors in the developing countries' economies) in *Classes and class struggle* II, 121

60 A.L. Batalov et al., 'Itogi razvitiya narodnogo khozyaistva' (Balance sheet of the development of the national economy), in *Problems of independent India* (Moscow, 1967) 23
61 R. Ulyanovsky, 'People's fight for democracy and social progress in India,' in R. Ulyanovsky and others, *Industrial Revolution and Social Progress in India* (New Delhi, 1970) 1
62 L. Vladimirskii, 'Gosudarstvennaya torgovaya korporatsiya Indii' (India's State Trading Corporation), *Vneshnyaya Torgovlya* 9 (Sept. 1959) 41
63 Ibid. 44
64 Yu. V. Potemkin and V.A. Sandakov, 'Problema nakopleniya v razvivayush-chikhsya stranakh' (The accumulation problem in the developing countries) in *Classes and class struggle* II, 44-5
65 Maev, 'Monopolies, the banks and politics,' 59
66 Ul'yanovskii, 'India's struggle for economic independence,' 38-40
67 Maev, 'Monopolies, the banks and politics,' 59
68 B. Brodovich, *Denezhno-kreditnaya sistema Respubliki Indiya* (The Republic of India's monetary and credit system) (Moscow, 1964) 202
69 A.P. Shastitko, 'Political struggles in India,' *New Times* 33 (1969) 3
70 Maev, 'Monopolies, the banks and politics,' 60
71 Brodovich, *India's monetary and credit system* 204
72 Maev, 'Monopolies, the banks and politics,' 61
73 M. Stasov, 'Nationalization of big commercial banks in India,' *International Affairs* 11 (Nov. 1969) 26
74 G. Mirsky, 'Changes in the third world,' *New Times* 39 (1969) 5
75 R. Ulyanovsky, 'India: main tendencies of socio-economic development,' *International Affairs* 12 (Dec. 1971) 53

FIVE / PLANNING

1 A.Z. Arabadzhyan, 'Vvedenie' (Introduction), in *Plany-Programmy ekono-micheskogo razvitiya stran Azii* (The economic development plans of the countries of Asia) (Moscow, 1966) 5
2 E.A. Bragina, 'Perspektivnye plany kak faktor razvitiya ekonomiki' (Long-term plans as a factor in economic development), in *Classes and class struggle* II (Moscow, 1967) 134
3 Arabadzhyan, 'Introduction,' 5
4 Bragina, 'Long-term plans,' 138
5 Arabadzhyan, 'Introduction,' 3
6 Bragina, 'Long-term plans,' 171
7 Ibid. 170-1

8 V.I. Iskol'dskii, 'Tailand' (Thailand), in *Plany-programmy* 424
9 G.G. Federova, 'Pakistan,' in *Plany-Programmy* 416
10 Bragina, 'Long-term plans,' 165-6
11 V.L. Bodyanskii, 'OAR' (UAR), in *Plany-programmy* 366
12 N.G. Lozovaya, 'Indiya' (India), in *Plany-programmy* 97
13 R.S. Gorchakov, 'Nekotorye voprosy razvitiya gosudarstvennogo kapitalizma v Indii v svyazi s tret'im pyatiletnim planom' (Some questions concerning the development of state capitalism in India in connection with the third five-year plan), *Vestnik Leningradskogo Universiteta* 23 (1961) 37
14 Arabadzhyan, 'Introduction,' 14
15 Gorchakov, 'Some questions on state capitalism in India,' 37
16 V.A. Kondrat'ev, 'Gosudarstvennyi kapitalizm i promyshlennoe razvitie sovremennoi Indii' (State capitalism and modern India's industrial development), *Kratkie Soobshcheniya Instituta Narodov Azii* 51 (1962) 24
17 Ibid. 25
18 I. Ivanov, 'Opyt gosudarstvennogo regulirovaniya ekonomiki v Indii' (The experience of state regulation of the economy in India), *Sovremennyi Vostok* 1 (1958) 51
19 R.A. Ul'yanovskii, 'Indiya v bor'be za ekonomicheskuyu nezavisimost' (voprosy goskapitalizma)' (India's struggle for economic independence: the problems of state capitalism), in *Nezavisimaya Indiya, 10 let nezavisimosti, 1947-1957. sbornik statei* (Independent India, 10 years of independence, 1947-1957. Collection of articles) (Moscow, 1958) 75
20 Ivanov, 'State regulation of the economy,' 51
21 Ul'yanovskii, 'India's struggle for economic independence,' 22
22 Ibid. 21
23 Gorchakov, 'Some questions on state capitalism in India,' 39
24 V. Vasil'ev, 'Ekonomika Indii: planirovanie, plany, deistvitel'nost'' (India's economy: planning, the plans and reality), *Mirovaya Ekonomika i Mezhdunarodnye Otnosheniya* 10 (1968) 53
25 'Proekt vtorogo pyatiletnego plana Indii' (The draft of India's second five-year plan), *Planovoe Khozyaistvo* 6 (1956) 88-90
26 M.I. Rubinshtein, 'Vtoroi pyatiletnii plan Respubliki Indii' (The Republic of India's second five-year plan), *Sovetskoe Vostokovedenie* 4 (1956) 28-30
27 Modeste Rubinstein, 'A non-capitalist path for underdeveloped countries,' *New Times* 32 (2 Aug. 1956) 7
28 Rubinshtein, 'India's second five-year plan,' 31, 17, 41
29 Ul'yanovskii, 'India's struggle for economic independence,' 76
30 A. Kutsenkov, 'Vtoroi pyatiletnii plan i problemy razvitiya vneshnei torgovli Indii' (The second five-year plan and the problems in developing India's external trade), *Vneshnyaya Torgovlya* 7 (1957) 12

31 Ul'yanovskii, 'India's struggle for economic independence,' 64
32 Gorchakov, 'Some questions on state capitalism in India,' 39
33 Ul'yanovskii, 'India's struggle for economic independence,' 63-4
34 Ibid. 52
35 Kutsenkov, 'The second five-year plan,' 13, 14, 21
36 Ul'yanovskii, 'India's struggle for economic independence,' 52
37 E.A. Bragina, 'Tretii pyatiletnii plan i ekonomika Indii' (The third five-year plan and India's economy), *Narody Azii i Afriki* 2 (1963) 37
38 Ibid. 38
39 E. Bragina, 'Tretii pyatiletnii plan Indii' (India's third five-year plan), *Mirovaya Ekonomika i Mezhdunarodnye Otnosheniya* 10 (1960) 122-4
40 Gorchakov, 'Some questions on state capitalism in India,' 40
41 Bragina, 'India's third five-year plan,' 125-6
42 Gorchakov, 'Some questions on state capitalism in India,' 42-4
43 Bragina, 'India's third five-year plan,' 127
44 Gorchakov, 'Some questions on state capitalism in India,' 45
45 Ibid.
46 Bragina, 'The third five-year plan,' 44-5
47 Lozovaya, 'India,' 140-2
48 Ibid. 158-9
49 Ibid. 100-8
50 Ibid. 104
51 Vasil'ev, 'India's economy,' 53-62
52 E. Gryaznov, 'India: main tendencies of socio-economic development,' *International Affairs* 12 (Dec. 1971) 54
53 V.A. Yashkin, 'Planirovanie v Indii: chetvertyi pyatiletnii plan, 1969/70 – 1973/74 gg' (Planning in India: the 4th five-year plan, 1969/70 – 1973/74), in *Strany 'Tret'ego mira': vneshneekonomicheskie svyazi, finansirovanie razvitiya* (Countries of the third world: External economic links, financing of development) (Moscow, 1974) 360
54 One exception is the mathematician S.A. Kuzmin's technical discussion *Sistemnyi analiz ekonomiki razvivayushchikhsya stran* (System's analysis of the developing countries' economies) (Moscow, 1972) an excerpt from which can be found in S. Kuzmin, 'Systems analysis of the developing countries' economies,' *Social Sciences* 4 (1973) 87-98
55 Arabadzhyan, 'Introduction,' 9
56 Ibid. 11
57 Bragina, 'Long-term plans,' 152
58 Arabadzhyan, 'Introduction,' 9
59 V.L. Tyagunenko, ed., *Industrialisation of Developing Countries* (Moscow, 1973) 10

60 Arabadzhyan, 'Introduction,' 12
61 Bragina, 'Long-term plans,' 155
62 Yu. V. Potemkin and V.A. Sandakov, 'Problema nakopleniya v razvivayush-
    chikhsya stranakh' (The accumulation problem in the developing countries),
    in *Classes and class struggle* II, 35-41, 61
63 V.L. Tyagunenko, 'Vvedenie' (Introduction), in *Classes and class struggle* II,
    15
64 Potemkin and Sandakov, 'The accumulation problem,' 62-3, 71, 74
65 Y.N. Cherkassov, *The Problem of Accumulation in Africa* (Moscow, 1967) 4-5
66 Ibid. 9
67 Bragina, 'Long-term plans,' 171
68 I.I. Egorov and V.G. Rastyannikov, 'Nakopleniya v Indii i problemy ikh
    realizatsii' (Accumulation in India and the problems of its achievement),
    Narody Azii i Afriki 2 (1966) 14
69 Lozovaya, 'India,' 115, 121
70 Arabadzhyan, 'Introduction,' 9, 12, 13
71 Bragina, 'Long-term plans,' 149
72 Arabadzhyan, 'Introduction,' 9
73 Tyagunenko, *Industrialisation* 10
74 S.A. Kuz'min, *The Developing Countries, Employment and Capital
    Investment* (New York, 1969) 5
75 Tyagunenko, *Industrialisation* 15
76 Ibid. 77
77 Ibid. 360-1
78 E. Gryaznov, 'India: main tendencies,' 54
79 Arabadzhyan, 'Introduction,' 6

SIX / THE PRIVATE SECTOR

1 A. Arzumanyan, 'Itogi mirovogo razvitiya za 100 let i aktual'nye problemy
   mezhdunarodnogo revolyutsionno-osvoboditel'nogo dvizheniya' (The results
   of world development over 100 years and the current problems of the international revolutionary liberation movement), *Mirovaya Ekonomika i
   Mezhdunarodnye Otnosheniya* 12 (1964) 84
2 V.L. Tyagunenko, 'Capitalist and non-capitalist development,' *International
   Affairs* 5 (May 1967) 56-7
3 R.A. Ul'yanovskii, 'Indiya v bor'be za ekonomicheskuyu nezavisimost'
   (voprosy goskapitalizma)' (India's struggle for economic independence:
   the problems of state capitalism), in *Nezavisimaya Indiya, 10 let nezamisi-
   mosti, 1947-1957, sbornik statei* (Independent India, 10 years of independence, 1947-1957. Collection of articles) (Moscow, 1958) 62

4 V.A. Kondrat'ev, *Promyshlennost' Indii. Osnovnye tendentsii razvitiya posle 1947 g.* (India's industry: the main development trends since 1947) (Moscow, 1963) 94

5 Ul'yanovskii, 'India's struggle for economic independence' (1958) 73

6 R. Ulyanovsky, 'India: new vistas of progress,' *New Times* 40 (Oct. 1971) 18

7 Ul'yanovskii, 'India's struggle for economic independence' (1958) 73

8 A.I. Levkovskii, 'Gosudarstvennyi kapitalizm i chastnokapitalisticheskoe predprinimatel'stvo v Indii' (State capitalism and private capitalist enterprise in India), in *Ekonomika sovremennoi Indii* (The economy of modern India) (Moscow, 1960) 211

9 Ul'yanovskii, 'India's struggle for economic independence' (1958) 68-70

10 L.A. Gordon, 'Polozhenie promyshlennogo proletariata Indii i nekotorye osobennosti bor'by rabochego klassa' (The Indian industrial proletariat's position and some specifics of the working class struggle), in *Polozhenie rabochego klassa i rabochee dvizhenie v stranakh Azii i Afriki (1959-1961)* (The working class' position and the worker movement in the countries of Asia and Africa – 1959-1961) (Moscow, 1962) 75

11 R.A. Ul'yanovskii, 'Indiya v bor'be za ekonomicheskuyu nezavisimost'; o gosudarstvennom sektore v ekonomike Indii' (India's struggle for economic independence: concerning the public sector in the Indian economy), *Sovetskoe Vostokovedenie* 4 (1957) 22

12 Ibid. 25

13 N.G. Lozovaya, 'Indiya' (India) in *Plany-programmy ekonomicheskogo razvitiya stran Azii* (The economic development plans of the countries of Asia) (Moscow, 1966) 95-6

14 O.V. Maev, 'Indiiskii monopolisticheskii kapital: zapadnoindiiskie gruppy' (Indian monopoly capital: Western groups), *Mirovaya Ekonomika i Mezhdunarodnye Otnosheniya* 8 (1966) 120

15 Yu. I. Loshakov, 'Indiiskii monopolisticheskii kapital' (Indian monopoly capital), *Vestnik Moskovskogo Universiteta* 3, Series VII (1967) 64-6

16 O.V. Maev, 'Indiiskii monopolisticheskii kapital' (Indian monopoly capital), *Narody Azii i Afriki* 1 (1964) 21

17 O.V. Maev, 'Indiiskii monopolisticheskii kapital: vostochnoindiiskie gruppy' (Indian monopoly capital: Eastern groups), *Mirovaya Ekonomika i Mezhdunarodnye Otnosheniya* 3 (1967) 123

18 Maev, 'Indian monopoly capital: Western groups,' 125

19 Loshakov, 'Indian monopoly capital,' 72

20 N.A. Savel'ev, 'Natsional'naya burzhuaziya' (The national bourgeoisie), in *Classes and class struggle* I (Moscow, 1967) 209-10

21 Maev, 'Indian monopoly capital: Eastern groups,' 123

22 N. Savelyev, 'Monopoly drive in India,' *International Affairs* (April 1967) 35
23 Savelyev, 'Monopoly drive in India,' 35
24 Ibid. 39-40
25 O.V. Maev, 'Ekonomicheskaya programma indiiskikh monopolistov' (The economic programme of the Indian monopolies), *Narody Azii i Afriki* 5 (1964) 161
26 A.G. Bel'skii, Review of H.D. Malaviya's *The Danger of Right Reaction, Narody Azii i Afriki* 3 (1966) 171
27 Savelyev, 'Monopoly drive in India,' 35
28 Maev, 'Indian monopoly capital' (1964) 30
29 O.V. Maev, 'Monopolii, banki i politika' (Monopolies, the banks and politics), *Mirovaya Ekonomika i Mezhdunarodnye Otnosheniya* 11 (1969) 58
30 Levkovskii, 'State capitalism and private capitalist enterprise,' 213
31 A. Levkovskii, 'Gosudarstvennyi kapitalizm v Indii – nekotorye osnovnye problemy' (State capitalism in India: some fundamental problems), *Sovremennyi Vostok* 5 (1958) 15
32 Ul'yanovskii, 'India's struggle for economic independence' (1958) 31
33 Savelyev, 'Monopoly drive in India,' 35
34 Ul'yanovskii, 'India's struggle for economic independence' (1958) 31
35 Levkovskii, 'State capitalism and private capitalist enterprise,' 211
36 Ul'yanovskii, 'India's struggle for economic independence' (1958) 32
37 Lozovaya, 'India,' 124-6
38 A.L. Batalov et al., 'Itogi razvitiya narodnogo khozyaistva' (Balance sheet of the development of the national economy), in *Problemy ekonomicheskogo i sotsial'nogo razvitiya nezavisimoi Indii* (Problems of economic and social development of independent India) (Moscow, 1967) 14-16
39 Yu. V. Potemkin and V.A. Sandakov, 'Problema nakopleniya v razvivayushchikhsya stranakh' (The accumulation problem in the developing countries), in *Classes and class struggle* II (Moscow, 1967) 51
40 G.K. Shirokov, *Industrialisation of India* (Moscow, 1973) 87
41 Ibid. 83
42 V.A. Yashkin, 'Problema zanyatosti i planirovanie v Indii' (The employment problem and planning in India), *Narody Azii i Afriki*, 1 (1967) 44
43 T.S. Pokataeva, 'Struktura rabochego klassa razvivayushchikhsya stran' (The structure of the working class in the developing countries), in *Classes and class struggle* I (Moscow, 1967) 86
44 L.R. Gordon-Polonskaya, 'Polozhenie rabochego klassa Pakistana (1947-1957)' (The situation of Pakistan's working class: 1947-1957), in *Pakistan. Istoriya i ekonomika* (Pakistan: History and Economy) (Moscow, 1959) 34

45 L.I. Reisner and G.K. Shirokov, *Sovremennaya indiiskaya burzhuaziya* (The modern Indian bourgeoisie) (Moscow, 1966) 206
46 Savel'ev, 'The national bourgeoisie,' 206-7
47 Reisner and Shirokov, *The modern Indian bourgeoisie* 206
48 M.A. Aleksandrov and S.M. Mel'man, 'Privlechenie resursov iz-za rubezha' (Attracting resources from abroad), in *Problems of independent India* (Moscow, 1967) 119-20
49 Batalov et al., 'Balance sheet of development,' 14
50 S.A. Kuz'min, *The Developing Countries, Employment and Capital Investment* (New York, 1969) 5 ff.
51 Ibid. 43
52 Ibid. 92
53 Ibid. 85
54 Ibid. 58
55 Ibid. 103
56 L.I. Reisner and G.I. Shirokov, 'The industrial revolution in contemporary India,' in R. Ulyanovsky et al., *Industrial Revolution and Social Progress in India* (New Delhi, 1970) 16
57 Ibid. 31
58 G.K. Shirokov, 'Industrialisation and the changing pattern of India's social and economic system,' in V. Pavlov et al., *India: Social and Economic Development (18th-20th Centuries)* (Moscow, 1975) 201-2, 232
59 B.V. Andrianov and L.F. Monogarova, 'Lenin's doctrine of concurrent socioeconomic systems and its significance for ethnography,' *Soviet Anthropology and Archaelogy* 14, No. 4 (Spring 1976) 20
60 V. Solodovnikov and V. Bogoslovsky, *Non-Capitalist Development: An Historical Outline* (Moscow, 1975) 93
61 Y. Rozaliyov, 'Specificities of capitalist development in Asian and African countries,' *International Affairs* 2 (Feb. 1976) 69
62 Y. Yudin, 'The social nature of the state in the newly-independent countries of Africa,' *Social Sciences* 4 (1973) 99
63 V. Solodovnikov and N. Gavrilov, 'Africa: tendencies of non-capitalist development,' *International Affairs* 3 (March 1976) 33

SEVEN / THE CLASS STRUGGLE
AND THE INDUSTRIAL REVOLUTION

1 V. Solodovnikov and M. Braginsky, 'The working class in the African countries' social structure,' *International Affairs* 10 (Oct. 1976) 47, 49
2 Y. Yudin, 'The social nature of the state in the newly-independent

countries of Africa,' *Social Sciences* 4 (1973) 101; V. Solodovnikov, 'Some aspects of non-capitalist development,' *International Affairs* 6 (June 1973) 47

3 A.I. Levkovskii, 'Gosudarstvennyi kapitalizm i chastnokapitalisticheskoe predprinimatel'stvo v Indii' (State capitalism and private capitalist enterprise in India), in *Ekonomika sovremennoi Indii* (The economy of modern India) (Moscow, 1960) 192

4 A. Levkovskii, 'Gosudarstvennyi kapitalizm v Indii – nekotorye osnovnye problemy' (State capitalism in India: some fundamental problems), *Sovremennyi Vostok* 5 (1958) 14

5 R.A. Ul'yanovskii, 'Indiya v bor'be za ekonomicheskuyu nezavisimost' (voporosy goskapitalizma)' (India's struggle for economic independence: the problems of state capitalism), in *Nezavisimaya Indiya, 10 let nezavisimosti, 1947-1957, sbornik statei* (Independent India, 10 years of independence, 1947-1957. Collection of articles) (Moscow, 1958) 45

6 Levkovskii, 'State capitalism and private capitalist enterprise,' 212

7 G. Mirsky, 'Changes in the Third World,' *New Times* 39 (1969) 5

8 A major thrust of Soviet indology is historical. For an extended treatment of the evolution of capitalism from feudalism and the growth of the major entrepreneurial castes during the colonial period, see V.I. Pavlov, *The Indian Capitalist Class. A Historical Study* (New Delhi, 1964).

9 N.A. Savel'ev, 'Natsional'naya burzhuaziya' (The national bourgeoisie), in *Klassy i klassovaya bor'ba v razvivayushchikhsya stranakh* (Classes and the class struggle in the developing countries) I (Moscow, 1967) 147-68

10 Rostislav Ulyanovsky, 'The developing countries: economic front,' *New Times* 34 (Aug. 1976) 18-19

11 Savel'ev, 'The national bourgeoisie,' 174-82

12 M.A. Aleksandrov and S.M. Mel'man, Review of L.I. Reisner and G.B. Shirokov's *Sovremennaya indiiskaya burzhuaziya* (The modern Indian bourgeoisie), *Narody Azii i Afriki* 1 (1967) 158

13 Savel'ev, 'The national bourgeoisie,' 205

14 Levkovskii, 'State capitalism and private capitalist enterprise,' 211

15 R.A. Ul'yanovskii, 'Indiya v bor'be za ekonomicheskuyu nezavisimost'; o gosudarstvennom sektore v ekonomike Indii' (India's struggle for economic independence: concerning the public sector in the Indian economy), *Sovetskoe Vostokovedenie* 4 (1957) 14

16 Savel'ev, 'The national bourgeoisie,' 216-20

17 R.A. Ul'yanovskii, 'Ob osobennostyakh razvitiya i kharaktere gosudarstvennogo kapitalizma v nezavisimoi Indii' (On the specific characteristics of the development and nature of state capitalism in independent India), *Problemy Vostokovedeniya* 3 (1960) 27

18 Ul'yanovskii, 'India's struggle for economic independence' (1957) 11
19 Ul'yanovskii, 'India's struggle for economic independence' (1958) 31
20 Savel'ev, 'The national bourgeoisie,' 221
21 Ul'yanovskii, 'On the nature of state capitalism in India,' 40
22 Savel'ev, 'The national bourgeoisie,' 226-65
23 Ibid. 205-6
24 L.I. Reisner and G.K. Shirokov, *Sovremennaya indiiskaya burzhuaziya* (The modern Indian bourgeoisie) (Moscow, 1966) 205-7
25 Savel'ev, 'The national bourgeoisie,' 206-88
26 K. Marx and F. Engels, *Sochineniya* 26, part I (Moscow, n.d.) 417-18
27 Ul'yanovskii, 'On the nature of state capitalism in India,' 40
28 G.I. Mirskii and T.S. Pokataeva, 'Sluzhashchie i intelligentsiya' (Civil servants and the intelligentsia), in *Classes and class struggle* I (Moscow, 1967) 289
29 Ibid. 288-329
30 T.S. Pokataeva, 'Struktura rabochego klassa razvivayushchikhsya stran' (The structure of the working class in the developing countries), in *Classes and class struggle* I (Moscow, 1967) 72
31 *Asia and Africa: Fundamental Changes* (Moscow, 1972) 177
32 Pokataeva, 'The structure of the working class,' 85
33 S.I. T'yulpanov, 'O nekotorykh osobennostyakh gosudarstvennogo kapitalizma slaborazvitykh stran' (Concerning some specific problems of state capitalism in the under-developed countries), *Vestnik Leningradskogo Universiteta* 11 (1961) 6
34 L.A. Gordon, 'Polozhenie promyshlennogo proletariata Indii i nekotorye osobennosti bor'by rabochego klassa' (The Indian industrial proletariat's position and some specifics of the working class struggle), in *Polozhenie rabochego klassa i rabochee dvizhenie v stranakh Azii i Afriki (1959-1961)* (The working class's position and the worker movement in the countries of Asia and Africa – 1959-1961) (Moscow, 1962) 57
35 Ibid. 58-72
36 Ul'yanovskii, 'India's struggle for economic independence' (1958) 52
37 M.V. Danilevich, 'Polozhenie rabochego klassa' (The position of the working class), in *Classes and class struggle* I (Moscow, 1967) 144
38 Reisner and Shirokov, *The modern Indian bourgeoisie* 207
39 Aleksandrov and Mel'man, Review, 158
40 Savel'ev, 'The national bourgeoisie,' 205-6
41 Reisner and Shirokov, *The modern Indian bourgeoisie* 204
42 A.L. Batalov et al., 'Itogi razvitiya narodnogo khozyaistva' (Balance sheet of the development of the national economy), in *Problemy ekonomiches-*

kogo i sotsial'nogo razvitiya nezavisimoi Indii (Problems of economic and social development of independent India) (Moscow, 1967) 24

43 P. Kutsobin, 'The Indian confrontation,' *New Times* 47 (1969) 6
44 V. Rymalov, 'Lenin's doctrine of imperialism and our age,' *International Affairs* 9 (Sept. 1969) 37
45 Editorial, 'India: 20 years of the republic,' *New Times* 4 (1970) 24
46 Yu. V. Potemkin and V.A. Sandakov, 'Problema nakopleniya v razvivayush-chikhsya stranakh' (The accumulation problem in the developing countries), in *Classes and class struggle* II (Moscow, 1967) 76, 16-17
47 Ibid. 14
48 Ibid. 66-7
49 L.I. Reisner and G.I. Shirokov, 'The industrial revolution in contemporary India,' in R. Ulyanovsky et al., *Industrial Revolution and Social Progress in India* (New Delhi, 1970) 10-31
50 G.K. Shirokov, *Industrialisation of India* (Moscow, 1973) 216
51 S.A. Kuz'min, *The Developing Countries, Employment and Capital Investment* (New York, 1969) 6
52 E. Gryaznov, 'India: main tendencies of socio-economic development,' *International Affairs* 12 (Dec. 1971) 55
53 Batalov et al., 'Balance sheet of the national economy,' 27
54 V.L. Tyagunenko, 'Capitalist and non-capitalist development,' *International Affairs* 5 (May 1967) 56
55 V.G. Solodovnikov, 'Africa's objective difficulties and contradictions,' *International Affairs* 5 (May 1967) 65
56 V. Bylov and M. Pankin, 'India's economy,' *International Affairs* 9 (Sept. 1967) 109
57 E.A. Bragina, Review of Charles Bettelheim, *Independent India, Narody Azii i Afriki* 3 (1965) 226
58 Bylov and Pankin, 'India's economy,' 111

EIGHT / INDEPENDENCE AND FOREIGN INVESTMENT

1 V.L. Tyagunenko, 'Vvedenie' (Introduction), in *Klassy i klassovaya bor'ba v razvivayushchikhsya stranakh* (Classes and class struggle in the developing countries) II (Moscow, 1967) 15
2 G.F. Kim, *National Independence and Social Progress* (Moscow, 1967) 8
3 B.N. Ponomaryov, ed., *World Revolutionary Movement of the Working Class* (Moscow, 1967) 325
4 E. Burlatsky, *Great October and the Developing Countries* (Moscow, n.d.) 13

5 Y. Khavinson, 'Conclusion,' in *Soviet Economists Discuss Parent States and Colonies* (Moscow, n.d.) 203

6 E. Khmelnitskaya, 'Colonialism old and new,' ibid. 16

7 L.V. Stepanov, *Problema ekonomicheskoi nezavisimosti* (The problem of economic independence) (Moscow, 1965) 4

8 Ibid. 10

9 R.N. Andreasyan, 'Developing countries and foreign capital,' *International Affairs* 5 (May 1967) 70

10 Stepanov, *Economic independence* 6

11 V. Tyagunenko, 'Aktual'nye voprosy nekapitalisticheskogo puti razvitiya' (Current questions on the non-capitalist path of development), *Mirovaya Ekonomika i Mezhdunarodnye Otnosheniya* 11 (1964) 16

12 A. Mileikovsky, 'Colonialism old and new,' in *Parent States and Colonies* 14

13 Stepanov, *Economic independence* 11 ff

14 Ibid. 14-122

15 Tyagunenko, 'Introduction,' 14

16 G. Mirsky and L. Stepanov, *Asia and Africa: A New Era* (Moscow, n.d.) 24

17 E. Alayev, 'Regional planning,' *Social Sciences* 5 (1974) 162

18 L. Alexandrovskaya, 'Africa: some tendencies in economic development,' *International Affairs* 7 (July 1974) 65

19 S.A. Kuz'min, *The Developing Countries, Employment and Capital Investment* (New York, 1969) 2 (italics added)

20 R.N. Andreasyan and V.A. Kondrat'ev, 'Razvivayushchiesya strany i miro-khozyaistvennye svyazi' (The developing countries and world economic links), in *Classes and class struggle* II, 351

21 V.G. Solodovnikov, 'Africa's objective difficulties and contradictions,' *International Affairs* 5 (May 1967) 67

22 Ibid.

23 R.A. Ul'yanovskii, 'Indiya v bor'be za ekonomicheskuyu nezavisimost' (voprosy goskapitalizma)' (India in the struggle for economic independence: problems of state capitalism), in *Nezavisimaya Indiya, 10 let nezavisimosti, 1947-1957, sbornik statei* (Independent India: 10 years of independence (1947-1957). Collection of articles) (Moscow, 1958) 22

24 Mirsky and Stepanov, *New Era* 50

25 V.I. Pavlov, *Imperializm i ekonomicheskaya samostoyatel'nost' Indii* (Imperialism and India's economic autonomy) (Moscow, 1962) 81 ff

26 Ibid. 88 ff

27 R.A. Ulyanovsky, *The Dollar and Asia: U.S. Neo-colonialist Policy in Action* (Moscow, 1965) 16

28 V.G. Solodovnikov, *Some Problems of Economic and Social Development of Independent African Nations* (Moscow, 1967) 9-12

29 Yu. I. Loshakov, 'Indiiskii monopolisticheskii kapital' (Indian monopoly capital), *Vestnik Moskovskogo Universiteta* Series VII 3 (1967) 67

30 Pavlov, *Imperialism and India's autonomy* 89

31 Loshakov, 'Indian monopoly capital,' 68

32 A. Maslennikov, 'Indiya: bor'ba vokrug ekonomicheskoi politiki,' (India: the struggle over economic policy), *Mirovaya Ekonomika i Mezhdunarodnye Otnosheniya* 11 (1966) 104-6

33 N. Savelyev, 'Monopoly drive in India,' *International Affairs* (April 1967) 35

34 Andreasyan, 'Developing countries and foreign capital,' 73

35 Ulyanovsky, 'India in the struggle for economic independence' (1958) 97

36 V.V. Rymalov, *S.S.S.R. i ekonomicheski slabo-razvitye strany* (The USSR and the underdeveloped countries) (Moscow, 1963)

37 N.A. Savel'ev, 'Natsional'naya burzhuaziya' (The national bourgeoisie), in *Classes and class struggle* I, 234

38 L.I. Aleksandrovskaya, 'Industrializatsiya razvivayushchikhsya stran i otnoshenie k nei razlichnykh klassov i sotsial'nykh sil' (The industrialization of the developing countries and its relationship with different social and class forces), in *Classes and class struggle* II, 254

39 A.V. Shpirt, *The Developing Asian and African Countries and the Scientific-Technical Revolution* (Moscow, 1967) 8

40 Savel'ev, 'The national bourgeoisie,' 250

41 Solodovnikov, *Some Problems of African Nations* 6

42 Pavlov, *Imperialism and India's autonomy* 98

43 I.S. Kazakevich and G.S. Matveeva, Review of *Aktual'nye problemy stran Azii: sbornik statei* (Current problems of Asian countries: collection of articles), *Narody Azii i Afriki* 1 (1967) 155

44 Pavlov, *Imperialism and India's autonomy* 101-3

45 Ulyanovsky, *The Dollar and Asia* 244

46 R.N. Andreasyan, 'Bor'ba protiv gospodstva imperialisticheskikh monopolii' (The struggle against the domination of imperialist monopolies), in *Classes and class struggle* II, 283

47 Solodovnikov, *Some Problems of African Nations* 5-13

48 Y.N. Cherkassov, *The Problem of Accumulation in Africa* (Moscow, 1967) 5

49 L. Aleksandrovskaya, 'Afrika: ekonomicheskie problemy 60-kh godov' (Africa: economic problems of the 60s), *Mirovaya Ekonomika i Mezhdunarodnye Otnosheniya* 5 (1968) 120

50 Solodovnikov, *Some Problems of African Nations* 6

51 Pavlov, *Imperialism and India's autonomy* 109-10
52 Rostislav Ulyanovsky, 'The developing countries: economic front,' *New Times* 34 (Aug. 1976) 12-30
53 N. Volkov, 'The developing countries and international economic relations,' *International Affairs* 9 (Sept. 1976) 63
54 Andreasyan, 'Developing countries and foreign capital,' 73
55 Ibid.

NINE / IMPERIALIST 'AID'

1 *Soviet Economists Discuss Parent States and Colonies* (Moscow, n.d.)
2 L. Stepanov, 'Modern colonialism's "economic balance,"' ibid. 116 ff
3 Y. Khavinson, 'Conclusion,' ibid. 199-206
4 V. Tyagunenko, 'Break-up of colonial empires and imperialism,' ibid. 191
5 V.L. Tyagunenko, 'Capitalist and non-capitalist development,' *International Affairs* 5 (May 1967) 58
6 Mileikovsky, 'Colonialism old and new,' in *Parent States and Colonies* 14
7 Khmelnitskaya, 'Colonialism old and new,' ibid. 21
8 V. Valkov, 'Break-up of colonial empires and the smaller countries of Western Europe,' ibid. 50
9 E. Khesin, 'After the loss of colonies,' ibid. 67
10 V. Kollontai, 'Significant changes,' ibid. 167
11 V. Rybakov, '"Enlightened neocolonialism,"' ibid. 181
12 Mileikovsky, 'Colonialism old and new,' ibid. 14
13 V. Pavlov, 'Imperialism adapts itself to the situation,' ibid. 115
14 G. Mirsky, 'Imperialism adapts itself to the situation,' ibid. 107
15 V. Rimalov, *Economic Cooperation between the U.S.S.R. and Under-Developed Countries* (Moscow [1964?]) 154
16 O.V. Maev, 'Ekonomicheskaya programma indiiskikh monopolistov' (The economic programme of Indian monopolists), *Narody Azii i Afriki* 5 (1964) 161
17 V.I. Pavlov, *Imperializm i ekonomicheskaya samostoyatel'nost' Indii* (Imperialism and India's economic autonomy) (Moscow, 1962) 135
18 V.S. Baskin, *Ekonomicheskoe sotrudnichestvo SSSR so stranami Afriki* (The USSR's economic cooperation with the countries of Africa) (Moscow, 1968) 187
19 Pavlov, *Imperialism and India's autonomy* 134
20 Baskin, *USSR's economic cooperation with Africa* 180
21 Rimalov, *Economic Cooperation* 52

22 B.N. Ponomaryov, ed., *World Revolutionary Movement of the Working Class* (Moscow, 1967) 325
23 Rimalov, *Economic Cooperation* 119
24 Pavlov, *Imperialism and India's autonomy* 133
25 Baskin, *USSR's economic cooperation with Africa* 189
26 R.A. Ulyanovsky, *The Dollar and Asia: U.S. Neo-colonialist Policy in Action* (Moscow, 1965) 189
27 Pavlov, *Imperialism and India's autonomy* 145
28 R.N. Andreasyan and V.A. Kondrat'ev, 'Razvivayushchiesya strany i mirokhozyaistvennye svyazi' (The developing countries and world economic links), in *Classes and class struggle* II (Moscow, 1967) 351
29 Pavlov, *Imperialism and India's autonomy* 111-12
30 Rimalov, *Economic Cooperation* 156-60
31 L.I. Aleksandrovskaya, 'Industrializatsiya razvivayushchikhsya stran i otnoshenie k nei razlichnykh klassov i sotsial'nykh sil' (The industrialization of the developing countries and its relationship with different social and class forces), in *Classes and class struggle* II, 267
32 V.V. Rymalov, 'Economic aspects of the current stage of the liberation revolution,' *International Affairs* 5 (May 1967) 61
33 Baskin, *USSR's economic cooperation with Africa* 188
34 Ibid. 193
35 V.G. Solodovnikov, *Some Problems of Economic and Social Development of Independent African Nations* (Moscow, 1967) 7
36 V. Panov, 'International financial organisations: their role in neocolonialist policy,' *International Affairs* 7 (July 1973) 68-9
37 Pavlov, *Imperialism and India's autonomy* 158
38 Ibid. 160
39 M.A. Aleksandrov and S.M. Mel'man, 'Privlechenie resursov iz-za rubezha' (Attracting resources from abroad), in *Problemy ekonomicheskogo i sotsial'nogo razvitiya nezavisimoi Indii* (Problems of economic and social development of independent India) (Moscow, 1967) 93
40 Pavlov, *Imperialism and India's autonomy* 163
41 Baskin, *USSR's economic cooperation with Africa* 191
42 N.G. Lozovaya, 'Indiya' (India), in *Plany-programmy ekonomicheskogo razvitiya stran Azii* (The economic development plans of Asian countries) (Moscow, 1966) 158
43 V.G. Rastyannikov, 'Price policy and food production,' *Amrita Bazar Patrika* (8 March 1968)
44 Ulyanovsky, *The Dollar and Asia* 206, 199

45 Baskin, *USSR's economic cooperation with Africa* 191-2
46 Pavlov, *Imperialism and India's autonomy* 135-6, 112-13
47 I.M. Shatalov, 'The third world and the scientific and technical revolution,' *International Affairs* (May 1967) 74
48 Baskin, *USSR's economic cooperation with Africa* 190-1
49 Lozovaya, 'Indiya,' 157
50 T.S. Pokataeva, 'Struktura rabochego klassa razvivayushchikhsya stran' (Working class structure in the developing countries), in *Classes and class struggle* I, 72
51 Shatalov, 'The third world and the scientific revolution,' 75; Solodovnikov, 'Africa's objective difficulties,' 67
52 V.I. Iskol'dskii, 'Tailand,' in *Plany-programmy ekonomicheskogo razvitiya stran Azii* (Economic development plans of Asian countries) (Moscow, 1966) 444
53 Pavlov, *Imperialism and India's autonomy* 115-16
54 Ibid. 118-23
55 R.A. Ul'yanovskii, 'Amerikanskaya strategiya v Indii' (American strategy in India), *Mirovaya Ekonomika i Mezhdunarodnye Otnosheniya* 5 (1963) 29
56 Ulyanovsky, *The Dollar and Asia* 216-22
57 Pavlov, *Imperialism and India's autonomy* 147-8
58 Panov, 'International financial organisations,' 68
59 A. Maslennikov, 'Indiya: bor'ba vokrug ekonomicheskoi politiki,' (India: the struggle over economic policy), *Mirovaya Ekonomika i Mezhdunarodnye Otnosheniya* 11 (1966) 105
60 Pavlov, *Imperialism and India's autonomy* 172
61 Rimalov, *Economic Cooperation* 160
62 Aleksandrova and Mel'man, 'Attracting resources from abroad,' 93
63 Rimalov, *Economic Cooperation* 54-5
64 Quoted in V. Rymalov, 'Economic competition of the two systems and the problem of aid to underdeveloped countries,' *Problems of Economics* 3 (Dec. 1960) 45
65 Rimalov, *Economic Cooperation* 55
66 I.S. Kazakevich and G.S. Matveeva, Review of *Aktual'nye problemy stran Azii: sbornik statei* (Current problems of Asian countries: collection of articles), *Narody Azii i Afriki* 1 (1967) 155
67 L. Stepanov, 'Odin protsent' (One per cent), *Mirovaya Ekonomika i Mezhdunarodnye Otnosheniya* 6 (1968) 68
68 Pavlov, *Imperialism and India's autonomy* 168
69 Baskin, *USSR's economic cooperation with Africa* 196
70 Solodovnikov, *Some Problems of African Nations* 15

71 M.A. Sidorov, Review of S.K. Bose, *Some Aspects of Indian Economic Development, vol. I, Narody Azii i Afriki* 2 (1964) 185

TEN / SOCIALIST AID

1 V. Rimalov, *Economic Cooperation between the U.S.S.R. and Under-Developed Countries* (Moscow, [1964?]) 6, 41
2 R.N. Andreasyan and V.A. Kondrat'ev, 'Razvivayushchiesya strany i mirokhozyaistvennye svyazi' (The developing countries and world economic links), in *Klassy i klassovaya bor'ba v razvivayushchikhsya stranakh* (Classes and class struggle in the developing countries) (Moscow, 1967) II, 370-1
3 Rimalov, *Economic Cooperation* 47
4 V.S. Baskin, *Ekonomicheskoe sotrudnichestvo SSSR so stranami Afriki* (The USSR's economic cooperation with the countries of Africa) (Moscow, 1968) 197
5 Andreasyan and Kondrat'ev, 'The developing countries,' 351-70
6 Rimalov, *Economic Cooperation* 50
7 Baskin, *Economic cooperation with Africa* 197
8 Andreasyan and Kondrat'ev, 'The developing countries,' 370
9 'India: 20 years of the republic,' *New Times* 4 (1970) 24
10 Y. Tsaplin, 'The sound foundation of Soviet-Indian ties,' *International Affairs* 8 (Aug. 1976) 71
11 V.V. Rymalov, *S.S.S.R. i ekonomicheski slabo-razvitye strany* (The USSR and the economically underdeveloped countries) (Moscow, 1963) 90-101
12 S. Skachkov, 'Economic cooperation of the USSR with developing countries,' *Social Sciences* 5, No. 3 (1974) 10
13 Rymalov, *USSR and under-developed countries* 103
14 I. Temirsky, 'Moscow and Delhi,' *New Times* 5 (1969) 10
15 Tsaplin, 'Soviet-Indian ties,' 71
16 B.N. Ponomaryov, ed., *World Revolutionary Movement of the Working Class* (Moscow, 1967) 328
17 Andreasyan and Kondrat'ev, 'The developing countries,' 370-1
18 'Independent Ceylon,' *New Times* 6 (1968) 7
19 Rymalov, *USSR and under-developed countries* 98
20 N. Kolesnikov, 'The importance of training national personnel,' *Social Sciences* 5, No. 2 (1974) 116; A. Vladin, *National Personnel: Its Importance for Developing Countries* (Moscow, 1975) 6
21 'Bhilai-2,' *New Times* 3 (1962) 81
22 Kolesnikov, 'Training national personnel,' 127
23 Rimalov, *Economic Cooperation* 48

24 B.N. Ponomaryov, 'Some problems of the revolutionary movement,'
    World Marxist Review 5, No. 12 (1962) 11
25 Ponomaryov, *World Revolutionary Movement* 3-7
26 Rimalov, *Economic Cooperation* 41-2
27 Marshall I. Goldman, *Soviet Foreign Aid* (New York, 1967) 115
28 Ibid. 93, 130
29 Y. Yershov, *India: Independence and Oil* (Moscow, 1965) 28-61
30 Ibid. 109 ff
31 P.R. Nayak, 'Collaboration in oil: some operational aspects,' *Indian Journal
    of Public Administration* 10 (1954) 473-80; Raj Narayan Gupta, 'Recent
    development in the oil industry,' *Economic Review* 14, No. 11 (30 Oct.
    1962) 19-23; M. Subhan, 'The government of India's oil policy,' *Revue du
    Sud-Est Asiatique* 1 (1962) 45-56
32 Nayak, 'Collaboration in oil,' 473 (italics added)
33 Gupta, 'Recent development in oil,' 19
34 Subhan, 'India's oil policy,' 45
35 Nayak, 'Collaboration in oil,' 475
36 Subhan, 'India's oil policy,' 53
37 Nayak, 'Collaboration in oil,' 487
38 Subhan, 'India's oil policy,' 53
39 Humayun Kabri, 'Role of oil companies in the economic development of
    India,' *Economic Review* 17, No. 7 (15 Sept. 1965) 13-39
40 Nayak, 'Collaboration in oil,' 476-9
41 K.D. Malaviya, 'Mineral oils in the Indian economy,' *Economic Review*
    8, No. 5 (1 July 1956) 7
42 Goldman, *Soviet Foreign Aid* 99
43 Ibid. 170
44 V.G. Solodovnikov, 'Africa's objective difficulties and contradictions,'
    International Affairs 5 (May 1967) 67-8
45 L. Stepanov, '"Odin protsent"' ('One per cent'), *Mirovaya Ekonomika i
    Mezhdunarodnye Otnosheniya* 6 (1968) 69
46 Philip E. Mosley, 'Communist policy and the third world,' *Review of
    Politics* 28 (1966) 231
47 Rymalov, *USSR and under-developed countries* 34-5
48 A. Kodachenko, 'An important form of economic cooperation,' *Inter-
    national Affairs* 11 (Nov. 1962) 43, 37
49 Rostislav Ulyanovsky, 'The developing countries: aspects of the political
    scene,' *New Times* 38 (Sept. 1976) 19
50 V.A. Kondrat'ev, 'Osnovnye problemy i tendentsii bor'by za preobrazovanie
    vneshnei torgovli' (The basic problems and trends in the struggle to trans-
    form foreign trade), in *Classes and class struggle* II, 430

51 Rymalov, *USSR and under-developed countries* 87-9
52 L.L. Klochkovsky, *Economic Neocolonialism: Problems of South-East Asian Countries' Struggle for Economic Independence* (Moscow, 1975) 298
53 Rymalov, *USSR and under-developed countries* 89
54 A. Vladine, 'L'Inde et le marché socialiste mondial,' *Temps Nouveaux* 44 (4 nov. 1963) 22
55 Tsaplin, 'Soviet-Indian Ties,' 72
56 Kondrat'ev, 'The struggle to transform foreign trade,' 431
57 Ulyanovsky, 'The developing countries,' 19
58 R.N. Andreasyan, 'Bor'ba protiv gospodstva imperialisticheskikh monopolii' (The struggle against the domination of imperialist monopolies), in *Classes and class struggle* II, 301
59 V.V. Rymalov, 'Economic aspects of the current stage of the liberation revolution,' *International Affairs* 5 (May 1967) 62, 76
60 Rimalov, *Economic Cooperation* 81
61 Indian Institute of Foreign Trade, *India's Trade with East Europe* (New Delhi, 1966) 1-4
62 Goldman, *Soviet Foreign Aid* 107-10

ELEVEN / BOTH TRUCK AND TRADE
WITH THE IMPERIALISTS

1 V.A. Kondrat'ev, 'Osnovnye problemy i tendentsii bor'by za preobrazovanie vneshnei torgovli' (The basic problems and trends in the struggle to transform foreign trade), in *Klassy i klassovaya bor'ba v razvivayushchikhsya stranakh* (Classes and class struggle in the developing countries) (Moscow, 1967) II, 382
2 L. Aleksandrovskaya, 'Afrika: ekonomicheskie problemy 60-kh godov' (Africa: economic problems of the 60s), *Mirovaya Ekonomika i Mezhdunarodnye Otnosheniya* 5 (1968) 119-20
3 V.G. Solodovnikov, 'Africa's objective difficulties and contradictions,' *International Affairs* 5 (May 1967) 66
4 Kondrat'ev, 'The struggle to transform foreign trade,' 43
5 V.V. Rymalov, *S.S.S.R. i ekonomicheski slabo-razvitye strany* (The USSR and the under-developed countries) (Moscow, 1963) 117
6 Kondrat'ev, 'The struggle to transform foreign trade,' 379-80
7 V.S. Baskin, *Ekonomicheskoe sotrudnichestvo SSSR so stranami Afriki* (The USSR's economic cooperation with the countries of Africa) (Moscow, 1968) 182
8 'Association of riders and horses,' *Pravda* (14 Dec. 1966) 4, in *Current Digest of the Soviet Press* 18, No. 50

9 L. Stepanov, '"Odin protsent"' ('One per cent'), *Mirovaya Ekonomika i Mezhdunarodnye Otnosheniya* 6 (1968) 67

10 'Association of riders and horses'

11 L. Stepanov, 'By whom and how are the newly liberated countries being assisted?' in *Internationalism; National-Liberation Movement and our Epoch* II (Moscow, n.d.) 195

12 A. Arzumanyan, *Crisis of World Capitalism* (Moscow, 1966) 39

13 E. Burlatsky, *Great October and the Developing Countries* (Moscow, n.d.) 76-8

14 Kondrat'ev, 'The struggle to transform foreign trade,' 375-420

15 O.E. Tuganova, 'The foreign policy of the developing countries,' *International Affairs* 5 (May 1967) 62-3

16 L. Vladimirskii, 'Gosudarstvennaya torgovaya korporatsiya Indii' (India's State Trading Corporation), *Vneshnyaya Torgovlya* 9 (Sept. 1959) 41

17 R.A. Ul'yanovskii, 'Indiya v bor'be za ekonomicheskuyu nezavisimost' (voprosy goskapitalisma)' (India in the struggle for economic independence: problems of state capitalism), in *Nezavisimaya Indiya, 10 let nezavisimosti, 1947-1957, sbornik statei* (Independent India: 10 years of independence, 1947-1957. Collection of articles) (Moscow, 1958) 78

18 R.N. Andreasyan, 'Developing countries and foreign capital,' *International Affairs* 5 (May 1967) 71

19 V. Kudryavtsev, 'Regionalism, the good and the bad,' *Izvestiya* (2 Feb. 1967) 2, in *Current Digest of the Soviet Press* 19, No. 5 (1967)

20 D. Volsky, 'Illusions are coming to an end. Contradictions in the common-wealth of nations are growing,' *Pravda* (16 Jan. 1967) in *Current Digest of the Soviet Press* 19, No. 3 (1967)

21 S. Borisov, 'The sterling area and British neocolonialism,' in *Soviet Economists Discuss Parent States and Colonies* (Moscow, n.d.) 100

22 L. Krasavina, 'Changes in the franc area,' ibid. 89-90

23 Solodovnikov, 'Africa's contradictions,' 67

24 L. Fituni, 'Disintegration of colonial system and West European integration,' *Parent States and Colonies* 74

25 E. Khmelnitskaya, 'Colonialism old and new,' ibid. 23

26 V. Pevzner, 'Developing countries and reproduction in parent states,' ibid. 37

27 Y. Olsevich, 'Can monopoly capitalism develop without colonies?' ibid. 137

28 Pevsner, 'Developing countries and reproduction,' 38

29 Karl Marx, 'The future results of the British rule in India,' *New-York Daily Tribune* (8 Aug. 1853), reprinted in K. Marx and F. Engels, *On Colonialism* (Moscow, n.d.) 84-7

30 R. Palme Dutt, *Modern India* (London 1927) 52-8

31 E. Varga, *Osnovnye voprosy ekonomiki i politiki imperializma posle vtoroi mirovoi voiny* (The fundamental questions of imperialism's economics and politics after the second world war) (Moscow, 1953) 345n.
32 Ibid., 2nd edn (1957), 399n.
33 E. Ablina, 'Imperialism and the developing countries,' *Social Sciences* 4, No. 4 (1973) 226
34 V.I. Pavlov, *Imperializm i ekonomicheskaya samostoyatel'nost' Indii* (Imperialism and India's economic autonomy) (Moscow, 1962) 133
35 Ablina, 'Imperialism and the developing countries,' 227
36 *Les principes du marxisme-léninisme* (Moscow, n.d.) 427

TWELVE / AGRARIAN REFORMS

1 David Mitrany, *Marx against the Peasant* (New York, 1961)
2 W.K., 'The agrarian question,' *Survey* 43 (Aug. 1963) 31
3 Alexander Erlich, *The Soviet Industrialization Debate 1924-1928* (Cambridge, Mass., 1960)
4 K.M. Varentsov and M.A. Maksimov, 'Klassovaya struktura derevni i polozhenie krest'yanskikh mass' (Class structure in the country and the position of the peasant masses), in *Klassy i klassovaya bor'ba v razvivayushchikhsya stranakh* (Classes and class struggle in the developing countries) I (Moscow, 1967) 364
5 Y. Frantsev, *50 Years of a New Era* (Moscow, 1967) 158
6 'Soviet notions about "the Peasant Commune" in Africa,' *Mizan Newsletter* 6, No. 2 (Feb. 1964) 7-20
7 V.G. Solodovnikov, *Some Problems of Economic and Social Development of Independent African Nations* (Moscow, 1967) 13-15
8 Varentsov and Maksimov, 'Class structure in the country,' 361
9 K. Marx and F. Engels, *On Colonialism* (Moscow, n.d.) 309
10 Ibid. 310
11 Ibid. 36
12 Ferenc Tokei, 'Le mode de production asiatique dans l'oeuvre de K. Marx et F. Engels,' *La Pensée* 114 (jan.-fév. 1964) 14, 16
13 George Lichtheim, 'Marx and "the Asiatic Mode of Production,"' St Antony's Papers No. 14, *Far Eastern Affairs* 3 (1963) 91
14 Jean Chesneaux, 'Le mode de production asiatique: quelques perspectives de recherche,' *La Pensée* 114 (jan.-fév. 1964) 38-9
15 E. Varga, 'Du mode de production asiatique,' in *Essais sur l'économie politique du capitalisme* (Moscow, 1967) 373-94. For a discussion of the debate in the 1920s and 1930s see also L.V. Danilova, 'Controversial

problems of the theory of precapitalist societies,' *Soviet Anthropology and Archeology* 9 (1971) 269-328

16 R.A. Ulyanovsky and V.I. Pavlov, 'Afterword,' in V. Pavlov et al., *India: Social and Economic Development (18th-20th Centuries)* (Moscow, 1975) 288

17 V. Rastyannikov, 'The agrarian evolution and class formation processes in India,' *Social Sciences* 4, No. 3 (1974) 139

18 A.L. Batalov and R.P. Gurvich, *Mozhet li Indiya prokormit' sebya?* (Can India feed itself?) (Moscow, 1961) 3-5

19 Ibid. 3-4

20 Marx and Engels, *On Colonialism* 84

21 Batalov and Gurvich, *Can India feed itself?* 6-9

22 G.G. Kotovskii, *Agrarnye reformy Indii* (India's agrarian reforms) (Moscow, 1959) 30

23 R.A. Ul'yanovskii, 'Reforma agrarnogo stroya' (Reform of the agrarian structure), in *Ekonomika sovremennoi Indii* (Contemporary India's economy) (Moscow, 1960) 53

24 Batalov and Gurvich, *Can India feed itself?* 11

25 Kotovskii, *India's agrarian reforms* 22

26 Ibid. 38

27 M.A. Maksimov and V.G. Rastyannikov, 'Predislovie' (Preface), in D. Torner, *Agrarnyi stroi Indii* (D. Thorner, India's agrarian structure) (Moscow, 1959) 5-6

28 Kotovskii, *India's agrarian reforms* 38-40

29 Ul'yanovskii, 'Reform of the agrarian structure,' 64

30 Ibid. 55

31 Kotovskii, *India's agrarian reforms* 50

32 G.G. Kotovsky and P.P. Moiseev, *Social and Economic Transition of the Rural East: Basic Trends. Some Problems of Methodology* (Moscow, 1967) 1

33 Ibid. 3

34 Kotovskii, *India's agrarian reforms* 4

35 Y. Kovalyov, 'Latin America: the struggle for agrarian reform,' *International Affairs* 2 (Feb. 1974) 64

36 Ibid. 61-2

37 V. Solodovnikov and N. Gavrilov, 'Africa: tendencies of non-capitalist development,' *International Affairs* 3 (March 1976) 36

38 Ul'yanovskii, 'Reform of the agrarian structure,' 64

39 Kotovskii, *India's agrarian reforms* 5, 77-8

40 Ul'yanovskii, 'Reform of the agrarian structure,' 64

41 Maksimov and Rastyannikov, 'Preface,' 4

42 Batalov and Gurvich, *Can India feed itself?* 15-16
43 Kotovskii, *India's agrarian reforms* 4-5
44 Varentsov and Maksimov, 'Class structure in the country,' 356
45 Kotovsky and Moiseev, *Social and Economic Transition* 6-7
46 A. Maslennikov, 'Agrarnye reformy v Indii' (Agrarian reforms in India), in *Agrarnye reformy v stranakh Vostoka* (Agrarian reforms in the countries of the East) (Moscow, 1961) 78
47 Kotovskii, *India's agrarian reforms* 81
48 Maslennikov, 'Agrarian reforms in India,' 78
49 Maksimov and Rastyannikov, 'Preface,' 13
50 Maslennikov, 'Agrarian reforms in India,' 86
51 Maksimov and Rastyannikov, 'Preface,' 13
52 Maslennikov, 'Agrarian reforms in India,' 86
53 Maksimov and Rastyannikov, 'Preface,' 16
54 Kotovskii, *India's agrarian reforms* 106
55 Kotovsky and Moiseev, *Social and Economic Transition* 7-8
56 R.P. Gurvich, *Sel'skoe khozyaistvo Indii* (India's agriculture) (Moscow, 1960) 96
57 Maslennikov, 'Agrarian reforms in India,' 86
58 Kotovskii, *India's agrarian reforms* 81
59 Ul'yanovskii, 'Reform of the agrarian structure,' 81
60 V.G. Rastyannikov and M.A. Maksimov, *Razvitie kapitalizma v sel'skom khozyaistve sovremennoi Indii* (The development of capitalism in independent India's agriculture) (Moscow, 1965) 9
61 R. Ulyanovsky, 'People's fight for democracy and social progress in India,' in R. Ulyanovsky et al., *Industrial Revolution and Social Progress in India* (New Delhi, 1970) 2
62 D.S. Layalpuri, 'Kapitalisticheskoe preobrazovanie sel'skogo khozyaistva Indii' (The capitalist transformation of Indian agriculture), *Narody Azii i Afriki* 4 (1963) 19-20
63 L. Stepanov, 'Why social reforms are inevitable,' in Y. Zhukov et al., *The Third World: Problems and Prospects* (Moscow, 1970) 132-3
64 Varentsov and Maksimov, 'Class structure in the country,' 381
65 V.G. Rastyannikov, 'Ekspluatatorskaya verkhushka derevni i formirovanie sel'skoi burzhuazii' (The exploiting summit in the villages and the formation of the agrarian bourgeoisie), in *Problemy ekonomicheskogo i sotsial'nogo razvitiya nezavisimoi Indii* (Problems of economic and social development of independent India) (Moscow, 1967) 192
66 'Izmeneniya v sotsial'no-klassovoi strukture Indii' (Changes in India's social and class structure), in *Problems of independent India* 121

67 R.P. Gurvich, 'Krest'yanstvo' (The peasantry), ibid. 139
68 Rastyannikov and Maksimov, *The development of capitalism* 280
69 Rastyannikov, 'The exploiting summit,' 178
70 L. Rudin, Review of V.G. Rastyannikov and M.A. Maksimov, *The development of capitalism*, in *Narody Azii i Afriki* 2 (1967) 178
71 Daniel Thorner, 'L'Inde aujourd'hui: le problème agraire,' *Annales* (jan.-fév. 1962) 72
72 Karl Marx, *Theories of Surplus Value* (London 1951) 192
73 Georges Plekhanov, *Oeuvres philosophiques* 1 (Moscow, n.d.) chap. 3
74 V. Lenin, *The Development of Capitalism in Russia* in *Collected Works* 3 (Moscow, 1964) 21-604, and *The Agrarian Question in Russia towards the Close of the Nineteenth Century*, in *Collected Works*, 15 (Moscow, 1965) 69-147
75 Thorner, 'L'Inde aujourd'hui,' 73
76 L.K. Orleanskaya, Review of A.M. Khusro and A.N. Agarwal, *The Problem of Cooperative Farming in India,* in *Narody Azii i Afriki* 4 (1963) 195
77 Maslennikov, 'Agrarian reforms in India,' 95-7

THIRTEEN / RURAL CLASS RELATIONS

1 G.G. Kotovsky and P.P. Moiseev, *Social and Economic Transition of the Rural East: Basic Trends. Some Problems of Methodology* (Moscow, 1967) 2-5
2 G. Kotovskii, 'Predislovie' (Introduction), in *Agrarnye otnosheniya v stranakh Yugo-vostochnoi Azii* (Agrarian relations in the countries of South-East Asia) (Moscow, 1968) 4
3 R.A. Ul'yanovskii, 'Reforma agrarnogo stroya' (Reform of the agrarian structure), in *Ekonomika sovremennoi Indii* (Contemporary India's economy) (Moscow, 1960) 77
4 G.G. Kotovskii, *Agrarnye reformy Indii* (India's agrarian reforms) (Moscow, 1959) 55-62
5 A.L. Batalov and R.P. Gurvich, *Mozhet li Indiya prokormit' sebya?* (Can India feed itself?) (Moscow, 1961) 19
6 A. Maslennikov, 'Agrarnye reformy v Indii' (Agrarian reforms in India), in *Agrarnye reformy v stranakh Vostoka* (Agrarian reforms in the countries of the East) (Moscow, 1961) 95-6
7 M.A. Maksimov and V.G. Rastyannikov, 'Predislovie' (Preface), in D. Torner, *Agrarnyi stroi Indii* (India's agrarian structure) (Moscow, 1959) 13
8 Ul'yanovskii, 'Reform of the agrarian structure,' 73

9   Maksimov and Rastyannikov, 'Preface,' 16
10 V. Rastyannikov, 'The agrarian evolution and class formation processes in India,' *Social Sciences* 5, No. 3 (1974) 141
11 V.G. Rastyannikov, 'On the evolution of share-cropping tenancy in India,' *New Age* 11, No. 9 (Sept. 1962) 12
12 V.G. Rastyannikov, 'Ekspluatatorskaya verkhushka derevni i formirovanie sel'skoi burzhuazii' (The exploiting summit in the villages and the formation of the agrarian bourgeoisie), in *Problemy ekonomicheskogo i sotsial'nogo razvitiya nezavisimoi Indii* (Problems of economic and social development of independent India) (Moscow, 1967) 178
13 Maksimov and Rastyannikov, 'Preface,' 17
14 Ul'yanovskii, 'Reform of the agrarian structure,' 91
15 Kotovskii, *India's agrarian reforms* 62-72
16 Batalov and Gurvich, *Can India feed itself?* 31
17 Maslennikov, 'Agrarian reforms in India,' 78
18 V.G. Rastyannikov and M.A. Maksimov, *Razvitie kapitalizma v sel'skom khozyaistve sovremennoi Indii* (The development of capitalism in independent India's agriculture) (Moscow, 1965) 271
19 Rastyannikov, 'The exploiting summit,' 185
20 L. Rudin, Review of V.G. Rastyannikov and M.A. Maksimov, *The development of capitalism,* in *Narody Azii i Afriki* 2 (1967) 178
21 Rastyannikov and Maksimov, *The development of capitalism* 28
22 Kotovskii, *India's agrarian reforms* 87, 114
23 Kotovsky and Moiseev, *Social and Economic Transition* 8-9
24 Maslennikov, 'Agrarian reforms in India,' 97
25 K.M. Varentsov and M.A. Maksimov, 'Klassovaya struktura derevni i polozhenie krest'yanskikh mass' (Class structure in the country and the position of the peasant masses), in *Klassy i klassovaya bor'ba v razvivayushchikhsya stranakh* (Classes and class struggle in the developing countries) I (Moscow, 1967) 381-3
26 Maksimov and Rastyannikov, 'Preface,' 7-8
27 Rastyannikov and Maksimov, *The development of capitalism* 272
28 Maksimov and Rastyannikov, 'Preface,' 8
29 Kotovskii, *India's agrarian reforms* 100
30 Rastyannikov, 'The exploiting summit,' 170-2
31 Rastyannikov and Maksimov, *The development of capitalism* 263-6
32 E.I. Mironova, *Prodovoi'stvennaya problema v Indii* (The food problem in India) (Moscow, 1967) 12
33 Rastyannikov, 'Class-formation processes,' 139-49
34 G.G. Kotovskii and V.A. Popov, 'Ot redaktsii' (Editorial), in *Krest'yanskoe*

dvizhenie v stranakh Vostoka (The peasant movement in the Orient) (Moscow, 1967) 3-4

35 A. Kiva, 'Experience of non-capitalist development in Africa,' *International Affairs* 5 (1972) 28

36 Kotovsky and Moiseev, *Social and Economic Transition* 6

37 R. Ulyanovsky, 'Burma's new path,' *International Affairs* 5 (1972) 20-1

38 Varentsov and Maksimov, 'Class structure in the country,' 376

39 Kotovsky and Moiseev, *Social and Economic Transition* 5-6

40 Maslennikov, 'Agrarian reforms in India,' 98

41 Rastyannikov and Maksimov, *The development of capitalism* 23-4

42 Batalov and Gurvich, *Can India feed itself?* 22

43 Kotovskii, *India's agrarian reforms* 69

44 Maslennikov, 'Agrarian reforms in India,' 82

45 Batalov and Gurvich, *Can India feed itself?* 18

46 Kotovskii, *India's agrarian reforms* 69

47 Ul'yanovskii, 'Reform of the agrarian structure,' 89

48 Kotovskii, *India's agrarian reforms* 66-7

49 L. Stepanov, 'Why social reforms are inevitable,' in Y. Zhukov et al., *The Third World: Problems and Prospects* (Moscow, 1970) 131

50 Maslennikov, 'Agrarian reforms in India,' 83

51 Kotovskii, *India's agrarian reforms* 101

52 Batalov and Gurvich, *Can India feed itself?* 19

53 Stepanov, 'Social reforms,' 131

54 Karl Marx, *Theories of Surplus Value* (London, 1951) 193-4

55 Kotovskii, *India's agrarian reforms* 41

56 Daniel Thorner, 'Peasant economy as a category in economic history,' *Economic Weekly* 15 (July 1963) 1243

57 Batalov and Gurvich, *Can India feed itself?* 19

58 Rastyannikov and Maksimov, *The development of capitalism* 41 ff

59 Ibid. 186

60 G.G. Kotovskii, 'Sel'skokhozyaistvennyi proletariat i poluproletariat' (The agrarian proletariat and semi-proletariat), in *Problems of independent India* (Moscow, 1967) 151-9

61 Rastyannikov and Maksimov, *The development of capitalism* 39

62 Kotovskii, 'The agrarian proletariat,' 147

63 N.I. Semenova, 'Bor'ba sel'skokhozyaistvennykh rabochikh Indii' (The struggle of India's agrarian workers), in G.G. Kotovskii and V.A. Popov, eds, *Krest'yanskoe dvizhenie v stranakh Vostoka* (The peasant movement in the eastern countries) (Moscow, 1967) 134

64 Varentsov and Maksimov, 'Class structure in the country,' 404-6

65 G.I. Mirskii, 'Ofitserstvo' (The officer class), in *Classes and class struggle* I, 354

66 Rastyannikov, 'The exploiting summit,' 192

67 Kotovskii, *India's agrarian reforms* 116

68 V.A. Popov, 'Nekotorye osobennosti krest'yanskogo dvizheniya v razvivayushchikhsya stranakh svyazennye s provedeniem agrarnykh reform' (Some special characteristics of the peasant movement in the developing countries in its connection with the implementation of agrarian reforms), in G.G. Kotovskii and V.A. Popov, eds, *Krest'yanskoe dvizhenie v stranakh Vostoka* (The peasant movement in the eastern countries) (Moscow, 1967) 45

69 Kotovskii, *India's agrarian reforms* 72, 100

70 Maksimov and Rastyannikov, 'Preface,' 25

71 Ibid.

72 Rastyannikov and Maksimov, *The development of capitalism* 270

73 Semenova, 'The struggle of India's agrarian workers,' 142

74 Kotovskii, 'The agrarian proletariat,' 164

75 Kotovskii, *India's agrarian reforms* 116

76 Batalov and Gurvich, *Can India feed itself?* 50

77 Y. Guzevaty, 'Population and the problems of developing countries,' in *Internationalism, National-Liberation Movement and our Epoch* 2 (Moscow, n.d.) 155

78 Kotovskii, *India's agrarian reforms* 111

79 Maslennikov, 'Agrarian reforms in India,' 87, 89

80 Batalov and Gurvich, *Can India feed itself?* 32

81 Maslennikov, 'Agrarian reforms in India,' 89-98

82 Batalov and Gurvich, *Can India feed itself?* 49-50

83 B.H. Farmer, 'Planning of land settlement schemes,' *Economic Weekly* 15, Nos 28-30 (July 1963) 1255

84 Batalov and Gurvich, *Can India feed itself?* 53-95

85 Stepanov, 'Social reforms,' 133

86 R. Ulyanovsky, 'People's fight for democracy and social progress in India,' in R. Ulyanovsky et al., *Industrial Revolution and Social Progress in India* (New Delhi, 1970) 2

87 V. Shurygin, 'India: on the road to democracy and social progress,' *International Affairs* 5 (May 1974) 48

88 E. Kovalyov, 'The Green Revolution: its technical and social aspects,' *International Affairs* 9 (Sept. 1972) 42-3

89 A. Shpirt, *The Scientific-Technological Revolution and the Third World* (Moscow, 1972) 75

90 A.B. Letnev, *Estimations of Agricultural Produce Marketing Systems in Connection with Agrarian Reforms: The Case of West Africa* (Moscow, 1967) 8

91 Ibid. 11-12

92 Mironova, *The food problem in India* 39-54

93 A.L. Batalov et al., 'Itogi razvitiya narodnogo khozyaistva' (Balance sheet of the national economy's development), in *Problems of independent India* (Moscow, 1967) 17

94 Mironova, *The food problem in India* 67

95 V.G. Rastyannikov, 'Price policy and food production,' *Amrita Bazar Patrika* (8 March 1968)

96 Batalov et al., 'Balance sheet,' 18-20

97 N.G. Lozovaya, 'Indiya' (India), in *Plany-programmy ekonomicheskogo razvitiya stran Azii* (The economic development plans of Asian countries) (Moscow, 1966) 143-5

98 Shurygin, 'India and social progress,' 48

99 Lozovaya, 'Indiya,' 153

100 Kotovsky and Moiseev, *Social and Economic Transition* 1

101 Varentsov and Maksimov, 'Class structure in the country,' 39-98

102 Maslennikov, 'Agrarian reforms in India,' 78

103 Kotovskii, *India's agrarian reforms* 4

104 Maksimov and Rastyannikov, 'Preface,' 25, 10

105 Batalov et al., 'Balance sheet,' 30, 35

FOURTEEN / ASSESSMENTS AND REFLECTIONS

1 M.A. Aleksandrov and S.M. Mel'man, 'Privlechenie resursov iz-za rubezha' (Attracting resources from abroad), in *Problemy ekonomicheskogo i sotsial'nogo razvitiya nezavisimoi Indii* (Problems of independent India's social and economic development) (Moscow, 1967) 105-7

2 R. Ulyanovsky, 'People's fight for democracy and social progress in India,' in R. Ulyanovsky and others, *Industrial Revolution and Social Progress in India* (New Delhi, 1970) 9

3 V.G. Gafurov, ed., *Politika S. Sh.A. v stranakh Yuzhnoi Azii* (US Policy in Southern Asia) (Moscow, 1961) 2

4 L. Reusner, 'Developing economies in terms of growth and reproduction,' *Social Sciences* 4, No. 4 (1973) 137

5 V. Solodovoikov and A. Letnev, 'Contemporary trends in the historiography of Africa,' *Social Sciences* 5, No. 1 (1974) 157

6 R.A. Ulyanovsky and V.I. Pavlov, 'Afterword,' in V. Pavlov et al., *India:*

Social and Economic Development (18th-20th Centuries) (Moscow, 1975) 274

7 R.A. Ulyanovsky, *The Dollar and Asia: U.S. Neo-colonialist Policy in Action* (Moscow, 1965) 6

8 M. Volkov, 'The developing countries: the choice of technology,' *Problems of Economics* 18, No. 4 (Aug. 1975) 11

9 Vladimir Kollontai, 'The scientific and technological revolution and the developing countries,' in *The Scientific and Technological Revolution: Social Effects and Prospects* (Moscow, 1972) 225-6

10 S.F. Levin, 'Ob evolyutsii musul'manskikh torgovykh kast v svyazi s razvitiem kapitalizma' (On the evolution of Moslem trading castes and their links with the development of capitalism), in *Kasty v Indii* (Castes in India) (Moscow, 1965)

11 Yu. V. Potemkin and V.A. Sandakov, 'Problema nakopleniya v razvivayush-chikhsya stranakh' (The problem of accumulation in the developing countries), in *Klassy i klassovaya bor'ba v razvivayushchikhsya stranakh* II (Moscow, 1967) 66-7

12 I.M. Shatalov, 'The third world and the scientific and technical revolution,' *International Affairs* 5 (May 1967) 74

13 G.G. Kotovskii, 'Introduction,' in *Kasty v Indii* 37, 40

14 Levin, 'On the evolution of Moslem trading castes'

15 A.G. Bel'skii, Review of H.D. Malaviya's *The Danger of Right Reaction* (New Delhi, 1965), in *Narody Azii i Afriki* 3 (1966) 174

16 See A.M. Dyakov, *The National Problem in India Today* (Moscow, 1966); V.I. Kazakov, *Bor'ba za sozdanie natsional'nykh shtatov v nezavisimoi Indii* (The struggle to found national states in independent India) (Moscow, 1967)

17 See *Obshchestvenno-politicheskaya i filosofskaya mysl' Indii* (India's philosophical and sociopolitical thought) (Moscow, 1962); L.R. Gordon-Polonskaya, *Musul'manskie techeniya v obshchestvennoi mysl' Indii i Pakistana (Kritika 'musul'manskogo natsionalizma')* (Moslem currents in India's and Pakistan's social thought: a critique of 'Moslem nationalism') (Moscow, 1963); *Ideologicheskie techeniya sovremennoi Indii* (Modern India's ideological currents) (Moscow, 1965); A.D. Litman, *Filosofoskaya mysl' nezavisimoi Indii (akademicheskie sistemy i religioznofilosofskie ucheniya)* (Independent India's philosophical thought: academic systems and religious-philosophical teaching) (Moscow, 1966)

18 S.A. Kuz'min, *The Developing Countries, Employment and Capital Investment* (New York, 1969) 2

19 A. Usvatov, 'Quarter-century of independent India,' *New Times* 33 (Aug. 1972) 9

20 Ranjit Sau, 'Non-capitalist path and all that,' *Economic and Political Weekly* 9, No. 15 (13 April 1974) 591, 593

21 Susanne Bodenheimer, 'Dependency and imperialism: the roots of Latin American underdevelopment,' in K.T. Fann and Donald C. Hodges, eds, *Readings in U.S. Imperialism* (Boston, 1971) 166

22 Theotonio Dos Santos, 'The structure of dependence,' ibid. 235

23 André Gunder Frank, 'The development of underdevelopment,' in Robert I. Rhodes, ed., *Imperialism and Underdevelopment: A Reader* (New York; 1970) 5

24 Jacques Lévesque, *L'URSS et la révolution cubaine* (Paris, Montréal, 1976) 79-89

25 O. Igho Natufe, 'Nigeria and Soviet attitudes to African military regimes, 1965-70,' *Survey* 22, No. 1 (Winter 1976) 97

26 Jerry F. Hough, 'The Soviet experience and the measurement of power,' *Journal of Politics* 37 (1975) 695

27 Robert H. Donaldson, *Soviet Policy Toward India: Ideology and Strategy* (Cambridge, Mass., 1974)

28 Bhabani Sen Gupta, *The Fulcrum of Asia: Relations among China, India, Pakistan and the U.S.S.R.* (New York, 1970)

29 Richard B. Remnek, *Soviet Scholars and Soviet Foreign Policy* (Durham NC, 1975) 49

30 John H. Kautsky, *Moscow and the Communist Party of India: A Study in the Postwar Evolution of International Communist Strategy* (New York, 1956)

31 Usvatov, 'Quarter-century of independent India,' 8

32 Pavel Victorov, 'India: amendment of the constitution,' *New Times* 46 (Nov. 1976) 10

33 Stephen Clarkson, 'Non-impact of Soviet writing on Indian thinking and policy,' *Survey* 20, No. 1 (Winter 1974) 10

34 Remnek, *Soviet Scholars and Soviet Foreign Policy* xi

35 Albert L. Weeks, 'Assessing the fundamental nature of Soviet foreign policy,' *Orbis* (1976) 1645-6

36 Remnek, *Soviet Scholars and Soviet Foreign Policy* 92

37 *Monthly Public Opinion Survey*, Nos 7, 8, 9 (1956)

38 William J. Barnds, 'Soviet influence in India: a search for the spoils that go with victory,' in Alvin Z. Rubinstein, ed., *Soviet and Chinese Influence in the Third World* (New York, 1975) 23-50

39 Wolfgang G. Friedmann, George Kalmanoff and Robert F. Meagher, *International Financial Aid* (New York, 1966)

40 Kautsky, *Moscow and the Communist Party of India* (1956)

41 Bhabani Sen Gupta, *Communism in Indian Politics* (New York, 1972)
42 Peter Sager, *Moscow's Hand in India. An Analysis of Soviet Propaganda* (Berne, 1966)
43 For details of the methodology and the complete research results, see Clarkson, 'Non-impact of Soviet writing.'
44 N.K. Chandra, 'The class character of the Pakistani state,' *Economic and Political Weekly* 7, Nos 5, 6, and 7 (Feb. 1972) 275-92
45 Paresh Chattopadhyay, 'Aspects of the growth of state capitalism in India,' in Government of Kerala, *Alternative Policies for the Fourth Five Year Plan* (Trivandrum, 1969) 71-89; Ranjit K. Sau, 'Indian economic growth: constraints and prospects,' *Economic and Political Weekly*, 7, Nos 5, 6, and 7 (Feb. 1972) 361-78; Ashwani Saith and Ajay Tankha, 'Agrarian transition of the peasantry; a study of a West UP village,' *Economic and Political Weekly* 7, No. 14 (1 April 1972) 707-23; S. Ganguli, 'Public sector and private sector: dynamics of the system,' in Government of Kerala, *Alternative Policies for the Fourth Five Year Plan* (1969) 207-25
46 Edward Shils, *The Intellectual between Tradition and Modernity: The Indian Situation* (The Hague, 1961) 83
47 Frank Moraes, *Jawaharlal Nehru* (New York, 1956) 473
48 *Planning and Statistics in Socialist Countries*, No. 19 in Indian Statistical Series (Calcutta, 1963)
49 S. Mohan Kumaramangalam, 'A new venture: a holding company for iron and steel,' *Socialist India* 14, No. 13 (19 Feb. 1972) 13-14
50 Arthur J. Klinghoffer, *Soviet Perspectives on African Socialism* (Rutherford NJ, 1969) 230

Index

CENTRE FOR RUSSIAN AND EAST EUROPEAN STUDIES
University of Toronto

Feeding the Russian Fur Trade by James R. Gibson. (University of Wisconsin Press, Madison, Wisconsin, 1969)

The Czech Renascence of the Nineteenth Century edited by Peter Brock and H. Gordon Skilling. (University of Toronto Press, Toronto, 1970)

The Soviet Wood-Processing Industry: a linear programming analysis of the role of transportation costs in location and flow patterns by Brenton M. Barr. (University of Toronto Press, Toronto, 1970)

Interest Groups in Soviet Politics edited by H. Gordon Skilling and Franklyn Griffiths. (Princeton University Press, Princeton, New Jersey, 1971)

Between Gogol' and Ševčenko by George S.N. Luckyj. (Harvard Series in Ukrainian Studies. Wilhelm Fink Verlag, Munich, Germany, 1971)

The Collective Farm in Soviet Agriculture by Robert C. Stuart. (D.C. Heath and Company, Lexington, Mass., 1972)

Narrative Modes in Czech Literature by Lubomir Dolezel. (University of Toronto Press, Toronto, 1973)

Leon Trotsky and the Politics of Economic Isolation by Richard B. Day. (Cambridge University Press, Cambridge, England, 1973)

Literature and Ideology in Soviet Education by Norman Shneidman. (D.C. Heath and Company, Lexington, Mass., 1973)

Guide to the Decisions of the Communist Party of the Soviet Union, 1917-1967 by Robert H. McNeal. (University of Toronto Press, Toronto, 1974)

Resolutions and Decisions of the Communist Party of the Soviet Union 1898-1964 General Editor, Robert H. McNeal. Four Volumes. (University of Toronto Press, Toronto, 1974)

The Slovak National Awakening: an essay in the intellectual history of east central Europe by Peter Brock. (University of Toronto Press, Toronto, 1976)

Czechoslovakia's Interrupted Revolution by H. Gordon Skilling. (Princeton University Press, Princeton, New Jersey, 1976)

The Russian Revolution: a study in mass mobilization by John L.H. Keep. (Weidenfeld and Nicolson, London, 1976; W.W. Norton and Co., New York, 1977)

Polish Revolutionary Populism: a study in agrarian socialist thought from the 1830s to the 1850s by Peter Brock. (University of Toronto Press, Toronto, 1977)

The Soviet Theory of Development: India and the third world in marxist-leninist scholarship by Stephen Clarkson. (University of Toronto Press, Toronto, 1978)